# The Detective as Historian

# The Detective as Historian: History and Art in Historical Crime Fiction

edited by

Ray B. Browne

and

Lawrence A. Kreiser, Jr.

Preface by Robin W. Winks

Bowling Green State University Popular Press
Bowling Green, OH 43403

Copyright 2000 © Bowling Green State University Popular Press

Library of Congress Cataloging-in-Publication Data

The detective as historian : history and art in historical crime fiction / edited
by Ray B. Browne and Lawrence A. Kreiser, Jr.
    p. cm.
   Includes bibliographical references.
   ISBN 0-87972-815-9 (cloth) -- ISBN 0-87972-816-7 (paper)
   1. Detective and mystery stories, English--History and criticism.
2. Detective and mystery stories, American--History and criticism.
3. Historical fiction, American--History and criticism. 4. Historical
fiction, English--History and criticism. 5. Literature and history--Great
Britain--History. 6. Literature and history--United States--History.
I. Browne, Ray Broadus II. Kreiser, Lawrence A., 1969-

PR830.D4 D39 2000
813'.087209358--dc21

                                        00-029245

Cover design by Dumm Art

*Dedicated to*

*Pat, Alicia, and Julia*

*for reasons only*

*they can fully understand*

# Contents

# Preface

## Robin W. Winks

Mystery and detective novels are the bestselling form of popular fiction today, certainly in the United States and Great Britain, and the "historical mystery" is the most rapidly growing branch of the genre. Clearly many readers find pleasure in seeing a mystery set in the past and solved by methods not always available in our times. Of course, logic, the careful accumulation of evidence, and knowing how to ask good questions were as essential in the thirteenth century as they are in the twenty-first, and the historical mystery is not greatly removed from a rousing puzzle set in the year 2000, but there are great differences in technique and in the tools available to both the detective and the criminal. One need think only of DNA, computers, and modern photography to dramatize the gap between the mainstream detective story and the historical mystery.

Why do so many readers enjoy historical mysteries? Surely there are many reasons. These will include a desire for the presumably more ordered world of the nineteenth century. But then why are novels about the disorderly world of the fifteenth century so popular? Surely there are readers attracted to the historical mystery because the bloodshed is, on the whole, less and certainly less gruesomely revealed in most cases; because the casual vulgarities of turn-of-this-century demotic speech are not to be found on the lips of even the most heinous villains of ancient Rome (though equivalents may be abundantly present, undetected by some readers): perhaps because the crimes are less threatening to us than are repetitive serial killings, accounts of wildings in Central Park, and corrupt police. Still, one notes these plot devices creeping into the historical mystery today, as they were certainly present in real life. Perhaps readers who do not much care for history as written by historians, but who enjoy thinking their way back into the past, rid themselves of any residual guilt they may have felt about discussing this subject in school.

I confess that until recently I have disliked historical mysteries. Not too long ago I wrote what I now recognize as a virtual hatchet job on Josephine Tey, exasperated by the number of times her *Daughter of Time* was praised as a good mystery novel. I still think it is a bad novel and quite misleading as to how historians ask and answer questions, but I now realize, especially having read the many essays in this pioneering volume, that she had no intention of representing herself as a historian and that she shoulders little blame if unwary readers take her to have posed as one. Read objectively, unburdened by the professional historian's regard for methodology, objectivity, and order, *Daughter of Time* is an intriguing if flawed book that represents the context and the world in which it was written: that is, it is a historical mystery on two levels.

In any case, there are now many superb writers of the historical mystery. There are, as with all crime fiction, also a goodly number of potboilers, badly researched books that introduce jarring anachronisms in every chapter. Why should the historical mystery be better than mainline popular prose? It need only be as good, and it has clearly become that, as the essays that follow frequently demonstrate. Seeing the detective be a historian is now as much pleasure as seeing the historian be a detective. Historians moved too far away from their origins, as storytellers; now storytellers may bring historians back to those roots, to the benefit of both ways of exploring the past.

Every reader of this intriguing volume will discover authors they did not know about, will learn of new sources for future pleasure, and will better understand the relationship between fact and fiction. Not every writer written of here is, as yet, significant or even, truth be told, interesting, but the historical mystery is still new, and a writer who has not yet found a voice, measured a pace, and taken up a piece of turf to make their own may do so in the future, soon, even yesterday, so that we may find pleasure in their future as they bring us pleasure to our past.

**Robin W. Winks** is Townsend Professor of History at Yale University, editor of *The Historian as Detective*, and author of several critical studies of the mystery and detective novel.

# Introduction

## Ray B. Browne and Lawrence A. Kreiser, Jr.

In recent years, historians—both professional and amateur—have given increased thought to the value and place of historical fiction in their research and teaching. A recent issue of the *American Historical Review* contains a Forum prefaced by the remarks, presumably by the editor, that "storytelling has returned to claim a prominent place in history." The return has not been without debate, for renewed interest in the narrative "has also rekindled controversies about the virtues and vices of recovering the past through the methods of historians and novelists, the pages of histories and historical fictions" (*AHR* 1502).

The Canadian novelist Margaret Atwood, whose novel *Alias Grace* (1996) serves as a point of discussion for the *AHR* Forum, says that historical fiction is about human nature. She itemizes the passions that drive, impede, unite, and divide humankind as: "pride, envy, avarice, lust, sloth, gluttony, and anger." Then she lists the subjects of historical novels: "They are about truth and lies, and disguises and revelations; they are about crime and punishment; they are about love and forgiveness and long suffering and charity; they are about sin and retribution and sometimes even redemption" (1516). She quite properly highlights "sin and retribution" and "crime and punishment" and mentions how these sins of the heart and flesh are particularly described in canonical historical fiction. Historians, in searching for reality and truth, are interested in documents and evidence—those that are dull and those that are lively, those that tell lies in the guise of truth as well as those that contain truth. It is the historian's job to separate truth from fiction, and, equally important, to discover the truth in fiction.

Popular culture—of which novels and storytelling are only two parts—has been a major source of knowledge for historians from Herodotus on. Daniel Boorstin, for example, used the various aspects of everyday culture for his several records of human cultures through the centuries. Other historians have recognized the importance of this aspect of life in their work. "Popular culture is a mainstream field in American history now," says David Thelen, editor of the *Journal of American History*. "It's at the center of a lot of interpretive issues in the humanities."

An excellent example of the way that historians use popular culture, sometimes against the grain of established opinion, is an account by Robert C. Davis in the acknowledgments to his *The War of the Fists: Popular Culture and Public Violence in Late Renaissance Italy*:

*1*

A few years ago, shortly after I had discovered the pleasures and challenges of the Chronicle of the *pugni* in Venice's *museo Correr*, I mentioned to a more experienced colleague how much I would enjoy the chance to write my own history of the city's *battagliole*. His immediate response was, in so many words, Why? Who would ever want to read about such a tasteless topic? . . . Happily, as I explored and worked out the principal themes of the *War of the Fists*, I discovered that my colleagues in Venetian history, and indeed in social history generally, were as likely to be as fascinated and attracted as I was by this cult of popular violence and public disorder that flourished for so many centuries in the heart of the world's Most Serene Republic. It is largely due to their constant encouragement, support and criticism—their understanding of the central role of popular culture in an absolutist society—that this book has been possible. (vi)

Historical fiction generally covers adventures of all kinds and deals with all aspects of culture. Historical *crime fiction*, though more narrow in its thematic treatment, is concerned with the major drives of human life as highlighted by Margaret Atwood's "crime and punishment" and "sin and retribution." If life is the assertion of the forces in society working with and against one another, then the analogy with football as a metaphor for society might be appropriate, with individuals striving both within the team and on their own against other individuals and groups. In this context, crime fiction becomes the official judging of the actions of the persons as they interact one against another in illegal ways. The role of such fiction is to catalogue, measure, and adjudicate the actions, point out infractions, and bring to penalty those who do not act according to the rules. Historical crime fiction registers the actions of the people of the past, recording how they influenced, both good and bad, their future—and our present.

Life is a search-and-reveal exercise, an account of growth and development. The historian Robin Winks, recognizing this three decades ago, commented on the similarity between the work of historians and crime fiction writers in his informative book *The Historian as Detective: Essays on Evidence* (1968): "The historian must collect, interpret, and then explain his evidence by methods which are not greatly different from those techniques employed by the detective, or at least the detective in fiction. . . . Obviously the author of such fiction does not construct his work as the historian does, for to one the outcome is known and to the other that outcome is at best guessed. But the reasoning processes are similar enough to be intriguing." Winks also comments on a practice much more widely engaged in now than it was thirty years ago, "It is not surprising then that historians often seem to relax with a so-called detective story, or that certain English dons and American professors are known not only to be addicts of the genre but sometimes even contribute to the literature" (xiii).

Winks's implied prediction has proved prophetic. More authors and scholars are recognizing the values of historical crime fiction and are producing it. Two recent publications by history professors, *Murder Most Foul:*

*The Killer and American Gothic,* by Karen Halttunen (1998) and *The Murder of Helen Jewett: Life and Death of a Prostitute in Nineteenth-Century New York,* by Patricia Cline Cohen (1998), have caused considerable stir in newspapers and the popular-professional press, with reviews in such publications as the *New Republic* and *Chronicle of Higher Education.*

Both authors realize that they are using historical crime fiction (or faction, as the combination of fact and fiction is coming to be called) for new outreaches in the study of human nature and behavior: "Mine is a study of the oral imagination," Halttunen says, calling it "the pornography of violence." The reviewer of Cohen's book for the *New Republic* said, "By reproducing her evidence in colorful detail, and by assessing its strengths and weaknesses frankly, Cohen draws readers into the excitement of the historian as detective" (47). Of her own book, Halttunen explains, "our intense interest implicates us, if only as voyeurs, in the crime, however much we assert the inhumanity of murder," and, according to Scott Heller, of the *Chronicle of Higher Education,* her book "should provide fodder for other historians to more fully comprehend individual lives and individual deaths" (A13) of the past.

"By looking at crimes that are way out there, you begin to open a window on a culture in a particular time," argues Amy Gilman Srebnick, author of *The Mysterious Death of Mary Rogers* (1995), a study of the murder case in New York that triggered one of Edgar Allan Poe's tales of ratiocination. "What the press did with the case tells us a lot about journalism. How the police handled the case tells us a lot about policing at the time," she says. But, even more important in the long run, opening the case tells us about the desires, needs, and feelings of the public of the time, a public which, intrigued by the power of logic, accepted Poe's short story on the same subject, which he called "The Mystery of Marie Roget" (1842-43), transferred in action to Paris and solved by Poe's name for logic—ratiocination, a term that has been consistently used as one of the tools of some crime fiction.

Authors of historical crime fiction take their work seriously. Barbara Mertz, who under the name of Elizabeth Peters writes about a Victorian Egyptologist-detective, has written two straight history books, *Temples, Tombs, and Hieroglyphs: A Popular History of Ancient Egypt* and *Red Land, Black Land: Daily Life in Ancient Egypt,* in addition to her historical crime fiction. In an interview published in the *University of Chicago Magazine* she says: "When people ask 'When are you going to write a serious book?' my response is 'Every book I have written is a serious book. Especially the mysteries'" (xv).

So the above authors summarize a growing seriousness among academics toward historical crime fiction. Several strands in the writing of history converge in accounts of murder. Scholars are interested in lives on the margin. Histories of gender and sexuality are clearly in vogue. At the same time, many scholars have put aside efforts to document social change empirically, turning instead to tell rich stories with full-blooded characters. Perhaps most significantly, crime-fiction writers reveal a page of life full of people and events that often are neglected in traditional history books.

History is a chronicling of facts and events. Medieval literature is filled with so many events that it is jokingly called ODTAA (One Damn Thing After Another). Historical crime fiction, because it is concerned with the details of life which in the past included countless acts of violence, should be called ODCAA (One Damn Crime After Another). In the recounting, such stories teach the uninformed and remind the professionals of the details of everyday life of the past that may not be known or might have been forgotten.

To be credible, crime fiction has to be authenticated by details. For example, who beyond a few specialists remembers that in sixteenth-century England-Scotland, when a member of the body, say a hand, was amputated, it had to buried "with a live rat tied to it to draw out any morbidus [disease]"? Or that the best firearms of the time were made at the Tower of London, in Newcastle or, in Scotland, at Dumfries? Further, those who despise the present-day fast food industry might profit by being reminded that people have always demanded easily obtained food: for example, at sixteenth-century Scottish outdoor gatherings, alewives and pie sellers "made stunning profits" selling their wares. Such details are integral to P. F. Chisholm's *A Surfeit of Guns* (22, 45, 53).

Another fascinating historical bit offered by Sharon Kay Penman in *Cruel Is the Grave* (181, 226) is that after a murderer had spent a fortnight in a church sanctuary in twelfth-century England, he could escape the noose. After confessing to his crime and leaving behind all belongings (although he often carried hidden resources on his person), he went directly to a port city. He then boarded the first ship leaving the realm, usually to France. The practice infuriated the French, because they did not have a similar law that allowed them to export their murderers to England. Penman also tells us that horse traps were used in twelfth-century England, especially in sieges, to cripple steeds (called a *caltrop,* it was a ball with metal spikes constructed in such a way as to always have spikes protruding upward to penetrate the horse's hooves). And in twelfth-century England, today's child's oath of "Cross your heart and hope to die," was "Swear it and then spit" (153, 211).

Who does not benefit from Candace Robb's explaining in *The Gift of Sanctuary* that, in Irish folklore, "a red birthmark on the hand [was] the sign of a Messiah"? Or that in fourteenth-century Wales, some people thought that mustard took away the ache of sword wounds (*Mustard heats the lingering ghost of the sword*)? That hawthorne leaves when slept on brought fertility, or contrariwise safeguarded a "young maid's virtue when temptation is near?" Or that there was a way for a woman to annul her marriage if she found it unsatisfactory for any several reasons. "Should a woman discover that she is dissatisfied with the legal persona that has been imposed upon her by marriage, or simply wishes to be separated from her husband," reads the medieval Law of Women, "she can do so legitimately under Welsh law by proving that he has been discovered with another woman not less than three times, has leprosy or bad breath, or is impotent" (56, 78, 139, 303).

Robb has an advanced degree in Anglo-Saxon and medieval literature, and authors a mixture of historical literature and crime fiction. In order to write convincingly and without having to explain her terminology, she prefaces each novel with a glossary that explains the period words she will use—such as *carody, houppelande, leman, mazer, nones* and dozens of other terms. Through this technique, Robb wraps the culture of the period around readers, immersing them in the very essence of medieval Britain.

Historical crime fiction often deals more with the lower aspects of historical life than does historical fiction. It is the streets of life. In Raymond Chandler's oft-quoted words, it is the "mean streets," down which more history passes than has generally been admitted. These are, furthermore, the byways of most people. As historical fiction makes at least amateur historians of us all, so historical crime fiction makes some-degree crime authorities of its readers by exposing the underbelly of the past. Such crime fiction fascinates and makes a worthy tool for both historians and users of history.

History can, of course, be taught or used by crime novelists in different ways and with varying degrees of success. The prominence of present-day historical crime novels has spawned another kind of crime novel about the past, written by people who use various kinds of artifacts—generally seen in museums or bought in antique stores—as a spur to investigate some aspect of a past culture. So we have present-day investigators revisiting, as it were, the past while standing in the present.

Lyn Hamilton's *The Moche Warrior* (1999), a so-called archaeological mystery, is an excellent case in point. The setting is among the Moche, an ancient people who lived on the north coast of Peru approximately A.D. 100-750 but about whom archaeologists knew virtually nothing until the 1980s and about whom there has been growing interest since. The Moche, according to Garth Bawden, possessed "splendid artistic and architectural creations." And as Bawden points out, "archeology often represents the only means of learning about ancient people and their accomplishments. However, in the modern era, the central themes of archaeology have hindered comprehensive study of human cultures" (4), and therefore any study which humanizes and casts light on the daily life of any people of the past is to be welcomed. The spur that drives the visit to the modern ruins of that culture in this novel is a box of "junky" artifacts uncovered in an antique store in Toronto which happen to be not junk but genuine relics that have been smuggled out of Peru. Hamilton teaches us about the burying practices of the elite of that period:

For the higher status individuals . . . large chambers were constructed, large enough to hold the individual, logs of grave goods, some very elaborate, and other sacrificed animals, like llamas or dogs, and individuals, perhaps their retainers in life. Sometimes there were even guardians, bodies placed in niches above the principal body.

So these graves are much larger, they have been known to have adobe walls, and they are more likely to have timber roofs. (240)

Crime literature and the investigator who searches for the perpetrator is as old as time. In the Garden of Eden two instances of the breaking of the law are recorded—Eve's eating of the Forbidden Fruit and Cain's murdering his brother Abel—and God was the first investigator ferreting out the guilty party and determining the reasons Eve and Cain had broken His law. In later times, the biblical Book of Daniel gives the story of Susanna and the two elders who accused her of infidelity, but were proved liars and would-be fornicators, and were executed. In classical times Herodotus the historian told a delightful story of how King Rhampsinitus (possibly Rameses III) was robbed blind by one of his trusted lieutenants and how the mystery was solved through detective work.

It is not the detective as historian, of course, but the author as historian that the following essays concern. The novels under examination differ in the degree to which they are about crimes of the past, but they essentially are of the classical or "locked door" type. Such works have always concerned the elite—royalty, military, professional people, and academics. The authors have admitted lower-class people, those on the streets and in the hovels, only as background or support for the lives of the elite. But increasingly, crime fiction authors have developed an interest in those people who supported the elite, who walked "the mean streets." Some authors love the life and people of the everyday world of the past. In *The Lucifer Contract,* discussed below, Annette and Martin Meyers, writing as Maan Meyers, have the Southern conspirators who have come to New York City dazzled by the richness of life they found there. "We are not surprised that our conspirators were dazzled by the amazing City of New York in 1864," they assert. "We were born here, and the City still has this effect on us" ("Footnote" 301).

Virtually all of recorded history—from ancient Egypt through classical Greece and Rome, and from medieval Europe through nineteenth-century England and America—is covered in the essays in this volume. All bring the past to life in a way that only death—and the means of committing it—can. In the following essays, death stalks always within breath's reach, in the arms of violence or natural disaster.

Ancient Egypt is a culture mysterious and attractive to Westerners. Since the discovery of King Tut and the riches of his burial site, the society that produced such wealth has taken on a new power and mysteriousness. In the first essay, Rita Rippetoe examines two authors of crime fiction who are reading the underside of Pharaonic Egypt—Lynda S. Robinson and Lauren Haney. The Egypt of these authors is the filthy and dangerous alleys of day and night and the fields far from the Pharaoh's palace and temple. They reveal the little-known world, but one that supported the life and culture of the time.

Across the Mediterranean in Egypt's declining days, Rome was in its ascendancy. Daily life was filled with wicked civilians, ambitious slaves, and better-born nobility, all trying, in their own ways, to improve their lots and to stay alive. Focusing on the lives of everyday Romans are stories by John Maddox Roberts and Steven Saylor, examined in an essay by Terrance L. Lewis. Lindsey Davis's eight novels set during the early Roman Empire are examined in an essay by Peter Hunt. The star of the series is Falco, who circulates throughout the several cultural and social levels of culture of Rome, spying and reporting to the nobility.

From Rome to seventh-century Ireland is a long leap in time and space, but we make it in the next essay, "Peter Tremayne: Sister Fidelma and the Triumph of Truth," by Christiane W. Luehrs and Robert B. Luehrs. Sister Fidelma, the heroine of the novels, belongs to the royal family of one of medieval Ireland's five kingdoms. She is a *dálaigh*, an agent of the Irish legal system, knowledgeable in poetry, science, and law. Her life touches virtually all aspects of the culture of her land and her time and provides an excellent vehicle for the authors to transmit that culture to us.

The next essay, "Ellis Peters: The Brother Cadfael Chronicles," by Edward J. Reilly, takes us to twelfth-century England and to the attractive and now-popular stories of Brother Cadfael, a slow and painstaking defender of religion and the poor. England two centuries later comes alive— or should we say, goes dead—in novels by the authors treated in the next two essays. With a PhD in history and a dissertation on fourteenth-century England, P. C. Doherty knows his cultures of the past, as displayed in his numerous novels. A PhD from Cambridge with a specialty in mammalian teeth and bones, Susanna Gregory found it interesting to broaden her areas of concern and to write on everyday people and their cultures, as she does exceedingly well in her *Chronicles of Matthew Bartholomew*.

The scene next moves to Italy with Judy Ann Ford's examination of Umberto Eco's contribution to this genre, *The Name of the Rose*. For its novelistic quality and historical fidelity, the book again comes out a winner and a wonder. Italian Renaissance culture comes to life in the historical crime fiction of Elizabeth Eyre, the subject of the next essay by Jeffrey A. Rydberg-Cox. Eyre ranges widely through society and gives us several well-crafted stories.

Geoffrey Chaucer's world is explored in Margaret Frazer's depiction of life in the fifteenth century, discussed here by Patricia Julius. It is a world of intrigue and ambition, of murder and, often enough, to advance one's position. Frazer's depiction, building on Chaucer and other historians of the period, helps to flesh out the world of the *Canterbury Tales*.

"Josephine Tey and Others: The Case of Richard III," by R. Gordon Kelly, takes up again the ever-constant question, addressed by several crime novelists, of the guilt or innocence of Richard III in the death of Edward's two sons in the Tower. Though many readers have already made up their minds on the subject, this new approach brings fascinating conclusions to bear that may tip the scales toward a new reading.

All interested in the role of women in medicine during the Middle Ages should be delighted with the novels of C. L. Grace (another of the several noms de plume of P. C. Doherty) and the essay by Jean Coakley. Grace outlines how women were usual practitioners of medicine in the fifteenth century until, Coakley says, "universities intellectualized the craft in the thirteenth century" and tried to exclude them. But despite such restrictions, women continued to practice medicine because they were good at it and were determined to persevere. Grace situates the stories in Canterbury and "portrays fifteenth century Canterbury life in all its warts and occasional glory," Coakley says.

Sixteenth-century England as presented by Michael Clynes is far from that in which the ordinary detecting searcher can look for truth. Clyne's world, as the authors of the next essay say, is one of nightmares, with Clynes "a true advocate of the conspiracy school of history." It is a fascinating world and Sir Roger Shallot's "memoirs," as revealed by Clynes, are fascinating.

The New World—seventeenth-century New York—is presented by Maan Meyers, whose works Frank A. Salamone explores in "Maan Meyers: The Saga of the Dutchman." Salamone gives us a detailed study of a family rich in the trappings of New Amsterdam and its culture.

We go back to London in the next essay by Donna Bradshaw Smith, and to the novels of Bruce Alexander. It is the Georgian period, in the heyday of the Bow Street Runners, the police force created by Henry and John Fielding. Alexander delights in recounting the adventures of the blind, compassionate, and brilliant magistrate Sir John Fielding, 1750-1780, and his unusual helper, thirteen-year-old orphan Jeremy Proctor, who is wise and experienced beyond his years. The two make a splendid pair—one doing the running and looking, the other the directing from his think tank.

"Keith Heller: A Genealogy of Detection in the Eighteenth Century," by Scott Christianson, looks at Heller's three almost-forgotten novels, which study "the emerging power/knowledge relations in 'The Age of Reason,'" and cast new light on the culture of the time.

The newly established United States is the setting for the next study, "Margaret Lawrence: An Eighteenth-Century Midwife," by Marie Nelson. Lawrence's stories are about an unconventional woman "educated above her station." The result, says Nelson, "is the illumination of an historical moment or era whilst also telling a good story."

One of the great stars of eighteenth-century English literature was Jane Austen, sharp observer and acerbic wit on the more prominent of her fellow citizens. Always an object of great interest, she comes alive in Stephanie Barron's series, which Anita Vickers explores in "Stephanie Barron: (Re)Inventing Jane Austen as Detective."

England during the Regency period (1811-1820) is the setting for four novels by Kate Ross, as discussed in "Kate Ross: Where Have All the Dandies Gone?" by Jerry L. Parker. The dandified artificial society of the Regency was a perfect setting for con people and crimesters. Parker's revisit to Dandyland, after Ross's death in 1998, is fascinating and informative.

The New York City of Teddy Roosevelt, Jacob Riis, Cornelius Vanderbilt II, Elizabeth Cady Stanton, and many other notable personages is the setting for the detective works of Caleb Carr. According to Douglas Tallack, Carr "makes highly imaginative use of the detective story genre to confront a tough historiographical challenge: how to write a history of sub-conscious fears and their occasional eruption into daily lives." In his essay "Caleb Carr: Running Away from the Darkness," Tallack suggests that Carr confronts the challenge and succeeds in his endeavor.

Victorian England is well presented by Anne Perry in her Charlotte and Thomas Pitt detective stories, here thoroughly analyzed by Linda Holland-Toll in "Anne Perry: Victorian 'Istorian and Murdermonger." "Perry uses her history superbly," Holland-Toll writes, "to allow the contemporary reader to connect with the time she 'has made her own literary preserve.'"

Reconstruction America, with its many political and social complexities, is the backdrop against which James Brewer delves into crime fiction. Brewer's fiction both instructs and entertains, says Lawrence Kreiser: "Brewer's attention to historical detail and accuracy throughout the series, and his willingness to tackle the too-long neglected period of Reconstruction greatly add to our understanding of the period."

Post-Reconstruction is the era of Peter Heck's informative series featuring Mark Twain as investigator. The subject is a natural since Mark Twain, jealous of the success of A. Conan Doyle in his newly arrived Sherlock Holmes, wrote several tales with Tom Sawyer and Huck Finn as detectives. Heck in his series is more successful than Twain was in his weaker detective stories and, sticking close to the general activities of Mark Twain in real life, gives a detailed and accurate picture of the underbelly of the Gilded Age.

Peter Lovesey's "historical mysteries have been unanimously praised for their authentic period flavor and solid historical research," writes Margaret Foxwell in "Peter Lovesey: No Cribbing on History." Sergeant Cribb and Bertie, Prince of Wales, offer "penetrating insight into the Victorian Age," she writes.

We come full circle to Egypt, around the turn of the century, with Elizabeth Peters's series featuring the redoubtable archaeologist Amelia Peabody. As the final contribution to the volume, Gary Hoppenstand analyzes Peters's *The Last Camel Died at Noon* in the broader context of "lost world adventure pastiche."

What, an amateur or professional historian might ask, do these twenty-five essays on the full sweep of history contribute to our knowledge and understanding? Is the full wash of known human existence covered and in such detail to be helpful in our understanding of the past? The answer can only be a resounding yes. Not all periods of the past are covered, Incan or Aztecan America, for example, as well as the Far East. Not all periods in history have become subjects for historical crime fiction. A few periods that have crime written all over them are not presented in these studies, and some excellent crime fiction of periods presented here are not covered.

There are several reasons for their omission (both human and intellectual), and the editors hope to correct those omissions, as well as explore new territories and times, in a second edition of this work.

Meanwhile, the essays presented below demonstrate the value of the fiction of everyday life of the past in adding a new depth and warmth of understanding to the world long gone. We see those people faced with the same problems and hoped-for solutions that we face today. The realization may be saddening, not comforting, but at least it may bring some hope and perseverance and urgency. As the space explorers are wont to say today on every possible occasion as they search space for other creatures like ourselves, historical crime fiction shows that we are not without precedent in a world of crime nor in our efforts to control it.

### Works Cited

"*AHR* Forum: Histories and Historical Fictions." *American Historical Review* 103.5 (Dec. 1998): 1502.

Atwood, Margaret. "In Search of *Alias Grace*: On Writing Canadian Historical Fiction." *American Historical Review* 103.5 (Dec. 1998): 1503-16.

Bawden, Garth. *The Moche*. Cambridge: Blackwell, 1996.

Chisholm, P. F. *A Surfeit of Guns*. New York: Walker, 1996.

Cohen, Patricia Cline. *The Murder of Helen Jewett: Life and Death of a Prostitute in Nineteenth-Century New York*. New York: Knopf, 1998.

Davis, Robert C. *The War of the Fists: Popular Culture and Public Violence in Late Renaissance Italy*. Oxford: Oxford UP, 1994.

Halttunen, Karen. *Murder Most Foul: The Killer and American Gothic*. Cambridge: Harvard UP, 1998.

Hamilton, Lyn. *The Moche Warrior*. New York: Berkley, 1999.

Heller, Scott. "Historians as Detectives: Revealing Society's Fault Lines." *Chronicle of Higher Education* 45 (13 Nov. 1998): A13-A14.

Mertz, Barbara. Interview. *University of Chicago Magazine* Feb. 1999.

Meyers, Maan. *The Lucifer Contract*. New York: Bantam, 1998.

Penman, Sharon Kay. *Cruel as the Grave*. New York: Holt, 1998.

Robb, Candace. *The Gift of Sanctuary*. New York: St. Martin's, 1998.

Srebnick, Amy Gilman. *The Mysterious Death of Mary Rogers*. Oxford: Oxford UP, 1995.

Taylor, Alan. Review of *The Murder of Helen Jewett*, by Patricia Cline Cohen. *New Republic* 12 Oct. 1998: 47.

Winks, Robin, ed. *The Historian as Detective: Essays on Evidence*. New York: Harper & Row, 1968.

# Lynda S. Robinson and Lauren Haney:
# Detection in the Land of Mysteries

## Rita Rippetoe

Ancient Egypt has long been regarded as a land of mystery. With its pyramids, its sphinx, its pantheon of animal-headed deities, the esoteric art of mummification and a history stretching back thousands of years. Currently, three authors have chosen Pharaonic Egypt as a setting for historical detective fiction. Lynda S. Robinson uses the short but famed reign of King Tutankhamun, as does Lee Levin, while Lauren Haney sets her fiction in the reign of the somewhat lesser known Queen Hatshepsut, one of the rare women to exercise kingly power in ancient Egypt.

Tutankhamun was the last pharaoh of royal blood in the Eighteenth Dynasty. A number of factors have worked together to make the last rulers of that dynasty fascinating to the modern world. According to Christiane Desroches-Noblecourt in *Life and Death of a Pharaoh: Tutankhamen*, Amenophis III appears to have been a typical pharaoh who worshipped the traditional gods of Egypt. In honor of his jubilee, he commissioned two statues of himself as god-king. Later known as the Colossi of Memnon, these immense seated figures feature in early travelers' accounts of the Theban necropolis, since legend has it that they sang at sunrise (Desroches-Noblecourt 125-26). However, Amenophis III's son and co-regent Amenophis IV (later Akhenaten) began religious and social reforms that earned him the label of the heretic king. These reforms included moving the capital from Thebes to a new site called Akhetaten (now known as Tell el Amarna). There he replaced the worship of Amun with that of the solar disc, Aten; decreed that the spoken form of the language replace the traditional written formulae in documents; and patronized a new, naturalistic style of art (Desroches-Noblecourt 127). Once he achieved full power, Akhenaten began to suppress the worship of gods other than Aten, especially the chief god Amun, whose priests were his most organized opponents. He sent workmen to disfigure statues of other deities and deface inscriptions that contained their names. While preoccupied with these reforms he neglected foreign affairs, ignoring appeals for help from Egypt's allies in Asia (Desroches-Noblecourt 156-58). Akhenaten made his brother Smenkhkare his co-regent, but they both died in the same year and in 1361 BC the throne fell to the youngest son of Amenophis III, Tutankhaten. At the age of nine, Tutankhaten succeeded to the office of pharaoh and was married to his niece, Ankhesenpaaten (Desroches-Noblecourt 170). Tutankhaten soon returned to his birth name of Tutankhamun and changed that of his wife to

Ankhesnamun, reflecting a turn away from the worship of Aten and back to Amun.

Much of the interest in the history surrounding Akhenaten results from his having been hailed as the first monotheist reformer. His modern admirers see him as an enlightened ruler, concerned with the common people, who replaced a dark, death-obsessed religion and its greedy and oppressive clergy with a god of light and life. Some have even claimed that Moses was inspired by Akhenaten's monotheism in the creation of the Hebrew religion. This is unlikely since Moses led the Hebrews out of Egypt in 1250 BC, almost 100 years after the death of Akhenaten and the restoration of the traditional gods of Egypt, whose priests had begun as soon as possible to efface the memory of the heretic king.

Despite his short reign and relatively minor part in Egyptian history, Tutankhamun has become probably the best known of the pharaohs to the average American. Archaeologists had long known from documents and tomb inscriptions that pharaohs were buried with a wealth of tomb goods. But centuries of tomb robberies had deprived archaeologists of the discovery of a fully equipped royal tomb. By an accident of fate, the entrance of Tutankhamun's tomb was buried in the rubble from the excavation of other tombs, and its location was forgotten until its discovery during the early twentieth century. The tale of the discovery became a major media event in 1922, the excitement heightened by the delays in excavation occasioned by World War I and by the fact that Howard Carter, financed by Lord Carnarvon, was in the last of five years of exploration when the discovery was made. Carter's exclamation, "Yes, wonderful things" ushered in an era of "Tut" madness during which a fad for all things Egyptian swept Europe and the USA. The gold and gem-inlaid death mask of the inner mummy case has become our dominant image of a pharaoh, and any book on Egyptian art or antiquities is virtually certain to feature some of the tomb's rich artifacts. These treasures remain on display in Cairo but were made familiar to many Americans by a national tour in the late 1970s.

This amount of knowledge of, and possible curiosity about, the period makes it a natural venue for the historical novelist. However, the details of this period in Egyptian history are much disputed. Akhenaten's fate is not known with any certainty; he is variously believed to have died of natural causes, accident, or assassination. Even his age at death is disputed, forty-seven by the most accepted calculations but as young as twenty-five according to other authorities (Desroches-Noblecourt 169). Two major non-royal figures play parts in this era. In Akhenaten's court, Ay served as Commander of the King's Horse, and Lieutenant-General of Chariots, Personal Scribe to the King and Royal Fan-Bearer, and was titled "Divine Father." Yet his origin and his relationship to the royal family remain obscure. He is generally believed to have been the husband of Queen Nefertiti's nurse, Tey. Others believe that Ay and Tey were Nefertiti's parents and Ay, therefoгᴄ, Ankhenaten's father-in-law. But there is no proof of this theory other than the status Ay achieved (Desroches-Noblecourt 124). Despite his apparent support of Akhenaten, he seems to have played some role in bringing Tutankhamun to the throne and encouraging his repudiation of Aten. Ay then succeeds Tutankhamun, reigning about four years. He was succeeded by General Horemheb, the leader of Egypt's armies in Asia. Thus the Eighteenth Dynasty ends with the rulerships of two pharaohs who acquire power without royal blood (Desroches-Noblecourt 170).

The fragmentary evidence concerning the events of this period, combined with the widespread awareness of the period on the part of the general public, works to the advantage of the historical novelist, who has a wide latitude to invent motivations and actions for historical characters without violating known history. Lynda S. Robinson makes full use of this latitude, constructing a setting for her characters during which private crime intersects with political intrigue in plots that display Egyptian society at all levels, from the king's audience chamber to seedy riverfront taverns.

The first volume of Robinson's series, *Murder in the Place of Anubis*, appeared in 1994. Her "detective," the fictional Lord Meren, friend and adviser to the fourteen-year-old Tutankhamun, holds the title of Eyes and Ears of the Pharaoh, a title that Robinson appears to have created for her purpose. Meren is a scion of a noble Egyptian family, whose father was killed by Akhenaten for refusing to worship Aten. Meren, only a teen at the time, was tortured into apostasy and branded on his inner wrist with the solar disk symbol of Aten. Years later he is still tormented by nightmares of the torture chamber and by the itching of the scar, which he usually conceals with a wide bracelet. He also suffers inner torment, suspecting his own motives in allowing himself to be sent to Libya despite his suspicions that Ay was plotting Akhenaten's death. Realistically he knows both that his vows to Akhenaten were forced and that the fanatical king was harming the nation, but he still feels guilt about his inaction. Meren is intensely loyal to the young Tutankhamun, determined to protect him against the endless plotting of various factions, including those who still worship Aten and resent the power of the traditional gods and their priests.

These factions include the royal wife, Ankhesanamun, who is portrayed as still loyal to her father's god. Historians know that shortly after Tutankhamun's death Ankhesanamun wrote to the Hittite king, offering to marry a Hittite prince and make him co-regent, an unprecedented step for Egyptian royalty. Desroches-Noblecourt considered the queen to have been a pawn of the vizier Ay, determined to keep his rival Horemheb off the throne (275-78). But Robinson makes the queen the plotter and moves her correspondence with the Hittites back to a time when her husband was still living. Thus we are led to expect that Tutankhamun's early death will prove to be the result of assassination, although his portrayal as a young man eager for the glory of battle leaves open the possibility that he will be slain leading troops against desert bandits. Nor are the supporters of Aten the only suspects in plots against the young king. Priests of Amun, including Meren's cousin Ebana, whose family was killed by the heretic king, have neither forgiven nor forgotten the damage done to their prestige by Akhenaten. They may be plotting against Tutankhamun, motivated by a desire for revenge and a craving for a larger share of royal revenues.

Meren himself is a widower with three daughters: Tefnut, Bener, and Isis. He also has an adopted son. Kysen was the abused son of a carpenter purchased by Meren because the eyes of the eight-year-old boy displayed in the slave market reminded him of his dead wife, Sit-Hathor. Because of his lower-class origins, Kysen struggles against a tendency to be diffident to those he sees as social superiors. But his origins become an advantage in questioning witnesses and suspects who would be awed into silence or incoherence by the Lord Meren, officer of the Pharaoh. Kysen can also leave off his charioteer's uniform and go undercover.

In theory, the pharaoh was personally responsible for all administration of justice in Egypt, since crime was an offense against the goddess Maat. In practice, most crime was punished at the village level by magistrates or citizens. Robinson constructs her novel around crimes that are brought to Meren's attention because of unusual circumstances or possible political ramifications. In *Murder in the Place of Anubis*, the first victim is a low-ranking scribe, but his body is found in the temple of Anubis, the funerary god. This aspect of sacrilege makes the apprehension of the culprit essential, since the embalming performed in this temple is essential to the afterlives of Egyptian nobles. Yet, as Meren says in reporting to Tutankhamun, " 'this evil touches a sacred place and involves priests. One must not capture suspicious ones and beat them in hopes of finding a culprit.' 'No,' the king said. 'It is not wise to beat priests'" (11-12). Robinson neatly combines the tasks of informing readers of the usual course of Egyptian law enforcement and presenting a reason for her protagonist to follow procedures more in keeping with modern sensibilities. Of course, in addition to fear of offending priests or nobles, Meren has his own experience to remind him that torture is a very fallible path to truth.

Robinson's Tutankhamun, although not present in many scenes in this first work, is an engaging character. The author portrays him as aware of his status as a living god, easily assuming his right to the homage and service due to him in that capacity, and yet as a normal young man who wearies of courtly duties, of being constantly on his guard. Meren is the only man before whom he can be a mere person, the fourteen-year-old boy he actually is; and hearing Meren's accounts of the crimes and their solutions gives him relief from the interminable details of diplomacy, taxation, administration, and religious ritual.

Robinson's Tutankhamun acquires our sympathy since he is impatient with the constraints of his ritual duties. He does not repudiate his status, but neither does he seem to crave the obsequiousness it begets in his courtiers, although in a later volume, *Eater of Souls* (1997), he does resent the thinly veiled insolence of the Hittite ambassador. For the historically knowledgable reader, sympathy for the character is increased by awareness that Tutankhamun's life and reign will be short; about five years remain to him at the beginning of the series. It will be interesting to discover whether

Robinson will have Meren survive the transition from Tutankhamun's reign to that of Ay and continue to serve as investigator to the throne.

In addition to the details of history, the historical novelist is responsible for conveying a feel for the texture of life in the chosen era. Robinson successfully describes a world that is physically quite different from modern Western cultures. This is a culture where men wear linen kilts, upper-class men appear in finely pleated robes, decked with jewelry and heavy makeup, and respectable women may appear in virtually transparent gowns. It is a world where keeping a concubine is condemned only because they "cost and make trouble" (Robinson, *Anubis* 22), where slavery is an accepted institution, and where lower-class people bow or grovel to those of higher rank. Even Meren kneels to kiss pharaoh's sandal and waits permission to stand and to speak. A witness questioned by Kysen is described in these terms:

The youth was one of the thousands of children of the poor who served in menial capacities in the temples, palaces, and households of the Two Lands. He would fear Kysen because he was common, landless, and of no importance to anyone but himself. (Robinson, *Anubis* 46)

Language aids in setting the scene. Just as characters in medieval mysteries swear by Christian saints, Robinson's characters exclaim "By Hathor's tits," refer to Egypt as the Two Lands (a reflection of the predynastic division of Upper and Lower Egypt), talk of the state of their *ka* (spirit), and fear desert nights haunted by the hostile spirits of the neglected ancient dead. Robinson also uses metaphors appropriate to the time and locale. Suspects shake like papyrus in a north wind; a vicious woman is compared to a cobra; a questioner is "as persistent as a goose after a fly." It is easy to use such techniques to excess; many readers probably have shuddered at crudely written novels in which dialogue seems to come straight from a B grade epic—"by the venomed fangs of Shem, the snake goddess, confess or I will make you scream like a qualla bird at dawn"—and so on. In her restraint with metaphor and profanity and in the sparing use of titles and honorifics Robinson maintains a balance, enough exotic language to remind us of the setting without annoying excess.

Robinson's portrayal of Egyptian culture widens with subsequent volumes in the series. The scenes in *Murder at the Place of Anubis* are divided between the royal palace and temple buildings and the workman's village near the Valley of the Kings on the west bank of the Nile. There the artisans who carve and paint tombs for nobles and royalty live in modest dwellings: usually four rooms of mud brick, whitewashed and furnished with stools, small tables and jars and chests for storage. Roofs are flat and served then, as they still do in the Middle East, as additional living space, especially as cooler sleeping space than the sun-heated interiors.

In *Murder at the God's Gate* (1995), we enter the world of the great temple complex of Amun, in which hundreds of pure ones, priests, lesser servants, workmen and worshippers come and go in a compound that is virtually a small city. Robinson also introduces more of the complexities of Egyptian politics. The plot centers on a rebellion planned by Prince Tenefer, son of Amunhotep III and a princess of Mitanni, a kingdom on the northern Euphrates. Tenefer would have inherited the rule of Mitanni had not Akhenaten's neglect of the alliance allowed it to fall to the Hittites. Ahiram, son of the now deposed king of Byblos, is also part of the plot. It was common for sons of subject or allied kings to be brought to the Egyptian court. There they were raised to fear and respect Egypt's power and aspire to its culture. Ahiram is bitter because Akhenaten failed to aid his father, who was deposed by Hittite-funded rebels, leaving Ahiram no kingdom to inherit. Tenefer and Ahiram have raided the tomb of Akhenaten and are using the treasure to recruit mercenaries for a planned coup which Meren discovers and foils.

Small details of Egyptian life emerge as well, such as the use of hunting cats to kill poisonous snakes. One of the murder victims, a lector priest, is trained in magic, and Robinson describes his tools and methods, implying that spells against foreign rulers were an accepted adjunct to war and diplomacy. The descriptions of the armor and weapons of Meren's charioteers and of workmen's tools remind us that Egypt was still a Bronze Age culture and that the poor continued to use flint tools for some tasks.

*Murder at the Feast of Rejoicing* (1996) takes us to the main country estate of Meren's family. There Meren hopes to rest and distract possible spies while Kysen oversees the secret removal and concealment of the desecrated and restored mummy of Akhenaten and that of Queen Nefertiti. But his sister, who manages the estate, celebrates his visit with a feast for relatives and neighboring nobles. The feast features an abundance of meats, including roasted quail, heron, duck, and beef; grapes, melons and sweet cakes; wine and fruit wine and the staples of bread and beer. The elaborately dressed guests are entertained by music, dancers, and acrobats. Robinson brings to life the beauties of a noble's country estate: walled gardens; ponds with lotus flowers, ducks and swans; shaded arbors and frescoed rooms; the family chapel with offering tables in front of statues of gods and ancestors; the surrounding fields and canals.

Robinson's fourth volume, *Eater of Souls* (1997), relocates Meren and Kysen and the court to the city of Memphis, oldest capital of Egypt. Across the river loom the Pyramids, and the old Necropolis, already ancient and abandoned for almost 1,000 years. Memphis, a port town, is more multi-cultural than Thebes. Greek sailors, Hittite traders, Cretan ships' captains, Mycenean pirates, and Syrian slaves mingle in markets and taverns, engaged both in legal business and underhanded dealings in stolen or smuggled commodities. In the twisted and dead-end alleys of the old city a serial killer stalks. Bodies are discovered with their throats marked by claw-like slashes, their chests hacked open, their hearts removed and a white feather, symbol of the justice of Maat, left in its place. Rumors spread that the demon, Eater of Souls, who consumes the souls of those who enter the underworld with sin in their hearts, is responsible. These murders go unreported to Meren until the Hittite emissary, Prince Mugallu, becomes a victim.

In most of the murders Meren investigates, a physical cause of death is obvious. Magic is mentioned as a possibility only to be dismissed. But in *Eater of Souls,* Meren and the pharaoh must deal with the possibility that an actual demon roams the streets of Memphis, either sent by the gods to punish the nation for its sins under the heretic Akhenaten, or summoned by a powerful magician to serve unknown purpose. While Meren pursues his investigations, Tutanhkamun leads the priests of the major deities in a ritual designed to imprison the demon. However, in adherence to the "rules" of the detective novel, the killer is revealed to be a minor noble, possessed of a demon or, in modern terms, psychotic, who dresses as the demon to kill those who affront his overweening pride.

In addition to expanding her picture of Egyptian society, Robinson uses each novel in the series to delve into the psychology of her characters. Meren must continue to deal with the guilt of not attempting to stop the plot against Akhenaten, and Kysen with the effects of having been an abused and unwanted child of poor parents suddenly transformed into a nobleman's heir. We also learn more of Meren's wife and how an arranged marriage was transformed into a marriage of love, leaving Meren unwilling to remarry after Sit-Hathor died in childbirth. Meren's memories of his parents further illuminate his character, as do his relations with his children. Meren's daughters also develop from book to book. Bener, in particular, attracts our interest as an intelligent young woman beginning to chafe at the restrictions of her culture. One could see this as an awkward attempt to impose modern feminist concepts on a culture to which they would have been foreign. However, the author may be reminding us that most cultures have harbored individuals who did not fit the roles assigned to them and that a full description of the culture should include such characters. In addition, Egyptian women had more personal freedom and legal standing than women in most other premodern cultures. Even married women could own, manage, and will property and act in their own interest in law courts.

Lee Levin's treatment of this period is quite different. *King Tut's Private Eye* (1996) is cast as a secret account by the co-regent Ay (here Eye, creating a punning title). He is challenged by Tutankhamun to discover who murdered Akhenaten, eight years after the fact. Furthermore, he is commanded to do so without the use of torture, a provision plainly intended to make his task impossible and to give Tut an excuse for dismissing him from office. As the tale begins, Tut is eighteen and in the process of wresting power from the co-regents Eye and Horemheb, who continue to vie for power and favor with the king. Levin's Tut is vain and capricious, possibly mad. This could be accepted as a variant reading of a personality of whom we really know virtually nothing with historical certainty. Mental instability in the pharaoh is not even particularly unlikely considering the excesses of his predecessor, who if not insane was certainly fanatically indifferent to the political fortunes of Egypt.

Despite a good start, Levin spoils his plot by badly mangling the generally accepted facts. His Tutankhamun is the son of Akhenaten and Nefertiti rather than brother to Akhenaten and brother-in-law to Nefertiti. Levin is also apparently unaware that Ankhesenpamun, Tutankhamun's queen, had earlier been married to Akhenaten (her father) and that Tutankhamun was her uncle, not her brother. Dates are also bent to the author's purposes. He introduces a Greek slave girl into Eye's household who is, we are meant to accept, the woman who will become known as Helen of Troy. Unfortunately for this scenario, the battle for Troy is 100 years in the future, as is the Exodus, revelations concerning which are promised in the next volume of Eye's memoirs. Speaking of the Hebrews, Levin has Eye exclaim against the practice of male circumcision, unaware that the Egyptians practiced it themselves. Levin is apparently under the impression that the Egyptians practiced female circumcision, which he has Eye mention with approval. In another error concerning established Egyptian custom, Levin has Eye express envy of the full head of hair the high priest Aanen retains despite his age. Egyptian priests, however, are known to have shaved their heads as well as their beards.

In the finale of the novel, Eye proves that it was Tutankhamun himself who, with the connivance of the royal food taster, procured poisonous mushrooms to have served to his father. However satisfying this solution may be in Levin's plot, it is unlikely to bear any relation to history, since Tutankhamun did not reside in the same palace as Akhenaten at the time of the latter's death. He was, as mentioned above, probably being reared in Thebes, or possibly in the North Palace with the estranged Nefertiti, whereas Akhenaten observed his vow never to leave the new capital and temple city of Akhetaten and did not appear with Nefertiti in the later years of his reign.

Although Levin's historical inaccuracy is annoying enough, his tone is even more so. Eye's pursuit of Akhenaten's killer is interspersed with sexual episodes recounted in a prurient and salacious tone, highly inappropriate to a society that seemed little concerned with sexual purity. Here is a sample:

Regarding appetites, considering that I was having trouble falling asleep anyway, I did give passing consideration to sending for one of my concubines. I had nothing as elaborate in mind as the games [shaving her pubic hair and painting her body with sexually explicit phrases] I'd played with poor Oudah [who has died of poison]. Really, it was the companionship I had in mind more than anything else. In fact, I even considered summoning Tey, and when a man seriously considers asking for his principal wife you know he's of a troubled mind indeed. (74)

Levin also tries to have his fun and mollify readers at the same time by inserting notes from the supposed translator of Eye's long hidden manuscript. For example:

If you are a woman you probably feel Eye to be a disgusting rogue and bounder. I, on the other hand, being a man, feel chagrin that he, living 3,400 years earlier, displayed so much more erotic creativity than has yet come to my own mind. (68)

Overall, Levin's version of Tut's world seems hardly worth seeking out by the reader interested in the particular pleasure afforded by well-researched and well-written historical fiction.

Lauren Haney has chosen an earlier period to set the adventures of Lieutenant Bak of the Medjay police. Nearly 150 years before the reign of Tutankhamun, the Pharaoh Tuthmosis II died. His chief wife and half-sister Hatshepsut had not borne him a son, but she became co-regent for her nephew/stepson Tuthmosis III (the son of Tuthmosis II and a minor wife), who was only a child when his father died. Hatshepsut then took the bold step of ruling in her own right, as a female king, rather than merely as regent.

Maatkare Hatshepsut is a remote figure for Bak and others stationed at the frontier fortress of Buhen, located at the second cataract, and political intrigue does not occupy the central place in *The Right Hand of Amon* (1997) that it does in Robinson's works. The Medjays were a Nubian people who had been recruited for police and frontier patrol duty after Egypt conquered the area that became the modern Sudan. Bak and his fellow Egyptians are described as bronzed or reddened by the sun, with dark eyes and black, brown, or red-brown hair. The Medjay troops and the neighboring Kushites are described as dark as night or as obsidian. However, race does not play a large part in the lives of the characters. Interracial marriage is accepted and the Kushites seem to be regarded as respected opponents and valuable allies.

The events of the story are set circa 1463 BC, twenty-seven years after Thutmosis II put down a rebellion of Kushite kings. The rebel king's heir, Amon-Psaro, was reared as a hostage in Waset (Thebes) and now rules his own kingdom as an ally of Egypt. Like Robinson, Haney has created a situation in which her protagonist must use evidence and intuition rather than confessions exhorted by torture to solve his case. The murder victim, Lieutenant Puemre, is an infantry officer of noble birth. The logical suspects are his fellow officers, whom he has alienated by his arrogance and clear willingness to be promoted at others' expense. Bak is obviously unlikely to intimidate battle-tested men or to beat confessions out of men of equal or superior military rank. A major subplot concerns the impending visit of the god Amon, in the form of his cult statue from Thebes, sent to heal the son of Amon-Psaro, who has petitioned for the god's help as the boy cannot be cured by Kushite physicians. Bak discovers that Puemre was killed because he learned of a plan to assassinate Amon-Psaro, an act that might ignite another war on Egypt's southern frontier. Bak must then learn who in the garrison has reason to hate Amon-Psaro, and then foil the attempt.

Nothing in Haney's plot or exposition appears to violate the known facts of Egyptian history. The role of the border police in controlling and protecting trade caravans is well attested, as is the Kushite rebellion, its defeat by Thutmosis II and continued peace during the reign of Hatshepsut, who is known to have expanded Egyptian trade with Africa.

Haney's evocation of the locale and the culture is effective. The Nile, broken at this point by islands, shallows, and rapids, is described in vivid detail. In contrast, the surrounding desert stretches into the distance, baking in the heat of Ra, the sun. Details include smells and tastes as well as sights and sound. Odors invoked include a savory dish of braised beef, the stench of an embalming shed, fish drying on a flat roof, and the rank sweat of men who have worked a day in the desert heat. The roar of the cataracts, donkeys pattering through the marketplace, and the noise of the crowd welcoming the arrival of the god's barge are skillfully described, as are the sights of the area: partially deserted cities of mud brick crumbling into neglected ruins, the pomp of the procession of Amon's image through reverent and enthusiastic crowds, and caravans with trade goods ranging from ebony to live baboons, ostrich eggs, and leopard skins.

The reverence of the characters for their gods is also well presented. In one scene, as Bak watches the procession of Amon, "he felt his breast swell with wonder and adoration" (58). Later, inspired by the efforts of a cat to protect her kittens, Bak comes up with an idea to protect Amon-Psaro from the dangers of traversing a city in which an assassin lurks. Bak offers a prayer of thanks to the lady Bast, the cat goddess (223).

Oddly, given her choice of periods, Haney makes no mention of the anomaly of a woman reigning as pharaoh. This can be partially explained by her frontier setting. Men serving far from the capital might be thought less likely to discuss the controversies of politics than those closer to the centers of power. But Bak, we are told, was raised in Thebes and might be expected to have some ideas about royal politics. Nor would such considerations be irrelevant to Haney's plot. In worrying that the assassination of a neighboring king might spark a war, soldiers would surely ponder whether Hatshepsut would lead the armies or whether she would permit Thutmosis III to assume command. But perhaps Haney intends to save such issues for later novels, preferring to establish her character Lieutenant Bak before delving into the puzzles of royal politics.

In the series of works devoted to Lord Meren, Robinson portrays the complexity of a particular period in Egyptian history and develops the inner psychology of her characters. Her writing is generally effective, conveying interesting and exotic scenes and actions without calling undue attention to itself. She is plagued by the problem common to any writer of a series, reintroducing the same information in each volume so that the new reader is not left disoriented, although she handles it about as well as can be expected. Her readers are apparently satisfied, since she has four books in print and another, *Drinker of Blood*, published after this essay was written.

Lauren Haney's work is also well written and especially impressive in its sensory detail. It remains to be seen whether her second book, *Face Turned Backward,* will continue the pattern started in *The Right Hand of*

*Amon,* with its view of an Egypt remote from the centers of power and court intrigue. Lee Levin's *King Tut's Private Eye,* however, seems like a parody of both the historical and the detective genres, rather than a true example of either.

Whether any fiction has value beyond its ability to entertain is a matter of opinion. Contemporary detective fiction can be said to reflect the tensions in our society, but whether it aids readers in dealing with these tensions is uncertain. Detective fiction set in societies as distant in time and values as ancient Egypt probably cannot reflect either the actual problems of the culture in question or contemporary problems with any accuracy. Do any readers of the Lord Meren series actually share his concern that chaos will result if the living god is harmed? Or worry that the Eater of Souls is an actual demon summoned from the underworld? If so, they are probably fantasy readers gone astray. On the other hand, it may be instructive to realize that the problems of greed, government corruption, jealousy, madness, and the crimes these problems generate have existed for centuries. And it may be some comfort to consider that, no matter what the problems we face, we do not have to kiss the feet of our rulers. Nor is it lawful for those rulers to solve crimes by beating a confession out of the nearest peasant. For all but the most dedicated antiquarian, time travel would probably serve only to confirm our preference for our own culture, "warts and all." Historical detective novels, like other historical novels, can cater to our curiosity about past times without waiting for the invention of time travel and with less effort than a college course in ancient history.

*Works Cited*

Desroches-Noblecourt, Christiane. *Life and Death of a Pharaoh: Tutankhamen.* New York: New York Graphic Society, 1963.

Haney, Lauren. *Face Turned Backward.* New York: Avon, 1998.

——. *The Right Hand of Amon.* New York: Avon, 1997.

Levin, Lee. *King Tut's Private Eye.* New York: St. Martin's, 1996.

Robinson, Lynda S. *Drinker of Blood.* New York: Ballantine, 1998.

——. *Eater of Souls.* New York: Ballantine, 1997.

——. *Murder at the Feast of Rejoicing.* New York: Ballantine, 1996.

——. *Murder at the God's Gate.* New York: Ballantine, 1995.

——. *Murder at the Place of Anubis.* New York: Ballantine, 1994.

# John Maddox Roberts and Steven Saylor: Detecting in the Final Decades of the Roman Republic

## Terrance L. Lewis

There are two standard ways of approaching the setting and writing of historical mysteries. One is to use a period and culture which few people know about and for which there are few sources, thus allowing the author wide scope for control and creativity. The other approach is to use a well-documented era, allowing for greater realism by incorporating the known social and political details. John Maddox Roberts and Steven Saylor have both opted for the second method in their respective mystery series, each set in the final decades of the Roman republic.

Although the eras depicted are essentially the same, the authors approach the declining decades of republican Rome from two very different perspectives. Roberts's sleuth in his SPQR series is Decius Caecilius Metellus, son of a relatively important (if fictional) Roman politician and scion of what was perhaps the most important plebeian family in the last 150 years of the Roman republic. This allows Decius to be involved in political intrigue from the top down in Roman society in the short stories and four novels which make up the canon in English.[1] While Decius the Younger usually starts his involvement by investigating crime at the street level, every story leads him to political connections and conspiracies, better reflecting most of the sources we have for murder and general violence, as they highlight the political cases more often than they do what we more commonly consider the purely criminal.

Steven Saylor's Roma Sub Rosa series detective, Gordianus the Finder, is from a very different stratum of Roman society than the aristocratic Decius Caecilius, moving up from skilled working-class status to the middle class so far in the series. Roman citizens were divided into six economic classes (five voting classes and the urban poor), and all members of the political and economic elites were from the first class. Gordianus starts the series off in the fifth class, eventually moving to the third because of an inheritance, although his early circumstances (wide-ranging travel, a large if run-down house, and above all the lack of a patron, almost unheard of even for most members of the first class who were not patricians or old nobility) suggest his family had once been wealthy, although not in the league of Rome's elites.[2] For although Gordianus mentions both Cicero and the fictional Lucius Claudius as former patrons, neither fulfills the role of a traditional patron in Roman culture; both were rather employers who spread the word of Gordianus's abilities. For once it is Roberts who strikes the stronger historical note, as the client system is much better used in the first SPQR novels (despite some minor problems noted below) than anywhere in Saylor's work.

Even when dealing with the same set of events (e.g., Catilina's revolt in 63 BC) and individuals, these class differences help shine very different combinations of light and shadow on Rome and its society. Class position and power are parts of the nature of Decius Caecilius, and so he may use his share of the public power of Rome and his family (*dignitas*) or ignore it, depending on his needs. On the other hand, while he has to be accorded respect because of his family, that also makes him more dangerous to the political elite, for as one of their own, Decius might be able to use any information he has against those concerned with the illegal plays of power politics in the future, a theme well illustrated in all the stories, especially the novel *The Sacrilege*. Both the crimes Decius investigates and the reactions he stirs are always at a higher level than anything Gordianus can be directly concerned with. Even in the events that overlap the two (Catilina's revolt), Decius is in the midst of the plot as an actor as well as investigator while Gordianus is much more a witness and involved bystander.

Although Saylor's series has the greater depth of social commentary, reading the two series together highlights the class differences of Rome wonderfully. Gordianus, a relatively poor private investigator, has to survive by understanding the interplay of the powerful forces and people around him, for he has only his wits and whatever assistance his current employers may choose to give him. Gordianus cannot directly affect the major course of events around him as Decius tries to do, except by learning the truth and revealing it (or not) to the powerful elite he reports to, although they are only interested in advancing their own ambitions. Except in a number of the Gordianus short stories, both series are more concerned with politics than they are crime—the crimes set the stage for the politics.

The main thing to remember about crime and detection in the reality of ancient Rome, especially during the republican period, is that both were primarily the concern of private citizens, not the state.[3] If a citizen was killed, it was really up to his family, friends, patron, or clients to find and accuse any suspects and then up to the patron or clients of the accused to support the suspect at any trial. These sets of conflicting allegiances would automatically invoke political alliances even when no political motivations were present in the original crime. The state was involved in all this by having courts set up to try crimes and electing various junior ranking elected officials, similar to Decius the Younger in the first novel of the series, *SPQR,* who were in charge of arrests and any executions or confiscations and fines as well as the various forms of watchmen who patrolled the streets at night looking for obvious criminals and fires. The state was primarily concerned with providing the apparatus of the court system and, to some degree, in preventing public disorder. Other than that, the "rule was that if you wanted justice, you had to get it yourself. If you had a grievance, you had to get satisfaction, or hire someone to help you get it" (Stambaugh 125).

This meant you either hired members of the different gangs which were gaining in political power by this period to exact private revenge, or you got yourself an advocate and brought a charge in court. Here, we have some of the judicial orations of Cicero and various ancient commentaries to guide us, and Saylor uses some of Cicero's cases as his guides—or at least starting points. What is missing in the historical records is exactly how cases were investigated, and into this gap Saylor places Gordianus, more convincingly perhaps than Roberts does Decius.

By using Cicero as his guidepost to many of Gordianus's cases, Saylor has a detailed end-product to base his stories around (Cicero's published versions of his court orations, polished and improved upon), as well as the centuries of glosses and commentaries on them. The basic events of three of Saylor's six current novels (*Roman Blood* [1991], *The Venus Throw* [1995], and *Murder on the Appian Way* [1996]) are based in large part on Cicero's court speeches, while two novels (*Catilina's Riddle* [1993] and *Rubicon* [1999]) and two of the short stories ("A Will Is a Way" and "The House of the Vestals") were partially inspired by various details Cicero provides in passing.[4] Saylor takes his inspiration from other ancient sources as well, and discusses his use of some of them in "author's notes" at the end of his books. Any reader with access to a public or college library should have no trouble finding most of the primary sources Saylor used.

Perhaps the best example of Saylor's use of Cicero and the associated ancient sources is *The Venus Throw*, a complicated story involving: political terrorism against a group of Egyptian envoys; a murder; the political maneuvers of Pompey, Crassus, Cicero, Clodius, and their minions; the complicated love affairs of Clodia, especially with the poet Catullus and Marcus Caelius; and the cult of Cybele. Many of the references in Cicero's defense oration for Marcus Caelius were difficult even for sources writing within a hundred years of Cicero to understand. Nevertheless, Saylor weaves the complicated story together brilliantly. Where Cicero is at his most tangled (the episode where Clodia's slaves and supporters try to catch the exchange of a box of poison in a bath house), Saylor presents a clear picture of the event, which allows the reader to see Cicero's talent for hiding damaging testimony yet which still remains believably reconcilable to Cicero's accounts.[5] Saylor even takes the opportunity to fill in what salacious story was circulating about the later use of the poison box, which Cicero hinted at but prudishly refused to give the details of in his published speech.[6]

Saylor does not, of course, merely flesh out Cicero's defense speeches. He provides a depth of characterization that is not always found in mystery writing, and a wealth of fairly accurate social detail, usually well integrated into all his stories.

That question of what to explain and what not to is, of course, one of the nagging problems in all literature. The need to explain seems more pressing, however, in dealing with historical settings. Writers trying to get the ambiance of modern San Francisco or New Orleans always try to add "local flavor" (and as often or not get the details wrong unless they currently live there), even though they need not explain much about current American society to their readers. Saylor, and to a lesser extent Roberts, fill in the details a Roman audience would already know. Some of the political detail is not quite as accurate as it should be (although probably at least as accurate as most citizens today could give about their own governments) and at times these explanations may be fairly ponderous to those readers just after a good mystery.[7] Roberts is less guilty of the ponderous explanation, although he is no more (or less) accurate than Saylor in historical detail.

One minor example of inaccurate detail in Saylor's work is the age of the recurring character of the patrician politician M. Valerius Messalla Rufus—if he had been sixteen during the events of *Roman Blood* as Saylor has it, he should not have been a candidate for praetor in *Catilina's Riddle* (199), for at thirty-three, he would have been at least four years too young to run for that office. Saylor does make Rufus thirty-three in *Catilina's Riddle*, thus staying consistent with the earlier story, but again that ignores the fact that he would have been too young to be a candidate for praetor—perhaps Saylor made his initial mistake because Messalla Rufus only became consul in 53 BC, several years after he was first eligible for that office, or because Saylor was basing Rufus's career on later Imperial custom instead of that of the late Republic. On the other hand, at his proper age (at least twenty), Rufus would have been too old to have acted as he did in *Roman Blood* without defying Roman custom and mores. As far as the stories themselves are concerned, of course, this detail is totally irrelevant, and also reveals how generally accurate the stories are.

Roberts makes the same type of minor mistake. In his first three novels, he makes Cicero's elder rival Quintus Hortensius the *princip* of the Senate and the patron of Decius' father. As Quintus Hortensius was not a patrician, he could not have been the princip. Nor would it have been likely that any of the long-ennobled Caecilius Metellus family would admit to having a patron, certainly not one from outside the clan. Another example would be in the later short story "The Etruscan House," when Decius claimed that his plebeian aedileship had been extended an extra year, and it is hardly likely in this period of ambitious politicians attempting to woo the crowds with games that such a major departure from custom would have been allowed.[8] Again, this type of detail may cause the historian to pause but would seem very natural within the context of the story.

Roberts's SPQR series covers a much narrower range, in terms of both time (70-53 BC, with three of the novels and the short story "The Statuette of Rhodes" occurring between 63-60 BC) and subject, although to date both series cover nearly an equally wide geographical area. In each case examined, Decius the Younger comes across a murder, which will lead him to a web of political intrigue. The first three cases (*SPQR* [1990], *The Catiline Conspiracy* [1991], and *The Sacrilege* [1992]) and later two short stories ("Mightier than the Sword" and "The Etruscan House") are centered in the city of Rome, the latter cases (*The Temple of the Muses* [1992], and "The Statuette of Rhodes") in Egypt and Rhodes, respectively.

While in the *Roma Sub Rosa* series, Gordianus's cases also often deal with the political power struggles of the elite, Gordianus himself is primarily an agent of justice, not an actor on the political stage, although to some degree the sixth novel, *Rubicon*, goes against these trends. Political rivals and even enemies all come to Gordianus, for in a sense, he is neutral in their struggles—something the elite find difficult to understand in the stories, and which does go against much of what the Roman political elite itself claimed was normal behavior in their writings.[9] Because he is not and can never be an actor on the political stage in his own right, Gordianus has the power to get the most powerful members of the Roman elite to open up to him and tell him more than they sometimes should. Stated baldly, it might sound like a simple literary trick of the author, yet Saylor makes this characteristic of Gordianus completely believable and natural. Gordianus is a seeker of truth, and the Roman elite who employ him recognize that as something admirable from their own rhetorical and philosophic education, even if they pay little attention to the truth in their political manoeuvering and ambitions.

Only Caesar admires that same quality in Decius. Others do not see it, because Decius the Younger, however much he denies it to himself in the stories, belonged to the firmly-entrenched moderate conservatives. This group generally opposed both the nullity of the party of Cato (the *boni*, or in many texts, the *optimates*) and the various rival generals and demagogues, while at the same time usually staying snobbishly away from both the business leaders and the moderate camp of Cicero. However much Decius Caecilius himself strives for pure justice, he more often than not ends up ensnared in the many political rivalries of his time period and only manages to escape by either his family or himself invoking his own political and family connections. Whatever justice there might be is only incidental, and truth is served only because Decius has learned it, although no one other than he may care. In this sense, the richer and more powerful young Senator Decius Caecilius could be seen as being far less free than the socially ambiguous Gordianus.

This can be seen in the wide range of cases Gordianus undertakes, working for Cicero, Crassus, Clodia, and Pompey in the novels, serving their interests however much he may have worked against them before. Gordianus works for Cicero in *Roman Blood* and in his interests in *Catilina's Riddle*, against him in *The Venus Throw* and *Murder on the Appian Way* and then uses Cicero and his staff in *Rubicon*; Gordianus works against Pompey's interests in *The Venus Throw* and yet is employed by Pompey in *Murder on the Appian Way* and *Rubicon*—Gordianus is useful to all, but never permanently a political threat to anyone, while Decius is a threat to everyone, including himself.

As mentioned above, Decius and Gordianus are both involved with Catilina's revolt in 63 BC. The sources for these events are particularly rich, as it was the defining moment of Cicero's career. Cicero's revised speeches against Catilina have survived, and for the final twenty years of his life Cicero could rarely let an opportunity pass to talk about his role in uncovering and destroying Catilina's rebellion. Ancient writers similarly rarely discuss Cicero at length without discussing Catilina. Writers such as Plutarch also have to deal with Catilina when discussing the other players, such as Crassus, Cato, and especially Caesar, and Caesar's adherent G. Sallustius Crispus (c. 86-35 BC) wrote a short historical monograph on the conspiracy.

Roberts and Saylor take two different interpretations of the origins of the conspiracy, both supportable by the evidence. Roberts, in *SPQR II: The Catiline Conspiracy*, takes the traditional interpretation: Catilina, hounded by political and personal enemies for several years in the law courts and disappointed and even humiliated by being defeated by Cicero for consul, launched a two-prong plan in the summer of 63 BC, hoping to be elected as one of the consuls but, failing that, planning a revolt, primarily in the city of Rome itself and in northern Italy, with aid from some of Sulla's unsuccessfully retired veterans and a disaffected Gallic tribe.

Except that Roberts has Catilina's supporters (Crassus and Caesar) still backing Catilina up to the last moment, though in the background (which is a suggestion supportable by some but not most of the evidence), Roberts's basic plot is a straightforward adaptation of the most generally accepted historical narratives. Decius's role of ferreting out the conspiracy from the inside is well plotted and believable. Roberts creates a number of threads that lead Decius to different aspects of the plot, for Roberts rarely uses a red herring in his stories. When he does, it is usually to provide historical verisimilitude, such as his excellent chapter on the October horse.

Saylor's interpretation of the conspiracy in *Catilina's Riddle* is more ambiguous. Other than Catilina's basically unexplained contacts with some of Sulla's retired veterans who are plotting a demonstration of some kind, it is left up in the air if Catilina had really plotted anything, or if Cicero, looking to make himself a hero and win acclaim, had forced Catilina into a corner where he had no choice but to revolt or be destroyed. The latter is what Catilina claims throughout the novel, but he has been loose enough with the truth elsewhere in the novel to prevent the reader from taking him at his word. In fact, nearly everyone in the novel including, for once, Gordianus, is playing several roles and, except for Gordianus, the reader can never be certain who is currently trying to fix the games being played. At the end, even Gordianus is left pondering his role as well as the roles the others played.

Unlike Roberts, Saylor devises many plot twists and red herrings throughout his novel. Like poor Gordianus, the reader is led astray by the plottings of Cicero, Catilina, and those playing off both sides to wonder who might be responsible for a pair of bodies left at Gordianus's rural retreat until quite late in the novel. Even more than Roberts, Saylor also manages to integrate a great deal of social detail into his longer novels, although Saylor's commentaries and asides are slightly less likely to have a direct connection to the plot.

While the major players in the other works often overlap, the other stories cannot be as easily compared. However, since Clodius and Milo figure so highly in *SPQR, SPQR II: The Catiline Conspiracy*, and *The Sacrilege*, it is likely Roberts was originally planning a novel on the death of Clodius, which then could have paralleled Saylor's *Murder on the Appian Way*. Roberts would have had a brilliant opportunity, as the irony of Decius having to investigate the death of his arch-rival Clodius, supposedly at the hands of Decius's good friend Milo, would have provided the author a fine canvas. Unless the series is revived in English however (the series has a further five novels in German as of 1999), this excellent opportunity is lost, as are the direct comparisons in their use of the historical sources.

The authors do treat their major historical figures in characteristically different ways, however. Most of Saylor's major Romans who show up in Roberts's series (such as Crassus, Pompey, Caesar, Clodius, and Clodia) may be ambitious, self-satisfied and self-centered, and not above bending the letter of the law to help themselves or to serve what they consider to be the best interests of Rome, but they are nobler than the conniving, power-mad gangsters of Roberts's vision. The reputations of Crassus and Pompey, and above all Clodius, suffer greatly as they plot murder and treason in *SPQR* and *The Sacrilege*. Although Crassus and Pompey make very limited appearances in the pages of *SPQR* and *The Sacrilege*, they are the prime instigators in the plots Decius is trying to unravel and their mores are seen by their methods. Their agents also figure into the plot of *The Catiline Conspiracy*, while Pompey is behind the plot of the short story "The Statuette of Rhodes." In Saylor's work, Crassus (who is featured in *Arms of Nemesis*) and Pompey (*Murder on the Appian Way*) are merely tough and ruthless, not outright criminals.

This is even more true in the case of the rabble-rousing patrician Clodius and his sister Clodia. In Roberts's work, they typify nearly all that was wrong with the late Roman republic in the eyes of a traditionalist like Decius. In *SPQR* and *The Sacrilege*, Clodius is more than a demagogue and general troublemaker who has questionable relations with his own sister (as he appears in Saylor's *The Venus Throw* and from what the reader learns of him in *Murder on the Appian Way*), he is truly maniacal and is opposed (and contrasted) with the moral and sympathetic Decius. And while both Saylor and Roberts give credence to every innuendo about Clodia's sexual exploits, she comes across as a hardened, cruel, ambitious amoral hedonist in *SPQR* and as passionate and sympathetic in *The Venus Throw* and *Murder on the Appian Way*.

Only Caesar, the power lurking deep behind Roberts's series and the last four of Saylor's novels, seems to have defeated their powers of portrayal so far, as he hovers enigmatically just in view, always planning but never at a loss. Saylor, however, plans to continue his series until at least the assassination of Caesar (just as Roberts gives hints in *The Sacrilege* that he plans on doing the same), and so may yet deal with the phenomenon of the genius of the late Roman republic.

Unlike the other major players in Roman history, Cicero has a more set, yet ambiguous, place in both series. In the SPQR novels where he appears, he is helpful and friendly to Decius's causes, giving advice and help to a degree, although determined not to take on more opponents than he needs to. To Gordianus, Cicero is a generous employer and yet far too morally ambiguous to trust after their first case together.[10] Marc Antony is the one historical figure who comes across very similarly in both series (appearing in Saylor's novels *Murder on the Appian Way* and *Rubicon* and Roberts's short story "The Etruscan House"): tough, hard-drinking, and Caesar's loyal follower. Only Milo, an actor in only one of Saylor's novels (*Murder on the Appian Way*), comes across as a more likable character in Roberts's version of ancient Rome.

The reader of both the SPQR and the Roma Sub Rosa series would therefore be left with a wealth of commentary on the political and social mores of Rome, but would also be left wondering which interpretation is the more correct. The answer, of course, can never be decisively given, which explains why historical fiction can be so popular, as then the reader is given an answer to history's unanswered questions. Providing the novels are as well done as Roberts's and Saylor's, the historian has little cause for complaint.

### Notes

1. As Roberts goes to great lengths to explain, Decius was not a Roman praenomen. It might have been better to have named Decius (father and son) Lucius instead, as a Lucius Caecilius Metellus was consul in 68 BC, rather than invent the improbable story of how Decius became their praenomen. Decius Caecilius the Elder was supposed to have been consul in 67 BC, when Manius Acilius Glabrio and Gaius Calpurnius Piso were actually consuls.

Unfortunately, it seems likely that the SPQR series has ended in English, although some five more novels exist in German and Roberts continues to contribute short stories to anthologies.

2. Gordianus discusses his economic class and the class structure of Rome (with only minor errors) in Saylor's *Catilina's Riddle*.

3. For the best brief description of policing and the justice system, see Stambaugh, 124-27; for the best current monograph, Nippel.

4. *Roman Blood* is based on Cicero's "Pro Roscio Amerino" (*Cicero VI* 122-54); *The Venus Throw* on the "Pro Caelio" (*Cicero XIII* 406-522); *Murder on the Appian Way* on the "Pro Milone" (*Cicero XIV* 6-123 [with the early commentary of Q. Asconius Pedianus, 124-36, which Saylor also used in his material]. The "Pro Caelio" and "Pro Milone," as well as the four speeches against Catilina (which lend details to *Catilina's Riddle* and "The House of the Vestals") are also found in *Cicero Selected Political Speeches*. Although most of the historial background for *Rubicon* concern Caesar and Pompey, Cicero's collected letters from the period add details, while his letters to Tiro are also important to the story line. Cicero's letters are found

in two sets of three volumes each in the Loeb edition: *Letters to Atticus* and *Letters to His Friends* (Cambridge, vol. I 1927, vol II 1929, vol. III 1929). The letters to Tiro are found in *Friends*, vol. III 316-81.

5. *Cicero XIII* 483-93; *Venus Throw* 194-202, 362-64.

6. *Cicero XIII* 493; *Venus Throw* 267-68, 364-65.

7. For further commentary on this point, especially in regard to *Murder on the Appian Way*, and an even harsher evaluation of Cicero's actions in Saylor's works than I think is justified, see Mary Beard's review of four of the Saylor novels (*The Venus Throw* is not included), "Cicero the Bad Guy."

8. Roberts, "The Etruscan House" 21.

9. For the best examples, see Steven Saylor, *Murder on the Appian Way* 142-44, 148, 282, and *Rubicon* 16-21, 30-31, 41-42, 141-42, 171-72, 197-98, 236.

10. Saylor makes this clear in the (chronologically) early short story "Archimedes' Tomb."

## Works Cited

Beard, Mary. "Cicero the Bad Guy." *Times Literary Supplement* 8 May 1998: 23.

Cicero, M. Tullius. *Cicero Selected Political Speeches*. Trans. Michael Grant. London: Penguin, 1989.

——. *Cicero VI*. Trans. J. H. Freeze. Cambridge: Harvard UP, 1984.

——. *Cicero XIII*. Trans. R. Gardner. Cambridge: Harvard UP, 1987.

——. *Cicero XIV*. Trans. N. H. Watts. Cambridge: Harvard UP, 1992.

——. *Letters to Atticus*. 3 vols. Trans. E. O. Winstedt. Cambridge: Harvard UP, 1912-18.

——. *Letters to His Friends*. 3 vols. Trans. W. Glynn Williams. Cambridge: Harvard UP.

Nippel, Wilfried. *Public Order in Ancient Rome*. Cambridge: Cambridge UP, 1995.

Roberts, John Maddox. "The Etruscan House." *Crime through Time II*. Ed. Miriam Grace Monfredo and Sharon Newman. New York: Prime Crime, 1998.

——. "Mightier Than the Sword" *The Mammoth Book of Historical Whodunnits*. Ed. Mike Ashley. New York: Carroll & Graf, 1993.

——. *The Sacrilege*. New York: Avon, 1992.

——. *SPQR*. New York: Avon, 1990.

——. *SPQR II: The Catiline Conspiracy*. New York: Avon, 1991.

——. "The Statuette of Rhodes." *Classical Whodunnits*. Ed. Mike Ashley. New York: Carroll & Graf, 1997.

——. *The Temple of the Muses*. New York: Avon, 1992.

Saylor, Steven. "Archimedes' Tomb." *Crime through Time*. Ed. Miriam Grace Monfredo and Sharon Newman. New York: Berkley, 1997.

——. *The Arms of Nemesis*. New York: Ivy, 1992.

——. *Catilina's Riddle*. New York: Ivy, 1993.

——. *The House of the Vestals*. New York: St. Martin's, 1997.

——. *A Murder on the Appian Way*. New York: Ivy, 1996.

——. *Roman Blood*. New York: Ivy, Rubicon, 1999.

——. *The Venus Throw*. New York: Ivy, 1995.

——. "The White Fawn" in *Classical Whodunnits*. Ed. Mike Ashley. New York: Carroll & Graf, 1997.

Stambaugh, John E. *The Ancient Roman City*. Baltimore: Johns Hopkins UP, 1988.

# Lindsey Davis:
# Falco, Cynical Detective in a Corrupt Roman Empire

## Peter Hunt

Histories and historical novels both present worlds distant from their readers. Historians can do this explicitly; historical novelists must populate a world with appropriate individuals, social organization, and culture without becoming didactic. When a historical novel is also a detective novel, advantages accrue to its author because of the resemblance between detectives and historians.

The author of a modern detective novel often describes a society foreign to her readers, a world of police and criminals, blackmail, fallen high-society, illicit affairs, and murder. Even the more respectable cast of a who-done-it often experience their murder or theft in Egypt, on the Orient Express, or in an isolated mansion in the country. These worlds require description and explanation as surely as the Roman Empire does. So their narrators, often the detectives themselves, are meticulous about details of clothing, food, houses, and persons. They will often pause to speculate on the rules and motivations of the society into which they have transported their readers. Such a narrator is ideal for a historical novel, where—especially in the case of an ancient society such as Rome—a different world and mentality must be elucidated without the intrusion of patent lectures on social or cultural history.

The world of detective novels is not merely a different world that requires explanation. It is often a fallen and deceptive place that the detective must unveil. To begin with, the genre requires a crime; more important, the whole world of the detective novel is one of corruption, immorality, ruthlessness, and, most important, false appearances. The Roman Empire has special attractions to an author trying to evoke this atmosphere. Notwithstanding the efficiency its survival attests and the pristine morals claimed for its early years, in the popular imagination Rome is a place of arrogant power, murderous intrigue, open sexuality, and secret liaisons. The contemporary historian Tacitus describes the period of his *Histories*: "Things holy were desecrated, there was adultery in high places . . . those who had not an enemy in the world were ruined by their friends" (1.2). We could be in the "The Big Sleep" or "Chinatown." Rome is a detective's world.

Historians are like detectives in the attitude that they take to their quarry: they do not merely describe a world but unmask it. They strip away illusions and the outward appearances that hide actual events, causes, and motives. This strain of historical writing—which Hayden White calls ironic

(36-38)—dominates the historiography of ancient Rome. A desire to reveal hidden and unpleasant truths, already clear in the Romans Sallust and Tacitus, is apparent in modern treatments. In the mid-nineteenth century, Theodor Mommsen felt that the pedestal of antiquity upon which Roman politicians stood needed to be removed (Gay 202). The most influential Roman historian of the twentieth century, Ronald Syme, insisted that "the Roman constitution was a screen and a sham." He was interested in describing the forces that lay "behind or beyond it" (15).[1] So Roman history is a detective history.

Lindsey Davis's novels, narrated in the first person by the detective Falco, present the reader with a rich and varied picture of the early Roman Empire in 70-73 AD.[2] This essay treats three topics. First, a consideration of the plots of Davis's novels should aid the prospective reader and trace some generic affinities of the series, not all of which are straight detective novels. Second, the historical accuracy of Davis's world is impressive, although characters, including Falco himself, sometimes display modern attitudes. Third, Davis, as a historian, presents a fallen and hypocritical Rome; the detective Falco is the unmasker of the reality behind the facade. Nevertheless, despite the trappings of the bitter, skeptical, and alienated detective, we shall see that Falco's cynicism is limited.

Although the greatest joy of the Falco novels lies in their wit and their local and historical color, their plots are also well constructed. For the most part the development depends not on stunning turnabouts or major surprises, but rather on a gradual and entertaining accumulation of information and narrowing of suspects. Admittedly, Falco has a few clumsy moments. For example, he assumes an implausibly stupid murderer, when he jumps to the conclusion that a woman is having her husband's gravestone engraved in advance of killing him (*Venus* 66).

Davis's novels fall into a variety of modern genres. In *The Silver Pigs, Shadows in Bronze*, and *A Dying Light in Corduba*, Falco performs missions for the emperor à la James Bond. *The Silver Pigs* is Falco's fast-paced debut and should not be missed. He ends up thwarting a threat to the emperor that is plausible and has historical parallels: the bribing of the praetorian guard. *Shadows in Bronze* involves a less likely plot to suborn the navy and cut off the grain supply to Rome. *A Dying Light in Corduba* involves the investigation of a supposed olive oil cartel in Baetica in Spain. From the beginning the reader wonders how Baetica will raise prices and devastate the empire's economy when there are so many other sources of olive oil. In these two cases, one might invoke in Davis's favor the "James Bond principle": don't look too closely at a scheme to destroy the world.

*Time to Depart* is more of a police novel than a detective novel, since Falco is fighting an organized crime boss in conjunction with the *vigiles*, the closest thing in Rome to a police department. This was my least favorite of the novels. The criminal organization seemed anachronistic: for example, why would the mob concentrate on prostitution in a society where this was legal? Despite a minor traitor within the *vigiles*, the novel also lacks the sense of trust betrayed or good intentions corrupted that can make this genre so haunting.

*Venus in Copper*, quite an enjoyable read, fits the most neatly into the classic detective story mode: insincere clients, wealth and betrayal, a *femme fatale*, and unscrupulous businessmen. *Poseidon's Gold* also features an intricate plot, but this time involves the fallout from an illicit art deal on the part of Falco's dead brother. In addition to *Silver Pigs*, my personal favorites are *The Iron Hand of Mars* and *Last Act in Palmyra*. In *The Iron Hand of Mars*, Falco investigates a legion of dubious loyalty in the war-ravaged borderlands of Roman and Free Germany. The writing is crisp, the wit biting, and the atmosphere chilling. Set on the wild and colorful eastern fringes of the Roman Empire, *Last Act in Palmyra* resembles an Agatha Christie. A detective must decide among a fixed group of murder suspects, many of whom seem to have good motives for the deed.

Like a historian, like a detective, Davis explains a new world to her readers. In some cases this explanatory impulse is a bit transparent. It's hard to imagine a well-educated, high-ranking imperial freedman asking, "Do set me straight about the *vigiles*. I confuse them with the Urban Cohorts" (*Time* 64). Falco's concern about the danger involved in his long-time girlfriend Helena's giving birth is historically quite accurate.[3] Falco states that it is the "high rate of mother and infant mortality" that worries him (*Dying* 205). Such a formulation, however, is more likely from a social historian than a member of a society that knew no other mortality rate. Falco's fear and concern would have been sufficient. Although Davis's desire to instruct sometimes gets the better of her, in a vast majority of cases, the careful description expected of an observant detective allows crucial information to be conveyed more subtly.

The vividness and veracity of Davis's world is extraordinary, especially in the depth and accuracy of the details of daily life. Her achievement appears even more impressive when one considers the nature of our ancient sources. The basic political and military history of the Roman Empire depends primarily on a few sources, which explicitly tell the stories of the emperors, their courts, and their armies. In contrast, our knowledge of daily life is drawn from off-hand remarks scattered throughout Latin literature, from legal texts, from inscriptions, and from archaeological remains. Davis certainly consulted existing works that draw together these sources of information, but the breadth of her knowledge indicates wide reading in the ancient sources. Although I shall be detailing some of her mistakes—and have certainly missed others—her general level of historical authenticity is high.[4] There are, after all, eight books, with few anachronisms and a wealth of accurate detail. Had I read eight scholarly books on Roman social history, I might well have had at least as many quibbles and objections.

Falco lives in Rome itself and several of the novels take place there; thus it is important for Davis to accurately describe the material culture and atmosphere of this huge pre-industrial city. Since Falco is relatively poor, he, like the vast majority of the city's inhabitants, lives in an *insula*, an apartment building.[5] Davis's descriptions of *insula* life are all on the mark: "No balcony; no view; no garden, of course; no cooking facilities. Water from a fountain a street away. A public latrine at the end of our own street. Baths and temples on the Aventine" (*Time* 83). Davis also knows that the top floor of an *insula* was the cheapest (*Venus* 14) and that *insulae* had no heating (*Poseidon's* 165). Fires were common (*Time* 388-93). The dangerous height of Roman apartments was regulated repeatedly and apparently without complete success by several emperors. In *Venus in Copper*, a building is sabotaged; Davis describes the reaction of spectators on the street when it comes down, "There is a procedure to follow. In Rome, buildings often come falling down" (*Venus* 233).[6] Davis also catches a Roman's paradoxical pride in "the astonishing height of the gimcrack apartments" (*Shadows* 293). One huge apartment building, "the *insula* of Felicula" was famous around the Mediterranean (Carcopino 26).

The only significant flaw in Davis's Rome is that it is sometimes too small. Low estimates give Rome a population of 450,000 (Storey 966, 975). Falco would hardly have to avoid "my banker, a girl I preferred not to recognize, and several of my brothers-in-law" during a walk across town (*Poseidon's* 29). The arch-villain of *Time to Depart* is discovered and then killed when his hideaway, coincidentally adjacent to Falco's, catches on fire, a weak conclusion (*Time* 394).

Several of the novels take Falco to the ends of the Roman empire: *The Silver Pigs* brings him to Britain; *Shadows in Bronze* to Campania; *The Iron Hand of Mars* to Rome's German frontier, *Last Act in Palmyra* to the Hellenistic cities of Roman Syria; *A Dying Light in Corduba* to Roman Spain. In all cases the local color is rich, the result of careful research and, no doubt, enjoyable autopsy. Falco's perambulations reflect the concerns of modern scholars who often attempt to counter the Romanocentric view of our sources and to focus on the provinces that made up most of the empire.

In addition to the tone of daily life that Davis so richly conveys, her research on extraneous details seems to have been thorough. I investigated a variety of claims, including trifling, off-hand remarks by minor characters. They all seemed to check out. Germanicus made a grave for the corpses from the destruction of Varus's legions by the Germans. Of the three grounds for Tiberius's criticism of him, one was indeed that as a priest Germanicus should not have touched anything contaminated with death (*Iron* 218; cf. Tacitus, *Annals* 1.62). Falco's brother was in the Fifteenth Legion Apollinaris, which did indeed take part in the Jewish war and spent a winter in Scythopolis (*Last* 183). The army did take Gophna and Acrabata before moving on to Ephraim and Bethel, where Falco's brother died (*Poseidon's* 84, 316). The First Legion Adiutrix was indeed formed from the men from the Misenum fleet (*Iron* 256). Triremes, which I had wrongly associated only with classical Athens, were also the "workhorses" of the Roman fleet (*Shadows* 270). Aristophanes' *Birds* did indeed take second place when it was first produced, and it did lose to the *Revelers*, now lost (*Last* 206). This type of attention to detail is probably less of an accomplishment than the avoidance of anachronism, but is equally remarkable in Davis's series.

Davis turns out to be a bit weaker on straight political or military history. One must admit that the political background to the whole series is well chosen. The history of the early empire was punctuated by a complex series of civil wars in 69 AD, the "Year of the Four Emperors." This bloody interlude, which revealed weaknesses of the imperial system, adds a sense of urgency to Falco's missions for the new emperor, Vespasian. Nobody could have known at the time that Vespasian was to usher in a period of 120 years without civil war. Unfortunately, Davis makes two of her worst mistakes in her accounts of 69 AD. In *The Iron Hand of Mars*, an admittedly highly condensed account of the year ends with the statement that, "When Galba died, Otho took over in Rome, but the Rhine legions rejected him and decided to elect their own emperor" (24). In fact, Otho assassinated Galba *after* the German legions had elected their own emperor, Vitellius. In *A Dying Light in Corduba,* the claim is made that, "It was only three years since two Hispanic provinces played their part in the legendary Year of the Four Emperors: Tarraconensis in backing Galba, then Lusitania in supporting Otto [*sic*]" (144). Otho was the governor of Lusitania when Galba was first proclaimed emperor. At that time Otho, and thus Lusitania, backed Galba. Otho's successful coup against Galba depended on discontented soldiers in Rome and had nothing to do with Lusitania. A third lapse in political history comes in *A Dying Light in Corduba*: "I had to endure a rambling discussion of whether the Society had been founded by Pompey the Great (whom the Senate had honored with control of both Spanish provinces) or Pompey the rival of Caesar (who had made Baetica his personal base)" (5). This is at best confusing: Pompey the Great, given the right to govern Spain through legates, was the rival of Caesar. Although Pompey's two sons later based their last campaign against Caesar in Baetica, neither is aptly identified as "the rival of Caesar."

A historical detective novel requires a detective, even in societies such as Rome that had no such profession. Falco, indeed, does the typical work of the modern detective: "commissions for commercial surveillance, gathering court evidence, and finding ground for divorces" (*Poseidon's* 19). Although snooping is not attested as a specialized skill, aspects of the modern detective's job did become professional. Former gladiators worked as bodyguards. More interesting are "slave-catchers," whose job was to recover fugitive slaves; they show up as the perpetrators of a number of scams in legal texts (Daube). Social differentiation, a complex legal system, and most especially the size of Rome make a Roman detective plausible without much violence to historical veracity. In addition, under Roman law a husband was allowed to keep one-sixth of his wife's dowry on divorce, if she was shown to have committed adultery (Treggiari 464); Falco might well have had business of a seemingly modern nature.

But Falco is often less of a Sam Spade than a James Bond, performing special missions for the emperor. An emperor would typically employ detached centurions for military or police missions and imperial freedmen for more delicate tasks. A freedman sent on a delicate mission for Domitian is described as coming "from the more private of his attendants" (Tacitus, *Agricola* 40). Falco's similar mission in *Shadows in Bronze* would have been performed more quickly and efficiently by such an imperial freedman. None of our sources mention a secret police in the Early Empire, but some scholars feel that such an organization is *a priori* likely and would naturally leave little evidence (Rudich 134-35). Davis does include such an organization in her books, but it is under the command of Anacrites, a rival of Falco.

Falco calls himself an informer, a term which does not correspond to a modern informer, but seems to translate the Latin *delator*. Although *delator* can mean either somebody who brings information or somebody who brings an accusation, Davis seems to be thinking especially of the *delatores*. These men were notorious for accusing senators of conspiracies against the emperor. Since these charges were often trumped up and played on the fears of insecure emperors, *delatores* were unpopular with the senatorial class: Falco envisages the punishment he would receive at the hands of "a judge who hated informers—as most of them did" (*Poseidon's* 52; cf. *Time* 144). Falco contrasts himself with these informers, "political parasites who, before Vespasian purged public life, had put fear into the whole senate" (*Poseidon's* 111). But Falco is really not even in the same category. The *delatores* were almost always of the senatorial class or closely linked to the imperial family: ex-consuls, governors, and procurators are all attested as *delatores*. Their accusations were not the results of investigative skill, but resulted from opportunities arising from social contact or from ambition on the part of men who found traditional senatorial careers too confining (Rudich 25).[7] The plot requirement that Falco be not only a private detective, but a secret agent, presents Davis with a difficult, if not insoluble, problem: in what capacity should Falco serve the emperor? Calling him an informer does not succeed very well, since, as Davis is aware, he does not even resemble a *delator*.

When we get beyond the *realia* and their chronology to ancient attitudes and mentality, the problem of historical fidelity becomes a difficult one. Historical veracity to the mores of a radically different time can make characters alien and unsympathetic. Thus historical novels set in radically different cultures tend to fall on a continuum from a realistic and alien narrator and world to a sympathetic, but modern, one. For example, Colleen McCullough's Roman novels present the most bloody and superstitious aspects of the Roman world with an unswerving gaze; as a result her characters seem a bit monstrous. In Davis's novels, we get a world and characters that are sympathetic, accessible, and readily understood. As a result its attitudes are sometimes less historically accurate. Let us examine this issue in more detail in the case of Roman religion and slavery.

There are a couple of anachronisms in Davis's treatment of Roman religion.[8] Falco explains that "besides, as a priest I was too pious for witty street chat" (*Shadows* 57). Roman priests were expected to do their rituals correctly and with solemn reverence. Other than specific ritual limits on certain priests, there was no demand that priests be serious or solemn in their daily life. Davis seems to be thinking of Christian clergy, whose whole lives are sometimes supposed to be steeped in devotion and serious piety. In *Last Act in Palmyra*, Falco deposits a corpse in a temple of Nemesis for the evening (169). Death, however, involved pollution that would be kept out of temples whenever possible. In fact, Christians were criticized for burying their dead within their church precincts.

More important than these minor slips is the tendency for Falco to be either condescending or openly skeptical of Roman religion. Falco characterizes the sober, rustic simplicity of one character as follows: "It would not surprise me if he was the serious sort who quietly cleansed his stables each Parilia with a private lustration" (*Dying* 181). His skepticism is most explicit in *Last Act in Palmyra*: "There can't be much difference between being a priestess and an actress, except for public status. They both involve fooling an audience with a ritual performance in order to make the public believe in the unbelievable" (*Last Act* 131). Skepticism was strong among the highly educated elite at Rome, where it was usually combined with a respect for traditions and with approval of religious rituals that helped to maintain the social structure.[9] Falco's attitude is not tempered by either consideration. The motivation for Falco's skepticism and Davis's general neglect of religious feeling probably stems from two sources.

First, until recent decades, the predominant model of Roman religion depended on an implicit comparison with Christianity. Roman religion was—and still often is—represented as being a matter of empty ritual without the personal belief and devotion required by the "mystery cults" and eventually Christianity. Falco, a detective, an unmasker and despiser of empty form, naturally has no use for such a religion. This conception of Roman religion, however, denies the strength of Roman piety, amply attested in their festivals, dedications, and sacrifices. Skeptics were probably outnumbered by the devout even among intellectuals. In Davis however, it is mainly non-Romans who are strongly religious: Musa, a priest of an outlandish Eastern cult in *Last Act in Palmyra*, or Veleda, a German priestess, even more sinister, in *The Iron Hand of Mars*, or some Christians, whom Rome's Falco beats up (*Last Act* 282-83).

Second, skimming over this aspect of Roman life keeps Davis's world and characters from becoming too alien and difficult to understand. Davis does miss out on some of the interest that, for example, Tony Hillerman's *Skinwalkers* derives from a deeper exploration of the traditional Navajo mental world, one quite alien from that of the average reader. Nevertheless, a pious and, to our minds, superstitious narrator might detract from the light tone and fast pace of Davis's novels.

Slavery presents another dilemma for the historical novelist of Rome, who must bridge the gap between modern condemnation and ancient acceptance of the institution.[10] Davis is typically well informed about the roles and ubiquity of slaves in ancient Rome; as we shall see, she avoids one crucial and realistic step in order to avoid alienating modern sensibilities.

Some Roman slaves attained their freedom and Roman citizenship. These slaves were numerous and conspicuous in our sources, although probably only a small proportion of slaves escaped bondage. Those that did were sometimes prominent for their wealth—earned rather than inherited wealth was looked down upon—or in the imperial bureaucracy. Davis correctly emphasizes the importance of ex-slaves to Roman government and the resentment their power evoked: "Laeta was top of the heap: an imperial ex-slave, born and trained in the Palace of the Caesars amongst the cultivated, educated, unscrupulous orientals who had long administered Rome's Empire . . . (They mass together like woodlice)" (*Dying* 2, 5). Roman hostility towards ex-slaves, often "orientals" from the Greek-speaking eastern Mediterranean, turns out to be relatively easy to deal with, since it is easily assimilated to modern snobbery towards the *nouveaux riches*: "by New Men I mean ex-slaves and foreign immigrants; people with overflowing coffers but no education who want to appear cultured . . . In the shifting social strata of Rome there was plenty of scope for applying gloss to upstarts" (*Poseidon's* 129).

Toward actual slaves Falco shows an authentic condemnation of specific abuses with an unreflective acceptance of slavery itself. A noble woman, to whom Falco is teaching the cithara, sells off one of her maids who had propositioned Falco: "Helena's prophecy about the maid was correct. The daft chit had been sent to the slave market! Incredible. I hoped she found a more charitable mistress; I never saw her again" (*Shadows* 183). Falco complains because "I thought there must be better ways of keeping discipline" (*Shadows* 184). On the other hand, Falco is quite callous about the prospect of sale in another case: he mentions "Chysosto, a Levantine secretary who would sell for a high price once we released him for auction, though at present I was using him to make up inventories" (*Shadows* 20)—note that Davis correctly comes up with Greek names for her educated, urban slaves. Also accurate and contrary to modern sensibility is the assumed superiority of the free: "Groups of uncouth slaves stood blocking the pavement while they gossiped, oblivious to free citizens wanting to pass" (*Time* 314).

The step that Davis is unwilling to take is to supply her main characters with slaves. Although Falco envisions a future when their children will have "an escort of extremely prissy slaves" (*Dying* 255), neither Falco nor his girlfriend Helena is typically accompanied by slaves. Perhaps Falco, relatively poor, might not have owned a slave; Helena, a senator's daughter, would have been surrounded by slaves from her birth and certainly would take slaves on her journeys. Rich Romans bragged about their frugality, if they went on a trip with only a few slaves. The ultimate symbol of Pompey's fall from greatness was that he might have to untie his shoes himself—he was fortunately saved from this fate at the last moment (Plutarch, *Pompey* 73). Davis herself is aware of this inconsistency: "Most expected Romans to be traveling with an entourage" (*Dying* 113).

The reasons that Helena and Falco have no slaves are various. No doubt a skilled novelist such as Davis could circumvent the problems of extra witnesses or participants in almost every scene—privacy was a very different concept in a slave society. The alienation of the reader's sympathy would be hard to avoid, especially since Falco's appeal depends in part on his being the impoverished underdog, contemptuous of authority. Helena, too, is a rebel against convention, bucking Roman patriarchal control. Modern readers would have trouble swallowing an independent detective teamed up with his independent girlfriend with three or four slaves to take care of them.

As detective, Falco seems at first to fit into the category of the hard-nosed narrator of classic "American detective" fiction, cynical about the world and suspicious of the powers that be: "Not all the fine civic building programs in the world would ever displace the raw forces that drive most of humankind. This was the true city: greed, corruption, and violence" (*Time* 233). In a similar vein, *Venus in Copper* begins with the aphorism: "Rats are always bigger than you expect"—Falco turns out to be describing an actual rat in his prison cell (*Venus* 1). Falco can be as callous as any modern detective: on seeing the corpses of two men he had seen before in a heated argument, he observes, "Whatever had made these two so angry, fortune had found a decisive way of helping them get over it" (*Iron* 60). Nevertheless, Falco's hard front fades a bit too easily for the genre: always a righteous defender of women and children, he's even a soft touch for stray dogs (*Time* 77-79, 81, 200).

Falco's cynicism also turns out to be superficial.[11] The rot in his world does not go all the way to the top. The emperor Vespasian, however tight-fisted, is an admirable, self-made man, who succeeded through his ability despite "Establishment prejudice" (*Time* 58). Titus, the emperor's son, is enamored of Helena, but pursues honorably and politely his rivalry with the lowly Falco. Like the Russian peasant with faith in the czar, Falco has a good emperor, however corrupt and venal his minions. Nor is Falco the rootless detective in the big, anonymous city. He has a large and close family. He has a steady, loving, and beloved girlfriend of the senatorial class, who occasionally bails him out of trouble. Despite superficial trappings of the detective of urban alienation, Davis aims to amuse and educate, but not to disturb her readers.

Falco's lechery has a similar flavor. Many male detective characters have a keen appreciation of women's appearances, if not a predatory attitude. Falco certainly shares this trait: "Finding men, like chasing women, was my way of life. I had learned to approach both in a relaxed mood" (*Shadows* 89). In a more modest moment, he explains that "being a private informer . . . is less glamorous than you think—it's not all hard knocks and easy women" (*Shadows* 113). His actual philandering turns out to be rather limited, since he has only one true love, Helena. Even the "frank young women in the pink of condition, relaxed and plumped up in the warm sea-side air, each one wearing very little and just looking for a reason to take it off" cannot take his mind off Helena, whom he idolizes (*Shadows* 102; *Iron* 179). He is never unfaithful to this paragon despite numerous opportunities, albeit often dangerous ones. Not that his relationship with Helena is a smooth one, especially given their different statuses. A patently formulaic aspect of the series is that the two quarrel or separate in every novel only to be reunited at the end. Sometimes the reader shares Falco's bewilderment, "as usual I was not entirely certain what the quarrel was about" (*Last Act* 28-29).

As narrator too, Falco often focuses on the sexual. Insinuations or descriptions of licentiousness are legion: he describes one of his sisters as giving herself "to anybody with the bad taste to have her" (*Shadows* 106).[12] Despite Helena, Falco looks at women with the eye of a man on the prowl: "Her figure was as watchable as her face, small and curvaceous, and hinting of unrevealed possibilities . . . a tantalizing neck" (*Last Act* 131). Falco's sexual preoccupation gives the series a racy tone and accords well with Rome's reputation: what would Rome be without sex? Usually the tone is light and entertaining, but when the wit fails, Falco's prurience seems more adolescent than urbane: "The girl was in the saddle. I quipped, 'Glad to see you're on top of things!' and whipped the door shut on them" (*Time* 345). Another low point occurs when an extended fight and interrogation scene is spiced up with a naked female model: "Hey, Marcus, do you think I should take her out in the back and ask her some questions privately?" (*Poseidon's* 249).

Davis's world is not entirely that of the lusty and callous male detective. Falco does not gloss over the possibility and consequences of pregnancy: "She's just realized why her mother always warned her: she'll spend the next fifty years paying for this mistake . . . Now you will appreciate why women who can afford it are prepared to risk abortionists' drugs" (*Shadows* 255). Falco and Helena usually use birth control: they reject the hairy spider amulet "mainly because its success seemed doubtful; my sisters had huge families . . . she endured the humiliating sticky procedure with the costly alum in wax" (*Last Act* 92, *Time* 36).[13] Nevertheless, Helena has a miscarriage in *Shadows in Bronze* and gives birth at the end of *A Dying Light in Corduba*.

In addition, the books contain a vast array of strong and sympathetic female characters. Indeed Roman patriarchy is repeatedly presented as a thin facade barely concealing the fact that the women really called the shots—and often with good results.[14] So we not only have the *femme fatale* of *Venus in Copper*, but Falco's insulting but good-hearted mother, his land-lady, Lenia, and the formidable snake dancer, Thalia. Silvia, the wife of Falco's best friend, is a typical Davis woman: "tiny and tough. Petronius endured her with his easy good temper, but she terrified me" (*Shadows* 94).

Most important to the series, Helena herself is strong-willed, rich, and intelligent. So although Falco resembles the bitter and predatory detective, Davis's world is, in the end, a far friendlier one, generally more amusing and titillating than disturbing or sexist.

The historical accuracy of Davis's novels is high. Plot and character considerations lead to a few anachronisms of mentality. The narrator Falco plays at the cynical, sexually predatory detective, but neither attitude seems to go very deep. The plots and settings are varied and amusing. Few readers will want to go through all eight novels in a couple of months as did this reviewer. But it is evidence of their high quality and variety that, despite this potential overdose, I enjoyed the last novel as much as I did the first.

### Notes

1. In reaction to this ironic historiography, recent histories of Roman mentalities, often by French scholars or inspired by anthropology, have consciously deferred the process of unmasking. They seek to understand the mental world and categories of the Romans rather than immediately trying to get "behind" them, e.g. Veyne and Price.

2. Davis's novels are usually published a year later in the United States so I was unable to read *Three Hands in the Fountain* and *Two for the Lions*, her most recent works.

3. On Roman demography, see Saller.

4. Fred Mench notes references to windmills (anachronistic) and Hittites (unknown in classical antiquity and only rediscovered in this century) (74-78).

5. Although it is admittedly modern usage, I wish Davis did not equate plebian and poor, e.g. *Time to Depart* 37. In a Roman context, the word "plebian" suggests the Plebians, whose status, increasingly irrelevant even in the late Republic, depended on birth not wealth: the Plebian nobility became as wealthy and included as many senators and high officials as the Patricians.

6. Of course, we have no statistics on how often apartments actually fell down. Nevertheless, today far more people know "women and children first" than have ever been on a sinking ship; so a few standard rules of what to do when a building falls down are entirely plausible.

7. A certain Paetus dug up records of old debts to the treasury, but these were not connected with his accusations as *delator*. Even Paetus must have been a rich man, since his business was to buy up confiscated property at official auctions (Tacitus, *Annals* 13.23).

8. For a detailed and accessible account of Roman religion in daily life and personal belief, see Ogilvie. For more scholarly accounts see Frend and Momigliano.

9. See, for example, Cicero, *De divinatione* 2.148.

10. For Roman slavery see Bradley, which also contains a bibliographical essay.

11. Compare Mary Beard's view of Davis's novels as utterly undermining the mythology of Roman grandeur.

12. The ubiquity of brothels and prostitutes could be attributed to the prurient interests of Falco, but seem also to reflect accurately Roman realities. There were over twenty brothels in the town of Pompeii, which probably had a population of less than 20,000. Davis is also cognizant of the surprisingly low social class of many brothel customers: slaves probably visited brothels (*Time to Depart* 110). See McGinn on Roman prostitution.

13. On this subject, see Hopkins.

14. The extent to which this general picture is historically accurate is largely irrecoverable. Although male complaints about uppity women cannot be taken at face value (e.g., Juvenal, *Satires* VI), the property and divorce rights of Roman women made some such individuals plausible.

## Works Cited

Beard, Mary. Review of Lindsey Davis. *Times Literary Supplement* 4663 (Aug. 1992): 19.

Bradley, Keith. *Slavery and Society at Rome*. Cambridge: Cambridge UP, 1994.

Carcopino, Jérôme. *Daily Life in Ancient Rome*. Ed. Henry T. Rowell. Trans. E. O. Lorimer. New Haven: Yale UP, 1968.

Daube, David. "Slave Catching." *Juridical Review* 64 (1952): 12-28.

Davis, Lindsey. *A Dying Light in Corduba*. New York: Mysterious, 1998.

——. *The Iron Hand of Mars*. New York: Crown, 1992.

——. *Last Act in Palmyra*. New York: Mysterious, 1994.

——. *Poseidon's Gold*. New York: Crown, 1992.

——. *Shadows in Bronze*. New York: Crown, 1990.

——. *The Silver Pigs*. New York: Crown, 1989.

——. *Time to Depart*. New York: Mysterious, 1995.

——. *Venus in Copper*. New York: Crown, 1991.

Frend, W. H. C. *The Rise of Christianity*. Philadelphia: Fortress, 1984.

Gay, Peter. *Style in History*. New York: Norton, 1988.

Hopkins, Keith. "Contraception in the Roman Empire." *Comparative Studies in Society and History* 8 (1965): 124-51.

McGinn, Thomas A. *Prostitution, Sexuality, and the Law in Ancient Rome*. Oxford: Oxford UP, 1998.

Mench, Fred. Review of Ancient Roman Historical Novels. *Classical World* 86 (1992/3): 74-78.

Momigliano, Arnaldo. *On Pagans, Jews, and Christians*. Middletown, CT: Wesleyan UP, 1987.

Ogilvie, R. M. *The Romans and Their Gods in the Age of Augustus*. New York: Norton, 1969.

Price, Simon. *Rituals and Power: The Roman Imperial Cult in Asia Minor*. Cambridge: Cambridge UP, 1984.

Rudich, Vasily. *Political Dissidence under Nero: The Price of Dissimulation.* London: Routledge, 1993.

Saller, Richard. *Patriarchy, Property, and Death in the Roman Family.* Cambridge: Cambridge UP, 1994.

Storey, Glenn. "The Population of Ancient Rome." *Antiquity* 71 (1997): 966-78.

Syme, Ronald. *The Roman Revolution.* Oxford: Oxford UP, 1939.

Tacitus. *The Histories.* Trans. Kenneth Wellesley. Harmondsworth: Penguin, 1976.

Treggiari, Susan. *Roman Marriage.* Oxford: Oxford UP, 1991.

Veyne, Paul. *Bread and Circuses: Historical Sociology and Political Pluralism.* Ed. Oswyn Murray. Trans. Brian Pearce. Harmondsworth: Penguin, 1990.

White, Hayden. *Metahistory.* Baltimore: The Johns Hopkins UP, 1973.

# Peter Tremayne:
# Sister Fidelma and the Triumph of Truth

## Christiane W. Luehrs and Robert B. Luehrs

Peter Tremayne is actually London journalist and historian Peter Berresford Ellis, who, over the last three decades, has published some seventy books along with scores of essays, articles, and short stories. As Tremayne, one of the two pseudonyms he generally uses when writing fiction, he has made worthy contributions to horror and fantasy literature, his Dracula trilogy for example.[1] However, his most notable fictional creation is the seventh-century Irish detective Sister Fidelma, outspoken, sarcastic, supremely logical, and impatient with pretense or arrogance. Tremayne introduced her in a 1993 story, "Murder in Repose"; her adventures have since been chronicled in a number of further stories as well as, to date, six novels.[2]

Tremayne describes Fidelma as tall, red-haired, attractive but not beautiful, "well-proportioned," and, for all of her sagacity, relatively young.[3] He has given her a plausible biography. She belongs to the royal family of Munster (Muman), one of medieval Ireland's five kingdoms; she is the daughter of one king and the sister of another. She is a *religieuse* and, until the sixth book, *Valley of the Shadow,* a member of the religious community founded at Kildare by the revered St. Brigid. Having studied eight years at a nonecclesiastical bardic school in Tara, she received the second highest degree, *anruth,* and possesses knowledge of poetry, literature, science, medicine, and especially law. She is recognized as a *dálaigh,* an agent of the Irish legal system.[4] As such she is authorized to investigate crimes, evaluate evidence, interrogate witnesses, and, as she puts it on one occasion, to act as "an advocate, qualified to plead before the law courts of my country, to prosecute or defend those summoned to answer to the law before our judges, the Brehons" (*Absolution* 44-45). Under certain circumstances she can even sit as a judge herself (*Spider's Web* 9-10). Tremayne once compared her to Perry Mason, but clearly her powers far exceed those of that redoubtable attorney.[5] All in all, Fidelma very much embodies key elements of Celtic culture and the early Middle Ages.

Not surprisingly, Tremayne's accounts of that period in his Fidelma series mirror the perceptions offered in his purely historical studies, so that Fildema's world rings true. He casts historical figures as supporting players: King Oswy of Northumbia, the several rulers of Munster, Archbishop Deusdedit of Canterbury, Abbess Hilda of Whitby, Archbishop Ultan of Armagh, the monk missionary Colmán, and the cleric Wighard, to name a few, were real individuals. Since the extant records are sketchy, Tremayne endows these figures with appearances and personalities that best serve his plots. Besides being meticulously accurate in describing the dress, adornment, and deportment of his characters, Tremayne occasionally pauses in his narration for brief essays on pertinent historical topics ranging from medieval water clocks through the intricacies of Christian theology or Irish law to Celtic bathing habits.

He frequently ties his mysteries to actual events. Thus the great debate waged at the Synod of Whitby in 664 between representatives of Celtic and Roman Christianity, each group extolling the merits of its version of the faith for the benefit of King Oswy, provides the backdrop for *Absolution by Murder*. A passing mention by Bede, England's first historian, of the death of Wighard, struck down by plague in 664 after he journeyed to Rome to be consecrated as Archbishop of Canterbury, inspired Tremayne to base *Shroud for the Archbishop* on the premise that Wighard really had been murdered in revenge for past iniquities (Bede 198). That same year was also the year in which a strange disease known as the Yellow Plague, probably smallpox, ravaged the British Isles; many of the Fidelma stories set at that time take this deadly epidemic into account.[6] Further, Tremayne is adept in evoking a believable atmosphere for his settings: the petty bickering and animosities that made the proceedings at Whitby less than Christian; the nasty political intrigues in Rome; the isolation and hardships of Irish village life; the friction, tensions, and anxieties which marred religious houses.

The era in which Fidelma lives, the "Dark Ages" for much of Europe, was a period of brilliance for Celtic culture, especially that of Ireland. There monastic libraries preserved the literature of antiquity, and schools attracted students from Britain and the continent. Irish medical facilities were justly famous. Irish artisans and craftsmen enjoyed international demand for their creations. Irish missionaries carried Christianity to the German tribes.[7] So the monasteries mentioned in the Fidelma series, including her own house at Kildare, have impressive manuscript collections, some written in ancient Ogham script on rods or bark.[8] The locale for "A Canticle for Wulfstan" is the great school at Durrow. Tremayne's Celtic princes, whatever their flaws, are generally well educated. Fidelma herself symbolizes the Celtic renaissance in her demeanor, her intellectual cultivation, her tendency to quote pagan authors as much as Scripture, and, above all, her confidence in the wisdom of her Irish heritage, a blend of old beliefs with the new concepts of Christianity.

Tremayne points out that this heritage is endangered by two new forces. One is outside barbarism, personified in the invading Jutes, Angles, and Saxons, who ruthlessly carve out their domains in Britain by defeating, expelling, and even exterminating the native Celtic Britons. The other threat is the authoritarianism, bigotry, theological narrowness, and crude superstition of Rome, where the pope increasingly finds the outlook of Celtic Christianity unacceptable. For Tremayne, Celtic Ireland was equivalent to civilization, and by the mid-seventh century it was coming under siege, although the real calamities would not occur until later with the Viking raids of the ninth and tenth centuries and the intrusion of the Norman English beginning in the 1100s.

Just as Fidelma often feels obliged to defend the superiority of Celtic tradition against challenges from Anglo-Saxon barbarity and Roman Catholic revisionism, so Tremayne is an open advocate for Celtic culture and institutions. Tremayne writes history under his given name for a general audience, but many academic historians, even in our postmodern epoch, would fault him for his extreme partisanship.[9] He is well versed in the ancient and medieval sources for Celtic history and in the contemporary controversies among the interpreters of those sources. He does not falsify the material, but he does view Celtic historiography in terms of dichotomies. In the early Middle Ages, for him, the Celts manifested a galaxy of virtues, while their opponents in England and Italy exemplified the opposite. From his standpoint what is called British history is in fact the story of attempts by the English descendants of the Anglo-Saxons to treat Celtic Ireland, Scotland, and Wales as colonies and to obliterate the indigenous, distinct culture of these regions.[10]

On this basis, Tremayne's picture of Fidelma's world is comprehensible.[11] In his fiction and nonfiction alike the Celts emerge as having had an idyllic and essentially ideal society, motivated by humanism and a *joie de vivre*. In Ireland law was founded on the principle of compensation paid by the convicted offender to the victim. Kings and chieftains were elected from designated families and held accountable for their actions. Land ultimately belonged to the tribe, which regulated its use.[12] There was no slavery, though criminals sometimes lost their civil rights, and the community felt responsible for the care of the ill, elderly, and handicapped.[13] Women were accorded considerable respect and rights and could enter most professions, including those of warrior, judge, and ruler.[14]

The Anglo-Saxons, in contrast, were crassly materialistic and rapacious.[15] Their legal system, deemed "unjust" by Fidelma the *dálaigh*, emphasized brutal punishments for transgressors, death or mutilation being common.[16] Their kings were absolutist warlords who claimed office by primogeniture or divine gift.[17] The rights of property were unlimited; slavery existed; and the less fortunate members of society were often killed as useless.[18] Women were but decorative chattel for breeding purposes.[19] To the Anglo-Saxons war was a lifestyle, while to the Celts it was more an affair of honor, self-defense, or amusement.[20] Tremayne finds it ironic that Anglo-Saxon chronicles and later commentators thought the Celts to be uncivilized; it was Irish missionaries who brought their Germanic neighbors such cultural refinements as literacy, education, and Christianity (Ellis, *Celt and Saxon* 16, 137, 156).

For the most part, Anglo-Saxon characters in the Fidelma mysteries are "not likable," to use the words of the Briton prince Talorgen in "A Canticle for Wulfstan."[21] His Anglo-Saxon rival in the story, Prince Eadred, is typical of the breed: arrogant, boorish, hostile, and superstitious. At first Eadred refuses even to respond to Fidelma's questions about the murder of his cousin because it "is not the custom of princes of our race to discourse with women if they be not of equal royal rank"; when Fidelma's own royal pedigree is revealed to him, he still talks with her only reluctantly ("Canticle" 37-42).

While the conversion of the Anglo-Saxons from paganism to Christianity was an onerous process, the Celts achieved the same transition with little turmoil and no martyrs, a phenomenon Tremayne, with justice, attributes to similarities in the two faiths (Ellis, *Celtic Inheritance* 82). The details of ancient Celtic spiritual life are elusive and must be pieced together from archaeological evidence, often unsympathetic Greco-Roman authors, and later medieval legends. Still, there is agreement that the priests were the Druids, who also acted as judges, counselors, educators, philosophers, bards, physicians, scientists, seers, and magicians.[22] Druids could be either male or female.[23] They constituted the intellectual class, learning their many skills through studying with masters or at special schools (Ellis, *Druids* 157-62).

Beyond veneration for a host of gods and heroes and the need for seasonal celebrations, the essential Druid message seemed to include man's unity with nature, the great sanctity of truth, the necessity of avoiding immorality, and the immortality of the soul, which after death resides for a time in the Otherworld before being reincarnated in this world.[24] Doubtless the Druidic tendency to envision many deities as triune and to accord great powers to the number three prepared the way for the acceptance of the Christian trinity among the Celts.[25] Strabo, Cicero, and Julius Caesar to the contrary, Tremayne denies that the Druids practiced human sacrifice.[26]

Christianity adapted Druid institutions. Christian monks, nuns, and priests took over most of the functions of the Druids. Druidic schools metamorphosed into bardic colleges. Druid shrines became chapels and monasteries, and their holy wells likewise became Christianized. The elder gods, the *áes sidhe*, turned into the fairies and diminutive nature spirits of folklore.[27] St. Brigid, who founded Fidelma's religious order around 500, was said to have begun as a Druid and to have built her monastery on a site sacred to her namesake, the goddess of crafts, poetry, childbirth, and regeneration. The legends of the two Brigids became so intertwined that they ended up sharing the same feast day (February 1, Imbolc to the Celts) and many of the same symbols.[28]

Tremayne suggests something of the range of attitudes which might have been found in those who clung to the old beliefs with three decidedly Druidic characters. Erca, the master of herbs in "Murder in Repose," is a wild-eyed, disheveled recluse who loathes the Christian intruders (345-46). The ungainly Druid priest Murgal is a Brehon and adviser to his unstable chieftain Laisre in *Valley of the Shadow*. Murgal deeply mistrusts Christians, including Fidelma, because he sees only paganism as welling from the soul of his people and as guaranteeing their traditions of freedom, morality, and self-reliance (66-67, 76, 121-24, 296). Gadra in *The Spider's Web* possesses the wisdom of the ages, exhibits more compassion than the Christians around him, and is at peace with the realization that in the cycle of the universe, the time for his religion has passed (167-68, 251-52, 334-37).

Even so, Fidelma's world continues to harbor remnants of Druidism. In *The Subtle Serpent*, to take but one work, Sister Brónach, doorkeeper of the Abbey of the Salmon of the Three Wells, muses about her parents' gods. She joins her fellow nuns to intone the eerie *caoine*, the pre-Christian lament for the dead at the funeral of Sister Almu, decapitated by her killer in the style of ancient warriors; the funeral includes the pagan customs of smashing the corpse's bier and dropping birch branches into the grave to ward off evil spirits. One of the items found on each murder victim is an Ogham rod, its text referring to Mórrígú, the terrible warrior goddess of death and violence. Even Fidelma speaks of heaven as the Otherworld.[29] As the shrewd Sister Berrach observes: "In these remote places, away from the great cathedrals and towns, you should know that people still dwell close to nature, keep to the old well-trodden paths. Scratch a Christian here and you will find the blood is pagan" (*Subtle Serpent* 162). Berrach's insight has particular application to Fidelma.

Tremayne sometimes depicts Fidelma walking with downcast eyes and demurely clasped hands as befits a nun, but she is no adherent of Christian orthodoxy; "there was scarcely concealed humour behind her enforced solemnity which hinted at a joy in living rather than being weighted down by the sombre pensiveness of religious life" ("High King's Sword" 131). She favors the world over the cloister and relishes worldy pleasures. She is rarely shown at worship, and when she does attend services, her mind invariably wanders to secular matters.[30] If she prays, it is quickly and quietly. She evinces skepticism about the possibility of miracles or other supernatural intrusions into everyday life.[31] Those "rebellious" strands of red hair that forever struggle to escape her headdress symbolize her relationship to the Christian faith.[32] She is a traditional, aristocratic, Celtic intellectual, who is a Christian *religieuse* because in seventh-century Ireland becoming a Druid has ceased to be a viable option for her kind.

Fidelma's sympathies and educational background are Druidic. When she rides horseback she experiences a mystical communion with nature (*Spider's Web* 224). She practices *dercad*, Druidic meditation techniques, to induce tranquillity.[33] She gives her ultimate loyalty less to God than to truth for "by Truth the earth endures and by Truth we are delivered from our enemies" (*Spider's Web* 173). Fidelma has more rapport with the pagan Gadra than with conventional Christians; chided about this, she responds: "Perhaps the differences are not so much once we remove the names we give things. We are all sprang from the same common ancestry" (*Spider's Web* 172). Later she says to Gadra: "I recognize in you the same virtues we all have." "Bless you for that, sister," he replies. "After all, do not all the tracks lead to the same great centre?" (*Spider's Web* 336). Here the aged Druid is echoing Fidelma's comment from earlier in the book about many paths leading to God, certainly not a standard Christian sentiment (*Spider's Web* 119). Murgal's ultimate judgment on Fidelma is: "If I did not see that you carry the symbols of the new Faith, Fidelma of Cashel, I would swear that you were of the old Faith. Perhaps you are wearing the wrong cloak?" (*Valley* 183).

Even Fidelma's name and personality betray her connection with the old religion. Celtic mythology is filled with powerful, independent females who exhibit the same strengths and foibles as their male counterparts. There are many mother goddesses, frequently warriors as well as guardians of knowledge and prosperity. One who may have originated as such a mother goddess is the passionate, devious, strong-willed Queen Mebd or Maeve of Connacht in the epic of the *Táin Bó Cuailgne* (*The Cattle Raid of Cooley*). Preparing to lead her armies against the hero Cœchulainn, she encounters an armed prophetess from the Otherworld who, correctly, predicts disaster for Mebd's military adventure. The prophetess's name is Fidelma.[34] Both Fidelmas possess noteworthy eyes. Those of the prophetess have multiple irises, a sign of a supernatural being (Green 101). Tremayne's Fidelma has eyes that likewise vary, seeming green or blue depending on the occasion.[35] His Fidelma's home kingdom, Munster, is closely associated with the Otherworld and with more goddesses than any other part of Ireland (Ellis, *Dictionary of Celtic Mythology* 164). Fidelma is very much a mortal but does put one in mind of the inhabitants of the Otherworld, the gods and spirits, in her uncanny omniscience and her power to manipulate both people and events in order to bring forth the truth. She divines truth from its traces, the physical evidence and the words of those she interviews; in so doing she is a seer, a mundane equivalent of the *Táin*'s Fidelma.

As Fidelma is well aware, the ultimate menace to her version of Christianity comes not from the Druids but from Rome, and Tremayne often reminds his readers of the areas of conflict.[36] One was administration. The Celtic Church was a loosely knit affair, with authority resting in abbots not bishops; the pope desired a more centralized, uniform organization. There were numerous differences in practice. Each church computed the date of Easter in its own fashion, and that was the main issue at the 664 Synod of Whitby. Rome objected to the Celtic tonsure, which involved shaving the forehead in the "Druid style," and to Celtic confession, a voluntary, informal sharing of confidences with a "soul friend," who could be a layperson. Although seventh-century Rome was not yet insisting on clerical celibacy, it increasingly looked askance at Celtic married priests and bishops and Celtic monasteries, like the one at Kildare, which housed men and women together.[37] Unlike its brother in Rome, the Celtic Church allowed women into leadership positions. Tremayne accepts the story that St. Brigid was consecrated as both a priest and a bishop—and, as an illustration of the sexual emancipation of Celtic women, that she was a lesbian to boot.[38]

Finally and more problematically, Tremayne speaks of a fundamental theological divergence. He describes the Celtic Church as deeply influenced by the ideas of Pelagius, a fifth-century Briton.[39] Pelagius argued that God had given man the ability to choose a moral course by his own efforts, a principle that Tremayne supposes Pelagius borrowed from the Druids. Since

Pelagianism was contrary to the doctrines of original sin and irresistable divine grace, it earned St. Augustine's wrath and condemnation as heresy by various popes, synods, and councils.[40] Likely it was not a significant element in seventh-century Ireland, but by making it so in his Fidelma mysteries, Tremayne adds a wonderful edge to the Celtic-Roman conflict. Fidelma is, of course, thoroughly Pelagian. In *The Spider's Web* she sharply defends Pelagius's logic against the obnoxious Father Gormán, a partisan of Rome; without man's free will, God becomes the author of sin, an unthinkable proposition (126-28).

A hint of what the eventual victory of Rome over the Celtic Church was to mean for women such as Fidelma is offered in *Shroud for the Archbishop,* when the papal official, Bishop Gelasius, tells Fidelma that only her habit allows her free access to the shops and sights of Rome. Roman women are otherwise kept secluded and under the control of either their fathers or their husbands. "Then this is a sad city for women," she comments. Gelasius replies: "It is the city of the Blessed Peter and of Paul who brought us light in the darkness of our paganism and it was given to Rome to spread that light throughout the world" (13-14). Unfortunately, the light in question included the subjugation of women and the triumph of patriarchal values.

Tremayne's Roman Catholic characters, whether real or fictional, for the most part fare no better than the Anglo-Saxons. They are usually shown as intolerant, ambitious, violent, poorly educated, and prone to embrace absurd beliefs. Father Agatho in *Absolution by Murder* has thin lips and cold, hooded eyes. He thinks that he has found a piece of the true cross in an English woods and that Christ speaks through him (170-73). Wighard, secretary to the ailing Archbishop of Canterbury in *Absolution by Murder* and murder victim in *Shroud for the Archbishop,* strikes Fidelma as having a face displaying "the cunning of a wolf, in spite of its cherubic, chubby roundness. The eyes were too close together and forever searching as if seeking out enemies" (*Absolution* 65). Since the Roman Church required celibacy for its higher officials, Wighard, when younger, paid to have his wife and children killed so that he might advance in his career (*Shroud* 306-7). The overweening Abbess Draigen in *The Subtle Serpent* hates men, prefers retribution to the evenhanded justice offered by Brehon secular law, and through her daughter, Sister Lerben, incites a mob against a supposed witch (107-8, 137, 163-65, 168-74, 188). Father Gormán is a crazed fanatic, devoid of Christian mercy. He is also part of a scheme to steal a gold mine from an unsuspecting parishioner and a murderer, responsible for four deaths (*Spider's Web* 117-28, 304-5, 330-33).

In contrast to these disturbed agents of Roman Catholicism is the Celtic Christian Abbot Laisran of Durrow, one of Fidelma's mentors and distant relatives.

His face proclaimed a permanent state of jollity, for he had been born with that rare gift of humour and a sense that the world was there to provide enjoyment to those who inhabited it. When he smiled, it was no fainthearted parting of the lips but an expression that welled from the depths of his being, bright and all-encompassing. And when he laughed it was as though the whole earth trembled in accompaniment. ("Canticle" 27)

Tremayne is too able a writer to rest content with broad stereotypes. He populates his admirable Celtic society with many less than admirable characters, endowed with a full range of vices, weaknesses, and flaws. Eber, a chieftain in *The Spider's Web*, has committed incest with his sisters and daughter, outrages his wife willingly ignores as she enjoys his wealth and power (314-16, 327-28). The unpleasant Celtic chaplain, Febal, in *The Subtle Serpent* kills two nuns in his futile attempt to secure a legendary idol of a golden calf (327-32). Members of Ireland's ruling houses pursue their various ambitions, conspiring against one another and their superiors.[41] Even Murgal, despite whatever spiritual depth Fidelma senses in him, is really more of a politician than a priest, with a personality marred by his tendencies to be both an obnoxious drunk and a lecher (*Valley* 90-93, 317-18, 328). On the other side, however, there is even one consistently engaging Anglo-Saxon Roman Catholic, Fidelma's colleague Brother Eadulf, a foil for the detective's superior intelligence but nevertheless patently beloved by her in more than the Christian sense of the word.

Fidelma the *dálaigh*, agent of secular power, relentlessly pursues truth, which she regards as "more serious than any other consideration," even justice (*Absolution* 78). She realizes that the two may diverge when, in order to save her own Abbey of St. Brigid, she must hide Abbess Ita's complicity in a murder and a suicide. To atone for serving justice but not truth, Fidelma uncharacteristically does penance with a pilgrimage to St. Patrick's shrine ("Hemlock" 21, 23-27).

Study of classical philosophy, which teaches that reason should subordinate and control passion, and her own experience with loss of emotional control, make Fidelma's concentration on the rational even more understandable. When a very young student at Tara she fell in love with a young man who jilted her, making her wary of giving way to emotion (*Spider's Web* 259-60). In *Suffer Little Children* Fidelma's uncontrolled anger results in the murder of Cass, her companion in investigation and member of her brother's royal bodyguard (278-79). To Fidelma, warrior for truth, reason is therefore not only a weapon but also a shield.

Fidelma assumes every mystery has a logical solution. She says, "For every action there is a motive" (*Subtle Serpent* 286). Fidelma also believes in scientific explanation for seemingly supernatural phenomena, for example the solar eclipse during the Synod of Whitby. She marvels at the superstitious Anglo-Saxons who, with no knowledge of astronomy, regard the eclipse as a "portent of evil," God's condemnation of the proceedings (*Absolution* 69-73). With such an outlook, Fidelma is well prepared for her legal profession, about which she remarks, "To present a clever and polished argument is no great art. To perceive and understand the truth is a better gift" ("Murder" 358).

Tremayne rescues his heroine from appearing to be merely a gender-less thinking machine by endowing Fidelma with female attributes—as a male author understands them. She is openly affectionate to family and close friends, delighted with children, compassionate toward others, fastidious about her person, pleased with a gift of perfume from an admirer, and romantically attracted to men. Though she considers herself unlikely to marry, she enjoys the company of men, particularly Eadulf.

However, human arrogance and evil do not automatically recognize or welcome either Fidelma's femininity or professionalism. Whether her talents are exercised in a village, or royal or ecclesiastical court, she often has to impress the local authority figures with her credentials in the face of their unwillingness to believe that the young nun is a *dálaigh*. In "Murder in Repose" Fidelma must resort to showing the tribal judge her official certificate (339). In *Shroud for the Archbishop* she counters the arrogance of Bishop Gelasius, the papal secretary, with her usual self-assured demeanor and observance of Irish etiquette, which does not include kissing his ecclesiastical ring (9-17). In *The Subtle Serpent* Fidelma has to disclose her royal status as well as her legal qualifications in order to be acceptable to Abbess Draigen and Adnar, the local chieftain (35-38).

Once accepted as a competent *dálaigh*, Fidelma reveals her investigative technique. She familiarizes herself with the circumstantial facts of a case and then surveys the scene of the crime. She sees the scene of crime "as a piece of parchment on which the transgressor must make some mark," and her task is "to spot it and interpret it" (*Absolution* 91). Here, Fidelma's knowledge of medicine allows her to identify the poison in Brother Fergal's medication and later to discern that Sister Eisten was tortured before being murdered and thrown into the sea.[42] Her keen eye allows her to discover the locked room method of Wulfstan's murder ("Canticle" 36-37, 53-55). She further demonstrates her thoroughness in searching for hidden clues at a crime scene when she discovers Augustine of Canterbury's sandals and staff under Wighard's bed (*Shroud* 76-77).

Armed with physical evidence and knowledge of how a crime was committed, Fidelma begins to search for the motive. Realizing that logic can at times prove faulty, Fidelma believes what feels false is false (*Spider's Web* 134), and she makes leaps of intellect, exercising her intuition about both crimes and criminals. Although Fidelma demonstrates in the first story her capability in apprehending criminals on her own, it is her association in investigation with Eadulf, the Anglo-Saxon monk, which truly highlights Fidelma's process of bringing criminals to the bar of justice.

Eadulf, former heir to the office of *gerefa* (magistrate) in Seaxmund's Ham, England, is well educated and a lover of learning as well as puzzles. An herbalist and apothecary by training, he does not possess Fidelma's creative intelligence. Eadulf acknowledges her superior mind in his statement that he is but "a simple man," one who does "not see the subtleties of which you speak" (*Spider's Web* 203). Eadulf is earthbound and plodding, a meat-and-potatoes Englishman much like Poirot's Captain Hastings. He offers masculine security and strength, protecting Fidelma physically if necessary, as he does with sturdy English bow and arrow in *The Spider's Web* (43). Eadulf helps with the questioning of witnesses, his placid demeanor calming those awed by Fidelma's admittedly "bludgeoning" techniques (*Spider's Web* 133, *Subtle Serpent* 101). However, Eadulf's primary function is to provide Fidelma with an audience for her hypotheses about her cases and to argue with her when her theories become too abstruse. Fidelma values Eadulf's comments and reactions, realizing that his patient practicality is a counter to her own impatient creativity. Even when in *Valley of the Shadow* Eadulf proves adept enough as an advocate at a hearing to get the murder charges against Fidelma dismissed, he violates the spirit of Irish law in behalf of a practical outcome, much to Fidelma's distress (209-35). He remains throughout, as Fidelma specifically notes in that work, one who calls her attention to the obvious, an admittedly necessary service (166, 234-35).

The stories are replete with subterranean forays, into caves, mines, cellars, wells, passageways, catacombs, and crypts, symbolizing Fidelma's search for truths hidden from the light of day, some of them at the center of a labyrinth. In "Hemlock at Vespers" the key to the mystery lies in the gold mine underneath St. Brigid's Abbey (23-26). In *The Subtle Serpent* the original resting place for the sought-after golden calf is under the chapel (330-31). In *Shroud for the Archbishop* part of the solution to the puzzle lies in the ancient catacombs of Rome (193-208). In *Valley of the Shadow* it is deep in a cave where Ibor, the High King's agent, reveals to Fidelma an elaborate conspiracy to subvert the ancient government of Ireland (256-78). In *Absolution by Murder* the truth resides within the psyche of Sister Gwid, namely, her lesbian affection for Étain (253-58). Each shred of cloth, fragment of wood, splash of candle grease, bloodstain, or example of handwriting picked up along the path to truth provides Fidelma with a piece of the mosaic of her solution (*Shroud* 133).

Fidelma's investigations culminate in courtroom scenes in which she, much like twentieth-century fictional detectives, gathers her witnesses and unfolds the plot of the crime and the motive of the murderer, describing how various bits of evidence fit together to form her solution to the crime. Additionally, Fidelma often reveals multiple crimes in a case, ones that are not necessarily connected by motive. For example, Wighard's daughter murdered him, but Cornelius's desire for rare medical texts provided the reason for the theft of the gold and silver chalices and the death of Osimo (*Shroud* 300-5, 310-23). In the end, the murderer invariably confesses, whether in anger or remorse, and for Fidelma, compensation has been paid and truth has delivered society from its enemies.

Although Fidelma has been rightfully considered comparable to two other fictional medieval religious detectives, Ellis Peters's Brother Cadfael and Margaret Frazer's Dame Frevisse, Tremayne's character differs from these two in significant ways. Cadfael and Frevisse act from within their Benedictine Rule, a choice both have freely made, and both are amateur sleuths who deliver miscreants to the secular authorities. Presumably both

Cadfael and Frevisse could be situated in the Roman Catholic culture of any century. In contrast, Fidelma operates as a secular authority not under the rule of her abbey. She cannot exist outside seventh-century Irish Celtic civilization; the historical setting of the Fidelma stories is a major theme of Tremayne's works. Fidelma exemplifies the ideals of early medieval Celtic culture as Tremayne the historian interprets them. As he says in *Absolution by Murder*, "Sister Fidelma was possessed of a spirit of time and place, of history and man-kind's place in its unfolding tapestry" (49).

*Notes*

1. *Dracula Unborn* (London: Bailey Brothers and Swinfen, 1977), *The Revenge of Dracula* (London: Bailey Brothers and Swinfen, 1978), and *Dracula My Love* (London: Bailey Brothers and Swinfen, 1980).

2. "Murder in Repose" appears in *Great Irish Detective Stories*. The six novels are: *Absolution by Murder* (1994); *Shroud for the Archbishop* (1995); *Suffer Little Children* (1995); *The Subtle Serpent* (1996); *The Spider's Web* (1997); and *Valley of the Shadow* (1998). Since this essay was written, Tremayne has published other Fidelma mysteries.

3. Tremayne, *Absolution* 18; Tremayne, *Shroud* 9; Tremayne, *Suffer* 1; Tremayne, *Subtle Serpent* 15-16; Tremayne, *Spider's Web* 9; Tremayne, "Murder" 337-38; Tremayne, "Hemlock at Vespers" 1; Tremayne, "The High King's Sword" 130-31; Tremayne, "A Canticle for Wulfstan" 27.

4. Tremayne, *Absolution* vii-viii; Tremayne, *Shroud* ix-x; Tremayne, *Subtle Serpent* vi-vii; Tremayne, *Valley* xi, 13. Fidelma is a member of the Eóganacht dynasty which dominated Munster from the fifth to the twelfth centuries.

5. Haining, *Great Irish Detective Stories* 337; Ashley, *Mammoth Book of Historical Whodunnits* 130.

6. On the Yellow Plague, see: Creighton 4-9, and Shrewsbury 5-47. Tremayne refers to the Yellow Plague in "The High King's Sword," "A Canticle for Wulfstan," *Absolution by Murder, Shroud for the Archbishop*, and *Suffer Little Children*. He may have indulged in an anachronism by having his characters call the disease the Yellow Plague because the first literary use of the term dates from the twelfth century. Of course, the name could have originated much earlier. Tremayne calls the Yellow Plague "an extreme form of jaundice" in *Absolution* 153.

7. Ellis, *Celtic Empire* 189-90; Ellis, *Celt and Saxon* 127, 153; Tremayne, *Absolution* viii; Tremayne, *Shroud* x-xi; Tremayne, *Subtle Serpent* vii; Tremayne, *Suffer* xi-xii. The existence of an early medieval Irish "Golden Age" is a generally accepted concept, with scholars focusing on its extent. A recent popular book that addresses the topic is Thomas Cahill, *How the Irish Saved Civilization* (New York: Talese, 1995).

8. Supposedly introduced by Ogma, the god of literature and eloquence, the Ogham alphabet involves a series of slashes or strokes on a base line. Its antiquity is uncertain. The only surviving examples are inscriptions on stone dating from the fifth and sixth centuries, AD, but Tremayne argues it is much older than that, with

whole libraries of Ogham texts existing in pre-Christian times. Ellis, *The Druids* 163-67; Ellis, *Dictionary of Celtic Mythology* 174; Ellis, *A Dictionary of Irish Mythology* 187-88; Ellis, *Celtic Inheritance* 81-82; Ellis, *Celtic Empire* 178, 216-17; Tremayne, *Suffer* 13-14, 55-56, 142-43; Tremayne, *Valley* 194, 201.

9. In recent years there has been a fierce debate between two schools of Irish historians. One, the nationalists, essentially assume the existence of an Irish identity, dating back to antiquity and struggling through the centuries to nationhood. The other school, the revisionists, disagree and call for an Irish history that is more value-free and demythologized, a scholarship less concerned with grand heroes and great villains. Tremayne's views place him in the nationalist camp. For this historiographical controversy, see Bradshaw; Steven G. Ellis; and especially Brady.

Tremayne's Brother Ségán, chief professor at the abbey college of Ros Ailithir, notes: "Some historians are as trapped in history as history is trapped in them." Tremayne, *Suffer* 139-40.

10. Ellis, *Celt and Saxon* 11-14, 43-44, 91-100, 158-59, 215-51; Ellis, *Dictionary of Celtic Mythology* 48-50.

11. Brief overviews of Celtic culture and early medieval Ireland may be found in Richter; Chadwick; Thomas; and Cremin.

12. Ellis, *Celtic Inheritance* 13, 16, 20; Ellis, *Celt and Saxon* 25, 28-29, 37-38, 52, 138, 155; Ellis, *Druids* 189-99; Tremayne, *Absolution* v-vi, 25; Tremayne, *Subtle Serpent* v, 59, 130, 220, 300; Tremayne, *Suffer* ix, 15-24, 54-55, 114, 291-92, 325-26; Tremayne, *Shroud* vii-viii, 53; Tremayne, *Spider's Web* 10-16, 50, 116, 140-44, 151-60; Tremayne, *Valley* 105-7.

13. Ellis, *Celtic Inheritance* 16-19; Ellis, *Celt and Saxon* 138-39; Tremayne, *Absolution* 97-98; Tremayne, *Shroud* 28; Tremayne, *Spider's Web* 31, 79-83, 96-97, 101, 114, 184; Tremayne, *Valley* 283.

14. Ellis, *Celtic Women* 76-141; Ellis, *Celtic Inheritance* 20-21; Ellis, *Celt and Saxon* 54; Ellis, *Dictionary of Irish Mythology* 115-16; Ellis, *Dictionary of Celtic Mythology* 96; Tremayne, *Absolution* vi-vii, 105-6; Tremayne, *Subtle Serpent* vi, 55, 231; Tremayne, *Suffer* x, 225; Tremayne, *Shroud* viii-ix, 13, 17, 135, 174, 180; Tremayne, *Spider's Web* 55-58, 110-11, 151, 269.

15. Ellis, *Celt and Saxon* 52, 54; Tremayne, *Shroud* 53.

16. Ellis, *Celt and Saxon* 54, 138; Tremayne, *Absolution* 21-23, 179; Tremayne, *Spider's Web* 83.

17. Ellis, *Celt and Saxon* 38, 53; Tremayne, *Absolution* 78.

18. Ellis, *Celt and Saxon* 55, 139; Tremayne, *Absolution* 25, 61, 154; Tremayne, *Shroud* 151, 308-9, 314-16; Tremayne, *Spider's Web* 50, 82, 96.

19. Ellis, *Celt and Saxon* 53; Tremayne, *Absolution* 45, 105; Tremayne *Shroud* 124, 174.

20. Ellis, *Celt and Saxon* 39, 137, 140; Tremayne, *Subtle Serpent* 252.

21. Tremayne, "Canticle" 49. Fidelma has similar sentiments in *Absolution* 179-80.

22. Ellis, *Dictionary of Celtic Mythology* 84; Ellis, *Druids* 162-250; Ellis, *Celtic Inheritance* 9-10.

23. Ellis, *Dictionary of Celtic Mythology* 84; Ellis, *Druids* 91-112; Ellis, *Celtic Women* 68-71, 94-96.

24. Ellis, *Celtic Inheritance* 10-15; Ellis, *Druids* 113-31, 167-80; Tremayne, *Spider's Web* 168-70. Diogenes Laertius, who lived in the third century, rendered the Druid credo as "Worship the gods, do no evil and exercise courage." Ellis, *Druids* 168.

25. Ellis, *Celtic Inheritance* 15-16; Ellis, *Druids* 128; Ellis, *Celt and Saxon* 124; Tremayne, *Suffer* 14-15.

26. Ellis, *Dictionary of Celtic Mythology* 85; Ellis, *Druids* 143-56; Tremayne, *Valley* 69-70. Both Caesar in Book VI of *The Gallic Wars* and Strabo in Book IV of his *Geography* refer to Druidic rites involving sacrificial victims being put into a colossal image of a man, made of straw or wicker, which was then set on fire as an offering to the gods.

27. Ellis, *Celtic Inheritance* 13, 81-82; Ellis, *Dictionary of Celtic Mythology* 39, 220. Useful overviews of the Christian appropriation of elements from Celtic paganism may be found in MacKillop; Dames; and Hutton.

28. Ellis, *Celtic Women* 27-29, 146-49; Ellis, *Druids* 102-3; Tremayne, *Spider's Web* 164; Tremayne, *Subtle Serpent* 189. See also the interesting account by Condren.

29. Tremayne, *Subtle Serpent* 4-6, 62, 66-68, 82-83, 131, 145, 151, 230-32.

30. For example, Tremayne, "Hemlock" 2-4; Tremayne, *Subtle Serpent* 176-79; Tremayne, *Absolution* 120-21; Tremayne, *Suffer* 185-87.

31. Peter Tremayne, "Abbey Sinister" 128; Tremayne, *Subtle Serpent* 20, 24, 163-66, 173-74; Tremayne, *Shroud* 21-22, 33, 137-38. Fidelma comments to Murgal: "We are born to doubt. Those who know nothing, doubt nothing." Tremayne, *Valley* 183.

32. This adjective for Fidelma's hair is repeatedly employed by Tremayne. Tremayne, *Subtle Serpent* 15; Tremayne, *Absolution* 18; Tremayne, *Shroud* 9; Tremayne, *Suffer* 1; Tremayne, "Hemlock" 1; Tremayne, "Canticle" 27; Tremayne, "Murder" 338; Tremayne, "High King's Sword" 130.

33. Tremayne, *Subtle Serpent* 31; Tremayne, *Suffer* 3; Tremayne, *Shroud* 214-15.

34. Tremayne supplies a translation of the *Táin*'s description of Fidelma in *Druids* 100; here he identifies her as a Druid. A somewhat different translation may be found in Hyde 321-23.

35. Tremayne, *Absolution* 43-44; Tremayne, *Subtle Serpent* 16; Tremayne, *Spider's Web* 9; Tremayne, *Valley* 9.

36. Valuable introductions to the Celtic Church include Hughes, Mackey, and de Paor.

37. Ellis, *Celtic Inheritance* 45-47; Ellis, *Celt and Saxon* 119-23, 147-48; Tremayne, *Subtle Serpent* vii-viii, 76, 176-80, 184-87, 196, 221-22; Tremayne, *Spider's Web* 17, 144-45, 304; Tremayne, *Suffer* xii-xiii, 94-95, 104-5; Tremayne, *Absolution* viii-x, 42, 67, 137-44, 193-94; Tremayne, *Shroud* xi-xii, 30, 175, 184.

38. Ellis, *Celtic Women* 147-49; Tremayne, *Subtle Serpent* 189.

39. On Pelagius, see M. Forthomme Nicholson, "Celtic Theology: Pelagius," in Mackey 386-413.

40. Ellis, *Celt and Saxon* 23-25; Ellis, *Celtic Inheritance* 33-36; Ellis, *Druids* 181-86.

41. For instance, the effort to deny Sechnasach his right to be High King in "The High King's Sword;" the dispute between Munster and its neighbor, the kingdom of Laigin, over a border territory in *Suffer Little Children;* and the rebellion against Fidelma's brother, King Colgú, in *The Subtle Serpent.* The initial murders in *Valley of the Shadow* are part of a scheme devised by the ruler of the Northern Uí Néill to foment civil war, destroy Munster, and establish his own supremacy over the other Irish kingdoms.

42. Tremayne, "Murder" 353-54; Tremayne, *Suffer* 160-61.

### Works Cited

Ashley, Mike, ed. *The Mammoth Book of Historical Whodunits.* London: Robinson, 1993.

Bede. *A History of the English Church and People.* Trans. Leo Sherley-Price. Harmondsworth: Penguin, 1965.

Bradshaw, Brendon. "Nationalism and Historical Scholarship in Modern Ireland." *Irish Historical Studies* 26 (Nov. 1989): 329-51.

Brady, Ciaran, ed. *Interpreting Irish History: The Debate on Historical Revisionism 1938-1994.* Dublin: Irish Academic P, 1994.

Chadwick, Nora. *The Celts.* Harmondsworth: Penguin, 1970.

Condren, Mary. *The Serpent and the Goddess: Women, Religion and Power in Celtic Ireland.* San Francisco: Harper and Row, 1989.

Creighton, Charles. *A History of Epidemics in Britain* Vol. I. 1894. New York: Barnes and Noble, 1966.

Cremin, Aedeen. *The Celts.* New York: Rizzoli International, n.d.

Dames, Michael. *Mythic Ireland.* London: Thames and Hudson, 1992.

de Paor, Máire, and Liam de Paor. *Early Christian Ireland.* London: Thames and Hudson, 1960.

Ellis, Peter Berresford. *Celt and Saxon: The Struggle for Britain, AD 410-937.* London: Constable, 1993.

——. *The Celtic Empire: The First Millennium of Celtic History c. 1000 BC–51 AD.* London: Constable, 1990.

——. *Celtic Inheritance.* London: Muller, 1985.

——. *Celtic Women: Women in Celtic Society and Literature.* 1995. Grand Rapids: Eerdmans, 1996.

——. *Dictionary of Celtic Mythology.* 1992. New York: Oxford UP, 1994.

——. *A Dictionary of Irish Mythology.* 1987. Santa Barbara: ABC-CLIO, 1989.

——. *The Druids.* 1994. Grand Rapids: Eerdmans, 1994.

Ellis, Steven G. "Historiographical Debate: Representations of the Past in Ireland: Whose Past and Whose Present?" *Irish Historical Studies* 27 (Nov. 1991): 289-308.

Green, Miranda. *The World of the Druids.* London: Thames and Hudson, 1997.

Haining, Peter. *Great Irish Detective Stories.* 1993. New York: Barnes and Noble, 1998.

Hughes, Kathleen. *The Church in Early Irish Society.* Ithaca: Cornell UP, 1966.

· Hutton, Ronald. *The Pagan Religions of the Ancient British Isles: Their Nature and Legacy.* Oxford: Basil Blackwell, 1991.

Hyde, Douglas. *A Literary History of Ireland.* 1899. London: Ernest Benn, 1967.

Mackey, James P., ed. *An Introduction to Celtic Christianity.* Edinburgh: T. and T. Clark, 1989.

MacKillop, James. *Dictionary of Celtic Mythology.* Oxford: Oxford UP, 1998.

Richter, Michael. *Medieval Ireland: The Enduring Tradition.* Houndmills and London: Macmillan Education, 1988.

Shrewsbury, J. F. D. "The Yellow Plague." *Journal of the History of Medicine and Allied Sciences* 4 (1949): 5-47.

Thomas, Charles. *Britain and Ireland in Early Christian Times, AD 400-800.* New York: McGraw-Hill, 1971.

Tremayne, Peter [Peter Berresford Ellis]. "Abbey Sinister." *The Mammoth Book of Historical Detectives.* Ed. Mike Ashley. London: Robinson, 1995.

——. *Absolution by Murder.* 1994. New York: Penguin, Signet, 1997.

——. "A Canticle for Wulfstan." *Ellery Queen Mystery Magazine* May 1995: 27-59.

——. "Hemlock at Vespers." *Murder Most Irish.* Ed. Ed Gorman, Larry Segriff, and Martin H. Greenberg. 1996. New York: Barnes and Noble, 1996.

——. "The High King's Sword." *The Mammoth Book of Historical Whodunnits.* Ed. Mike Ashley. London: Robinson, 1993.

——. "Murder in Repose." *Great Irish Detective Stories.* Ed. Peter Haining. 1993. New York: Barnes and Noble, 1998.

——. *Shroud for the Archbishop.* 1995. New York: St. Martin's P, 1995.

——. *The Spider's Web.* London: Headline, 1997.

——. *The Subtle Serpent.* 1996. New York: St. Martin's P, 1998.

——. *Suffer Little Children.* 1995. New York: St. Martin's P, 1997.

——. *Valley of the Shadow.* London: Headline, 1998.

# Ellis Peters:
# Brother Cadfael

## Edward J. Rielly

Ellis Peters is the pseudonym that Edith Pargeter used for most of her detective fiction, including the Chronicles of Brother Cadfael, on which her fame will primarily rest. Not to acknowledge Pargeter's other writings, however, would be to undervalue her accomplishments. Pargeter published at least ninety-one books in addition to short stories. Margaret Lewis, author of *Edith Pargeter: Ellis Peters*, so far the only book-length study of the author, lists thirty-six works of fiction by Pargeter, thirteen George Felse detective novels, twenty Chronicles of Brother Cadfael, three nonfiction books, three collections of short stories, and sixteen translations of books from Czech into English.[1]

Pargeter, who was born in 1913 and died in 1995, began her writing career in her native Shropshire, England, in the 1930s and continued her extraordinarily productive career until shortly before her death, her final published book being the twentieth Cadfael novel, *Brother Cadfael's Penance*, in 1994.[2] Certainly her early novels, six of which appeared in print by 1939, do not represent her finest writing. Already, though, she had begun using pseudonyms, employing either Jolyon Carr or Peter Benedict for three of these early novels.[3]

World War II took Pargeter temporarily away from Shropshire. She volunteered for the Women's Royal Naval Service (Wrens) and was posted to Plymouth, and later to Liverpool, to serve as a teleprinter operator helping to administer Allied convoys across the Atlantic. Pargeter's war experiences produced such fiction as *She Goes to War* (1942), featuring a Wren named Catherine Saxon; and a trilogy—*The Eighth Champion of Christendom* (1945), *Reluctant Odyssey* (1946), and *Warfare Accomplished* (1947)— about a soldier, Jim Benison, from Midshire (a fictional Shropshire).

Pargeter's war service also led to friendships with Czech servicemen and a lifelong interest in the literature, history, and political fate of Czechoslovakia. The novelist later visited Czechoslovakia several times; wrote about the country, e.g., the novel *The Fair Young Phoenix* (1948), in which the phoenix is the Czech Republic, and a memoir of her travels in the country, *The Coast of Bohemia* (1950); set one of her George Felse mysteries, *The Piper on the Mountain* (1966), in Czechoslovakia; and completed the sixteen translations mentioned above, including both classics and contemporary works. Over the years, Pargeter received various awards honoring her Czech interests, including a Gold Medal and Ribbon from the Czechoslovak

Society for International Relations and honorary membership in the Prague Branch of P.E.N., the international writers' association.

Edith Pargeter's most successful writing, however, came within the genres of historical fiction and detective fiction. Pargeter began writing detective fiction as a young woman and achieved her greatest pre-Cadfael fame through a series of contemporary detective novels featuring George Felse, a Criminal Investigation Department detective based in Midshire, from *Fallen Into the Pit* (1951), the only one in the series published with her real name (the remaining twelve appearing from Ellis Peters) to *Rainbow's End* (1978). *Death and the Joyful Woman* (1961) earned its author an Edgar Allan Poe Award from the Mystery Writers of America.

Unfortunately, Felse does not come through as a fully realized character. Pargeter falls well short of the ideal that she enunciates in a short but important essay called "The Thriller Is a Novel," where she stresses "that the thriller is a paradox. It must be a mystery. And it must be a novel" (214). She adds, regarding characterization:

A book about half-people is not for me. If I have written such books, they were simply failures on my part. What I want is to make my people live, breathe, speak, act with such conviction that the reader may know them as he knows his own kin. (217)

The more one creates "three-dimensional, calculable" characters, she points out, the more successful as a novel the book becomes, but at the same time, the reader's ability to understand the character as a fully realized person also undermines the thriller's intent to surprise the reader (216). The ideal, Pargeter argues, is "to show the reader every inflection of every character's personality, and yet come up at the end of everything with a solution that both startles and rings true" (217). That, she says, is virtually impossible, but it is the goal toward which she strives.

Pargeter comes up well short of that ideal in the Felse mysteries as a whole, although the books do entertain, especially through the human relationships, legends, and topographical details of the Shropshire setting, "with its border ambivalence and western frontier of mysterious hills," as she writes in *Shropshire* (161).

*Shropshire* (1992), to which Roy Morgan, husband of one of her cousins, contributed many beautiful photographs, is important to understanding Pargeter/Peters and her work, including the Cadfael mysteries. She declares at the end of the book:

Shropshire will be found, some evanescent glimpse, some oblique reflection of it, in everything I have written, and everything I shall write in the future, and I suspect I have left a faint trace of it everywhere I have been. (165)

Pargeter's love for the shire in which she was born and spent her entire life, except for her war service and occasional trips elsewhere in England and

abroad, helps to explain the success of her next series of detective novels. In creating Cadfael, Pargeter turned explicitly to Shropshire and neighboring Wales, the latter the home of her maternal grandmother. In fact, the grandmother, Emma Ellis, provided Pargeter with part of her most famous pseudonym (as well as her brother Edmund with his middle name). The "Peters" surname, as Margaret Lewis points out, was derived from "Petra," name of a Czech friend's daughter (17). Pargeter, using her real name, had for some time been writing successful historical novels set in the region, including *The Heaven Tree* trilogy (1960-63), *A Bloody Field by Shrewsbury* (1972), *The Brothers of Gwynedd* quartet (1974-77), and *The Marriage of Meggotta* (1979). Pargeter placed these novels between 1200 and 1403 (date of the Battle of Shrewsbury).

With *A Morbid Taste for Bones* (1977), first of the Cadfael novels, Pargeter, writing as Ellis Peters (a name used from now on in this essay because all of the Cadfael Chronicles are written over that pseudonym), stepped back a bit farther into time. The twenty Cadfael novels are set between 1137 and 1145, a particularly turbulent period in English and Welsh history. It is also a time that Ellis Peters knew well, for she was a historian as well as novelist. In fact, her native Shropshire and neighboring Wales, and their history, were part of her own life and heritage. She grew up, absorbing, with her elder siblings Edmund Ellis and Margaret, the history of the area, almost through her pores. Her comments about this "research" are worth quoting at length:

> Being limited chiefly to our own county meant that we got to know it very well. Towns, villages, museums, churches, mansions and ruins, railways and canals, all were grist to our mill. It always startles me when people ask about my research, since I am scarcely aware of ever having to do any, at least as far as Shropshire is concerned.
>
> I have used this landscape, native and familiar to me, in all my books, sometimes in its veritable shape and by its own names, sometimes with its edges diffused into a topography between reality and dream, but just as recognizable, for those who know it as I do, as if it had been mapped with the precision of an Ordnance Survey sheet. I did not set out deliberately to make use of my origins. Shropshire is simply in my blood, and in the course of creation the blood gets into the ink, and sets in motion a heartbeat and a circulation that brings the land to life. (*Shropshire* 26)

Ellis Peters's intimate knowledge of the shire included Shrewsbury, location of the Abbey of St. Peter and St. Paul, the Benedictine abbey whose monks included the fictional Brother Cadfael. While growing up, she visited Shrewsbury for its annual flower show and regularly for treatment of an eye problem. During these visits, she roamed with her mother through "every church, every museum, every alley and cobbled street within the town" (*Shropshire* 26, 43-45).

Over the years, Peters did in fact do much research into the times and places she wrote about, but it was reading bred of love for her native habitat, perhaps why she did not consider it research. She writes in *Shropshire*, the closest she would come to an autobiography, that at the age of fifteen she noticed an advertisement in a local paper for a used copy of Owen and Blakeway's *History of Shrewsbury*, first published in 1825. Purchasing this two-volume work, covering both the secular and ecclesiastical histories of Shrewsbury, was she writes, "the bargain of a lifetime" (45-46). No readers of Cadfael would quarrel with that assessment. Other sources of information included the Shrewsbury Abbey charter, published as *The Cartulary of Shrewsbury Abbey*, which provides the names of Shrewsbury abbots and priors, names Peters uses in her novels, as well as ideas for story lines.

Peters did not begin planning her first Cadfael novel with the protagonist. She points out in the introduction to *A Rare Benedictine* (1988), a collection of three short stories about Cadfael, including "A Light on the Road to Woodstock," chronicling Cadfael's decision to enter a monastery, that her original interest was in "deriving a plot for a murder mystery from the true history of Shrewsbury Abbey in the twelfth century" (3). Also in the introduction, she explains how she fashioned her protagonist. In addition to being a brother with intimate knowledge of abbey life, the detective, she decided, must "be a man of wide worldly experience and an inexhaustible fund of resigned tolerance for the human condition" (4). One cannot overestimate the importance of these characteristics. If Cadfael is to solve mysteries, he must know a broad range of humanity and the various motives that drive individuals to crime. He must be a student of people, and most monks, "these cloistered, simple souls who had put on the Benedictine habit as a life's profession," as Peters describes them in *A Morbid Taste for Bones* (3), would lack the experience and insights necessary to resolve life's darker mysteries. Cadfael, however, is a man of the world, a crusader who accompanied Godfrey de Bouillon on the First Crusade in 1098 and who took part in the siege of Jerusalem and the slaughter of its inhabitants the following year. He later was a ship's captain for a decade, primarily in the eastern Mediterranean. Cadfael returned to Normandy and finally to England as a man-at-arms under Roger Mauduit.

Cadfael had known war, violence, intrigue, and killing; countless times he had watched men die. He had encountered many types of men—evil, heroic, self-serving, or simply trying to survive—and he had known women as well, sometimes intimately, a type of experience obviously not shared by most members of Shrewsbury Abbey. Cadfael's first love, an English woman named Richildis, finally had tired of waiting for him to return from his wanderings and married someone else. Cadfael occasionally feels some regret about that but never blames her. On the contrary, he later proves of help to her in *Monk's-Hood* (1980) as he demonstrates her son's innocence of a murder he had been accused of committing. Even as a monk fifteen years into his monastic life and fifty-seven years of age at the time of his first fictional appearance in *A Morbid Taste for Bones*, he remembers the women who entered his life and provided "encounters pleasurable to both parties, and no harm to either":

Bianca, drawing water at the stone well-head in Venice—the Greek boat-girl Arianna—Mariam, the Saracen widow who sold spices and fruit in Antioch, and who found him man enough to replace for a while the man she had lost. The light encounters and the grave, not one of them had left any hard feelings behind. (3)

One of these relationships, though, the one with Mariam, had left behind a son whom Cadfael discovers in *The Virgin in the Ice* (1982), and who returns into Cadfael's world, temporarily turning that world upside-down, in the last of the chronicles, *Brother Cadfael's Penance* (1994).

Also crucial to Cadfael's success as a medieval detective is his "resigned tolerance for the human condition." Were he otherwise, the wide range of individuals who place their confidence in him would certainly not do so, from Hugh Beringar, who appears first in *One Corpse Too Many* (1979) and serves throughout the novels, as Andrew Greeley has said, as "a more or less permanent Dr. Watson to Brother Cadfael" (242); to the townsmen, young lovers, Welsh farmers, and assorted folk who take refuge in the wisdom and compassion of the aging brother.

Peters decided to have her detective be a Welsh native speaking the Welsh language, initially because most of the first novel is set in Wales. It proved a wise choice, for, as she says in her introduction to the collection of short stories, the action of subsequent novels "went back and forth freely across the border, just as the history of Shrewsbury always has" (3-4). Also important is the trait described in the final paragraph of the introduction regarding Cadfael and the Rule of Saint Benedict: "Thereafter, on occasions and for what he feels to be good reasons, he may break the rules. He will never transgress against the Rule, and never abandon it" (7).

Cadfael does not flee the world to bury himself in the abbey, and he sees no contradiction between his earlier, often violent life and his new existence tending the abbey's herb garden, where he grows plants for medicines to heal the sick and injured, both within and outside the abbey walls.[4] He sees himself as "like a battered ship settling at last for a quiet harbour" (*Morbid Taste for Bones* 2). He finds his new state peaceful and satisfying, although he does not like every aspect of it. As he reflects on his monastic life, again in the first novel, "he could not complain even of those parts of it he found unattractive, when the whole suited him very well, and gave him the kind of satisfaction he felt now"; however, he still likes life "spiced, to be truthful, with more than a little mischief when he could get it" (1-2). He therefore is willing to break the rules from time to time, usually rules relating to the daily Office. Otherwise, he would lack the mobility needed to solve the mysteries he encounters. Nonetheless, he usually seeks permission to absent himself from the daily devotions that were (and remain) an essential part of life for the Benedictine monk.[5]

With Cadfael, Ellis Peters approaches that ideal union of verisimilitude and surprise—books that are both mystery and novel—that she considers in her essay "The Thriller Is a Novel." Cadfael is a deeply developed character to whom readers return as to an old and helpful friend. And Cadfael operates within the historical frame of a time especially interesting to Peters, a time that elicits her best, most profound, and most realistic writing.

Peters states that "when writing history, even in the form of fiction, every documented and ascertainable fact must be respected, and an effort made to present events and locations as truly as possible" (*Shropshire* 160). Turning more directly to the Cadfael novels, she notes:

> The novels of Brother Cadfael, centered round the monastic life of Shrewbury's Benedictine abbey in the twelfth century, obviously adhere, as completely as possible, to what is known of the house and the town of that time. We have been very lucky in preserving the Cartulary of the abbey to be edited and published in full, as well as possessing a number of fine antiquarian works on the town and the county. Every tiny, detailed fact discovered adds to the pleasure of writing about places well known lifelong and well loved. In these books the topography is as true as I can make it, with some speculation on the changes the centuries have made. (160-61)

Peters managed to learn many "tiny, detailed" facts that add considerably to the pleasure also of reading the novels.

*A Morbid Taste for Bones* is especially important because, as the first of the twenty novels, it introduces Cadfael to readers. In its historical setting and use of actual historical conditions to propel the story forward, however, it is typical of the Cadfael novels. In this case, the novel is driven by the importance attached to relics of Christ, the Virgin Mary, and saints in the Middle Ages. Devotion to relics survived the Protestant Reformation and continued within the Catholic Church throughout the first half of the twentieth century, minus the financial abuses that helped to produce Luther's break with the Church of Rome. Even today, fascination with the Shroud of Turin is a reminder that the practice is far from dead.

In the twelfth century, saints' relics attracted the faithful in large numbers. Pilgrimages to shrines housing the saints' relics, usually in churches, were common. Perhaps the greatest example was the shrine to Thomas à Becket in Canterbury Cathedral, where he was murdered in 1170 in the very cathedral that he served as archbishop. Glastonbury Abbey, also late in the twelfth century, was the site of a spurious excavation of the supposed remains of King Arthur and Queen Guinevere. Not coincidentally, the remarkable Glastonbury finds came shortly after a great fire in 1184 had reduced the abbey church to ashes, along with its earlier relics. Both Glastonbury and Canterbury officials knew that nothing attracted funds quite so well as a famous saintly patron resting within the walls of their church. Canterbury itself had suffered a major fire four years after Becket's death, which confirmed in people's minds both the sinfulness of the murder and the importance of venerating the saint's physical remains. The money needed to rebuild Canterbury Cathedral certainly would have taken much longer to raise without the motivating factor of making amends both to Becket and to God.

Some churches claimed even greater relics, such as fragments of the True Cross on which Christ was crucified or a container of Christ's blood. Most churches, however, had to make do with lesser saints and in some cases tried to compensate in quantity for what they lacked in quality. The ideal, naturally, was both quality and quantity, for one could never be quite sure which saint might look most favorably upon a particular penitent. The Benedictines of Reading, in Berkshire, for example, accumulated by the late twelfth century approximately 240 relics, including twenty-nine of Christ, six of Mary, and assorted relics of such saints as diverse as Thomas à Becket, Brigid of Kildare, and St. Aethelmod. The remains of Brigid, St. Patrick, and St. Columba, meanwhile, had only recently been discovered at Downpatrick. Reading even boasted a piece of bread from Christ's feeding of the five thousand, and Canterbury claimed a bit of original clay out of which God had shaped Adam.[6]

This indiscriminate collecting of relics and the use made of them was not universal within the Catholic Church, as made clear by the Fourth Lateran Council in 1215. The council, under the leadership of Pope Innocent III, ordered that relics be displayed only within their reliquaries, that they not be sold, and that no newly discovered relics be offered for veneration without approval from Rome (Platt 80).

Relics obviously could mean much to the financial success of a monastery and, therefore, to the success of a monastic official who acquired such relics. It is within the context of these historical conditions that the story of *A Morbid Taste for Bones* occurs, and within which it fits so successfully. Shrewsbury Abbey is led in the year 1137 by the aging, gentle, ascetic Abbot Heribert. Next in line is Prior Robert Pennant. Prior Robert is ambitious and longs to become the next abbot of Shrewsbury. He sees his opportunity to make a name for himself by bringing to the abbey a saint to rival another saint recently acquired by the nearby Cluniac priory of Wenlock, their foundress, Saint Milburga. The names of both abbot and prior appear in the Shrewsbury *Cartulary* (Lewis 96), although many personal characteristics of the abbey officials are invented, along with other fictional brothers whose actual identities and actions, though invented, faithfully adhere to the historical boundaries of what such individuals did in specific monastic roles in the twelfth century.[7]

Prior Robert gains permission to head an expedition, including the Welsh-speaking Cadfael, into Wales to acquire the remains of St. Winifred, who had conveniently appeared in a vision to Brother Jerome, the prior's clerk, who sees his own future success closely tied to that of his immediate superior. The account of Milburga is historically true, as is the acquisition of Winifred, although many details of the latter are the creation of Ellis Peters. It is especially satisfying that Peters goes well beyond the historical as mere backdrop to incorporate important aspects of twelfth-century life, in this book especially religious life, into the fabric of the novel. That is Peters at her best, and it is something that characterizes the entire set of Cadfael Chronicles, although not always, of course, to the same degree. The reader follows the search for Winifred's remains and the mysteries (and crimes) that arise in response to the effort to acquire the saint's bones from an unwilling Welsh community. Ultimately, what almost everyone except Cadfael and his Welsh friends believe to be Winifred's remains are brought to the abbey church at Shrewsbury, St. Peter and St. Paul, and deposited in their reliquary atop the main altar. St. Winifred's relics will continue in that location until flooding of the Severn River forces removal in Chronicle nineteen, *The Holy Thief* (1992).

The presence of twelfth-century Shropshire and Wales within the novel is felt in many other ways as well. The details of character assigned to both Heribert and Robert fit well both ideals and concerns expressed by St. Benedict in his Rule. Heribert is a kind abbot, so that "novices and pupils were easy in his presence" (6), very much a father figure. The characterization fits the ideal of an abbot, a name derived from Aramaic *abba*, meaning father. The abbot is to be the spiritual father of the monastic community; in fact, St. Benedict, departing from the usual designation of Christ by the term "Son" refers to the Savior as "Father," and associates the abbot's spiritual fatherhood with Christ. The Benedictine abbot is to live within the community and provide leadership in the three major endeavors of prayer, study, and work. The abbot expects absolute obedience from his monks and in turn is to use his position always for the spiritual welfare of the monks within his community. That many abbots did not live up to this high standard does not detract from the importance of the ideal (Kardong 116-31; Knowles 39-48). Peters chooses to make her abbots, despite natural imperfections, on the whole admirable leaders of their Shrewsbury community. Heribert's successor, Radulfus, more severe in appearance and more interested in the financial management of the abbey than his predecessor, nonetheless serves effectively in his role. Among his accomplishments is a willingness to permit Cadfael wide latitude in solving the ongoing mysteries that surround the abbey, although he is less likely than Heribert to be fooled by his detective's small violations of the rules.

Prior Robert is another matter. As mentioned earlier, he is an ambitious, grasping individual, a climber one might say today. Although not evil, and the recipient of occasional praise from Cadfael, perhaps more owing to Cadfael's capacity for tolerance than Robert's own deserts, he is the type of person St. Benedict worried about when creating his Rule. Benedict even argues against the position of prior, fearing an inevitable power struggle with the abbot (Kardong 19). Ellis Peters's prior thus fits well the historical concerns about the position.

*A Morbid Taste for Bones* offers a range of other cultural details that make the story historically credible. To cite just a few: the honored Welsh profession of ox-calling, where the ox-caller precedes the oxen, urging them on by voice as another farmer follows behind them and the plough; the poet-harpist, a revered guest at homes of prominent individuals, who also comforts the family of a deceased member by singing the man to his grave; the role of the *alltud*, or outlander, in Welsh society; and the practice of proving an individual guilty of murder by seeing whether the corpse bleeds when the accused touches it. All of these practices, historically based, play significant roles within the novel.[8]

Crucial to the second novel in the series, *One Corpse Too Many* (1979), is the civil strife occurring within England at the time—a time when it appeared, according *The Anglo-Saxon Chronicle*, "that Christ and His saints slept" (265). The action of this novel follows shortly after that of the previous one, as the story lines in all twenty chronicles move forward chronologically, befitting the traditional concept of a chronicle. The turmoil was occasioned by a struggle for the Crown of England after the death of Henry I, youngest son of William the Conqueror, in 1135. Henry's male heir, William, had drowned at sea in 1120, leading Henry to designate his kingdom for his daughter, Matilda, the Empress Maud of Peters's novels. To prepare her for the throne, Henry arranged the marriage of his daughter to Geoffrey, son of the Count of Anjou, a long-time Norman enemy. Henry was operating within an ancient practice of forming political alliances through marriage, but instead he inadvertently fostered distrust toward Matilda by the Norman powers in England. On the death of Henry, his nephew Stephen, a favorite of the deceased king and son of Henry's sister, Adela, claimed the throne. Stephen enjoyed considerable popularity in England and was crowned by the Archbishop of Canterbury on December 22, 1135. During the following Easter season, he received sworn allegiance from most of the barons. Matilda, however, landed in England during the autumn of 1139, with her powerful half-brother, Robert of Gloucester.

The invasion guaranteed a long and tragic civil war during which powerful barons switched allegiances, many churches fell victim to a general climate of civil disorder, and countless innocent individuals lost their lives to random violence. After Robert's death in 1147, Matilda retreated to Anjou. By that time, her husband, Geoffrey, had conquered most of Normandy, and their son Henry took up the English cause of his mother. Henry, now Duke of Normandy and growing increasingly popular, landed in England with an army in 1153, and many barons joined him. Fearing a continued fight into the next generation, both sides finally compromised, and an agreement permitted Stephen to live out his days as king and be succeeded by Matilda's son, Henry. Stephen died on October 25, 1154, and Henry II and his famous wife, Eleanor of Aquitaine, succeeded to the throne.[9] The Cadfael chronicles take place within the height of this civil war, from 1137 until late 1145, with no end of the conflict in sight.

Stephen is an important player within the plot of *One Corpse Too Many* as his forces capture the castle of Shrewsbury, putting to death all who resisted, except for two escaped leaders. As Cadfael and other monks prepare the ninety-four victims for burial, Cadfael discovers one extra corpse. The rest of the story moves forward within the larger struggle for control of England. As always, Peters has her history correct and uses it for both backdrop and narrative engine within the plot.

Cadfael himself is not particularly political, seeing justification on both sides. When his new assistant, disguised as a boy but actually the daughter of one of the escaped supporters of Maud, vehemently denounces Stephen to Cadfael, the monk responds: "In my measure there's little to choose between two such monarchs, but much to be said for keeping a man's fealty and word" (6).

The student of history will again find much to appreciate in this novel in addition to the importance of the civil war. As is typical of Peters, she moves among details great and small to create a realistic impression of events. For example, she offers a portrait of Stephen that generally agrees with historical accounts of the king as a man more naturally attuned to tolerance than violence despite his angry order to execute the castle's defenders (Brooke 167; *Anglo-Saxon Chronicle* 263); Hugh Beringar triumphs over the murderer, Adam Courcelle, through the still accepted proof by combat, in which victory and truth are viewed as one and the same; and, to cite the type of small detail repeatedly present, caltrops (a medieval device with four projecting spikes) are used to disable a horse and thus place its rider in the way of being murdered.

In *St. Peter's Fair* (1981), the fourth Cadfael novel, there is considerable intrigue among the competing parties in the civil war as Maud's supporters attempt to enlist Earl Ranulf of Chester. The intrigue leads to murder and the abduction of a young woman. The Earl of Chester was, in fact, an actual person who saw himself as a king-maker and used his powerful position to exact benefits from both sides until his death in 1153 (Brooke 169). In addition to the political background, the novel is much concerned with abbey finances, especially relative to the neighboring town.

Early in the novel, a delegation from Shrewsbury visits Abbot Radulfus to request relief from the strict provisions governing income related to travelers arriving for St. Peter's Fair, an annual occurrence held in the horse-fair area and along the foregate to the abbey. The provost of the town reviews the regulations surrounding the three-day fair:

> For all that time all shops in the town must be shut, and nothing sold but ale and wine. And ale and wine are sold freely here at the fairground and the Foregate, too, so that no man can make his living in the town from that merchandise. For three days, the three busiest of the year, when we might do well out of tolls on carts and pack-horses and man-loads passing through the town to reach the fair, we must levy no charges, neither murage nor pavage. All tolls belong only to the abbey. Goods coming up the Severn by boat tie up at your jetty, and pay their dues to you. We get nothing. And for this privilege you pay no more than thirty-eight shillings, and even that we must go to the trouble to distrain from the rents of your tenants in the town. (5-6)

The summary by the town's provost is historically accurate and says much about ways in which the abbey made its money. Shrewsbury, which had just suffered heavy damage during Stephen's assault on the city castle, had considerable rebuilding to do. The town desperately needed assistance of the sorts mentioned above, such as murage, a toll levied to finance building or rebuilding of walls in the town, and pavage, a toll allocated to pave streets or highways.

The Abbey of Shrewsbury by charter had the right to hold this annual fair, which usually was both large and lucrative. Although Benedictine monks took the vow of poverty, the abbey as a whole needed considerable revenue to support its continued existence. The fair was an important source of this income, as were the mills that the abbey operated, a common monastic source of income at the time. Abbeys also often owned property in neighboring towns, which they were likely to rent out, as did Shrewsbury Abbey (Burton 241-45). The provost refers to this ownership of homes in town when he speaks of collecting the thirty-eight shillings from the abbey's tenants. Still another revenue stream, to borrow a modern term, but also a possible expense, was the tradition of accepting corrodians into the abbey precincts. Corrodians were lay men and women who resided in abbey buildings and received room and board from the abbey. In some cases the corrodians were servants working for the abbey for wages and keep, or individuals foisted off on the abbey by government officials or benefactors. Other corrodians resided within the abbey grounds, receiving their residence and food in exchange for having signed over their property. One example recorded in the Shrewsbury *Cartulary* is of an Adam of Bispham and wife who agreed to give their possessions to the abbey at death in exchange for specified allotments of food and other services during the interim (Burton 177). A similar situation arises in *Monk's-Hood* when Gervase Bonel and his wife, Richildis, Cadfael's early love, trade land for room and board. The abbey, for such people, became a medieval retirement home. As with other practices found in twelfth-century society, this one also demonstrates Ellis Peters's considerable knowledge of the period and her ability to incorporate these practices into her mystery novels.

Examples of Ellis Peters's in-depth use of twelfth-century history and society could be multiplied many times over in the remaining Cadfael novels. Cadfael himself, of course, is very much a monk of that time in many ways. But he also is different. One of the challenges facing the historical novelist in general, and the writer of historical mysteries in particular, is to combine readers' recognition of the authenticity of the historical milieu presented within the book (that is, recognition of differences between then and now) with a simultaneous, but on the face of it contradictory, recognition that despite the differences, and within the differences, there is a strong commonality of values and experiences between then and now.

This second recognition goes far toward explaining Cadfael's increasing popularity through twenty novels. Cadfael is of the Middle Ages, but he also is of the twentieth century. An important element of this modernism is to be found in Cadfael's belief system. Brother Cadfael's theology has been called a "patchwork theology" (Spencer 67), which is another way of saying that his set of beliefs is both flexible and nondoctrinaire. Indeed, it could hardly be any other way in a man so tolerant of others. It would be incorrect, though, to argue that his beliefs are not firm. Cadfael has an abiding belief in God and God's providence, a faith all the stronger for having been developed and tested repeatedly in the world—what Mary McDermott Shideler has called "an earthly holiness" (14). Many times he reminds others to trust in God, although at the same time he believes in helping God out a bit. He will do what he can to assist those in need, but finally one must have faith. Thus Cadfael reassures Emma Vernold, whose uncle has died unshriven in *St. Peter's Fair*:

> God knows the record without needing word or gesture. It's for the soul facing death that the want of shriving is pain. The soul gone beyond knows that pain for needless vanity. Penitence is in the heart, not in the words spoken. (59)

This response to Emma's fears is somewhat unusual for the time in which the action takes place. In fact, this departure from strict, legalistic orthodoxy would have been on the unusual side at any point among Catholics until the Second Vatican Council, the gathering of church leaders under Pope John XXIII from 1962 until 1965 that brought about, among other alterations, major liturgical changes and an exanded understanding of the role of the laity.

Brother Cadfael, while a man of the twelfth century, also comes across as a post–Vatican II Catholic. Among the documents that came out of the Vatican Council was the revolutionary *Pastoral Constitution on the Church in the Modern World*, also known by its Latin title *Gaudium et spes* ("Joy and Hope"). The preposition "in" is all important, for it marks a sharp turning away from the traditional view of church and state as essentially two different realms. The *Pastoral Constitution* argues that the Church exists within the world and must consider its role within and in relation to that world. It therefore affirms connections between religious faith and earthly duties. Cadfael would have been very comfortable with the teachings of the *Pastoral Constitution on the Church in the Modern World*, for he lives his life within Ellis Peters's novels in a manner consistent with the attitudes and values evidenced in the twentieth-century document.

It already has been shown that Cadfael saw no contradiction between his earlier life of action in the world and his current position within the abbey. The one is not a repudiation of the other but, for Cadfael, a natural next step in his life. He continues, though, to welcome his occasional forays into the outer world, and he certainly continues to use his wealth of experience gained in that world. Without it he could not solve the mysteries that he solves, and he would not be able to help those many individuals, most of whom are not Benedictine brothers, that he assists throughout the twenty chronicles.

Although next to other monks of his time, Cadfael might be viewed as skeptical, in reality, as stated above, he possesses deep faith, but a faith joined to a realism bred of a life lived within the world. He has seen good and evil, and he has seen it in many types of people. Cadfael knows, because he has lived within the world, that all people have much in common and have similar capacities for virtue and vice. "Both men and women partake of the same human nature," he says in *A Morbid Taste for Bones* (153), and he has known enough strong and wise women to be sure. Thinking of a fellow crusader, Guimar de Massard, in *The Leper of St. Giles* (1981), Cadfael says, "I have always known that the best of the Saracens could out-Christian many of us Christians" (196) and continues his reflections:

> One nobility is kin to another, thought Cadfael. There are alliances that cross the blood-line of families, the borders of countries, even the impassable divide of religion. And it was well possible that Guimar de Massard should find himself closer in spirit to the Fatimid caliphs than to Bohemond and Baldwin and Tancred [three Crusaders], squabbling like malicious children over their conquests. (197)

That virtue and salvation are as available to pagans as to Christians was a radical notion in the twelfth century, but it is the sort of conclusion to which a man of the world might come.

That same man of the world journeys out into it one final time in the twentieth and last book in the series, *Brother Cadfael's Penance*, the final book that Edith Pargeter wrote before her death on October 14, 1995. Cadfael, who had bent the rules occasionally, now violates the Rule itself, as he abandons the abbey to rescue his son Olivier. The pull of blood proves stronger than the pull of obedience to his abbot and the Rule of St. Benedict. Cadfael succeeds, finally, in saving his son, and, unsure of what awaits him, returns to Shrewsbury Abbey. He enters the nave of the Church of St. Peter and St. Paul, "this shell of an ageing, no, an old man, subject to all the ills humanity inherits" (252). He lies upon the cold floor, arms spread in a crucifixion posture, and prays

> without coherent words, for all those caught between right and expedient, between duty and conscience, between the affections of earth and the abnegations of heaven . . . for Cadfael, once a brother of the Benedictine house of Saint Peter and Saint Paul, at Shrewsbury, who had done what he had to do, and now waited to pay for it. (253)

In something between dream and vision, he seems to see St. Winifred, with whom the twenty novels began. She stoops to touch him as the bell in the dortoir rings for Prime.

Abbot Radulfus, rising earlier than the other brothers and entering the church before them, approaches Cadfael and speaks to him of events that have transpired. He adds simply, "It is enough. . . . Get up now, and come with your brothers into the choir" (255). Radulfus, like the good spiritual father a Benedictine abbot should be, welcomes back the prodigal son, knowing that Cadfael has followed the dictates of his conscience and has done good for others even through his disobedience. Cadfael is at home again in the abbey, and he will return to his herb garden. Perhaps, had Ellis

Peters lived longer, he would also have continued solving mysteries and attracting readers who, while appreciating the detailed differences between Cadfael's world and theirs, would have found much pleasure in perceiving the similarities within those differences—an identification in this modern world with a time and place brought to life by a skilled writer of historical detective novels and her creation, a monk of the church in the world.

*Notes*

1. I am indebted to Margaret Lewis's book for much of the biographical data presented in this essay. Also of great value is Robin Whiteman's *The Cadfael Companion*, which catalogues people and places in the novels and offers other useful information.

2. Publication dates given in the text refer to first publication of the book, usually in London, and not necessarily to the publication date of the edition used for this essay. The editions used in this essay are the readily available paperback versions.

3. Pargeter also used the pseudonym John Redfern.

4. See Robin Whiteman's *Brother Cadfael's Herb Garden* (photographs by Rob Talbot) for discussion of Cadfael's herb garden and traditional monastic gardens, and for an extensive textual and photographic journey through the many plants that Cadfael uses in his ministrations to the ill and wounded. The book demonstrates another way in which Ellis Peters has brought historical accuracy to her narratives.

5. Saint Benedict, who died about AD 550, placed great importance on the *Opus Dei*, or Divine Office, in his Rule. Monks are to engage in communal choir prayer during certain set hours of the day (the *horarium*), spread out from the first office, Prime, at dawn, through various morning, afternoon, evening, and late-night offices, the latter interrupting sleep and requiring that the *dortoir*, or dormitory, be close to the portion of the abbey church, usually the east end, where the monks gathered for their prayer. For discussions of Saint Benedict, his Rule, and the Benedictines' history, see Maynard; Kardong; Knowles, *The Benedictines*; and Dickinson, the latter for the physical layout of monastic buildings and grounds.

6. I am indebted for much of this information about collections of relics in the Middle Ages to Colin Platt, especially from pp. 77-86.

7. A more readily accessible book that includes names of abbots is *The Heads of Religious Houses: England and Wales 940-1216*, edited by Knowles, Brooke, and London. Shrewsbury abbots, including Heribert (Herbert in this listing) and his successor Radulfus (Ranulf), who succeeds Heribert in 1168 and, correspondingly, near the conclusion of the third Cadfael novel, *Monk's-Hood*, are listed on p. 71.

8. Two of the best histories of Wales are John Davies's *A History of Wales*, covering Welsh history from ancient times into the 1950s; and R. R. Davies's *Conquest, Coexistence, and Change: Wales 1063-1414*, especially strong on Anglo-Welsh relations during the centuries noted in the subtitle.

9. Many fine histories of England exist, including the accurate and readable Norton Library History of England series. The relevant volume for the time period

examined here is Christopher Brooke's *From Alfred to Henry III: 871-1272.* The nonspecialist who wishes a quick overview of the English monarchs might make good use of Josephine Ross's *Kings and Queens of Britain.*

10. Readers may gain considerable understanding of the importance of the Second Vatican Council and the *Pastoral Constitution on the Church in the Modern World* in Richard P. McBrien's two-volume *Catholicism,* especially chaps. 3 and 19 (1: 83-99; 2: 657-90).

## Works Cited

*Anglo-Saxon Chronicle.* Trans. G. N. Garmonsway. 1972. London: Dent, 1982.

Brooke, Christopher. *From Alfred to Henry III: 871-1272.* The Norton Library History of England. New York: Norton, 1969.

Burton, Janet. *Monastic and Religious Orders in Britain, 1000-1300.* Cambridge: Cambridge UP, 1994.

*The Cartulary of Shrewsbury Abbey.* 2 vols. Trans. and ed. Una Rees. Aberystwyth: National Library of Wales, 1975.

Davies, John. *A History of Wales.* New York: Penguin, 1993.

Davies, R. R. *Conquest, Coexistence, and Change: Wales 1063-1415.* Oxford: Clarendon P, 1987.

Dickinson, J. C. *Monastic Life in Medieval England.* London: Adam & Charles Black, 1961.

Greeley, Andrew M. "Ellis Peters: Another Umberto Eco?" *Armchair Detective* 18.3 (1985): 238-45.

Kardong, Terrence. *The Benedictines.* Wilmington: Michael Glazier, 1988.

Knowles, Dom David. *The Benedictines.* New York: Macmillan, 1930.

——, C. N. L. Brooke, and Vera London. *The Heads of Religious Houses: England and Wales 940-1216.* Cambridge: Cambridge UP, 1972.

Lewis, Margaret. *Edith Pargeter: Ellis Peters.* 1994. Bridgend, Wales: Poetry Wales P, 1997.

Maynard, Theodore. *Saint Benedict and His Monks.* New York: P. J. Kennedy & Sons, 1954.

McBrien, Richard P. *Catholicism.* 2 vols. Minneapolis: Winston, 1980.

*Pastoral Constitution on the Church in the Modern World. Vatican Council II: The Conciliar and Post Conciliar Documents.* Ed. Austin Flannery. Collegeville, MN: Liturgical P, 1975. 903-1014.

Peters, Ellis. *Brother Cadfael's Penance.* 1994. New York: Warner, 1996.

——. *The Leper of St. Giles.* 1981. New York: Ballantine, 1985.

——. *A Morbid Taste for Bones.* 1977. New York: Warner, 1994.

——. *One Corpse Too Many.* 1979. New York: Warner, 1994.

——. *A Rare Benedictine.* 1988. New York: Warner, 1991.

——. *St. Peter's Fair.* 1981. New York: Warner, 1992.

——. "The Thriller Is a Novel." *Techniques of Novel Writing.* Ed. A. S. Burack. Boston: The Writer, 1973. 213-18.

Peters, Ellis, and Roy Morgan. *Shropshire.* New York: Warner, 1993.

Platt, Colin. *The Abbeys and Priories of Medieval England.* New York: Fordham UP, 1984.

Ross, Josephine. *Kings and Queens of Britain.* London: Artus, 1982.

Shideler, Mary McDermott. "The Whodunnit Is Fiction's Most Moral Genre." *Books and Religion* 15.5 (1987): 11-14.

Spencer, William David. "Welsh Angel in Fallen England: Ellis Peters' Brother Cadfael." *Mysterium and Mystery: The Clerical Crime Novel.* Ann Arbor: UMI Research P, 1989. 61-70.

Talbot, Rob, and Robin Whiteman. *Brother Cadfael's Herb Garden: An Illustrated Companion to Medieval Plants and Their Uses.* Boston: Little, Brown, 1996.

Whiteman, Robin. *The Cadfael Companion: The World of Brother Cadfael.* Rev. ed. Intro. by Ellis Peters. New York: Warner, 1995.

# P. C. Doherty:
# Hugh Corbett, Secret-Agent and Problem-Solver

## Edward L. Meek, Theron M. Westervelt, David N. Eldridge

P. C. Doherty is currently one of the most popular British writers of historical crime and detective fiction; he is also one of the most prolific, having written over thirty books set in a wide variety of periods. In having such an active pen, Doherty has made himself one of the most familiar names to readers both of histories and of mysteries. As a trained historian and a longtime fan of detective stories, from Agatha Christie to Raymond Chandler, his involvement in these genres has a strong basis. After years of taking on the titans of history, from kings to bishops to knights, and taking on the realm of detective fiction, Doherty now looms so large in his own right that his work requires critical analysis of how much he adds to history and crime fiction.

Doherty's interest in historical fiction has its origins in his PhD thesis at Oxford, which he wrote on early fourteenth-century England. It was therefore natural that his first series of books, set in the reign of Edward I, was written about this period (Interview). Chaucer's *Canterbury Tales* provided the inspiration for Doherty's second series of books set (mainly) in the fourteenth-century.[1] These, by Doherty's own admission, are more fantastical than historical; they are in many cases based around gaudy tales of Satanism (Interview). More recently, however, Doherty has begun to write on more diverse topics ranging from late fifteenth-century England to Ancient Egypt during the reign of Hatusu.[2] The fifteenth century has provided Doherty with two historical detectives, one fictional and the other based on a known historical character, Luke Chichele and Viscount Lovell respectively. Much of Doherty's detective fiction expresses a desire to open up widely known historical mysteries, and then to present a possible explanation for many of them. One of Doherty's fifteenth-century detective novels, *The Fate of Princes*, presents one version of what might have actually happened to Edward V and his brother Richard during the turbulent year of 1483.

However, Doherty's historical detective fiction is mainly represented by his Corbett novels; this popular series of mysteries follows the exploits of Edward I's keeper of the secret seal, Hugh Corbett, who acts as the king's secret-agent and problem-solver.[3] Corbett is in the standard tradition of many fictional detectives, being neither a pathologist nor a policeman. In fact, Doherty explicitly remarks that like Holmes, Corbett has no medical training (Interview). Despite this assertion Corbett frequently orders the exhumation or examination of a victim to determine the cause of death.

*Crown in Darkness* (1988) provides a typical example in which Corbett checks the state of decomposition of the body of one of the victims in order to prove that the murder took place by poisoning (132-32). Corbett usually proves to be a ruthless logician whose application of logical principles (and often Ockham's Razor) leads to the uncovery of the truth. The puzzles with which Doherty tests Corbett's abilities as a logician are effective, though quite standard; the locked-room mystery is a particular Doherty favourite and occurs in *The Assassin in the Greenwood* (1993), amongst others. In this case, the murderer was able to kill a well-protected man (in a locked room) by the cunning means of a poisoned napkin. Corbett determined that the poisoned napkin had been switched for an innocent duplicate after noticing that the sores on the victim's mouth would have left blood stains amongst the food stains; this was not the case with the switched napkin (200). Other slightly overworked plot devices are also used by Doherty, such as Corbett's final revelation of the truth to a gathering of suspects, usually at a sumptuous dinner (188-207). In general, however, Doherty's own cunning devices (such as the poisoned napkin) are more than enough to prevent the reader's dissatisfaction at some of the more unoriginal aspects of the murder plots.

The Hugh Corbett novels can be split into four distinct types in which Doherty's use of historical, or factual, information is quite different. The first variety includes such books as *The Devil's Hunt* (1996) in which Doherty's reasonably predictable murder-mystery is set, in Oxford, within what might be termed a historical background. In this novel the factual background to the story is based upon Edward I's clampdown upon supporters of Simon de Montfort, long after de Montfort's death. The crime which Corbett is delegated to solve, however, is entirely fictional, though the motive for one of the murderers is well grounded in its historical context: a man whose mind has been unhinged by experience of the violence of Edward I's campaigns against the Welsh (184). Likewise, *The Assassin in the Greenwood* sees Corbett investigating a series of fictional murders within the historical background of marauding gangs of traitorous royal officials and the "secret diplomatic war preceding [the battle of] Courtrai."[4] Directly connected to this group of books is another set in which Corbett's investigation of a fictional murder or series of murders eventually leads to the solution to a long-standing medieval mystery. Chief amongst these is *Song of a Dark Angel*; this follows Corbett's investigation, in 1302, of a bizarre series of murders along the Norfolk coast, which eventually leads to his discovery of the whereabouts of part of king John's treasure, lost near the sea-coast of Norfolk in 1216.

A few of the Corbett mysteries also deal with documented crimes from the early fourteenth century. *Murder Wears a Cowl* (1992), for instance, describes Corbett's investigation of a number of slayings of London prostitutes, murders for which Doherty has found evidence in contemporary London court records (248). A second plot contained within the same book concerns Corbett's discovery of the culprits responsible for stealing royal treasure from Westminster Abbey in the early 1300s. The fourth type of

Corbett novel is one in which the crime that Corbett investigates is a well-known and documented mystery from Edward I's reign, such as the mysterious death of Alexander III of Scotland. Each of these mysteries is then eventually solved by Corbett, who puts forward what Doherty calls a "possible or logical" explanation for the mystery (Interview). *The Crown in Darkness*, for example, sees Corbett being commissioned to investigate Alexander III's suspicious fall from his horse, near Kinghorn Manor, in 1286 (7-8). *Spy in Chancery* also deals with another famous episode from the reign of Edward I, the treason of Sir Thomas Turberville in 1295. Doherty suggests in an Author's Note that the details of Turberville's capture are "shrouded in mystery" and therefore is able to portray Corbett himself as the man responsible for the capture of this French spy working on behalf of Philip IV of France in Edward's own court and administration.

In all four types of Corbett novel, Doherty's wide-ranging knowledge of English society during the early 1300s is readily apparent, particularly in his depictions of the practicalities of the every-day life of an administrative clerk (Hugh Corbett).[5] Doherty's careful description of the process of writing a formal administrative document is impressive, with reference to the essential tools of pumice, inkhorn and knife (Tout 77, Bischoff 18-19). Furthermore, the attempt to accurately portray urban living in the later Middle Ages is central to Doherty's fiction, for most of his Corbett novels are set in an urban context. He is quite willing, for example, to point out factual inaccuracies in descriptions of late medieval town life in the work of other authors of medieval detective fiction (Interview). Doherty himself spares us none of the grisly details of much of the urban squalor in late medieval England,[6] and his own research, based upon Adam of Monmouth's chronicle has provided the exemplar for Doherty's own, accurate, depictions of executions carried out by town authorities.[7] Doherty also draws some enlightening contrasts between the squalor of lay town-dwellings, with foul-smelling tallow candles, and the perfumed scent of beeswax candles that most lay people would have experienced in church (Prince 58). It is presumably through such contrasting descriptions of life in medieval England that Doherty feels he is able to portray accurate "pictures, or windows of medieval life" (Interview).

Doherty's "picture" of late-medieval Oxford in *The Devils's Hunt* is particularly successful, well-researched and perhaps grounded on the author's personal knowledge of present-day Oxford (Interview). The site of the fictional murders, Sparrow Hall, is well-documented; and the general descriptions of other Oxford colleges are quite accurate, particularly Hugh Corbett's own assertion that each Hall (or College) existed virtually as a separate village and was jealously protective of its own rights.[8] At one point, Corbett further suggests to his side-kick, Ranulf atte-Newgate, that "the University hates the town; the town resents the University" (*Devil's* 46). This town-gown rivalry, apparent throughout the book, is also nicely representative of both late medieval Oxford and Cambridge. The fourteenth century was a particularly violent time in Oxford; the St Scholastica's riot of

1355 lasted three days and caused deaths on both sides (Cobban 260-63). The care with which Doherty researches the background to each novel is further suggested by his provision of references to secondary material which he has used to provide an accurate context for his plots—notably his reference to further reading on the development of artillery which provides the justification for his assertion in *Satan's Fire*, that gun-powder could well have spread to England by the early fourteenth century.[9]

Doherty attempts to provide more than just a series of windows through which the reader may view a detailed historical context; he also gives us a valid type of "speculative history," in which the novels' detective-plots (rather than the novels' setting) are speculative, though mainly based on historical fact (Interview). Doherty's intention is made clear by the wide variety of historical sources which he uses to provide information upon which his Corbett plots are based. *Murder Wears a Cowl*, for instance, weaves together and embellishes two separate documented historical episodes which Doherty turns into the plots for his story. As we have seen, the first is a series of murders of prostitutes and the second is the theft of royal treasure by an errant clerk named Puddlicott. Doherty quotes his chief sources ranging from manuscripts held in the Chetham Library (Manchester), the British Library, to the Public Record Office at Kew.[10] *Assassin in the Greenwood* provides another example of Doherty's research leading to a murder mystery which, although fictitious, is plausible and based upon well-founded factual evidence. Here Doherty interweaves the diplomatic war between Edward I and Philip IV with a fictitious and murderous conspiracy amongst shire officials in Nottingham castle; Doherty's evidence for this "secret diplomatic war preceding Courtrai" comes from the Chancery Miscellanea at the Public Record Office (call-number C47) (215). Evidently a great deal of research has gone into producing complex plots, often either based on real crimes or plots based on fictitious crimes set within an effective (and well-researched) historical framework. Doherty then directly attempts to persuade the reader of the historical validity of his historical setting, or the actual plot itself, by means of Author's Notes or Historical Introductions, present in all of the Corbett novels.

It is clear that Doherty has taken a great deal of care in producing complex "speculative" Corbett mysteries with some foundation in fact and hence there is very little factual inaccuracy in the obviously historical components of most of the books; Doherty's historical interpretation is often extremely sound. However, not all of the Corbett novels are so successful in this regard. This is particularly the case with those Corbett novels that are based upon the more established historical mysteries of the period, notably those books dealing with the treason of Sir Thomas Turberville, and the infamously obscure death of Alexander III of Scotland in 1286. *Spy in Chancery*, dealing with the first of these episodes, seems to place the entire uncovery of the Turberville treason in 1296, rather than 1295, which wreaks havoc with the complex chronology of events constructed in the book. Doherty attempts to weave Turberville's treason into the plotting of John

Balliol, titular king of Scotland in 1296. This cannot possibly have been the case when Turberville's treason had already been discovered in the previous year.[11] Also, whilst Doherty claims that the capture of Turberville is "shrouded in mystery" (*Spy* 146) (and therefore feels able to attribute his capture to the fictional Hugh Corbett), the man whose actions may well have brought Turberville to the attention of the authorities, Robert de Crowland, receives no mention at all (Edwards 306). In fact, the previous example may bring into sharper focus the problems inherent within Doherty's idea of speculative history; Doherty's convincing knowledge of much of the fourteenth-century source material and persuasive justifications in the form of Author's Notes may well persuade the unwary that they are reading not just a logical possibility (what Doherty calls historical speculation or a "what if?"), but a more definite historical account. The problem then is further compounded if Doherty's historical speculation is based upon unreliable foundations.

This issue is to be seen most clearly within *Crown in Darkness*. Corbett has been commissioned (somewhat implausibly) to act as the Chancellor of England's detective and investigate the reasons for, and find the possible perpetrators of, the death of Alexander III (10-16). Corbett eventually finds that Alexander III has been murdered by a fanatical servant of Edward I, whose intention was to ensure that Edward's secret desire to overwhelm and control Scotland would actually take place (162-63). Most professional historians, however, suggest that his death came about because of an unfortunate riding accident in bad weather (Gillingham 136). Since, as Doherty suggests, "It is a matter of speculation whether the king's fall was an accident or murder," he is perfectly within his rights to point out the more dramatic possibility that historians have ignored. Doherty himself might suggest that they might have done so because, as a profession, he believes they tend to steer away from anything "which could ruin their reputation" (Interview). Doherty's Author's Note, however, suggests very strongly that the Scottish king's death may well have been brought about by foul-play, and a historical introduction to the book also promises to unravel "the fascinating mysterious truth behind the Scottish king's death" (*Crown* 185-87, 7-8). However, it is very important to note that this "mysterious truth" (ie Alexander's murder) is merely Doherty's speculation on the subject, and in any case it will be seen that this speculation is based on weak foundations.

In fact, there is no evidence to suggest that any servant of Edward I would ever have acted on his own initiative to kill the Scottish king in order to fulfil his master's desire for mastery over Scotland. It is widely believed that early on in his reign Edward I had no such consistent policy of empire building within the British Isles that Doherty credits him with (Prestwich 357-59). Factual errors within *Crown in Darkness* have led to this perhaps unwise characterisation of Edward's policies towards Scotland, Wales and Empire. For instance, it is suggested by Doherty that the issue of Alexander's homage to Edward was raised at the coronation (in 1274) and later, in 1278; it is actually the case that the issue was not raised in 1274 and raised only obliquely on the latter occasion (Prestwich 357). It is also unlikely that personal relations between Edward I and Alexander III had been soured by such constant wrangling (as Doherty suggests), for friendly relations were maintained throughout the period concerning Alexander's lands in Cumberland (Prestwich 357-58). Doherty's historical speculation may well be accused of taking the "logical possibility" of Alexander's murder further than the facts would seem to allow. And furthermore, by using such phrases as "mysterious truth" in the setting of a purportedly informative historical introduction, Doherty may leave the reader with a strong, although unlikely impression of the entire episode.

These occasional lapses in the Corbett novels develop into a more constant theme of errors and misinterpretations in Doherty's detective fiction based on the reign of both the Yorkist kings, Edward IV and Richard III. The two novels concerned are *Dove Amongst the Hawks* (1990, Edward IV) and *The Fate of Princes* (Richard III). Both of the novels are based upon the results of fictional commissions of enquiry set up by both Edward IV and Richard III to investigate the deaths or disappearances of Henry VI and Edward V respectively. Despite Doherty's claim that many aspects of the novels are "based on fact," it is important to state at the outset that neither Edward nor his brother would have had any need for such commissions, as they more than any other people would have known the precise fates of Henry VI and the Princes in the Tower (*Dove* 159). Most historians have accepted Edward IV's direct or indirect responsibility for Henry VI's death. Doherty's suggestion that the murder might have been carried out by Elizabeth Woodville (without Edward's knowledge or consent) is unlikely (Ross, *Edward IV* 175-77). Equally, Doherty's suggestion that Richard III was not responsible for the deaths of the Princes in the Tower seems to be based on faith rather than the weight of historical evidence. Two lines of argument in particular need to be criticised. Firstly, that Richard III would have gained nothing from the deaths of the princes is absurd. Edward V (the elder of the two princes) was already *de facto* king of England, and Richard III, would have benefited more directly than anyone else from the princes' removal from the political scene (*Fate* 190). Second, that the princes could have been smuggled out to obscurity in Burgundy is even more unlikely; given the strong support that Margaret, dowager duchess of Burgundy, later gave to pretenders against Henry VII, it is unreasonable to suggest that she would have allowed them any sort of obscurity at all (*Fate* 97).

So we can see clearly that much of Doherty's historical interpretation in the fifteenth-century novels can be seriously questioned, and unlike in the Corbett novels, some of the facts crucial to Doherty's plots may also be seen as faulty or questionable. In *The Dove Amongst the Hawks*, Doherty proposes that Elizabeth Woodville, and her supporters, were directly responsible for the deaths of Henry VI, George, duke of Clarence, and a host of fictional characters (143-47). Doherty bases this on the assumption that the Woodvilles were eliminating those with "knowledge" of Edward's pre-contract to Eleanor Butler; in order to support this theory he suggests in an

Author's Note that the pre-contract story "is also to be based on fact" (159). This assertion is extremely questionable as there was *no* concrete evidence for the story until after Edward's death, when the alleged pre-contract came to be used by Richard III in a wholly corrupt piece of propaganda to assert the bastardy of Edward's children (Ross, *Richard III* 91). Secondly, that Elizabeth Woodville would ever have sought the murder of those with the knowledge of this supposed pre-contract is very unlikely. Even if the pre-contract story were true, it would carry very little legal weight, on its own, for disinheriting Edward V (Ross, *Richard III* 89); as in any case, Edward IV's sons were later disinherited by Richard III for a variety of reasons other than pre-contract, such as Edward's own bastardy (Ross, *Richard III* 89-91). It is therefore less than clear why the Woodville clan would ever have considered the murderous actions that Doherty credits them with (and it is even less clear how Doherty can claim to suggest that the pre-contract story is "based on fact").

Many of Doherty's problems in the fifteenth-century novels seem to stem from the fact that his knowledge of historical source material for the reign of Edward IV is less comprehensive than his knowledge of such evidence for the reign of Edward I. As we have seen, in the Corbett novels Doherty uses to powerful effect a wide variety of printed and manuscript sources upon which to base his stories. However, for the fifteenth century, many of his facts seem to come from standard chronicle sources, using the more salacious aspects of commonly-known standard political history, presumably to appeal to a wide readership. It is clear that much of the information upon which Doherty bases his story concerning Edward IV's pre-contract is derived from the gossipy corpus of chronicle evidence for the reign of Edward IV and Richard III, notably the *Croyland Chronicle* which provides specific evidence of the pre-contract story. It might be suggested that seemingly uncritical acceptance of the more scandalous observations of Yorkist chroniclers lead Doherty into trouble. The eclectic variety of primary sources chosen to prop up Doherty's plots is also seen with reference to his characterisation of Henry VI in *Dove Amongst the Hawks*. Doherty uses Father Ronald Knox's edition of a sixteenth-century collection of miracle stories attributed to Henry VI to assert in an Author's Note that "Henry VI's sanctity seems well demonstrated."[12] However, many historians working rather more recently than the 1920s have begun to pick apart the idea of Henry VI's sanctity and replace it with the idea of Henry VI as mentally-backward from the very start of his reign. Doherty's suggestion that Henry's foundation of Eton and King's College Cambridge are representative of the king as being a "clever scholar" (*Dove* 53), perhaps shows nothing more than the educational aspirations of a close-knit circle of advisors surrounding the king and using his authority to found such institutions (Watts 168-69). In the light of this recent scholarship, Doherty's use of such spurious source material, composed thirty to sixty years after Henry's death, seems an unwise starting-point to base the characterization of a major historical figure.

In conclusion, Doherty's most successful novels, by far, are the Corbett series. Peppered with (sometimes) ingenious plot-devices, the novels present a vivid and often stimulating picture of life in England during the reign of Edward I. In these novels Doherty has often made a successful and valid attempt to use his own research amongst a variety of fourteenth-century source material, either to provide an accurate historical framework for his plots, or to provide specific crimes around which he weaves his tales. In very few of the Corbett novels may either his facts or most of his historical interpretations be questioned. However, in the novels set outside of the reign of Edward I (and in the Corbett novels which are exceptions to this rule), Doherty's claims that the stories are "based on fact" are left looking very unreliable indeed. In some cases problems occur with both his facts and interpretations which leave the reader with blurred "pictures, or windows of medieval life," and bring into question Doherty's avowed desire for historical validity.

*Notes*

1. See P. C. Doherty, *Ghostly Murder* (London: Headline, 1997) for a full list of the Chaucer inspired series of historical fiction. Doherty is currently writing a fifth volume in the series entitled *The Hangman's Hymn,* to be published shortly.

2. See for example: P. C. Doherty, *The Fate of Princes* (London: Hale, 1990), and his *The Mask of Ra* (London: Headline, 1998). The authors are grateful to Dr. Doherty for permitting us to consult a proof copy of *The Mask of Ra.*

3. Doherty has suggested that Hugh Corbett is based on Edward I's own trusted administrator, John de Droxford, successively cofferer, controller, and keeper of the king's wardrobe. P. C. Doherty, *Murder Wears a Cowl* (London: Headline, 1992), 249; for John de Droxford see M. Prestwich, *Edward I* (London: Methuen, 1988), 140.

4. The battle was fought on July 11, 1302. See G. Duby, *France in the Middle Ages,* trans. J. Vale, (Oxford: Blackwell, 1991), 265; Doherty, *The Assassin in the Greenwood,* 215.

5. Corbett is also "Keeper of the King's Secret Seal"; there is some evidence for this position although it is uncertain. See T. F. Tout, *Chapters in the Administrative History of Medieval England,* vol. 5 (Manchester: Manchester UP, 1920-23), 161-64.

6. See, for example, the description of Nottingham's market place in which chicken carcasses were plucked, their entrails emptied into open sewers and then washed in "huge vats of scalding water"; Doherty, *Assassin in the Greenwood,* 68.

7. Transcript of Interview, 12; for a typical description of medieval capital punishment, see Doherty, *Assassin in the Greenwood,* 41.

8. For Sparrow Hall, see A. B. Cobban, *The Medieval English Universities: Oxford and Cambridge to c. 1500* (Aldershot: Scholar P, 1988), 155.

9. The book Doherty refers to is H. W. Hime, *Gunpowder and Ammunition: Their Origin and Progress* (London: Longmans, 1904). It is to be noted that Doherty's bibliographical reference is incorrect; he wrongly refers to Henry W. Hine, rather than Hime.

10. The manuscripts are quoted as Chetham No. 6712, B. L. Cott. Nero D. ii, fol. 192d & P.R.O. Exchequer Accounts K.R. 322/8.

11. For a full account of the events surrounding Turberville's capture, see J. G. Edwards, "The Treason of Thomas Turberville, 1295," in R. W. Hunt, ed., *Studies in Medieval History Presented to F. M. Powicke* (Oxford: Clarendon P, 1948), 304-06.

12. Doherty, *A Dove Amongst Hawks*, 159; for the edition of miracle stories see R. Knox, ed., *The Miracles of King Henry VI* (Cambridge: Cambridge UP, 1923). The edition is based on an ecclesiastical investigation of the miracles attributed to Henry VI; Knox dates the manuscript to c. 1500-1530. It may be consulted in the British Library, B.L. Royal Mss 13 C.VIII.

## Works Cited

Bischoff, G. *Latin Palaeography: Antiquity and the Middle Ages.* Reprint. Cambridge: Cambridge UP, 1990.

Cobban, A. B. *The Medieval English Universities: Oxford and Cambridge to c. 1500.* Aldershot: Scholar P, 1988.

Doherty, P. C. *An Ancient Evil.* London: Headline, 1994.

——. *The Assassin in the Greenwood.* London: Headline, 1993.

——. *Crown in Darkness.* London: Hale, 1988.

——. *The Devil's Hunt.* London: Headline, 1996.

——. *Dove amongst the Hawks.* London: Hale, 1990.

——. *Fate of Princes.* London: Hale, 1990.

——. *Ghostly Murders.* London: Headline, 1997.

——. *Murder Wears a Cowl.* London: Headline, 1992.

——. *Prince of Darkness.* London: Headline, 1992.

——. *Spy in Chancery.* London: Hale, 1988.

Duby, G. *France in the Middle Ages.* Trans. J. Vale. Oxford: Blackwell, 1991.

Edwards, J. G. "The Treason of Thomas Turberville, 1925," in R. W. Hunt, ed. *Studies in Medieval History Presented to F. M. Powicke.* Oxford: Clarendon P, 1948.

Gillingham, J. "The Early Middle Ages (1066-1290) in K. O. Morgan." *The Oxford Illustrated History of Britain.* Oxford: Oxford UP, 1984.

Hime, H. W. *Gunpowder and Ammunition: Their Origin and Progress.* London: Longmans, 1904.

Interview, P. C. Doherty. Conducted June 24, 1998, by David Eldridge, Edward Meek, and Theron Westervelt.

Knox, R., ed. *The Miracles of King Henry VI.* Cambridge: Cambridge UP, 1923.

Prestwich, M. *Edward I.* London: Methuen, 1988.

Ross, C. *Edward IV.* Reprint. London: Eyre and Methuen, 1984.

——. *Richard III.* London: Metheuen, 1981.

Tout, T. F. *Chapters in the Administrative History of Medieval England.* vol. 5. Manchester: Manchester UP, 1920-23.

Watts, J. L. *Henry VI and the Politics of Kingship.* Cambridge: Cambridge UP, 1996.

# Susanna Gregory:
# Doctor Matthew Bartholomew,
# Master of Medicine and Detection

## Jean Coakley

Readers familiar with places where small minds rise to high positions should find themselves right at home in mid-fourteenth-century Cambridge University, where murder hastens promotion, tradition reigns supreme, and town and gown are at daggers drawn. It is an institution whose political and pedagogical rituals author Susanna Gregory (pseud.) knows intimately. A Cambridge Ph.D. with specialties in mammalian teeth and bones and a Fellow of one of its colleges since 1987, she has also written widely on castles, cathedrals, historic houses, seals, marine pollution, medical demographics, the cultural consequences of AIDS, and a variety of related historical and scientific topics. She has "always been interested in medieval architecture," she says, and "love[s] looking at old maps and working out how cities have changed and developed over the centuries."[1] This, coupled with her previous experience in a coroner's office and "as a police officer . . . involved with identifying the odd body through forensic means,"[2] adds an accuracy and richness of detail which makes her mysteries extraordinarily interesting and believable.

Set during the Black Death and its aftermath, 1348-1353, Gregory's four "Chronicles of Matthew Bartholomew"—*A Plague on Both Your Houses* (1996), *An Unholy Alliance* (1996), *A Bone of Contention* (1997), and *A Deadly Brew* (1998)—recreate medieval Cambridge in microcosm.

Beginning with *A Plague on Both Your Houses*, which sets the scene, introduces Gregory's *dramatis personae*, and establishes their motivations and frailties, each novel features a progression of carefully articulated subplots which contextualize contemporary personal, professional, institutional, ethical, and religious concerns. As a teacher, a physician, and above all a good man trying to lead a virtuous life while determining where he stands, Doctor Matthew Bartholomew is the logical protagonist to examine the questions at issue in this era of medical, institutional, and social change. A junior faculty member in minor orders teaching a marginalized discipline, accused more than once of heresy, and a townie to boot, he is caught up in a system where collegiality is at best a polite fiction and political intrigue a fine art. When greed and ambition metastasize into murder, jeopardizing the University's survival and threatening to reveal the skeletons in its closets, he is dragooned to discover the cause and dispense a cure.

Except for occasional forays to near-by Trumpington, Saffron Waldon, Denny Abbey, and the Fens, the action takes place mainly in Cambridge,[3] focusing largely on the University's then endowed colleges[4] and the less prestigious student lodging houses called "hostels" owned and/or managed by senior faculty as profit-making ventures. In order of their founding, these colleges are: Peterhouse (1280)—where Dr. Bartholomew began his education; Michaelhouse (1324)—where he now teaches medicine and serves as reluctant detective in residence; Clare Hall (1325); King's Hall (1337); Pembroke Hall—called Valance Marie in the narratives after its foundress (1346); Gonville Hall (1348); Trinity Hall (1350); and Corpus Christi (1352)—founded by the local merchant guild and called Bene't College in the series.[5] Conceived as orderly venues for educating "non-monastic scholars, who were mostly secular clergy and at least in minor orders" (Crawley 2), in theology, civil and canon law, and the newly intellectualized practice of medicine, they quickly developed internal and external rivalries which erupted into violence at the slightest provocation. University hegemony over municipal decision-making intensified town-gown friction, as did scholars' lax punishment under canon law while townsmen faced the full rigor of the King's harsh justice for the same offenses.

Complicating this already explosive mix was the plague, which originated in China and by 1346 had made its way inexorably across Asia Minor to Europe, carried ironically by European traders fleeing its ravages. Philip Ziegler quotes one contemporary chronicler's description of these refugees' fate in *The Black Death*:

> "In January of the year 1348 . . . three galleys put in at Genoa, driven by a fierce wind from the East, horribly infected and laden with a variety of spices and other valuable goods. When the [Genoese saw] . . . how suddenly and irremediably they infected other people, they were driven forth from that port by burning arrows and diverse engines of war; for no man dared touch them. . . . Thus, they were scattered from port to port."
>
> But by the time . . . the Genoese authorities reacted, it was too late. The infection was ashore and nothing was to stop it. By the spring of 1348 the Black Death had taken a firm grasp in Sicily and on the mainland.[6]

In April 1349, as the narrative shows, the contagion was well abroad in the diocese of Ely, where it leap-frogged from village to village without rhyme or reason, sparing some completely, devastating others, killing most individuals who contracted it while leaving others completely untouched. Little remains to show the plague's real impact on Cambridge University. If the chancellor or his deputies tallied how many faculty and students died in Cambridge colleges and hostels between May and September 1349, these records did not survive the fiery town-gown riots of 1381.

According to Ziegler,

> The only College which furnishes any useful material is King's Hall where sixteen out of forty resident scholars died between April and August. But one can deduce

that the losses among students must have been severe by what is known of events in the town of Cambridge. Though some of the damage may have been done by the second epidemic of 1361, an idea of the devastation is given by a letter from the Bishop of Ely written in 1366 which suggested the amalgamation of two of the city parishes on the grounds that there were not enough people to fill even one of the churches. Practically the whole of the town on the Castle side of the river, "The Ward beyond the Bridge," seems to have been wiped out. Most people in All Saints in Castro also died and the few parishioners left alive moved out. The nave of All Saints' church fell into ruins, leaving "the bones of the dead exposed to the beasts." (Ziegler 136-37)

University-trained physicians like Chaucer's "Doctour of Physic,"[7] who relied on conventional approaches like bleeding, natural magic, and astrology, were ill-equipped to deal with the pestilence when it reached them. The problem, Robert S. Gottfried argues in *Doctors and Medicine in Medieval England*,[8] was that medical education was locked into the Paris format established a century earlier which valued exegesis and disputation over clinical practice. Students held to this curriculum strove to master authorities like Galen, Hippocrates, Dioscorides, and occasional snippets of Avicenna and other Islamic commentators but rarely if ever interacted with patients. Since death and disease were widely construed as ruled by the heavens and recovery attributed to God's will, departure from standard practice was discouraged as heresy bordering on witchcraft. Thus, when England's physicians were called upon during the Black Death to treat sufferers or at least ease their passing,

[m]any refused to see the afflicted, or insisted on treating them, literally, at arms length. . . . A few prominent physicians did advocate change, and beseeched their colleagues to learn anatomy and practice surgery. But the reformers were a minority. Most physicians, secure in their social positions if not always in their practices, refused to consider new methods. The result was a century and a half of stagnation. (Gottfried 168-69)

Gregory's hard-working protagonist, Doctor Matthew Bartholomew, Michaelhouse's local-born Master of Medicine who values clinical experience above ability to debate ideas, is modeled after these brave reformers. Sent to Peterhouse as a prologue to joining his wealthy brother-in-law, Sir Oswald Stanmore, in the cloth trade, he instead ran away to Oxford and later to the University of Paris. There he studied under Ibn Ibrahim, an innovative Arab physician whose passionate regard for cleanliness and the links between sepsis, causality, and contagion distinguished him from his more conventional colleagues. Instead of the usual lackluster course of study which was replicated in England at Oxford and Cambridge, Bartholomew learned anatomy, physiology, diagnostics, *materia medica*, and surgical procedures, mastering his craft through observation and hands-on clinical experience rather than windy disputation.

Although he is naive in many respects, particularly with regard to women, Matthew Bartholomew has a dogged respect for truth, a demonstrated concern for the well-being of his fellow men regardless of economic status, and a clearly articulated duty to his students. He must give them the best medical education he can yet assure at the same time that they know enough astrology and traditional physic to pass muster with their examiners. Bartholomew's dilemma is clear when Bulbeck and Grey, who saved his life during the plague using his innovative surgical technique (*Plague* 174-82), point out their unease with the usual correlation between astrology and contagion:

"It is this notion of heavenly bodies. I know you are skeptical of the role played by the stars in a patient's sickness—and the little I have seen of medical practice inclines me to believe you are right. So why must we waste time with such nonsense? Why do you not teach us more about uroscopy or surgery."

"Because if you want to pass your disputations and graduate as a physician, you will need to show that you can calculate the astrological charts that can be used to determine a course of treatment. What I believe about the worth of such calculations is irrelevant."

"The medical faculty at Paris told King Philip the Sixth of France that the Death was caused by a malign conjunction of Saturn and Jupiter," said [his student] Gray from the doorway.

"I know," said Bartholomew. "And this malign conjunction was said to have occurred at precisely one o'clock on the afternoon of 20 March 1345. The physicians at the medical school of Montpellier wrote *Tractatus de Epidemia*, in which they explained that the reason some areas were more affected than others was because they were more exposed to evil rays when 'Saturn looked upon Jupiter with a malignant aspect." (*Bone* 134-35)

Bartholomew is in a quandary, dissatisfied with the traditional medicine he is forced to teach but reluctant to jeopardize his job, his students' safety, and even his life by speaking out:

He had been accused of heresy more times than he could remember for his unorthodox thinking, and was ever alert to the possibility that too great an accumulation of such charges might result in his dismissal from the University. In the past, he had not cared much about what his colleagues thought about his teaching, assuming that the better success rate he had with his patients would speak for itself. But he had moderated his incautious attitude when he realised that his excellent medical record would be attributed to witchcraft if he were not careful, and then his hard work and painstakingly acquired skills would count for nothing. . . . [He] recalled how he had felt when his Arab master in Paris had insisted that he learned astrology, even if he had not believed in its efficacy. So Bartholomew had learned his traditional medicine, and answered questions about poorly aligned constellations in his disputations. But he had also learned Ibn Ibrahim's unorthodox theories on hygiene and contagion, and so his patients had the benefit of both worlds. (*Bone* 135-36)

Compounding Bartholomew's dilemma about his teaching and practice of medicine is his loneliness: there is literally no one with whom he can share his innermost doubts and concerns. Although he has a warmly affectionate family in his sister Edith and brother-in-law Sir Oswald Stanmore who raised him, they move in a different milieu and cannot understand why he persists in treating the poor and angering constituted authority.

Bartholomew's chamber-mate, Philosophy Master Giles Abigny, and pretty Phillipa Abigny, Bartholomew's betrothed, are no help either. Giles is too erratic in temperament and self-indulgent to be trustworthy. Phillipa, an heiress widowed in childhood and consigned to the nuns at St. Radegund's[9] after her father died, wants a more satisfying life than treating the poor will provide.

Bartholomew's self-indulgent Michaelhouse colleagues present an even worse prospect. From selfish Roger Alcote who basks in comfort while others freeze, to self-aggrandizing Thomas Wilson the prototypical petty administrator who succeeds Bartholomew's murdered patron Sir John Babington as Master of Michaelhouse, to bigoted Father William whose fanaticism is so extreme even the Inquisition sent him packing, each is too self-absorbed and engaged in empire-building to have compassion for a colleague. The one who comes closest to fulfilling the role of confidant is Brother Michael, Michaelhouse's bent Benedictine Master of Theology, Bishop of Ely Thomas de Lisle's confidential spy, who is later named Proctor of the University. An academic Friar Tuck whose intelligence, agility, and physical strength belie his great bulk, he remains an enigma throughout the series, leaving readers as well as Bartholomew guessing about his origins until king's agent Ralph de Langelee unmasks Michael's resourceful grandmother in *A Deadly Brew*:

"Dame Pelagia is one of the greatest and most respected of all the King's agents, and it is said that she is one of the few people who knows all the details of the mystery surrounding the death of Edward the Second[,] . . . our current King's father. . . . It is not mere chance that Queen Isabella, whom we all know played a role in her husband's murder, spends her days at Castle Rising near a Franciscan nunnery—a house of the Poor Clares, which is Dame Pelagia's order. It is common knowledge at Westminster that the King would entrust the wardenship of his murderous mother to no one but Dame Pelagia."

Bartholomew looked at the old lady with renewed suspicion. No wonder Michael was unwilling to take a post as a mere head of a University College with those kinds of connections! (332-33)

Ironically, Bartholomew's most dependable friends are those at the bottom of the pecking order: Cynric ap Huwydd, his canny Welsh book-bearer; Agatha, Michaelhouse's cook, laundress, and sole female-in-residence; and the Lady Matilde, Cambridge's most elegant prostitute, a woman of parts one hopes he will eventually marry.[10]

Gregory's first "chronicle," *A Plague on Both Your Houses*[11] lays the groundwork for the series by exposing the dynamics of town-gown politics, using real people, familiar place names, and maps to enhance verisimilitude, and a prologue and epilogue to further contexualize conflict and action. From the discovery of Sir John Babington, Michaelhouse's well-liked Master, dead in a nun's habit and rumored a suicide, to Bartholomew's last fiery confrontation with his murderer, we are totally immersed in a medieval microcosm where tradition holds the upper hand and truth is difficult to separate from duplicity. When two of Michaelhouse's emeriti are found dead under grotesque circumstances, and others die mysteriously during the new master's installation feast, Doctor Bartholomew and Brother Michael are drawn into a complex intrigue involving Sir John's missing seal and a supposed plot to kill Cambridge masters as a means of insuring Oxford's survival. Fostered by a rogue administrator who owns many of the hostels and Sir Oswald Stanmore's jealous younger brother, its true object is to prevent the colleges from expanding. As Brother Michael explains at the novel's conclusion:

The colleges will be powerful forces in the University, Matt. There are five of them now, and there are plans to found another two next year. That will mean there will be seven institutions with Fellows and their own property. The Fellows will be more secure in their futures than the teachers in the hostels, and the longer they remain at the Colleges, the more power they will accrue. The hostels own no property, and are therefore inherently unstable, and, in time, the Colleges will take their power. (*Plague* 367)

When the Black Death arrives in November 1348, carried by a local man fleeing London, Cambridge physicians are at a loss to deal with it. Hypothesizing surgical intervention may help, Bartholomew lances the buboes as they ripen, giving sufferers a fighting chance. Septicemic plague is beyond him; by the time its spots manifest themselves, its victims are beyond help. When his colleagues die or opt out, he struggles on, battling fatigue, until he too contracts plague and Gray saves him by lancing his buboes. By novel's end, Bartholomew has validated his inclusion of clinical medicine, fingered the killers, and developed a growing trust in Brother Michael's friendship.

Gregory's second "chronicle," *An Unholy Alliance*, set in 1350, finds Cambridgeshire wrestling with the psychological fallout of the Black Death. Sure their reprieve is temporary, the survivors hedge their bets, some petitioning God, others Satan, some both, to save them. Prudent travellers walk wide of the hamlet of All Saints near the castle, where corpses rotted in their homes until Bartholomew burned them, and the church now stands open to the sky. Masterless dogs and cats haunt the streets seeking food, while thieves and women without mates ply their trades after curfew. When a whore is slaughtered near St. Botolph's, a supposed murderer disappears from sanctuary, and a strange Dominican turns up dead in a closed University chest, Bartholomew and Michael are handed a classic "locked room" mystery. Summoned to St. Mary the Great by Chancellor DeWetherset[12] to examine the corpse, they reveal the mechanism that killed him and discover the missing murderer nailed to the beams in the belfry. Witchcraft, fraud, and highway robbery abound in this adventure, which takes Bartholomew to the depths of graves to exhume corpses, to crypts to conduct postmortems, and to the creaking rafters of All Saints at midnight to view a cleverly staged but bogus black mass.

Gregory's third "chronicle," *A Bone of Contention*, set in 1352 with a flashback to 1327, examines the medieval preoccupation with relics Chaucer's Pardoner exploits so enthusiastically. When human bones are found in the King's Ditch near Valance Marie[13] during a long overdue cleaning, Chancellor DeWetherset calls upon Bartholomew to stipulate they are not the bones of Simon d'Ambrey, a local man reputedly martyred there in 1327.

Bartholomew [was] to use his medical expertise to crush, once and for all, the rumours that the bones of a local martyr had been discovered. He did not want the University to become a venue for relic-sellers and local gawpers, especially since term was about to start and the students were restless. . . . The Sheriff . . . was in complete agreement. . . . Both, however, suspected this might be easier said than done.

The Hall of Valance Marie had been founded five years earlier . . . and the Chancellor and the Sheriff were only too aware of the desire of its master to make the young Hall famous. The bones of a local martyr would be perfect for such a purpose: pilgrims would flock to the shrine [Robert] Thorpe[14] would build and would not only spread word of the miraculous find . . . but also shower the College with gifts. (*Bone* 12)

When these hoped-for relics turn out to be sheep bones, Thorpe and his minions persist, first dredging up the bones of a teen-ager too small to be the missing martyr, then manufacturing a giant skeletal hand to fill the bill. As Michael tells Bartholomew,

"There is money aplenty to be made from pilgrims these days. People are so afraid the Death will return and claim everyone who escaped the first time, that they cling to anything that offers hope of deliverance. The pardoners and relic-sellers' businesses are blossoming, and shrines and holy places all over Europe have never been so busy." (*Bone* 15)

Later, when a Scottish student is killed near the same ditch, Bartholomew learns Thorpe is just the first of many plotters in this complex tale of deception, revenge, riot, and greed.

Gregory's fourth and most recent "chronicle" in this series available in the United States,[15] *A Deadly Brew*, is easily the most complex of her four network novels. It begins with six deadly bottles of smuggled French wine stolen from a dank cellar and hawked by a sneak-thief to unwitting purchasers. The first to die is an apprentice, followed soon after by the new Master of Valance Marie, who expires at his installation banquet, casting suspicion on the unsuccessful candidate. When Michael and Bartholomew inquire too closely about the smuggled delicacies flooding Cambridge and the degree to which the whole town seems involved, they are suckered into the Fens, where an attack on their lives luckily goes awry. Taking shelter at Denny Abbey, ironically the smugglers' storehouse, they cheat death once again with the help of Michael's canny grandmother, Dame Pelagia. Bartholomew learns a humbling lesson about women and appearances from this feisty old nun and the Lady Matilde which may one day change his life as he battles with the master smuggler in a surprise-a-moment ending.

While it may shock readers unfamiliar with modern academic life, universities have changed very little since the fourteenth century. The high tables and academic regalia which set scholars apart from the common herd are still very much with us—at least on ceremonial occasions. Degree candidates must still prove their orthodoxy in structured "disputations" now called defenses. And, while murder has grown rarer and AIDS succeeded plague as the current scourge, institutional politics remain byzantine, casuistry flourishes, and town and gown still riot over slights real and imagined. Concerned that casuistry and cynicism never overwhelm ethics and reason, teachers like Bartholomew still value truth and compassion as ethical yardsticks for themselves, their colleagues, and their students as well as for the characters they encounter in fiction.

A master story-teller with an excellent understanding of the era and its history, Gregory educates her readers painlessly about her medieval milieu and its variables. She throws them no curves, grounds her narratives in verifiable reality, provides clues in a timely fashion, and eschews anachronisms and ideologies. In the process, we learn that scholars have always had the same frailties as the rest of humanity and that high offices and advanced degrees guarantee neither peace nor probity.

*Notes*

1. Personal correspondence, June 23, 1998.

2. Personal correspondence, June 23, 1998.

3. For an excellent overview of the area and its social and economic history, see "Medieval Cambridgeshire" in *The Victoria History of the County of Cambridge and the Isle of Ely*, L. F. Salzman, ed. (London: University of London Institute of Historical Research, 1967), 2: 58-72, called hereafter the *V.C.H. Cambridge*.

4. Near the end of *A Plague on Both Your Houses* Brother Michael counts five with two more soon to follow (367).

5. Michaelhouse and King's became part of a refounded Trinity College in 1546 after Henry VIII's dissolution of religious establishments. See Charles Crawley, *Trinity Hall: The History of a Cambridge College, 1350-1992* (Cambridge: Cambridge UP, 1992), 1-2.

6. Philip Ziegler, *The Black Death* (Phoenix Mill, Gloucestershire: Alan Sutton, 1991), 3-18. See also Colin Platt, *King Death: The Black Death and Its*

*Aftermath in Late-Medieval England* (London: University College London P, 1996), which has an excellent bibliography; Rosemary Horrox, ed., *The Black Death* (Manchester: Manchester UP, 1994), which presents contemporary documents; and J. M. W. Bean, "The Black Death: The Crisis and Its Social and Economic Consequences," in *The Black Death: The Impact of the Fourteenth-Century Plague,* Daniel Williman, ed. (Binghamton: Center for Medieval and Early Renaissance Studies, 1982), which has an excellent introduction by Nancy Siraisi.

7. Geoffrey Chaucer, "The General Prologue," *The Canterbury Tales,* ll. 413-46.

8. Robert S. Gottfried, "Traditional Physic," *Doctors and Medicine in Medieval England* (Princeton: Princeton UP, 1986), 168-69. For an excellent overview of medieval practice with a good bibliography, see David C. Linberg, ed., *Science in the Middle Ages* (Chicago: U of Chicago P, 1978), which includes articles on "Medicine" by Charles H. Talbot (391-428) and "The Institutional Setting" by Pearl Kibre and Nancy Siraisi (120-44).

9. See the description of St. Radegund's in *The V.C.H. Cambridge,* 3: 358-60.

10. See *A Deadly Brew* (345-46), where Brother Michael suggests this to Bartholomew.

11. Gregory's first novel was published in England but not in the United States, where her second, *An Unholy Alliance,* is called "The First Chronicle of Matthew Bartholomew."

12. As volume three of *The V.C.H. Cambridge* demonstrates, both the church and the chancellor are real. For St. Mary the Great, see 3: 129-31; for St. Michael's, Michaelhouse's college church, see 3: 131-32. DeWetherset appears as Chancellor 1349-51 and again, after the second plague, from 1360 through 1361 (3: 331-32).

13. See *The V.C.H. Cambridge,* 3: 346-55, for a full overview of Pembroke College, founded in 1347 by Marie de St. Pol, Countess of Pembroke, and called Valance Marie in this series.

14. Robert Thorpe is shown in *The V.C.H. Cambridge,* 3: 355, as the first Master of Pembroke College.

15. Since this chapter went to press Gregory has published two new chronicles not yet available in the United States. These are *A Wicked Deed* (1999), set in 1353 Suffolk, and *A Masterly Murder* (2000), which uncovers more dirty Michaelhouse secrets (London: Little, Brown). Three earlier works are newly out in Spanish: *Muerte en la Universidad* [*A Plague on Both Your Houses*], *La Sangre del Abad* [*An Unholy Alliance*], and *Matirio o Asesinato* [*A Bone of Contention*] (Barcelona: Plaza & Janes, 1999). Swiat Ksiazki (Warsaw) has brought out the same three in Polish: Robaczwe jabtko [*A Plague on Both Your Houses*], trans. Filip Kabulski (1998); Wspólnicy piekiet [*An Unholy Alliance*], trans. Wtadystaw Masiulanis (1998); and Ko ść niezgody [*A Bone of Contention*], trans. Jedrzej Polak (1999). Not to be outdone, Gregory's historian husband, Simon Beaufort [pseud.], has begun a strong new series starring Crusader Sir Geoffrey Mappestone: *Murder in the Holy City* (1998) and *A Head for Poisoning* (1999), both published by St. Martin's Press.

## Works Cited

Bean, J. M. W. "The Black Death: The Crisis and Its Social and Economic Conse-quences." *The Black Death: The Impact of the Fourteenth-Century Plague.* Ed. Daniel Williman. Binghamton: Center for Medieval and Early Renaissance Studies, 1982.

Chaucer, Geoffrey. "The General Prologue." *The Canterbury Tales.* 2nd ed. Ed. Helen Cooper. Oxford: Oxford UP, 1996.

Crawley, Charles. *Trinity Hall: The History of a Cambridge College*, 1350-1992. Cambridge: Cambridge UP, 1992.

Gregory, Susanna. *A Bone of Contention*, New York: St. Martin's P, 1997.

——. *A Deadly Brew*, London: Little Brown, 1998.

——. *A Plague on Both Your Houses*, London: Warner, 1996.

——. *An Unholy Alliance*, New York: St. Martin's P, 1996.

——. *A Wicked Deed.* London: Little, Brown, 1999.

Gottfried, Robert S. "Traditional Physic." *Doctors and Medicine in Medieval England.* Princeton: Princeton UP, 1986.

Horrox, Rosemary, ed. *The Black Death.* Manchester: Manchester UP, 1994.

Interview, Susanna Gregory, June 23, 1998

Linberg, David C., ed. *Science in the Middle Ages.* Chicago: U of Chicago P, 1978.

Platt, Colin. *King Death: The Black Death and Its Aftermath in Late-Medieval England.* London: U College London P, 1996.

Salzman, L. F., ed. *The Victoria History of the County of Cambridge and the Isle of Ely.* London: University of London Institute of Historical Research, 1967 [usually called the *V.C.H. Cambridge*].

Ziegler, Philip. *The Black Death.* Phoenix Mill, Gloucestershire: Alan Sutton, 1991.

# Umberto Eco:
## *The Name of the Rose*

### Judy Ann Ford

*The Name of the Rose* (1983) is a beautifully written and complex novel. Unlike many murder mysteries, it has already been subjected to considerable scholarly analysis. Interest in the book stems not only from its enormous popularity and engaging story but also from the reputation of its author, Umberto Eco, who was already a well-known scholar of semiotics when he wrote this, his first novel. In light of Eco's prominence in semiotics, a branch of communication theory, it is not surprising that most analyses of *The Name of the Rose* have been written from the perspective of literary and linguistic theory. These approaches have been and no doubt will continue to be fruitful, as there is much that can be said about this novel both in terms of traditional categories of literary criticism, such as plot and character, and in terms of theories of representation, such as semiotics. In this essay, I will be considering *The Name of the Rose* from a somewhat different perspective, namely, that of a medieval historian. This approach is amply justified not only because the novel is set in the Middle Ages, namely in a fourteenth-century Benedictine abbey, but also because its author began his academic career not as a semiotician but as a medievalist, writing a doctoral dissertation on medieval art and aesthetic theory.

From the perspective of a medieval historian, *The Name of the Rose* is compelling both because of the accuracy of its medieval setting and because of the disquieting commentary it offers on the profession of writing history. *The Name of the Rose* resonates with historical scholarship, especially in its brilliant use of non-fictional medieval characters and the glorious detail in which the intellectual world of fourteenth-century religion is constructed. Paradoxically, the novel presents the act of interpreting history, or at least, the act of committing such interpretation to writing, as presumptuous, arrogant and dangerous—not a very pleasant assessment for those of us who are professional historians.

Eco foregrounds the issue of historical scholarship at the very beginning of the novel. In the preface, a fictitious "author" tells the story of how he obtained a nineteenth-century book which "claimed to reproduce faithfully a fourteenth-century manuscript, that . . . had been found in the monastery of Melk" (xiii). The body of the novel consists of a new translation which the fictive author claims to have produced. On one level, the preface is simply employing a common strategy for creating verisimilitude. But this fictive author is not an unmarked individual who made a lucky find in his grandmother's attic; he is clearly a medieval historian. His concerns are quite specifically those of a historian: he tries to date the events in the manuscript by internal evidence, and he tries, though without success, to find archival documentation to validate its accuracy. Moreover, by claiming acquaintance with "illustrious medievalists such as the dear and unforgettable Étienne Gilson" the fictive author of the preface indicates that he too is a medievalist (xv). Eco could have chosen to begin the novel in the fourteenth-century setting in which all subsequent events take place, but did not. The inclusion of a preface in which a medieval historian presents the story as an historical text indicates that the profession of history is a central concern of the novel.

The remainder of the novel is narrated by Adso, an elderly Benedictine monk writing a chronicle about events that occurred when he was very young. His chronicle concerns the brief period in 1327 when he served as secretary to the Franciscan friar William of Baskerville. The story Adso tells is actually confined to seven days that he and William spent at a Benedictine abbey renowned for its famous library. William's mission at the abbey was to represent the interests of the Holy Roman Emperor at a meeting between representatives of the Franciscan Order and representatives of the pope. The purpose of this meeting was to establish the conditions for a future meeting between the head of the Franciscan Order and the pope at Avignon. Although William, Adso, and the abbey are fictional, the relations between the Franciscan Order and the papacy described in the novel accurately reflect the history of the period. As Adso relates, the two were in conflict at this time over scriptural interpretations of the poverty of Christ: the Franciscans insisted on Christ's absolute poverty, while the papal court argued against it. Although the matter may seem trivial to some twentieth-century observers, it became part of the greater contest between the emperor and the pope for supreme political authority in Europe. The Holy Roman Emperor, traditionally a friend to those who clashed with the pope, supported the Franciscans in this dispute in order to undermine the papacy.

Upon arriving at the abbey, William is asked by the abbot to look into the recent death of one of the monks whom the abbot suspects was murdered. As William investigates, a new dead body is discovered each day. Brother William pursues a number of possibilities to explain the murders: that they are the result of a love triangle among the monks who work in the library, that they are an attempt to conceal the heretical pasts of some of the monks, and that they involve efforts to locate a copy of Aristotle's yet unrecovered *On Comedy* in the abbey's library. On the last day he determines that the guilty party is an elderly blind monk named Jorge, who was indeed trying to hide a copy of Aristotle's *On Comedy*. Jorge did not, in fact, commit all the murders, but his designs were responsible for setting them in motion. When William confronts him, Jorge destroys the book and starts a fire that destroys the abbey. William and Adso survive the fire and soon after part, never to see one another again.

William of Baskerville is a character as much in the spirit of Sherlock Holmes as the word "Baskerville" suggests. Eco underlines the similarities between the two detectives in many ways, perhaps most obviously in the description that Adso provides in the first chapter:

Brother William's physical appearance was at that time such as to attract the attention of the most inattentive observer. His height surpassed that of a normal man and he was so thin that he seemed still taller. His eyes were sharp and penetrating; his thin and slightly beaky nose gave his countenance the expression of a man on the lookout. (8)

Adso even describes an addiction whose symptoms should be familiar to all Sherlock Holmes fans:

His energy seemed inexhaustible when a burst of activity overwhelmed him. But from time to time, as if his vital spirit had something of the crayfish, he moved backwards into moments of inertia, and I watched him lie for hours on my pallet in my cell, uttering barely a few monosyllables, without contracting a single muscle of his face. On these occasions a vacant, absent expression appeared in his eyes, and I would have suspected he was in the power of some vegetal substance capable of producing visions if the obvious temperance of his life had not led me to reject this thought. (9)[1]

From the opening chapter, the reader is encouraged to think of Brother William in the model of Sherlock Holmes, and William's subsequent behavior proves this first impression correct. He embodies the ideal of a rational, logical detective who makes a virtue of deductive reasoning.

Brother William, in being this sort of detective, is also like a modern historian in that he evaluates evidence and searches for causal connections between events in order to construct an accurate narrative of the past. In response to Adso's questions about his methods, William explains that he solves mysteries by thinking of a number of different hypotheses which could explain events, and then eliminating each hypothesis as he encounters a piece of evidence which makes it unworkable, eventually leaving only one which seems to fit all the known facts. The final hypothesis is probably closest to the truth. He tells the disappointed Adso that "for the events of the abbey I have many fine hypotheses, but there is no evident fact that allows me to say which is the best" (367). Adso is disturbed by William's method of reasoning, remarking that "it seemed to me quite alien to that of the philosopher, who reasons by first principles, so that his intellect almost assumes the ways of the divine intellect" (367). Adso's reply reflects a mode of thinking that one might expect from a member of the long-established and very tradition-bound Benedictine order. But what he encounters in William is not the mindset of a post-industrial thinker inappropriately dropped into the fourteenth century: Eco carefully communicates to the reader that William's approach to explaining causality is grounded in a branch of thought developed in the relatively new Franciscan Order.

In various conversations throughout the novel, William explains that he is a follower of William of Ockham and Roger Bacon, both famous English Franciscan philosophers (11, 59). Roger Bacon was an early proponent of the scientific method, which directly contradicted the type of natural philosophy familiar to Adso. Bacon wrote: "Experimental science controls the conclusions of all other sciences. It discloses truths which reasoning from general principals [the favored method of the Paris theologians] would never have discovered."[2] While Bacon is probably better known to the general reader, Ockham was even more influential in medieval philosophy as the founder of nominalism. The nominalists held that reality was founded in individual things, whereas mainstream medieval scholastic philosophy held that individual things were real because they participated in the reality of divine ideas. Ockham thus reasoned that one could not draw conclusions about divine truths from observing physical phenomena. In other words, he posited "a radical distinction between empirical facts and Christian doctrine . . . The existence of God had to be taken on faith. It could not be proven, and all efforts to create a rational theology were doomed. The scope of human reason was limited to the world of visible phenomena."[3] In light of these models, Brother William can be seen as equally an advocate of deductive reasoning and as a man of his times.

As one might expect from a follower of Ockham, William claims to distrust long chains of reasoning leading back to God. For example, when he first agrees to look into the murders for the abbot, William insists on considering the matter as a crime as opposed to an act inspired by the devil. He argues with the abbot:

Let us suppose a man has been killed by poisoning. This is a given fact. It is possible for me to imagine, in the face of certain undeniable signs, that the poisoner is a second man. On such simple chains of causes my mind can act with a certain confidence in its power. But how can I complicate the chain, imagining that, to cause the evil deed, there was yet another intervention, not human this time, but diabolical? I do not say it is impossible . . . But why must I hunt for these proofs? (27)

William thus confines himself to drawing conclusions about the human past; in other words, to the realm of history. Much later in the book he tells Adso: "at a time when as a philosopher I doubt the world has an order, I am consoled to discover, if not an order, at least a series of connections in small areas of the world's affairs" (476).

William approaches the murders like a modern historian, searching for small connections in order to construct a finite chain of causality, a story whose outlines he does not know until the end of the investigation. In the novel, this approach is contrasted to a number of other ways of knowing, but the most sustained contrast is between William's rationalism and what might best be called apocalyptic thinking.

Apocalyptic thinking may be described as an understanding of causality in which human, scriptural, and sacred history are combined and viewed from a teleological perspective, that is, in light of how they relate to the end of the world. In this mode of thinking, the outline of the historical narrative from the beginning to the end of time is believed to have been already revealed through prophesy. In trying to make sense of a series of events, a detective—or historian—like Brother William would speculate on a number of different causal relationships, search for as much evidence as possible, and then eliminate all the hypotheses that were contradicted by facts, leaving, ideally, the one hypothesis that must be true. In contrast, an apocalyptic thinker would believe that he already knew the correct hypothesis because all history had already been revealed through prophesy; he would merely have to figure out where these particular events fit into the story. In other words, the former method begins with events and builds to a narrative, the later begins with a narrative and sets events into it.

Apocalyptic thinking was a significant element in the dispute between the Franciscan Order and the pope which first brought William and Adso to the abbey. The dispute centered around the theory and practice of Franciscan poverty.[4] Francis of Assisi and his earliest followers had lived in utter poverty without possessions. But the Franciscan Order grew rapidly and soon the practices of the earliest Franciscans were seen as incompatible with the administration of a large international organization. Changes were made: the Order began to own property and individual houses were allowed to have a higher standard of living. Some friars were unable to accept the changes and the Franciscan Order began to fracture. By the late thirteenth century the friars who rejected the ownership of property had become a separate faction called the Franciscan Spirituals, who came to identify poverty as the essential and obligatory condition of all true Christians. Over time, more radical groups began to splinter off from the Spirituals. Such groups, collectively known as the *fraticelli,* sometimes expressed their love of poverty by destroying private property and murdering those who possessed it. The *fraticelli* were considered heretics. The poverty controversy in Franciscan history is a significant element in *The Name of the Rose.* One of the Spiritual's most important leaders, Ubertino de Casale, appears as a major character in the novel, while two fictional characters, Remigio and Salvatore, had belonged to the *fraticelli* and were condemned as heretics because of it.

The Franciscans frequently set their disputes about poverty within an apocalyptic framework. They drew upon the prevailing medieval traditions, especially from the apocalyptic expectations of Joachim of Fiore.[5] Allegories between history and scripture had long supplied material for predictions of the future; the Book of Revelation in particular had been combed for clues about the last days. Joachim combined a concept from the Book of Revelation, namely, the idea of a universal apocalypse signaling the end, with the millenarian concept of an age of peace and perfection occurring before the final destruction of the human race. The Joachimite tradition focused on speculation about the final sequence of events: the time and structure of the apocalypse and the nature of the final period of peace—the millennium—which was known in Joachimite terminology as the *status* of the Holy Spirit, or simply the third age. Joachim's theory included the idea of precursors: each age, period, and *status* was foretold by the appearance of certain persons or events. He predicted that among the precursors of the third age would be two orders of *viri spirituali*. The Franciscans identified these orders with the two great mendicant orders: themselves and the Dominicans.[6] Their appearance meant that the second age was giving way to the third age. In the Joachimite tradition and other branches of apocalyptic thought, the sequence of events leading to the third age was conceived as seven days, based on imagery from the Book of Revelation, although each "day" could last several years. Each day featured a tribulation, or persecution by the Antichrist. During the time in which the novel is set, most apocalyptic thinkers believed that they were living in the sixth day.

An expectation of the apocalypse permeates *The Name of the Rose*. The abbey's most prized possession, the library collection, contains an enormous number of works on the apocalypse (378). The great Spiritual leader, Ubertino de Casale, talks at length to William throughout the novel about his millenarian beliefs, such as the idea that they are living in the sixth day, and his expectations of the Antichrist and the angelic pope who was to come (66-67). The very structure of the novel mirrors the great apocalyptic texts of the Spirituals, such as the *Seven Tribulations* of Angelo of Clareno, in that it is divided into seven days instead of into chapters, and each day is marked by a tribulation in the form of a murder.

Apocalyptic thought is not confined to the Franciscans in the novel. One of its greatest proponents is Jorge, the monk responsible for the murders. Upon learning Adso's name, Jorge compliments him on it because one of the most important early works on the Antichrist was written by another Adso, Adso of Montier-en-Der (93). When Jorge berates the monks in the scriptorium for wasting their time with trivia, he employs the warning: "Do not squander the last seven days!" (93). Later, when given the opportunity to address the community, Jorge delivers an apocalyptic sermon that lasts nine pages (481-89). In it he describes what will happen on each of the seven days, concluding:

And on the seventh day Christ will arrive in the light of his Father. And there will be the judgment of the just and their ascent, in the eternal bliss of bodies and souls. But this is not the object of your meditation this evening, proud brothers! It is not sinners who will see the dawn of the eighth day, when . . . all the angels will advance together . . . seated on a chariot of clouds, filled with joy . . . to set free the blessed who have believed, and all together they will rejoice because the destruction of this world will have been consummated! (489-90)

Despite the presence in the novel of one of the greatest leaders of the Spirituals, it is Jorge, not Ubertino, whom the reader most completely identifies with apocalyptic thinking.

Brother William, not surprisingly, rejects apocalyptic thinking. His attitude is not obvious to Adso during William's conversations with Ubertino because William admires and sympathizes with Ubertino; after all, even though they follow very different schools of thought, they are both Franciscans. When Adso comes to realizes that William does not share the millenarian expectations of the other Franciscans, he is perplexed: " 'But the third age, the Angelic Pope, the chapter of Perugia.' I said, bewildered. [William replies] 'Nostalgia. The great age of penitence is over' " (134).

Despite Brother William's rejection of it, apocalyptic thought nonetheless intrudes into his investigation as a clue to solving the murders. Alinardo, a elderly monk and contemporary of Jorge, offers a theory in which he interprets the murders as part of an apocalyptic prediction. William and Adso question him after the first two murders, in which the first body was found at the bottom of a cliff and the second in a vat of pig's blood. Alinardo explains:

Did you not hear how the other boy died, the illuminator? The first angel sounded the first trumpet, and hail and fire fell mingled with blood. And the second angel sounded the second trumpet, and the third part of the sea became blood . . . Did the second boy not die in the sea of blood? Watch out for the third trumpet! (182-83)

After the third and fourth murders also seem to conform to apocalyptic imagery, even Brother William begins to accept the hypothesis, although, in his version, the murderer is choosing to follow an apocalyptic pattern (439). Even then, William follows his own methods by keeping other explanatory hypotheses in mind. He wonders, in regard to the murderer: "But if he were pursuing another design? And if, especially, there were not *a* murderer?" (506). But it is the connection to apocalyptic thinking that leads him to suspect Jorge. With Jorge and William, the reader seems to be presented with a clear contrast: a murderer who follows apocalyptic thought and a detective who prefers deductive reasoning.

The antithetical approaches adopted by William and Jorge to determine the meaning of events are mirrored in their respective attitudes towards knowledge. Human knowledge, for William, can and should be extended. He believes that it is the sacred duty of learned men both to increase the sum of information and understanding about the natural world and to actively use their knowledge to improve the quality of life. He espouses the opinion, held by Roger Bacon, that one should "study the secrets of nature, use knowledge to better the human race" (68). While discussing his eyeglasses with Nicholas, the master glassier, William praises the imaginative transformation of nature, saying: "there is a magic that is divine, where God's knowledge is made manifest through the knowledge of man, and it serves to transform nature" (97-98). Jorge, in contrast, believes that knowledge is static and that the duty of learned men is to preserve it without alteration. He asserts that knowledge "is a divine thing . . . complete and . . . defined since the beginning, in the perfection of the Word which expresses itself to itself" (482). He condemns those who "seek anxiously to discover new codicils to the words of the truth, distorting the meaning of that truth already rich in all the scholia, and requiring only fearless defense and not foolish increment" (484).

Jorge's conception of knowledge as a fixed entity had determined the policies of the library and scriptorium. As William says to Jorge:

> When you realized you were going blind . . . you acted shrewdly. You had a man you could trust elected abbot; and as librarian you first had him name Robert of Bobbio, whom you could direct as you liked, and then Malachi, who needed your help and never took a step without consulting you. For forty years you have been master of this abbey. (565)

Both the abbot and the chief librarian had been chosen by Jorge long before the events of the novel to ensure that the library was not used to attempt to increase human knowledge. In fact, Malachi may have been selected to be the librarian precisely because he was good at copying scripts without understanding their meaning (509). The abbot demonstrated his allegiance to Jorge's ideology when he explained the purpose of the library to William by saying: "until the triumph, however brief, of the foul beast that is the Antichrist, it is up to us to defend the treasure of the Christian world, and the very word of God, as he dictated it to the prophets and to the apostles, as the fathers repeated it without changing a syllable" (35). The monks who use the library are not allowed to do pure research, or in the words of the abbot, they are "not to pursue every foolish curiosity . . . whether through weakness of intellect or through pride or through diabolical prompting" (36). Jorge, who repeatedly asserts that it is the purpose of the monks in the scriptorium to copy texts without alteration, even disapproves of those who paint creative illustrations in the margins (85). The marginalia constitute the only imaginative transformation of knowledge taking place in the library, so not surprisingly, while Jorge deplores them, William praises them, saying that "Marginal images often provoke smiles, but to edifying ends" (88). William greatly dislikes the repressive policies of the abbey's library, which he claims is "an instrument not for distributing the truth but for delaying its appearance" (343).

The principles that William and Jorge adopt in regard both to knowledge in the abstract and to understanding a specific chain of past events are each internally consistent. William accepts the growth of knowledge and encourages its imaginative use. Thus he is willing to imagine more than one hypothesis, or reconstruction of events, when trying to create a true and meaningful narrative about the past. For Jorge, who believes that knowledge is static, immutable and wholly revealed by God, there can be only one explanatory narrative. And that narrative was not created by human detectives or historians; it was revealed by God through the prophets: it is the historical narrative of the apocalypse.

The opposition between the conceptual frameworks of Jorge and William is carried through their concepts of the proper organization of political authority. This is not surprising, for one's understanding of the operation of history often determines one's orientation towards politics—which is why, even in our own time, national histories can be so politically controversial. For Jorge, there can be only one acceptable political organization, which was ordained by God and is, like knowledge, immutable. Not surprisingly, in Jorge's conception of the divinely established order the Church, and in particular the Benedictine Order, holds supreme authority. During the fourteenth century, medieval society was undergoing substantial changes that were reducing the power of the Benedictine Order. Traditional monasticism had emphasized cloistered communal living and the virtues of humility and obedience, qualities highly valued by early-medieval culture in which power derived, not from wealth, but from noble blood and military prowess. Early medieval culture valued gold chalices and jeweled Bibles as laudable signs of veneration for God. Consequently, traditional monastic orders, such as the Benedictines, habitually employed a remarkable luxury as part of their worship. During the high Middle Ages, this notion of religious virtue was challenged because the rise of towns and development of proto-capitalism made money a significant source of power. Greed for money began to be seen as a more dangerous vice than lust for power, especially by townspeople most effected by the commercial revolution.[7] Townspeople frequently transferred their allegiance away from traditional monasticism in favor of the newer religious orders which embraced poverty, such as the Franciscans, and preferred secular learning to monastic education. Thus the principal enemies of Jorge's conception of the divinely ordained order are the towns. The abbot explains this view to William:

The [Benedictine] order is still powerful, but the stink of the cities is encroaching upon our holy places, the people of God are now inclined to commerce and wars of faction; down below in the great settlements, where the spirit of sanctity can find no lodging, not only do they speak (of laymen, nothing else could be expected) in the vulgar tongue, but they are already writing in it, though none of these volumes will ever come within our walls—fomenter of heresies as those volumes inevitably become! Because of mankind's sins the world is teetering on the brink of the abyss. (34)

Writing learned works in Italian had certainly begun: Dante was alive and writing Italian during the time of the novel's setting. In the judgment of Jorge and the abbot, the political order, being divine, is elevated to the status of revelation, and "heretics are those who endanger the order" (176).

William, not surprisingly, supports a political order in which supreme authority is held by a secular politicians and the church has no political power (423-29). He advocates rule by an emperor with "an elective general assembly . . . empowered to interpret, change, or suspend the law" (424). William, after all, is at the abbey to represent the Holy Roman Emperor. While his opinions may appear modern, they are an accurate reflection of the medieval political theorist Marsilius of Padua, who William claims as a colleague in the imperial court (416-17). It is in this context that William places the pope's opposition to, and the Emperor's support of, the Franciscan Order's declarations regarding the poverty of Christ. He explains to Adso: "But the question is not whether Christ was poor: it is whether the church must be poor. And 'poor' does not so much mean owning a palace or not; it means, rather, keeping or renouncing the right to legislate on earthly matters" (416). The respective political ideals of William and Jorge are thus opposite in both their composition and their justification. The former advocates an authority which comes from the people, albeit with a more restrictive definition of that term than one might see in the late twentieth century, while the latter sees authority as something imposed upon the people. And as in the case of knowledge and historical explanation, Jorge will entertain only one conception of political authority while William considered many and chose the one which seemed to him to be the best.

Most of the Benedictine characters in the novel place a very high value on submission to authority, a quality that William believes to be destructive of natural perception. A conversation between the abbot and Adso, both Benedictines, near the end of the novel, makes clear the connection between obedience to authority and the acceptance of the idea that there is only one licit interpretation—of politics, knowledge, history, or anything else of importance. The abbot, talking of the symbolic significance of gems, tells Adso:

The language of gems is multiform; each expresses several truths . . . according to the context in which they appear. And who decides what is the level of interpretation and what is the proper context? You know, my boy, for they have taught you: it is authority, the most reliable commentator of all and the most invested with prestige, and therefore with sanctity. Otherwise how to interpret the multiple signs that the world sets before our sinner's eyes, how to avoid the misunderstandings into which the Devil lures us? (549)

William's critique of the Benedictine acceptance of authority is expressed near the beginning of the novel and is phrased in a more circuitous manner. Upon reaching the abbey, William impresses several Benedictine monks by deducing the location, size, speed, color, appearance and name of the abbot's missing horse. He explains to Adso, in a most Sherlockian fashion, how he interpreted the hoofprints and other clues. When Adso realizes that these clues could not have revealed the detailed description William provided, he asks: "but what about the small head, the sharp ears, the big eyes . . . ?" (19). William replies:

"I am not sure he has those features, but no doubt the monks firmly believe he does. As Isidore of Seville said, the beauty of a horse requires 'that the head be small, *siccum prope pelle ossibus adhaerente*, short and pointed ears, big eyes, flaring nostrils, erect neck, thick mane and tail, round and solid hoofs.' If the horse whose passing I inferred had not really been the finest of the stables, stableboys would have been out chasing him, but instead, the cellarer in person had undertaken the search. And a monk who considers a horse excellent, whatever his natural forms, can only see him as the auctoritates have described him, especially if"—and here he smiled slyly in my direction—"the describer is a learned Benedictine." (19)

William is telling Adso that a Benedictine will see things not as they are, but as authority tells him they should be. William, as a detective, a nominalist, and a follower of Roger Bacon, values the ability to observe things as they are; he believes that this ability is the necessary first step toward truth. Jorge, like the abbot, praises the ability to bend one's perceptions to the interpretation of authority, because natural senses can be deceived by the devil and the divinely ordained authority already knows all the truth there is to know.

The conflict between these two worldviews is illustrated most clearly in the scene in which William, the detective, reveals to Jorge his knowledge of Jorge's guilt, and Jorge, the murderer, reveals to William his reasons for the crimes. Jorge acted in order to keep secret the only extant copy of a book by Aristotle, *On Comedy*, which was hidden in the library. His reason for concealing the book is that "Aristotle sees the tendency to laughter as a force for good, which can also have an instructive value" (574). Jorge and William disagree about the value of laughter a number of times in the course of the novel. Jorge hates laughter because "Laughter foments doubt" (151). When William tells him, "But sometimes it is right to doubt . . ." Jorge replies, "I cannot see any reason" (151). William not only defends the medicinal value of laughter, he also claims that the ability to laugh is a sign of rationality (149). Jorge believes that laughter is base, a weapon of the poor and uneducated and thus inappropriate to the learned elites. He is sure that if the learned begin to laugh—and doubt—that the divine order will be lost forever (579). He tells William:

But on the day when the Philosopher's word would justify the marginal jests of the debauched imagination, or when what has been marginal would leap to the center, every trace of the center would be lost . . . if one day somebody, brandishing the words of the Philosopher . . . were to raise the weapon of laughter to the condition of subtle weapon . . . oh, that day even you, William, and all your knowledge, would be swept away! (578-79)

Jorge is referring to both the artistic marginalia created in the scriptorium and to the poor, who are socially and politically marginal. Earlier in the novel, William not only praises the marginalia of the scriptorium, but he also advocates the reabsorption of the socially marginal into the body of the church. He tells Adso that Francis of Assisi's "first decision was to go and live among the lepers. The people of God cannot be changed until the outcasts are restored to its body" (237). In climactic confrontation with William, Jorge asserts that the opposite had happened to Francis's order: instead of bringing the poor into the center, they joined forces with the learned. "They have rejoined our ranks, they no longer speak like the simple" (582). In the end, William and Jorge each find their devil in the other:

"You are the Devil," William said then . . . "Yes . . . The Devil is not the Prince of Matter; the Devil is the arrogance of the spirit, faith without smile, truth that is never seized by doubt. The Devil is grim because he knows where he is going, and, in moving, he always returns whence he came. You are the Devil, and like the Devil you live in darkness."

Jorge replies: "You are worse than the Devil . . . You are a clown, like the saint who gave birth to you all." (581)

This confrontation between the detective and the murderer, containing the murderer's confession and followed by his death, would signal the end in most detective novels. The reader would probably suppose that he or she was to conclude that William's philosophy was right because he was the "good guy" who solved the case and that Jorge's philosophy was wrong because he was the "bad guy" who murdered and got caught. But in *The Name of the Rose*, things are not so simple.

Almost immediately after Jorge confesses to William, the abbey is destroyed in a manner which seems to confirm the truth of Jorge's predictions. Jorge knocks over a lamp, setting the library on fire. Adso tries to organize the monks into a fire brigade, but they are slow to comprehend that there is something wrong in the library: "they could not understand that it was threatened by the sort of banal accident that might have befallen a peasant hut" (591). The rescue attempt fails because there is no single authority directing it: "If a man invested with authority had given these orders, he would have been obeyed at once" (592). Instead, "this horde of villeins and of devout, wise, but unskilled men, with no one in command, was blocking even what aid might still have arrived" (595). Combined with an earlier observation by William that the abbey is a microcosm of the world, Jorge's prediction is complete (230). A weapon associated with peasants attacks the confines of the learned, and because of a lack of obedience to authority, the world is destroyed.

Can the reader then confidently conclude that Jorge's philosophy was more accurate than William's? No, because both their ideologies are problemitized by Adso's commentary on them. In the middle of the confrontation between the detective and the murderer, Adso intrudes on the dialogue with the sudden realization that the two men are both alike and intrinsically connected to each other. He writes:

I realized, with a shudder, that at this moment these two men, arrayed in a mortal conflict, were admiring each other, as if each had acted only to win the other's applause . . . each of the two interlocutors making, as it were, mysterious appointments with the other, each secretly aspiring to the other's approbation, each fearing and hating the other. (575)

Of course, Adso is unarguably correct in regard to roles played by William and Jorge within the genre of murder mysteries: the detective cannot exist without the murderer. In a sense, the hunter and the hunted define each other. There are a number of such matched and mutually defining opposites recognized as such by characters in the course of the novel, including heretics and inquisitors, saints and sinners, heaven and hell, the seraphim and Lucifer, and, during the confrontation scene, Jorge even asserts that "the Prince of Darkness was necessary . . . to make the glory of God shine more radiantly" (52, 134, 71, 61, 580). But Adso's realization is not limited to a recognition of the mutual dependence of detective and murderer, he also recognizes an underlying similarity which unites them.

Adso reveals this similarity by contrasting William's "secret" relationship with Jorge to a brief sexual encounter Adso had with a village girl earlier in the novel.

The thought crossed my mind that . . . the simple and natural acts with which the girl had aroused my passion and my desire, were nothing compared with the cleverness and mad skill each [William and Jorge] used to conquer the other, nothing compared with the act of seduction going on before my eyes at the moment, which had unfolded over seven days. (575)

The girl is the only unnamed character in the novel, a fact that figures prominently in many interpretations of the book. Adso explicitly states that he never learned her name: "This was the only earthly love of my life, and I could not, then or ever after, call that love by name" (493). The girl represents, among other things, unnamed experience.

Within the context of the novel, naming is presented as the assertion of a type of dominion or control over the object named: one of the arguments presented by William in defense of secular government is based on God's having given Adam dominion over the earth, signified by his having commanded Adam to give a name to every animal and thing (425). Moreover, this Adamic naming was not arbitrary, it constituted an interpretation of the named object. William explains: "And though surely the first man had been clever enough to call, in his Adamic language, every thing and animal according to its nature, nevertheless he was exercising a kind of sovereign right in imagining the name that in his opinion best corresponded to that nature" (425). In light of Adso's contrast between, on the one hand, his relationship with unnamed experience, and on the other, the relationship between William and Jorge, it would seem that, to Adso, the detective and murderer share the identical presumption that they can accurately "name things according to their nature," that is, construct an accurate interpretation of events. This similarity transcends the differences in their methods of interpretation to make William and Jorge two sides of the same coin.

The similarity between William and Jorge is underlined by the unusual and ironic nature of William's solution to the mystery. After the first four murders, he came to suspect that the murderer was killing people in ways deliberately chosen to correspond with apocalyptic symbolism. He was wrong; Jorge was doing nothing of the kind. But when Jorge found out about William's hypothesis, he adopted that method and made it true.

William, upon realizing his mistake, tells Jorge: "I conceived a false pattern to interpret the moves of the guilty man, and the guilty man fell in with it. And it was the same false pattern that put me on your trail" (572). Jorge persists in acting out the apocalyptic pattern even in the method of his own death. He swallows the pages of Aristotle's book, on which he had spread poison, saying to William and Adso:

> You were awaiting the sound of the seventh trumpet, were you not? Now listen to what the voice says: Seal what the seven thunders have said and do not write it, take and devour it, it will make bitter your belly but to your lips it will be sweet as honey. You see? Now I seal that which was not to be said, in the grave I become. (585)

What emerges from the recognition of the similarity between William and Jorge is neither a triumph for the interpretation of events through rational observation and logical deduction nor a justification of apocalyptic thought, but the suggestion that the construction of any interpretation of events is dangerous. The danger lies partly in being in error, but more in running the risk of establishing a pattern that may alter the course of future events, that is, an interpretation that will exert dominance over experience. The novel suggests that patterns of this sort had, in fact, been created and endlessly repeated. For example, Adso comes upon description of love-sickness in a medical text in the library and for long afterward feels and acts as though he has the symptoms described in the book; the elder Adso writing about the experience comments that most people react to medical texts by experiencing the symptoms they read about (388-92). Even the library catalogue seems to represent such a pattern. Years after the abbey burns, but long before he chronicles his experiences, Adso revisits the site and gathers together as many scraps of burnt but legible parchment as he can. He then spends years trying to acquire all the books whose fragments he saved in order to reconstruct the abbey's collection (608-09). The most destructive example of a pattern determining experience is the one guiding the course of inquisitions in which both the inquisitors and accused heretics respond to each other in ritual patterns which may have nothing to do with the particulars of the case being tried, but which lead to tortures and fiery executions (63, 448). The elder Adso who writes about his experiences was well aware of the danger of establishing an interpretation which could overshadow events and come to substitute for reality. This awareness was manifest in Adso's melancholy complaint which closes the novel: "stat rosa pristina nomine, nomina nuda tenemus," that is, "set a name on the pristine rose, we hold name alone" (611).[8]

Yet this older and apparently wiser Adso, who eagerly looks forward to losing himself in divine silence, cannot himself keep silent. He chooses to write about the events he experienced in his youth. From the very beginning of his manuscript Adso denies that his chronicle will contain any historical interpretation:

Having reached the end of my poor sinner's life . . . I prepare to leave on this parchment my testimony as to the wondrous and terrible events that I happened to observe in my youth, now repeating verbatim all I saw and heard, without venturing to seek a design, as if to leave to those who will come after me (if the Antichrist has not come first) signs of signs, so that the prayer of deciphering may be exercised on them. May the Lord grant me the grace to be the transparent witness. (3-4)

But Adso cannot present a narrative of past events without interpreting them. No historian can, because the mere process of selecting events to relate constitutes an interpretation. Adso's text, far from refraining from interpretation, employs the methodologies of both William and Jorge. Adso frequently interrupts the narration of the incidents he experienced to explain at length historical events which he had not witnessed; he does so in order to provide his reader with a context for constructing causal relationships among events in the manner of Brother William. His intentions are clear in such phrases as: "Perhaps, to make more comprehensible the events . . . I should recall" (4). The formal organization of his material—in seven days, each containing a "tribulation" in the form of a murder—replicates the apocalyptic ordering of events which characterized Jorge's method of historical interpretation. Far from being a "transparent witness," Adso models the very behavior he believes he is trying to avoid. Adso, as chronicler/historian of his own youth, presents the reader with an interpreted, mediated view of events—thus risking the establishment of a false or pernicious pattern in the mind of the reader.

Eco could have chosen to write the novel from the point of view of the young Adso, relating the events as he experienced them, without the narrative frame of the elderly Adso as chronicler or the secondary narrative frame of the historian of the preface. The inclusion of these frames serves to raise questions about writing history. On first glance, the historicity of *The Name of the Rose* would seem to suggest a sympathetic bias towards historical scholarship. Unlike some historical crime fiction in which the setting seems almost incidental, this novel contains such abundant detail about the fourteenth century and presents the religious sensibilities of that era so well that it has been used in college history courses as a teaching tool. Paradoxically, upon closer reading the novel seems to denounce historical scholarship, characterizing the attempt to determine an accurate interpretation of past events as not only fraught with the likelihood of error but also as arrogant and dangerous. The fictional historian of the preface explains that he is presenting this particular manuscript as "an act of love" (xviii). The rest of the novel suggests that this motive may not, in fact, provide adequate justification for committing an act of written history.

Despite, or perhaps because of such thought-provoking paradoxes, *The Name of the Rose* will no doubt continue to be read, studied and enjoyed for many years to come. It constitutes a major contribution to the genre of historical crime fiction.

## Notes

1. Compare these to Watson's descriptions of Holmes: Sir Arthur Conan Doyle, *The Complete Sherlock Holmes* (Garden City, NY: Doubleday, 1969), 20.

2. Roger Bacon, as quoted in C. Warren Hollister, *The Making of England: 55 B.C. to 1399*, 4th ed. (Lexington, MA and Toronto: D.C. Heath, 1977), 201.

3. Hollister, 244.

4. Two of the best general accounts of early Franciscan history may be found in John R. H. Moorman, *The History of the Franciscan Order from Its Origins to the Year 1517* (Oxford: Clarendon P, 1968); and Vida D. Scudder, *The Franciscan Adventure: A Study in the First Hundred Years of the Order of Saint Francis* (London, Toronto, New York: Dent; Dutton, 1931).

5. The most complete work on the impact of Joachim of Fiore is Marjorie Reeves, *The Influence of Prophesy in the Later Middle Ages: A Study in Joachimism* (Oxford: Clarendon P, 1969). Joachim does not appear as a character in the novel, but he is mentioned: Eco, 51.

6. See Edward Peters, "The Spiritual Franciscans and Voluntary Poverty," *Heresy and Authority in Medieval Europe* (Philadelphia: U of Pennsylvania P, 1980), 238; and David Burr, *The Persecution of Peter Olivi*, Transactions of the American Philosophical Society, ns. 66, part 5 (Philadelphia: American Philosophical Society, 1976), 10.

7. L. K. Little, "Pride Goes Before Avarice," *American Historical Review* 76 (1971): 16-49.

8 This line is from a twelfth-century poem by Bernardi Morlanensis, also known as Bernard of Cluny or Bernard of Morlay: Bernard Morlanensis, *De Contemptu Mundi*, in *Mediaeval Latin*, edited by Karl Pomeroy Harrington, Allyn and Bacon's College Latin Series (Boston, New York, Chicago, Atlanta and San Francisco: Allyn and Bacon, 1925), 320.

# Elizabeth Eyre:
# Detection in the Italian Renaissance

## Jeffrey A. Rydberg-Cox

Elizabeth Eyre is the author of six Italian Renaissance Whodunnits that follow the escapades of the adventurer Sigismondo and his servant Benno as they investigate murder and conspiracy in the Renaissance courts of both fictional and real Italian cities.[1] These novels contain a fast paced succession of seemingly unrelated murders and other crimes that pose a direct threat to the society in which they take place. By the end of each novel, Sigismondo traces these seemingly unrelated crimes to a single perpetrator who, in each case, meets an appropriate end, thereby allowing social order to be restored. In each novel, Sigismondo adopts a wide variety of roles and crosses the accepted social boundaries of his society. Benno plays the role of the idiot with undying devotion both to Sigismondo and to his dog Biondello. With this configuration of the plot and the main characters, Eyre's novels follow the pattern of much modern detective fiction. These novels are not historical fiction in the sense that they portray their characters playing roles in well-known historical events or interacting with historical figures. Rather, these novels represent historical fiction because their settings are inspired by Renaissance history and supported by the addition of historical details. In the few cases where Eyre bases her characters on well-known historical figures or events, the relationship is quite loose; she transforms them freely to suit the purposes of her novels. In this paper, I will first explore the ways that Eyre draws upon the conventions of the modern detective novel. Second, I will examine the ways that she uses Renaissance humanism and approaches to war to support the settings of her novels and, in a few cases, adapts historical events to suit the needs of her mysteries.

Although Eyre's novels are set in Italy during the Renaissance, they lie firmly within the tradition of the modern mystery story. The genre of the mystery story is dominated by conventional formulae that originated with Edgar Allan Poe. As Dorothy L. Sayers pointed out in her introduction to *The Omnibus of Crime*, "It is doubtful whether there are more than half a dozen deceptions in the mystery monger's bag of tricks, and we shall find that Poe has got most of them" (60).[2] Sayers points to plot devices in Poe's works such as the mystery of the apparently locked room, the ruse of the most obvious place, and the solution by means of the most unlikely person. Eyre uses all of these devices in her novels. For example, in the *Murders in the Rue Morgue*, Dupin attempts to solve a murder that took place in the locked room. Investigating the possible ways that the murderer could have entered this room provides the stage for a virtuoso display of his detective abilities. A locked room plays a similar role in *Dirge for a Doge* (1996), when Niccolo Ermolin is stabbed in the study that he always kept locked. The various means of entry into this apparently locked room provide a venue for Sigismondo's display of his own investigative abilities. Eyre also uses the idea of the locked room in a slightly different manner in the *Death of the Duchess* (1991). In this case, Sigismondo must penetrate the apparently locked palace dungeons to free the unjustly condemned Leandro Bandini before his execution.[3] The challenge of gaining entry for himself, rather than determining how a murderer gained access provides the stage for Sigismondo's display of his abilities.

The ruse of the most obvious place first appears in Poe's *Purloined Letter*, which tells the story of a government minister who had stolen a sensitive letter. He hid the letter from the extensive police searches by simply leaving it on his mantle as if it were an ordinary letter. The key to this ruse, as Dupin points out, is that the police are so certain that they are looking for a hidden letter, that they fail to even consider those letters that are in plain sight. This ruse makes several appearances in Eyre's novels. For example, in *Axe for the Abbot* (1995), Sigismondo is drawn into a family feud about a jewel called La Feconda, thought to have magical powers to bring sons and riches to its owner. In this novel, two different branches of the Pantera family have engaged in a series of reciprocal murders while trying to gain possession of the jewel. As the novel opens, Olivero and Ferondo Pantera trick Sigismondo so that he fights and eventually kills their cousin, who is trying to steal the jewel. After a long series of events, the entire matter is referred to the Pope for adjudication. The Pope orders Sigismondo to deliver the jewel as an offering to a shrine of Mary in order to end the feud and to atone for his unwitting complicity in it. On the evening prior to the dedication of the jewel, the Pantera brothers arrange for Sigismondo and Benno to be drugged and searched so that they can steal the jewel. Sigismondo foils this plot by placing the jewel on another smaller statue of Mary as if it were an offering. Eyre describes Benno's reaction when Sigismondo recovers the jewel, "Benno was speechless. Sigismondo had often said, if you want to hide something, put it in the open" (319). Eyre also uses a version of this device in *Poison for the Prince* (1993). In this novel, Sigismondo asks Angelo—a fortune teller, performer, and mercenary who occasionally offers his skills to Sigismondo—to help him hide Lord Mirandola from Duke Grifone. Angelo accomplishes this by using Mirandola as an assistant for his fortune-telling act in the main square of the town. When Benno sees Mirandola in the main square, Sigismondo explains, "Angelo's doing what I asked. When you want to hide something, put it out in the open, where no one expects to see it" (199). This plan, however, backfires when Angelo's act attracts the attention of Lord Aster—Duke Grifone's son—and he decides to present the two men to his father for his entertainment (279-80).

The solution by means of the most unlikely person is also an important element in the modern detective novel and Eyre's books are no exception. The series of crimes in each novel are frequently committed by one of the closest advisors to an important person. For example, in *Death of the Duchess*, all of the crimes are committed or planned by Lord Paolo, Duke Ludovico's brother and chief advisor, as part of his attempt to take the throne from his brother. Likewise, in *Poison for the Prince*, the murders are traced to Michelotto, the chief lieutenant of the mercenary Gatta, who was motivated by the desire to see him gain power. In fact, Eyre follows a similar pattern in all six of her novels; unlikely criminals emerge as the perpetrators of every crime.

Eyre's novels fit the pattern of modern detective novels not only in their use of these plot devices, but also in the construction of their main characters. As Sayers points out, mystery stories are dominated by an "eccentric and brilliant private detective whose doings are chronicled by an admiring and thick-headed friend" (57). Sayers further points out that this eccentricity is frequently manifested in some nervous habit and distinctive physical characteristic like Holmes' fiddle playing and hawk-like features. Sigismondo's investigative skills are certainly complemented by both of these features. He is tall and broad shouldered with a shaved head while he has habit of humming to himself when he is investigating a crime. Similarly, although Benno is not the chronicler of Sigismondo's activities, he is certainly both admiring and thick headed. Benno also plays another important role traditionally allotted to the dim-witted sidekick in the detective novel; he or she allows the author to reveal clues and their interpretations without revealing their entire significance. Eyre frequently uses this convention to reveal clues to her readers. From the outset of their relationship, Sigismondo tells Benno that he should not ask any questions. However, at key points in every story, Sigismondo answers many of Benno's questions before cutting him off.

Finally, modern detective novels frequently follow conventional patterns that are larger than the individual devices employed for committing and solving crimes. W. H. Auden, in his essay "The Guilty Vicarage," argues that the detective novel, like the Greek tragedy, tells the story of a closed society disturbed by some crime that must be solved before that society can return to its normal state (16). While the crime remains unsolved, the fabric of the society is in danger. The detective, in the act of solving the crime, preserves and reconstitutes social order. Thus, the task of solving this crime bestows upon the detective the role of defender of social order while its attendant requirement for the detective to associate with the possible criminals bestows upon him or her a liminal quality that allows the detective to transcend the social boundaries and roles that constrain the other characters in the novel. Glenn Most argues that the detective is,

in every regard a marginal figure: his profession is not to have a profession but to investigate those who do; he derives his income not from a steady and productive job but, case by case, from those who have such jobs but require his services; he alone can move . . . through every stratum of society, from the mansions from which the poor are excluded to the slums that the wealthy abhor; he is almost always single or divorced; . . . his parents are almost never mentioned, and he is invariably child-less. It is his freedom from all such categories that permits him so clearly to see through their workings in all the other characters (343)

This sort of plot structure appears in each of Eyre's novels, all of which describe a closed society that is somehow threatened by a crime. Sigis-mondo is called upon to solve this crime and, thereby, to preserve the soci-ety. In his investigations, Sigismondo is compelled to adopt a wide variety of roles and to function effectively in many parts of society. A detailed examination of Eyre's first novel, *Death of a Duchess*, reveals and exempli-fies both themes. The novel opens in a society that is threatened by a feud between two noble families, the di Torres and the Bandinis. The most recent manifestation of this feud is the alleged abduction of Jacopo di Torre's daughter by the Bandini family. Ludovico, the Duke of Rocca, commissions Sigismondo to look into the abduction because this feud is disturbing the peace within his kingdom. While Sigismondo is investigating this crime, the Duchess is murdered at a wedding banquet for one of her courtiers. As the threat to the kingdom of Rocca thus escalates, Sigismondo is again commis-sioned to find the culprit. With such high stakes having been established, Sigismondo adopts his full role as the defender of society.

While carrying out these duties, Sigismondo also exhibits the liminal characteristics of his position. Throughout the novel, characters express both doubt and curiosity about Sigismondo's identity and social status. When set-ting the scene for the wedding banquet, Eyre writes,

Heads turned also to stare at the Duke's agent [Sigismondo], the man from nowhere, so hard to place socially that it had taken a directive from the Duke himself for his steward to find him room at one of the long side tables. Courtiers nearby eyed him as if an executioner sat at meat beside them, though he wore good velvet and linen and bore himself in modest quiet. . . . Someone had heard he was a soldier who had saved the Duke's life a good few years ago, before he inherited his present rank. Ladies pointed out, in support of this tale, the breadth of this man's shoulders. He was clearly a man of the sword. Others objected. His shaven head made him resem-ble a man of the cloth. One lady was visited by the conviction that he was a templar, and this gained credence: there was very little, after all that could not be believed of the templars. (34-35)

Sigismondo's ambiguous social position at the Duke's dinner foreshadows the wide variety of roles that he adopts throughout *Death of a Duchess*. As noted above, Sigismondo's distinguishing physical characteristic is his shaven head. Because of this, characters frequently think that Sigismondo is a priest. For example, when he comes to question the prime suspect, Lean-dro Bandini, about the Duchess' death in prison, Leandro is convinced that he is a priest come to hear his last confession (61).[4] Sigismondo is equally able to appear as an accomplished fighter. For example, when he stops at the house of the Widow Costa, he is received by the widow as an old battle comrade of her husband (113). Likewise, when he returns to the widow's house and is attacked by an assassin, Sigismondo displays his own martial skill. The fight ends when Sigismondo realizes that he has also fought alongside the man who has been hired to kill him (153). Aside from revealing Sigismondo's identity as a fighter, these events reveal that Sigismondo is known by a wide variety of names; the widow calls him Hubert (113) while Barley, the would-be assassin, calls him Martin (149). Sigismondo extends the position of a mercenary soldier so that he can adopt the role of headsman in a public execution (208-09) and even to be perceived as death himself when he arrives at Poggio's village (78). Sigismondo acts as an agent of death during Leandro's escape when he, having been admitted because the guard thinks that he is a priest, becomes an assassin who strangles one of the palace guards. Finally, in order to rescue Cosima di Torre from her captors in a convent, Sigismondo must dress as a woman and convince the women who offer him medical care in the convent of his gender. Eyre describes Benno's perception of this transformation,

As time went by, the person beside him seemed to become more and more feminine in bearing and behaviour. The voice modulated to a deep contralto, and, gradually, Benno began to see just such a woman as he had often met: big, somewhat masculine, but with a score of differences that Benno could not place but which made him all but lose sight of his master, and made him able to accept the transformation. (116-17)

As the above account of the Duke's dinner suggests, Sigismondo also adopts a variety of roles within the royal courts. At times, he is the consummate courtier giving deference and respect to the Duke. For example, when meeting the Duke to explain the results of his investigation into the abduction of Cosima di Torre, Sigismondo bows respectfully and kisses the Duke's ring (9-10). However, Sigismondo is able to breach the social hierarchy within the palace as well. This can be seen in the other courtiers' perceptions of Sigismondo when he is walking alongside Lady Violante and questioning her about the murders. Eyre describes how the chatter stops and how, "Corvine glances examined the man who surely ought to be following the lady, not pacing at her side" (99). Finally, Sigismondo presents himself as an equal to the Duke himself in the dénouement of the novel; when he is presenting witnesses to the Duke to prove who was responsible for the murders, he is able to bargain with the duke about the punishments and rewards that should be given to the different witnesses (222-23).

However, after the murders have been solved, Sigismondo must return to his proper social position as an obedient servant of the Duke. If he does not, Sigismondo becomes a figure like Will Kane in *High Noon*, a threat to the very society that he had saved. Eyre portrays this return to normalcy during another feast in the duke's palace. Eyre describes Sigismondo in a seat of honor wearing a valuable jewel that firmly establishes his social position, while also revealing his debt to the Duke. Sigismondo describes his new, more limited social role in an exchange with Benno. Benno asks, "You can do what you like, now the Duke is so grateful to you, can't you?" Sigismondo responds, "No. The gratitude of princes is limiting. You must be there to display it. Princes need it to be seen that deeds done for their advantage are rewarded" (241). Thus, offered a high but restricted social position in the court of Rocca, Sigismondo, following the pattern of other modern detectives, chooses to depart and seek adventure, on his own terms, elsewhere.

Just as Eyre both draws upon the conventions of the detective novel, so also does she consult elements of Renaissance history to suit the purposes of her novels. Eyre does not, however, describe her characters in known historical settings or interacting with known historical figures. Instead, she draws upon broad themes of Renaissance history to establish the settings for her novels and to convey the idea, rather than the substance, of the Renaissance. In English scholarship, the idea of the Renaissance is almost completely synonymous with humanism, the arts, and the social milieu of Florence. Elements of this idea of the Renaissance appear throughout Eyre's novels. For example, in *Death of the Duchess*, *Curtains for the Cardinal*, and *Bravo for the Bride*, Eyre describes central events that take place at royal wedding celebrations. In each case, the person who organizes the festival is a Florentine working either for the city's ruler or for one of the city's guilds anxious to impress the ruler. For example, in *Curtains for the Cardinal*, Eyre describes some difficulties that arose during the preparations for the arrival of Grifone, the Duke of Nemora, when a cast member did not want to wear the wig that was part of her costume. Eyre writes,

That her behaviour demonstrated her aptness for the role of fickle Fortune did not appease the director of the pageantry—who was, in fact, a Florentine and very expensive. The Merchants' Guild intended to impress the Duke with their loyalty . . . and were paying for him. (206-07)

This passage exemplifies Eyre's use of Renaissance history. The preparations for Grifone's arrival are a comic digression within the essential action of the story while the sketch of the Florentine and the reasons for his employment appear as an aside even within this digression. However, it draws on two aspects of Renaissance history to convey the idea of the period: Florence as an artistic center and the competition among different guilds as manifested in festivals and the arts. This placement of historical detail in a digression from the main plot allows Eyre to convey the idea of the Renaissance as the setting for her works.

This approach can also be seen in Eyre's presentation of the subject matter of Renaissance art. A major component of Renaissance historiography was a new interest in the ideals of the Roman empire. Humanists in Florence, Milan, and Venice all were anxious to connect their cities to the past glory of the Roman Empire (Chambers 12-13). This idealization of antiquity is reflected in the use of classical myths as the subject matter for works of art. Eyre draws upon this aspect of Renaissance society in many of her novels. For example, in *Axe for an Abbot*, the tapestries in Cardinal Tartaruga's banquet hall depict Heracles cleaning the Augean stables (244). Likewise, in *Curtains for the Cardinal*, Eyre describes a statue in the room of Father Torquato—nephew to the recently immolated Cardinal Petrucci as follows.

Extending behind the bed, a tapestry darkened the room with its dingy greens and browns. The subject, classical still but with sickening aptness, showed Heracles writhing in the fiery shirt of Nessus. Torquato stood beneath this without apparent consciousness of any allusion; it was probably some time since he had noticed the thing. (139)

With this final sentence, Eyre also accurately reflects the relative social value placed upon these sorts of objects. Evelyn Welch has demonstrated that the most valued objects in Renaissance Italy were rare natural objects such as coral, precious metals, and carved stones. Thus, Niccolo Ermolin's locked room in *Dirge for a Doge*, where he kept his most valuable possessions, is described as containing "account books, cloth-swathed dishes, cups and flagons of gold and silver, chests of rich clothes, coffers of coin and jewels hidden from sight" (324). This attitude is also reflected in the above passage from *Axe for an Abbot*; Eyre claims that the Cardinal's guests were surprised that he had not replaced the tapestries with more impressive decorations for such an important banquet.

Classical subjects, however, never replaced religious figures as a subject for art. In fact, much of the art in Renaissance Italy would have been commissioned for, and observed in, religious settings. These works of art thus would have also had a religious significance. As Welch points out, "Fourteenth- and fifteenth-century work of religious art were usually created for precise places, events, and audiences and many of the most important works of art spent much of their time in storage" (167). Certain images would have been displayed only on holy days or festivals and they would be thought to have particular powers. This is reflected in *Curtains for the Cardinal* when Benno is accused of a theft by a group of pilgrims and Sigismondo contrives to have him brought before a picture of St. Bernardina that was on display as a special event for a religious celebration to obtain forgiveness. When one of the pilgrims saw the picture of the saint move, it was understood as a miraculous sign of forgiveness and Benno was allowed to go free (90-91).

In addition to establishing the setting for her novels, Eyre also uses historical information as a key element in the development of her mysteries. This can also be seen in the way that Eyre treats humanistic material. For example, in *Bravo for the Bride*, an abbot friend of Sigismondo reports that he had recently seen a complete manuscript of Quintilian's *Institutio Oratoria.*[5] Quintilian's work was widely known in antiquity but there was no known complete copy of the work in the Middle Ages. However, Renaissance rulers were quite interested in the collection of manuscripts and employed humanists to search for copies of texts. In 1416, a complete manuscript of Quintilian's work was discovered and it had a wide-ranging influence on scholarship in the Renaissance and beyond (Kennedy 139-41). Eyre uses the discovery of this manuscript and its acknowledged importance as the key to unraveling the mystery in *Bravo for the Bride*. However, she uses only the idea of the Quintilian manuscript in her novel; she replaces the actual circumstances and people involved in the discovery of the manuscript with her fictional characters. In this novel, Lord Tebaldo, the young cousin of Duke Ippolyto of Altamura, focuses his energies on building the Duke's library of manuscripts. Tebaldo has freedom to acquire the works that he thinks are worthwhile, but he must ask the Duke for permission to purchase particularly expensive manuscripts. When an assassin tries to use the Quintilian manuscript to lure the Duke to his death in the library, Sigismondo's knowledge of the manuscript and the person who, in this fictional world, had purchased it allows him to foil this scheme (273-74).

Eyre's approach to the art of war in the Italian Renaissance echoes her approach to humanistic topics; she uses scattered facts to establish the setting and provide a general sense of the Renaissance while also adopting and transforming particular events to suit the needs of her novels. In Italy during the Renaissance, war increasingly became the activity of professionals, conducted by mercenary armies lead by *condottiere* (Taylor 1-28), a fact reflected in Eyre's novels. For example, in the *Death of the Duchess*, the key to Lord Paolo's plot against the Duke is the arrival of his mercenary army while he is denouncing his brother as the murderer (224-30). Similarly, in *Curtains for the Cardinal*, after Prince Livio's plan to assassinate Duke Grifone fails, Lord Astorre must ride out to announce Livio's death and offer to pay the army himself so that they will not plunder Colleverde (238-40). Finally, in *Bravo for the Bride*, when Altamura is faced with an attack by their rival Venosta, Duke Ippolyto is vulnerable because he has not retained a *condottiere* and there are not any in the region who are available for hire.

The conduct of war as a business enterprise by mercenary armies had several implications during the Renaissance. First, *condottiere* were not inclined to risk their armies in direct combat, favoring instead extensive maneuvers and posturing. Second, they would not fight during the winter because of the added discomfort and risk. These problems were described by Machiavelli in the *Prince*, who writes,

They use every means to spare themselves and their soldiers hardship and fear, not killing each other in their battles . . . ; they will not attack cities at night; and those in the cities will not attack the tents of the besiegers; they do not build stockades or trenches around their camps; and they will not campaign in winter. (XII)

Eyre portrays this sort of problem with mercenary armies in the dealings of Duke Guido of Montano with the *condottiere* Il Lupo in *Dirge for a Doge*. In this novel, Montano is under attack by a Venetian mercenary army that is trying to secure a mainland trade route for Venice. As this series of events opens, the city of Piombo is under siege and Guido rides out to oversee its defense. He arrives expecting to urge his troops into battle, but he must quickly come to terms with a new set of circumstances. Eyre explains the situation as follows.

> Battle, unless the outcome was a pushover, was altogether too dangerous an activity for a condottiere. They might, from time to time, be forced into it if taken by surprise of browbeaten by tyrannical employers, but not one would voluntarily take the chance of depleting his precious stock of men, his bargaining power. . . . The Duke's captains expected to effect a bargain with the enemy at some point and, when he arrived in their midst, they could be forgiven for supposing he had come to initiate such bargaining. (139)

Il Lupo eventually convinces Guido that the best course of action is not to engage in battle, but to sacrifice Piombo and bribe the Venetian army so that it would withdraw.

The events in *Dirge for a Doge* reveal a third repercussion of the reliance on mercenary armies for war; these armies often posed a threat to the ruler who hired them. As Machiavelli points out, "In peace, you are plundered by them [*condottiere*], in war, by your enemies" (XII). In *Poison for the Prince*, Eyre considers the implications of this sort of uneasy relationship between *condottiere* and those who hire them. In this case, she also transforms known historical events to suit the needs of her mystery stories. *Poison for the Prince* tells the story of Prince Scipione of Viverra who has hired the mercenary Gatta to subdue an upstart vassal. Scipione, however, must constantly concern himself with Gatta's loyalty. In fact, Scipione initially hires Sigismondo to spy on Gatta and test his loyalty. In the midst of this tension, Scipione's son, Prince Francesco, renounces his claim to the throne and leaves the city in a fit of religious zeal. In the convoluted series of events that surround his return to the city, Francesco meets Gatta's daughter, they fall in love, and Francesco declares his intention to marry her (273-74). At first, the prince's family expresses their shock and displeasure and offends Gatta. An attack by Gatta's army seems inevitable. However, amends are quickly made and preparations begin for Gatta's family to join the ruling family of Viverra. This story, in its broadest outlines, reflects the rise of the Sforza as the Dukes of Milan. In 1447, when Duke Filippo Maria Visconti died without a male heir, a group of noble families formed the oligarchic Ambrosian Republic. The nobles hired Francesco Sforza, a *condottiere* and husband to an illegitimate daughter of the last Visconti Duke, to protect the republic. Francesco, however, staged a coup and made himself Duke of Milan in 1450. The similarities between the history of the Sforza in Milan and Eyre's story are clear. Both Prince Scipione and the Visconti

Dukes were dependent on *condottiere* for their power. While Scipione did have a legitimate heir, Eyre replicates the situation in Milan by making the young prince leave the city in a fit of religious zeal. It is this transformation of the history of Milan that allows Eyre to restore order to the world of her novel without requiring Scipione's downfall.

Elizabeth Eyre uses historical material in two ways throughout her novels. She either uses historical details to support the settings for her novels or she freely transforms known historical events to suit the purposes of her mysteries. She does not adopt the approach of other historical detective novelists and portray her characters playing roles in well-known historical events or interacting with historical personalities. Eyre's approach is not confined to the areas discussed in this essay, but it also appears in her treatment of other topics, such as the papacy and other church officials, the historical identities of Rome and Venice, science and magic, and many others. The overriding structure of her novels, however, is that of the modern detective novel. The genre of the detective story is highly formulaic and Eyre follows and transforms these formulae in her individual plot devices, the configuration of her characters, and the structure of her novels. In fact, the study of Eyre's use of devices from the genre of the mystery could also be expanded to include an examination of other topics such as stolen letters, and the role of Benno in solving these mysteries. In this combination of elements of Renaissance history and the modern detective novel, the needs of the mystery story govern the selection and transformation of the historical information. This means that Eyre's novels are not effective windows into the history of the Italian Renaissance, but they are entertaining exercises in historical imagination.

*Notes*

1. Elizabeth Eyre is a pseudonym for the writing team of Jill Staines and Margaret Storey. For the sake of convenience, I will refer to them throughout this essay as Elizabeth Eyre. Eyre's novels were first published in Great Britain by Headline Press and subsequently in the United States by St. Martin's Press. They are *Death of a Duchess* (1991), *Curtains for the Cardinal* (1992), *Poison for the Prince* (1993), *Bravo for the Bride* (1994), *Axe for an Abbot* (1995), and *Dirge for a Doge* (1996).

2. The Poe stories discussed by Sayers are "The Murders in the Rue Morgue," "The Purloined Letter," "The Mystery of Marie Rogêt," "Thou Art the Man," and "Gold Bug."

3. In the *Death of the Duchess*, it might be said that Eyre follows the pattern of Dupin and turns the question of the means of egress into a question of the means of ingress.

4. In *Death of a Duchess*, Sigismondo is also taken for a priest when he and Benno discover the body of one of Cosima di Torre's servants (61), when he first meets Poggio's mother (81), and when he comes to break Leandro out of prison (184).

5. Quintilian was a noted teacher of rhetoric in the Roman Empire. The *Instituto Oratoria* describes the training of an orator beginning with childhood and ending with a successful career as a public speaker.

## Works Cited

Ady, C. A. *A History of Milan Under the Sforza.* London: Methuen, 1907.

Auden, W. H. "The Guilty Vicarage." *Detective Fiction: A Collection of Critical Essays.* Ed. R. W. Winks. Englewood Cliffs, NJ: Prentice-Hall, 1980. 15-24.

Chambers, D. S. *The Imperial Age of Venice: 1380-1580.* London: Harcourt Brace Jovanovich, 1970.

Duffy, E. *Saints and Sinners: A History of the Popes.* New Haven: Yale UP, 1997.

Eyre, E. *Axe for An Abbot.* London: Headline, 1995.

———. *Bravo for the Bride.* New York: St. Martin's P, 1994.

———. *Curtains for the Cardinal.* London: Headline, 1992.

———. *Death of the Duchess.* New York: Harcourt Brace Jovanovich, 1992.

———. *Dirge for a Doge.* London: Headline, 1996.

———. *Poison for the Prince.* London: Headline, 1993.

Hay, D., and J. Law. *Italy in the Age of the Renaissance: 1380-1530.* London: Longman, 1989.

Haycraft, H., ed. *The Art of the Mystery Story: A Collection of Critical Essays.* New York: Simon and Schuster, 1946.

Kennedy, G. *Quintilian.* New York: Twayne, 1969.

Most, G. W. "The Hippocratic Smile: John le Carré and the Tradition of the Detective Novel." *The Poetics of Murder: Detective Fiction and Literary Theory.* Eds. G. W. Most and W. W. Stowe. San Diego: Harcourt Brace, 1983.

Poe, E. A. *The Complete Works of Edgar Allan Poe.* New York: AMS P, 1979.

Sayers, D. L. "Introduction to the Omnibus of Crime." *Detective Fiction: A Collection of Critical Essays.* Ed. R. W. Winks. Englewood Cliffs, NJ: Prentice-Hall, 1980. 53-83.

Taylor, F. L. *The Art of War in Italy: 1494-1529.* Westport: Greenwood P, 1973.

Thomson, J. A. *Popes and Princes: 1417-117.* London: Allen and Unwin, 1980.

Welch, E. *Art and Society in Italy: 1350-1500.* Oxford: Oxford UP, 1997.

Winks, R. W. "Introduction." *Detective Fiction: A Collection of Critical Essays.* Ed. R. W. Winks. Englewood Cliffs, NJ: Prentice-Hall, 1980. 1-14.

# Margaret Frazer:
## Sister Frevisse and Medieval Mysteries

### Patricia W. Julius

Once upon a time, writers—particularly satirists or social critics—set their plots in imaginary places presented as unexplored lands, the better to make their point about the society in which they lived. Thomas More, following Plato's lead, created *Utopia* or "no place." Jonathan Swift placed Lemuel Gulliver, his literal but dense reporter, in the lands of Lilliputians and Brobinagians and Yahoos to make his comments about his own world. But soon the globe was explored and mapped. There were no more floating islands, no more mysterious lands. So writers found a new arena—the world of the future or of other universes. Some of the most perceptive of the social commentators found a home in science fiction—Isaac Asimov, Frank Herbert, and Alexei Panshin among others.

Recently, mystery writers have sought an environment through which to make their own statements about the events and attitudes of their time. Like Asimov and Herbert and Panshin and the others, they cloak their commentary in another time. However, these writers have chosen to place their action in the historical past. Since 1992 and the introduction of her nun-cum-detective Dame Frevisse, Margaret Frazer[1] has taken her place among the company whose social commentary is played out upon the stage of the Middle Ages.

One of the clichés of literary scholarship is that neither writer nor critic can leave his or her own time; that they cannot shake off the realities of the twentieth century; and if they could, they should not. Their audiences, after all, are firmly grounded in the present, and one of the requirements of historical fiction, whatever its genre, is to establish a link, no matter how tenuous, between that time and our own. Margaret Frazer in her seven medieval crime novels establishes that link through her mastery of the cultural minutiae as well as the larger history of the fifteenth century.

The dual issues of class and choice operate in all the books of this series. Early in *The Novice's Tale* (1992) Frazer makes her attitude toward class clear in the words of Thomas Chaucer, son of the poet and Frevisse's uncle: he says, "my place in the world would hardly change by my gaining a title. I'd simply add more duties to my life and my taxes would go up and that's an idiot's price for fancying my name" (9). Shortly after, the actions and words of Lady Ermentrude remove any doubt that nobility, in the hands of Margaret Frazer, is generally far less than noble. Ermentrude's values become apparent when she says of her son, Walter, "Lord Fenner is dying now, it seems, and since the title comes by right of blood to Sir Walter, he's there to make sure not too much is lost when Lord Fenner makes his will" (25). Nobility, as both Geoffrey and Thomas Chaucer knew, has to do with the heart and the mind and the character of a person, not with the robes and honors—or lack of them—that mark the public self. However, many of us, then as now, would eagerly pay the "idiot's price." In fact, untrammeled hunger for visible rank provides the foundation for the crime in *The Novice's Tale,* the 1992 opener of the series. None of the parties are innocent—not the victim, arrogant proud Lady Ermentrude, not the murderer, and not the bystander who made no move to stay the killer.

Such misplaced faith in the superiority of class is not the sole province of the laity, however. *The Novice's Tale* also introduces Dame Alys, the cellarer, whose pride in and allegiance to family far overshadow her commitment to God. Lady Ermentrude is a Fenner and Dame Alys a Godfrey. Ironically, both families are very minor aristocracy whose pretensions to grandeur have found a decades-long battleground in the issue of land. Dame Alys' character and priorities are clear from her first words, "Would it were in my power to serve her [Lady Ermentrude] as she deserves. Spoiled fish and rotten apples, with ditch water for a drink, that's what she'd have." When a lay servant comments, "That would be enough to start a real feud between the Godfreys and Fenners," Dame Alys responds, "There's been no bloodshed yet, but there's a feud all right. And the blood will come soon, too, if they don't stop pushing to take our property away from us" (49). The "us" here is her family. No vows, no years in the convent, have weakened Alys' first loyalty to things that are Caesar's. And the consequences of that misplaced obsession with class and family come home to roost in the seventh tale of the series, *The Prioress' Tale* (1997.) But that is later.

Frazer's second theme—that of choice—is as clearly laid out. *The Outlaw's Tale* (1994), the last tale set before Thomas Chaucer's death, is at heart about choices, their consequences, and the futility of trying to escape those consequences. Frazer allows no excuse for Nicholas, kinsman to Thomas Chaucer and Frevisse. Born to privilege if not peerage, Nicholas chose the path that led to his being named "outlaw" and turned out. For two decades, he lived as a highwayman, leader of his band of thieves and conjurers, until at age forty, the hardships weigh heavily and he seeks a royal pardon. But he still relies upon the tools of his trade, as it were: he kidnaps Dame Frevisse, with Sister Emma and Roger Naylor, their protector, to persuade her to beg Thomas Chaucer to speak for him at court. Even here, with pardon dependent upon proof of reformation, he continues in his old habits. When the victim of Nicholas' thievery beats the woman who trusts him, Nicholas is only angry because she, near dead, reveals his name. And this occurs after Frevisse has agreed to speak for him to Thomas Chaucer. Faced with his misdeeds, Nicholas never accepts responsibility. But Frazer does not allow the excuse that such behavior is a matter of habit. Evan, Nicholas's lieutenant, also eager to be pardoned, acts consistently and honestly. Redemption, then, is possible but difficult, and Nicholas has chosen the easy way. Neither kinship nor affection can shield him from the consequences of his choice.

This tale raises another troubling issue. Frazer implies that one's nature can be modified but not reversed, no matter how positive the nurturing. This, of course, is an issue with particular relevance to our own society. And in *The Outlaw's Tale*, Frazer argues that we cannot escape the truth of this moral, no matter how uncomfortable we find it.

However, in our interest in the issues that resonate in our own society, we must not ignore the artistry and skill with which Frazer sets those issues in the fifteenth century. *The Novice's Tale* exemplifies this particularly careful balancing act and the kind of risk that attends Frazer's use of the medieval setting: if it succeeds, it succeeds well; but if it fails, it fails resoundingly. There is little "in between" to such a decision. The choice of an abbey—in Frazer's tales, a cloistered convent—as setting allows a greater freedom than is available in other sub-genres but it also places greater limitations on the writer. Most obviously, using an abbey as setting means that the world—and most of the sources of the mystery—has to come there. Further, the mystery is of necessity domestic. And there is always the danger of redundancy, a danger Frazer circumvents in part by moving three of the tales—*The Outlaw's Tale*, *The Bishop's Tale* (1994), and *The Murderer's Tale* (1996)—outside of St. Frideswide, and in part by being a rollicking good storyteller.

There are advantages to her choice of setting. This circumscribed environment provides the luxury of developing sustaining characters that link each tale to the others of the series. Unlike standalone novels, the setting does not have to be reinvented or built from scratch with each new tale. The different strengths and personalities of the fellowship of nuns add richness and reality to the tales and contribute to the complexity of their plots. The developing characters of the individual members of the Priory provide continuity, and a sense of a real world, without the need for lengthy explanation or introduction. The most obvious and perhaps the richest use of these attendant nuns to move the plot occurs in *The Outlaw's Tale*, the third novel of this series. Dithery, self-absorbed, and silly, Sister Emma provides the force that sends the two kidnapped nuns into the manor of Master Oliver Payne, a wealthy merchant and reluctant partner of Nicholas, the outlaw of the title. This turn of events serves several purposes. First, Emma's illness forces Nicholas to move Emma and Frevisse indoors away from the forest fastness that would be safer but provide no means to further the plot. Second, Frevisse needs the help of the women of the manor to care for Emma. This of course allows her to learn of the workings not only of the women but of Master Payne as well. The doings of the village itself also become grist for Frevisse's investigation. The Franklin who is attacked and later murdered, the woman beaten, and the presence of Nicholas in the middle of all this piques Frevisse's interest. Trapped in the manor by Emma's illness, Frevisse's forced inactivity gives way to curiosity and curiosity leads to questions. The stage, then, is set for Frevisse's skill as a detective. And Emma has been the inadvertent catalyst for the action of the tale.

A second purpose is simply to provide a reminder that nuns were people before they took their vows and the personality they brought into the priory stays with them. The interrelationships within the priory, the tensions and alliances, force us to surrender the common stereotypical assumption that "all nuns look alike." Sister Emma is just one example of this fact. In *The Bishop's Tale*, the second of the series to take place outside of St. Frideswide, Dame Perpetua is spotlighted. Quiet and self-effacing within the priory, here she becomes a developed and commanding character. She has been chosen to accompany Frevisse to Thomas Chaucer's lavish manor because "she had been brought up in a home much like this, had learned to be both gentle and detailed in her manners" (28). Like Frevisse, she is literate and at home in the great library that was Chaucer's pride.

Dame Perpetua reminds us of another assumption that Frazer shatters in these tales and not, presumably, by accident. One of the things we "know" about this period is that the literacy rate was very low, limited mostly to the Church, which was the keeper of the books. There is some truth to this, of course. Until the printing press was invented, ownership of books was effectively limited to the Church and the very rich—the aristocracy as well as the rising merchant class. But literacy was more widespread than most of us believe today. In *The Outlaw's Tale*, Master Payne did ask if Dame Frevisse could read and write as a practical matter. But he evinced no great shock to learn that she could. His youngest son and daughter were being taught to read Latin and his eldest, Edward, was an Oxford scholar. As Thomas Chaucer's nephew, Nicholas was literate, of course, but so was Evan, his lieutenant in the outlaw band. Moreover, the nuns of St. Frideswide were also literate, coming as they did from families of substance. In fact, no one of the community was excused from reading aloud during the supper hour because she lacked the skill. However, that Thomas Chaucer's cook was literate was unusual (145). In fact, the rarity of this reminds us of the great gap between the estates and the peasants whose position was light-years below any consideration.

*The Servant's Tale* (1993) presents a closer look at the lives of those peasants in the person of Meg and her fellows. Here, Frazer turns to an examination of the consequences of a society based on class. In the fifteenth century, peasants had no redress but that found in religion, and what they knew of that depended on the wisdom and compassion of the priest who purveyed it. With no other source of comfort nor knowledge, it was easy to become obsessed with following an often erroneous and always limited interpretation of God's will. Meg survived hunger, disappointment, and beating and loss because she was stubborn and because she had faith in her soul's salvation. Any peasant, but particularly a woman, had no choice, no hope of change. For her, to endure was her only triumph. In *The Novice's Tale*, Domina Edith said, "Ignorance breeds fear" (38). And Frevisse recognized that "It was Meg's ignorance, not stupidity, that made her so easily frightened" (*Servant's* 58). Comfort or reassurance had no reality to her— she had no words that would admit the existence of compromise. Because she was doomed to ignorance by class and gender, she could not change the things she "knew." For Meg, to die unconfessed meant damnation, Heaven was the only escape. So, stubborn, obsessed with the souls of her husband and sons, she acted to ensure their salvation in the only way she could. Meg was as much a victim of the society that shaped her as were the objects of her ignorance and obsession. The real tragedy in this tale was that no one, not the nuns for whom she worked nor the priest whose words she believed so literally, ever understood or really even saw her.

Clearly *The Servant's Tale* demonstrates that Frazer's knowledge and understanding of the Middle Ages is deep as well as wide. Throughout this series, her use of the small details of ordinary life sets her apart from many authors of historical fiction. Moreover, these details are so casually and unobtrusively placed that readers hardly realize the erudition and research they represent. This attention to detail is most obvious in her delineation of the workings of a convent. For example, "St. Frideswide had never grown much beyond its small founding by a pious, wealthy widow in the last century, but without greatly prospering, neither had it dwindled. Within its outer wall were the ample barns, sheds, workshops, and storehouses given over to the priory's worldly necessities" (*Boys'* 24). Suddenly, we understand how much of what the priory uses comes from the efforts of its people, the laity as well as the religious. St. Frideswide is a self-contained entity. No supermarkets or convenience stores or even wealthy patrons exist to ease the way. When Frazer writes, "The hour between Vespers and . . . Compline was for recreation, when ordinary, even idle, talk was allowed," we recognize the luxury of the ordinary, as do the nuns whose "anticipated ease was already in their movements" (28). With such simple phrases, Frazer invokes a world which once was alien and makes us part of it.

She accomplishes the same kind of magic with her characters. When Frevisse is wakened by her sense of duty, "clinging to her bed's warmth a few minutes more, Frevisse thought regretfully of how very rarely a sense of responsibility was convenient" (*Novice's* 87). No reader could fail to recognize and share that regret. Moreover, it paints a picture of a very human woman—no romanticized picture of a martyred and selfless servant of God. The lesson here and elsewhere is that to serve God, one need not give up one's humanity nor one's individuality. But the novice Thomasine has still to learn this lesson. Apologizing for weeping for her aunt, Thomasine said, "I'm only supposed to pray for them, not cry," to which Frevisse answered correctly, "You cried because you were hurting for other people's hurt, and that's probably worth more than a hundred careful prayers with no feeling at all behind them" (154). That this lesson is as true in our time as in the fifteenth century adds to our sense of commonalty with Frevisse's world.

To draw us more easily into that world, Frazer adopts a technique used successfully by many historical novelists: that is, she superimposes historical figures into her fiction. Thomas Chaucer, of course, is the central such figure. The son of Geoffrey, and an astute diplomat, Thomas Chaucer was born in 1367 and died in 1434 at the advanced age of 67. Although, as

Frazer points out, he had refused knighthood, he died the richest commoner in England, wealthier than most knights. In 1395, he married heiress Maud Burghersh. She is known as "Matilda" in *The Bishop's Tale.* They had one daughter, Alice, whose third marriage was to William de la Pole, Earl of Suffolk and, "for a time, the most powerful man in England." Cardinal Bishop Henry Beaufort, the title character in *The Bishop's Tale* (1994), was Thomas Chaucer's cousin, the son of John of Gaunt, the preeminent peer in England and father of Henry Bolingbroke (Henry IV). He was certainly as influential as Frazer's portrait indicates (Pearsall 276, 284). Frazer's use of these figures, especially Thomas, provides added verisimilitude to the Tales as well as elevates Frevisse's importance. We realize that she is called Dame "in deference to her stature both within the cloister and without" (Swanson and Dean 110). Certainly her relation to the powerful Thomas Chaucer protects her from Lady Ermentrude's virulent tongue.

In addition to her use of historical characters, Frazer sets her scenes through the words of our best-known medieval figure, Geoffrey Chaucer himself. The passages from *The Canterbury Tales* that preface the matter of Frazer's novels are usually apt, though, like Chaucer's own poetry, their meaning is often two-layered. So, their aptness is often unexpected and ironic. For example, the couplet "Help us, Seinte Frideswyde! A man woot lytel what him shal bityde" that introduces *The Novice's Tale* and the series itself sets the tone. Saint Frideswide is the name and patron saint of the priory. And certainly, man knows little of what shall befall him, especially in a mystery novel. Moreover, Frazer warns us early in the book that the usual stereotypes do not apply. She says of the nuns, "despite being blended all together in a sea of black gowns and veils, their faces framed in white wimples, they were still individual. Especially Dame Frevisse" (3-4). Our recognition of this individuality is particularly important, considering the limitations Frazer's choice of place and time and character have placed upon her. Four of the seven Tales take place within the priory and its grounds. The ten nuns who are the sustaining actors in this series and whose characters are often central to the action are clearly distinctive.

That the Benedictine nuns of St. Frideswide follow the "rule" of the medieval *Ancrene Wisse* (*Rule for Nuns*) reflects the careful research which marks Frazer's work. Throughout, Frazer provides passing references and small tidbits of information to set the period as well as provide explanation to her readers. For example, Dame Frevisse turns the Latin of Vespers "to English in her mind, partly from the little Latin that she knew but mostly from her much treasured Bible, an object forbidden because it was a Wycliffe English translation" (*Novice's* 64). This brief, apparently casual passage is heavy with implication that may pass unnoticed by most modern readers. First, it emphasizes that Dame Frevisse can read. Literacy, as well as the possession of books, had by the fifteenth century become a symbol of class. Second, this passage tells us that, while there was an English translation of the Bible, that edition was forbidden and its translator labeled a heretic. Third, in a period before the invention of the printing press, Frevisse owned a book. Frevisse, then, is not the usual sort of nun—her independence of thought, as well as her unusual education, has its source in her place as Chaucer's niece. Dame Frevisse can legitimately think, speak, read differently than other nuns, and in fact other women, because of her experiences in the Chaucer household and her closeness to Thomas Chaucer. That this is so is iterated and emphasized throughout the series and goes far to explain her detective ability as well as the tension between Frevisse and the more conventional characters in the Tales. Frazer has blessed—or cursed—her with a cool and logical brain, an eye for detail, an insatiable curiosity, and an inability to suffer fools gladly.

Frazer's titles follow the form of Chaucer's *Canterbury Tales* but also reflect the structure and matter of each novel. The part the title character plays is different in each book but always that character is central. Each novel opens and closes with the title character. For example, Thomasine is present through the series but in *The Novice's Tale* she is central to the plot. And so her voice, and her name opens and closes the novel. Each of the Tales begins and ends with the title character—usually with that character's words. In this tale, for example, after a brief introduction establishing the month, year and place—September 1431, in the Benedictine Abbey, St. Frideswide—Thomasine, the novice, pauses "to gaze out the narrow window on the stairs to the prioress's parlor, a plate of honey cakes in her hands" (1). In two weeks, we are told, after nine years in the convent, this "desperately pious" seventeen-year-old will take her final vows (18). And the book ends as it began, with Thomasine. *The Servant's Tale* opens, "Meg's first task every morning since she had come as Barnaby's bride had been to scrub or broom the sill and stone" of the hovel which is her home, "with husband and two sons" (1). This tale too ends with Meg.

The pattern is set and it continues through the seven books of the series. However, there is more. *The Novice's Tale* sets the stage for the additional information provided in the later tales. The convent is not a rich one—a common state for the period. The convents (or monasteries) that were richly endowed and gloriously ornamented were the exception. Here and in the later tales, the exceptional and sometimes annoying ardor with which Thomasine seeks holiness becomes a recurring theme. While Frazer does not belabor the realities of medieval life, she does make the opportunity to provide small subtle and historically accurate reminders that the events of the novels take place in a time beyond our knowing. However, the lessons and values implicit in these stories have meaning to a present-day audience as well. The foundations of both society and those who populate it have not changed essentially with the passage of time. It is this fact which makes Frazer's tales of particular interest to popular culturists today.

A brief summary of the plot of Thomasine's tale makes this claim clear. The novice Thomasine's future is threatened when her aunt, the dowager Lady Ermentrude, worldly, domineering, hard-drinking, and unpleasant, presents a different plan. Surrounded by her attendants and angry for no apparent reason with Thomasine's sister and her husband, she descends upon the priory like a hurricane, demanding that Thomasine leave with her. The tensions and undercurrents that Ermentrude brings with her to the priory are echoed in the threat of scandal in the royal family. This threat is given substance later in *The Boy's Tale* (1995), the fifth book of the series. Here, it remains only a hint. Ermentrude's murder, Thomasine's possible guilt, and Frevisse's successful discovery of the real culprit is the substance of this tale. Underlying the plot, however, and as important, is the universality of the characters. People like Ermentrude and her effect on those about her are not unknown to us. Our recognition that hypocrisy and fear of disclosure, pride, and greed exist in our time as well as Frevisse's shrinks the 400 years that separate us.

Frazer's skillful interweaving of these universal human emotions and the history of the time into the activities of the priory provides continuity. We have seen that Frazer has set the stage for the political crime in *The Boys' Tale*. But the introduction of Dame Alys and her obsession with family as well as her distrust of Dame Frevisse provides motive for Frevisse's pilgrimage in *The Murderer's Tale*, as well as for the plot in *The Prioress' Tale*. In many ways, it seems as though the seven books of this series are simply one long continuing story. And this near-seamless linkage of her tales, likely, is the main element that sets Frazer apart from some other series authors.

In *The Murderer's Tale*, Frazer returns to the issue of class. In Giles Knyvet, she has created the most despicable villain since Iago. but he represents more than evil incarnate. He exemplifies the worst qualities of the aristocracy. No other tale, not even *The Boys' Tale*, presents a more detailed blueprint of the dangers of corrupted privilege, of power without conscience. To the very end, Giles shows no sign of remorse for his actions, only fury that he was uncloaked. From the first lines of this tale, Giles's hatred for a world that did not appreciate his superiority rules his life and shapes his plans. Jealousy of his cousin Lionel, an epileptic and heir to title and fortune, both of which Giles believes should be his, and his determination to remedy that error rule him.

His wife, Edeyn, "was the one thing of dear cousin Lionel's that Giles had taken for himself" (4)—and the only reason he treasured her. His cruelty to Edeyn, to servants, and even to dogs is steady and unceasing. He kills Martyn, Lionel's steward and friend, and frames Lionel for the murder. Cruelest of all, he convinces Lionel and everyone—everyone except Edeyn and Dame Frevisse— at Lovell Minster that Lionel committed the murder in a fit of madness brought on by an epileptic attack.

Throughout, Frazer never loses sight of the science of the Middle Ages. She does not step outside of the knowledge available to the most learned medieval citizen. This is particularly evident in the scene of Martyn's death. While Frazer details the superstition and dread surrounding epilepsy which marked the period, she also provides clues to prove Lionel's innocence, which citizens of that period could understand and accept. Corroborating evidence is there to be uncovered piece by piece, and the truth can be deduced from these clues. But first, the fear of the unknown, the fear of Lionel's possession, must be overcome. In the end, Giles is unmasked and dies, unrepentant. When Giles tried to kill Lionel, Edeyn and Frevisse break into the room and put their own lives at risk. An unarmed Lionel intervenes to save Edeyn's life and, in the ensuing fight, stabs Giles with his own dagger. But Giles had so convinced the company of Lionel's demonic possession that he would have been killed by the guards who broke into the room and found Giles's body. However, Edeyn pointed to Giles and cried, "He killed Martyn and he tried to kill us" (226). Edeyn's class, her status as a member of the aristocracy, more than her speech stops the guards in their tracks. Given time and an audience now willing to listen, Frevisse explains the evidence and Lionel is cleared.

In Lionel, Frazer presents the possibility of good that resides in the aristocracy. Lionel accepts the responsibility that accompanies privilege. He is devout, thoughtful, modest, and compassionate—all qualities which make him fair game for the kind of evil that Giles represents. So class, like money, is not itself a source of evil. However, the ability to do what one chooses with impunity, to buy things and men, and not count the cost, provides temptation that few can resist. But one does, and we take comfort in Lionel's virtue.

Law is not the issue in *The Murderer's Tale* but justice, which must be the end, the driving force for those whose service is to God. Frevisse accepts that in this tale, as she had earlier in *The Outlaw's Tale*. There, she subverted the law in favor of justice more directly. She protected Edward, at whose hand the Franklin died, from any punishment save that of his own conscience. That the death was an accident is, in this environment, irrelevant as is the fact that Frevisse's guilt was known only to God. Her pain and her need to expiate that guilt are very real. We, in our more secular time, accept Frevisse's reality without question because Frazer has joined our verities to those of the middle ages

This artistry can be seen in the clear links between the tales of Frazer's series mentioned above. Frevisse and Dame Claire's presence at Lovell Minster had its source in earlier tales. The animosity between Frevisse and Dame Alys has been a source of tension throughout this series, exacerbated by Alys's pride and Frevisse's inability to disguise her feelings. That animosity peaked when through a fluke, Alys was elected Prioress on the death of Domina Edith seven months before *The Murderer's Tale* opened (12-13). Although Alys's real power and corruption are not detailed until *The Prioress' Tale*, the tension between the two nuns threatens to damage the community and Frevisse herself. So she and Dame Claire apply to go on pilgrimage to "St. Frideswide's great shrine in Oxford town some thirty miles away" (29). Their meeting with Lionel's train, his invitation to the nuns to travel with them to Lovell Minster, and so Frevisse's presence in time to foil Giles's plot are not only explained but occur so naturally that we never notice the skill with which Frazer manipulates her characters and her audience. Insignificant threads from the first tale are woven together to become the main tapestry in *The Prioress' Tale*, seventh of the series. There, the scope of Domina Alys's allegiance to family over God, seen briefly in *The Novice's Tale*, takes physical form. As prioress, she nearly destroys the priory through her preferential treatment of the Godfreys. She allows family members the protection of the convent from which they can raid the Fenner holdings. She spends money she does not have on unnecessary luxuries for herself, and she undertakes a building program solely to prove her own importance. And her pride of place and name, her betrayal of her vows, lead inexorably to tragedy and her own destruction. But St. Frideswide survives and Dame Frevisse and the other nuns with it.

The popularity of these historical mysteries, particularly those set in the most distant past, is tied to that survival. In the end, good triumphs. The victory is seldom easy and usually incomplete. But it is victory. It usually comes at the cost of suffering and pain and loss. But it comes. In the best of these novels—and Margaret Frazer writes some of the best—we sense that the characters who further these plots and people these times are, in the end, not much different from ourselves. In our own society, there is too often a growing sense that we have lost even the illusion of control, that our world is spinning beyond our comprehension. In fiction, however, we see our own problems, set in a different time but still our problems and, perhaps, we can achieve the distance that allows us to find solutions or at least the comfort of shared striving. Perhaps the brief time spent away from our own uncertainties provides renewal. Perhaps survival is not only possible but triumphant for us as well. And perhaps that is enough.

### Glossary

1. Accidie. The sin of hopelessness, despair so deep it denies God; the failure to find pleasure in those things God meant to be pleasurable.

2. Assuarted. Land added on to original amount, claimed by tenant.

3. Aumbrys. Cupboard.

4. Cockchafer. Pheasant.

5. Chapter. Meeting of all members of Convent or monastery in which the business of the day is dealt with. In a cloistered Abbey like St. Frides-wide, the only time general speech is allowed to the whole community.

6. Croft. Peasant's cottage.

7. Crowner. Coroner. Originally, crowner investigated for and reported to the king (the crown).

8. Dorter. Dormitory.

9. Garderobe. A private room, usually one in which clothes or armor are kept.

10. Garth. A bit of land (lawn) between two walls.

11. Grave-bottomed. Gravel bottomed.

12. Henbane. A poisonous herb, used in small quantities for relief of toothache or similar pain.

13. Houppelande. A jacket or tunic, worn by either man or woman.

14. Likerous. Lecherous.

15. Liripipe. Scarf usually attached to a hat or cap. Very fashionable.

16. Malmsey. A strong sweet white wine.

17. Marchpane. Marzipan.

18. Milk sops. Bread soaked in milk with honey and, sometimes, mild spices.

19. Necessarium. Privy.

20. Obedientiaries. Official titles or duties within the Abbey. Example: Cellerer or Hospitaler.

21. 'Pothecaries (apothecaries). Herbalists; precursor of "pharmacist."

22. Prie-dieu. A prayer desk.

23. Psaltery. Stringed instrument, similar to a dulcimer.

24. Scurriers. Messengers.

25. Slype. A narrow passageway. Here, leading from cloister to garth.

26. Sumpter-horses. Pack horses.

27. Villeins. Legally freemen to all but their lord who has total authority over them. However, to be lordless is to be without any protection.

28. Wanhope. That despair so deep that it denies God.

29. Wasting disease. Usually assumed to be cancer.

30. Wimple. White cloth covering forehead, throat and chin, worn by both lay women and nuns. The traditional nun's habit was originally the ordinary clothing of medieval common women, plainer and in black and white instead of color, but otherwise the same.

31. Withies. Reeds for making baskets, etc.

*Note*

1. Pen name of Mary Monica Pulver and Gail Frazer.

*Works Cited*

Ashley, Mike. *Historical Whodunits*. New York: Barnes & Noble, 1997.

Frazer, Margaret. *The Bishop's Tale*. New York: Berkley Prime Crime, 1994.

——. *The Boys' Tale*. New York: Berkley Prime Crime, 1995.

——. *The Murderer's Tale*. New York: Berkley Prime Crime, 1996.

——. *The Novice's Tale*. New York: Jove, 1992.

——. *The Outlaw's Tale*. New York: Berkley Prime Crime, 1994.

——. *The Prioress' Tale*. New York: Berkley Prime Crime, 1997.

——. *The Servant's Tale*. New York: Berkley Prime Crime, 1993.

Pearsall, Derek. *The Life of Geoffrey Chaucer*. Oxford, UK: Blackwell, 1994.

Swanson, Jean, and Dean James. *Killer Books*. New York: Berkley Prime Crime, 1998.

Taylor, Henry Osbourne. *The Mediaeval Mind*. 2 vols. Cambridge: Harvard UP, 1962.

# Josephine Tey and Others:
# The Case of Richard III

## R. Gordon Kelly

Most people would consider Richard [III] a person about whom the truth can be known, but since, in popular culture, no clear principles exist to enable the interested to distinguish fact from fancy, the issue remains in doubt.

—Charles T. Wood, "Richard III and the
Beginnings of Historical Fiction"

On August 22, 1485, England's King Richard III lost his life at the Battle of Bosworth Field, defending his crown. He had ruled for just over two years. Five centuries later, however, controversy continues to swirl about the man and his nature.[1] Was Richard "Hell's black intelligencer," the "elvish-marked, abortive and rooting hog" of Shakespeare's play? Or was he the loyal brother, fond uncle, "mighty prince and especial! good lord," as his defenders have claimed, beginning as early as George Buck in the seventeenth century?[2] And why does the matter continue to evoke interest and passionate partisanship?

At the center of the controversy about Richard III lie questions about the means by which he came to the throne following the unexpected death of his brother, Edward IV, at the age of forty on April 9, 1483. Arguably the most contentious of these questions has to do with the fate of Edward's two young sons, whom Richard immured in the Tower of London. They were last seen there shortly after Richard's accession. Was he responsible for their deaths? Or were they still alive in the Tower on August 22, 1485, only to be quietly dispatched by Henry VII, who had defeated Richard at Bosworth? Professional historians have long argued that the boys died during Richard's reign, probably in the first summer, and probably at Richard's behest.[3] The contrary position—that one or both remained alive after Richard's death— has been pressed primarily by novelists and amateur historians such as Clements Markham, whose highly colored, turn-of-the century defense of Richard III (1906) inspired Josephine Tey's *The Daughter of Time* (1951). Popular culture remains overwhelmingly pro-Ricardian. Most of the more than forty novels about Richard published since 1960 "seek to exculpate their hero," according to A. J. Pollard, as do the two dozen or so plays written for stage or radio over a somewhat longer period. In 1984, London Weekend Television staged a mock trial during which two prominent barristers argued the case for and against Richard's having caused the deaths of the two princes. The twelve jurors found themselves unable to convict, even on the balance of probabilities (223, 228). More recently, two mock trials in the United States, one of them conducted by Supreme Court Chief Justice William Rhenquist, also concluded with Richard's acquittal, on the balance of probabilities.[4]

The question of Richard's role in his nephews' fate has been argued in several mystery novels, notably Josephine Tey's *The Daughter of Time*, which was hailed by Anthony Boucher at its publication as "one of the permanent classics in the detective field. . . . one of the best, not of the year, but of all time" (42, 46). Four novels published in the wake of Tey's critical and commercial success have achieved neither: Jeremy Potter's *A Trail of Blood* (1970), Elizabeth Peters's *The Murders of Richard III* (1974), Guy M. Townsend's *To Prove a Villain* (1985), and P. C. Doherty's *The Fate of Princes* (1990). With the exception of Townsend's novel, each urges a version of the revisionist thesis, namely that Richard had no hand in murdering his two nephews to secure his claims to the throne.

In *The Daughter of Time*, Josephine Tey mounts a passionate defense of Richard, following closely the argument laid down by Clements Markham. In doing so, she attacks historians generally for their credulity and ignorance of human nature, singling out for sustained criticism the early historians Thomas More and Polydore Vergil, as well as James Gairdner, Markham's chief adversary.[5] Against the failings of historians, she makes large claims for the ability of novelists and painters to uncover and represent the truth about persons and events. Tey's "arm-chair" investigator, the hospitalized Scotland Yard Inspector Alan Grant, is no sort of historian, amateur or professional. Rather, as a career police officer, he possesses analogous investigative skills and a deep understanding of human motivation honed by years of experience, observation, and reflection. *The Daughter of Time* exemplifies the pro-Ricardian tendencies in popular culture and is arguably the most widely circulated positive image of Richard III in the twentieth century.

Before turning to the novels, however, a brief historical review is in order. Whether Richard was responsible for the deaths of his two nephews is part of the larger question of how he came to be king three months after the death of Edward IV on April 9, 1483. Surviving Edward IV were two sons, Edward, Prince of Wales, now Edward V, and Richard, Duke of York, aged twelve and nine, respectively; five daughters, the oldest of whom, Elizabeth, was eighteen; and Edward's widow, Elizabeth Woodville, head of a politically powerful and ambitious family, which included her brother, Anthony Earl Rivers, to whom Edward IV had entrusted the care and tutelage of the Prince of Wales; and her son by an earlier marriage, Thomas Grey, Marquis of Dorset. On April 30, Richard, accompanied by Henry Stafford, Duke of Buckingham, met Edward V and Rivers on their way to London, where the young king's coronation had been scheduled for May 4. Richard arrested Rivers and two others, dismissed the rest of the king's entourage, and set out for London with Edward V under his control. When news of Richard's action reached London, Elizabeth Woodville, accompanied by her younger son, her daughters, and Dorset, immediately sought sanctuary in Westminster. On June 13, Richard interrupted a council meeting to order the arrest and summary execution of William, Lord Hastings, who had served as Edward IV's chamberlain and whose support had been crucial to Richard in the weeks following his brother's death. Three days later, Elizabeth Woodville permitted the Duke of York to leave sanctuary to join his older brother in the Tower of London, there to await Edward's coronation, which had been postponed from May 4, first to June 22 and then to November.

On Sunday, June 22, Ralph Shaw, the brother of London's mayor, preached a sermon at St. Paul's Cross during which he alleged that Edward's sons were illegitimate and hence had no valid claim to the throne. The allegation, together with other charges against Edward IV, were subsequently embodied in an act of Parliament in January 1484 designed to secure Richard's claim to the throne: *Titulus Regius*. On June 25, Richard had Earl Rivers executed for treason. The following day, he formally assumed the throne and was duly crowned Richard III on Sunday, July 6, 1483. The princes, meanwhile, were moved to inner apartments in the Tower, and their attendants were withdrawn, including their physician, Dr. Argentine, who reportedly described Edward V as fearing death. Precisely when the boys were last seen is uncertain, but there is no evidence that they were seen alive after mid-summer 1483. As early as mid-June, rumors that the princes were dead had begun to circulate. In October, a rebellion initiated to restore Edward V to the throne became instead an effort to depose Richard and replace him with the exiled Henry Tudor, Duke of Richmond. The attempt failed, and Buckingham, Richard's erstwhile ally, was executed for his role in the uprising. In March 1484, Elizabeth Woodville, at Richard's urging, agreed to leave Westminster and return to his court with her daughters but only after receiving his public pledge to guarantee their safety. A year later, following the death of his wife Anne, Richard appears to have considered marrying his niece, presumably with Elizabeth Woodville's approval, but sentiment against the rumored match proved so strong that Richard had to disavow it publicly.

Most students of the period, historians and historical novelists alike, accept the foregoing chronology.[6] They disagree, however, on the appropriate inferences to be drawn from these actions and events. How, for example, is Richard's arrest of Earl Rivers and seizure of Edward V on April 30, 1483, to be understood? Was he already aiming to make himself king, or was he improvising—countering a Woodville plot to deprive him of the protectorate promised by Edward IV? Elizabeth Woodville's behavior also raises questions. Her support for Henry Tudor in autumn 1483, her return to Richard's court in the following spring, and her willingness to marry her daughter to Richard have puzzled historians. If she knew or believed that Edward V and his brother were still alive in 1483, why would she have supported the claims of Henry Tudor to the throne?[7] If she thought them dead at

Richard's hands, how could she, as their mother, have agreed to leave sanctuary and return to court with her daughters, much less countenanced a match between her oldest daughter and Richard?

Various answers have been proposed to these questions, but whether offered by Josephine Tey or by a historian of the stature of A. J. Pollard, the answers depend finally on "probabilities"—judgements about what is likely or reasonable or rational to do in certain circumstances. These judgements, in turn, derive from and express fundamental—and fundamentally different—assumptions about the sources of human motivation and the nature of personal character. In her mysteries, Tey employs a universalistic psychology, putting her at odds with professional historians, who typically ground their explanations of Richard III's and Elizabeth Woodville's behavior in the context of the politics of the period, rather than in universal, i.e., ahistorical, psychological categories and assumptions.

Tey's claims for fiction, and art more generally, begin with her title, which derives from the proverb "Truth is the daughter of time." She develops these claims in her respectful treatment of a fictitious historical novel, *The Rose of Raby,* from which she "quotes," but especially in her handling of a painting, a portrait of Richard III, the seeming misidentification of which by Alan Grant, her fictional investigator, initiates the novel's action.[8] At Scotland Yard, Inspector Grant enjoys a reputation for his ability to " 'pick them on sight' ": it might not be possible "to put faces into any kind of category, but it was possible to characterize individual faces" accurately (29). Studying the portrait of a man dressed in the fashion of the late fifteenth century, one of several pictures given him by a well-meaning friend to speed his convalescence, Grant concludes that the man must have been "someone used to great authority"—a judge or soldier or prince. Turning the card over, he discovers to his dismay that he has made a mistake; the subject is one of history's arch villains, Richard III: "to have mistaken one of the most notorious murderers of all time for a judge . . . was a shocking piece of ineptitude" (33). He resolves to discover how his professional judgement could have miscarried so badly.

Beginning with school book treatments of Richard III, Grant works his way backward in time through various historical accounts, aided by Brent Carradine, a young American who serves as his research assistant and plays Watson to Grant's Holmes. In the process, they "discover" that Richard was not responsible for the deaths of the princes; the boys died instead at the hands of Richard's successor, Henry VII. The story of Richard's villainy, they learn, had its origins in the politically motivated hostility of the earliest historians, Thomas More ("the sainted More") and Polydore Vergil (Henry VII's "pet historian"), who, in Tey's view, were little more than propagandists for the Tudors. The myth received its most powerful expression in Shakespeare's *Richard III* and owed its persistence to the power and popularity of the play, as well as to the deficiencies of later historians, such as James Gairdner, whose credulity was matched only by their ignorance of human psychology. " 'Historians should be compelled to take a course in psychology before they are allowed to write' [Grant huffs]. 'Huh [Carradine replied]. That wouldn't do anything for them. A man who is interested in what makes people tick doesn't write history. He writes novels, or becomes an alienist, or a magistrate—'" (201).

Grant's apparent failure to categorize Richard's face strikes at the root of his professional identity He undertakes his investigation to learn whether or how he went wrong and discovers that he had been right about the face. In Tey's hands, the portrait is a crucial piece of evidence. Despite a lack of skill ("The expression in the eyes—that most arresting and individual expression—had defeated him"), the portraitist had sufficiently captured Richard's character to enable viewers to see its essence, provided they possessed the requisite experience—as Grant did. What Grant correctly recognizes in the portrait are not only essential elements of the subject's character but, by implication, settled, stable features—the man's enduring essence.

Tey's treatment of the portrait as historical evidence reveals two key psychological assumptions that underwrite her conclusion: "One could not say: Because Richard possessed this quality and that, therefore he was incapable of murder. But one could say: Because Richard possessed these qualities, therefore he is incapable of *this* murder. It would have been a silly murder . . . and Richard was a remarkably able man. It was base beyond description; and he was a man of great integrity. It was callous; and he was noted for his warmheartedness" (174).[9] Grant's assessment of Richard's character, based on the portrait, must be accurate, but more than that is required, if Tey's argument to hold, for these qualities might be true of Richard at one time but not at another. Unless character is assumed to be stable and enduring, the argument collapses in the face of the obvious objection that Richard changed when confronted with the possibility of becoming king.

Through Grant's efforts to understand his "mistake," Tey attacks historians and compares them invidiously with writers of fiction and artists more generally. She rejects the view that Richard had a motive for murdering his nephews and argues that they must have been alive on August 22, 1485. Finally, given the convention of the falsely accused suspect in a murder mystery, she argues that Henry VII had the princes killed as part of his otherwise well-documented policy of eliminating possible claimants to the throne. Much has been said about these theories but Tey's argument on the all-important issue of motive deserves brief discussion. Tey accepts uncritically the claim advanced by Richard and his supporters on the eve of his accession to the throne, namely that Edwards's children by Elizabeth Woodville were illegitimate owing to a pre-contract—in effect, a marriage—that Edward had entered into with an Eleanor Butler prior to marrying Woodville.[10] If bastards, the princes had no claim to the throne. Without any legitimate claim to the throne, they posed no threat to Richard. It would have been unreasonable for him to order them killed. The truth of the pre-contract story is essential to Tey's case, although whether there are good reasons for believing the story remains controversial.

Tey's argument that the princes must have survived Richard's death begins with her denying the existence of rumors alleging their deaths, despite the translation and publication in 1936 of the only truly contemporaneous account of events in summer 1483, *The Usurpation of Richard III* by Dominic Mancini, who had been in London from summer 1482 through July 1483. His account of what he saw and heard, for all its limitations (Mancini spoke little if any English), is an essential source.[11] Mancini reports hearing rumors of the princes' deaths, and he talked with their physician, Dr. Argentine, one of the last of their attendants to be withdrawn, who reported that Edward V feared imminent death. Tey goes on to argue from Elizabeth Woodville's decision to leave Westminster and return to court that the princes must have been alive that spring: "'Where would one have to go to meet a *woman* who became matey with the murderer of her boys,'" Grant asks (151 emphasis added). In this context, "woman" (really "mothers"?) functions as a timeless universal category, an ahistorical concept one element of which is the belief that a mother, any mother, could not be "matey" with the murderer of her children. By the same logic, Woodville's willingness to see her daughter married to Richard must mean that the princes were still alive in the spring of 1485.

In the final pages of *The Daughter of Time,* Tey springs a last surprise on her readers: Richard's innocence has been "known" for centuries: "'A man named Buck wrote a vindication in the seventeenth century. And Horace Walpole[12] in the eighteenth. And someone called Markham in the nineteenth' [Carradine reports]. 'And who in the twentieth?'" Grant asks (195). The answer, of course, is the book the reader is on the verge of finishing. Using the conventions of the detective story, the twentieth century's most popular form of narrative fiction, Tey sought to challenge Shakespeare's powerful and pervasive image of Richard as evil incarnate, also, while demonstrating the critical superiority of the novelist over the historian.

Guy M. Townsend's *To Prove a Villain* (1985) is an anomaly, a mystery novel that argues the traditionalist interpretation. Townsend aims to discredit Tey's handling of the historical evidence and defend historical professionalism. Townsend's protagonist, John Forest, is a young history PhD teaching at a small college. When a brilliant but abrasive colleague is murdered, Forest is drawn into the investigation conducted by a local police officer who is both a friend of Forest's and a student enrolled in his evening course in British history. Townsend, who holds a PhD in modern British history, castigates Tey's argument in a putative classroom discussion of Richard III's role in the death of the princes. Her work is hopelessly unprofessional and untrustworthy for her "slavish" following of Clements Markham's argument, her failure to acknowledge her debt to his work, her "colossal carelessness" over an important fact, and her failure to take account of evidence contrary to her thesis, namely Mancini's contemporaneous account of events leading to Richard III's accession.

Townsend draws explicitly on works by professional historians in mounting his critique of Tey. Following Levine, for example, Townsend dismisses Titulus Regius, with its argument for the princes' illegitimacy, as little more than a "legal technicality."[13] Townsend's approach can be gauged by his treatment of Elizabeth Woodville's decision to permit the Duke of York to leave sanctuary in June 1483 to join his brother in the Tower, given Richard's summary execution of Lord Hastings just three days earlier. Her decision has puzzled some historians, who have asked, as one of Forest's students does: How "'can anyone possibly believe that a mother would do that?'" (100). Forest acknowledges that this is a "telling argument," suggesting that Townsend finds nothing objectionable about framing the question in terms of a universal category "mother." The rest of his reply makes clear, however, that he favors a far more situated, circumstantial form of explanation that takes account both of dominant character traits—Elizabeth Woodville's well-documented appetite for wealth and power—together with the realities of her situation—that Richard had the power, and family precedent, to violate sanctuary and seize the boy if she refused to let him leave Westminster.[14]

Townsend's argument raises difficulties not unlike the problems he exposes in Tey's. Two examples must suffice. Following Edward IV's death, the actions of the "Woodville faction," Forest declares, "'caused Richard to take drastic actions to preserve the rightful powers of lord protector which had been granted in Edward IV's will'" (96). According to Charles Ross, however, whose work Townsend almost certainly knew, Edward's wishes were not as clear as the foregoing suggests, and even if they had been, the council was not bound to follow them (67). Similarly, in his zeal to counter Tey and convict Richard III, Townsend surely overstates the evidence afforded by two skeletons unearthed in the Tower in 1674 and analyzed in 1933, endorsing without qualification the summary identification offered by one of the investigators, a distinguished anatomist: "'Their ages were such that I can say with complete confidence that their death occurred during the reign of their usurping uncle, Richard III'" (115).[15] Wondering at Tey's failure to mention this well-publicized analysis of the Tower skeletons or Mancini's *Usurpation,* both of which undercut her argument, one of Professor Forest's students asks "'But why haven't historians exposed the fallacies of the Richardist position in a popular forum?'" (116). The two chapters Townsend devotes to correcting Tey are clearly intended to be just such an exposé—using the "popular forum" Tey herself so effectively exploited: the conventional murder mystery.

The three novels still to be discussed argue versions of the revisionist thesis. Two, both historical novels, merit brief discussion: Jeremy Potter's *A Trail of Blood* (1970) and P. J. Doherty's *The Fate of Princes* (1990). Elizabeth Peters's *The Murders of Richard III* (1974) is a contemporaneous English country house mystery in which the pro-Ricardian material serves primarily as a backdrop. Potter and Doherty both possess historical credentials. Potter was the former chairman of the Richard III Society and the author of *Good King Richard: An Account of Richard III and His Reputation* (1983). Doherty, an Oxford-trained historian, has written a number of mystery novels with medieval settings, in addition to *The Fate of Princes*. Their novels embody the same premise, namely that Richard had no motive for murdering his nephews and, given the fragmentary and sometimes contradictory nature of the surviving sources, it is plausible that at least one of the princes survived Richard's death at Bosworth. Both make the argument, though imagining different explanations and outcomes.

In a prefatory note to *A Trail of Blood* (1970), Jeremy Potter acknowledges Paul Murray Kendall's biography *Richard III* (1955) as his principal source of historical fact and *The Daughter of Time* as a source of inspiration, adding that his version of the events of Richard's reign is as "plausible" as More's or Shakespeare's. Potter's tale begins in 1536, with Henry VIII threatening the dissolution of the monasteries and abbeys, including the abbey at Croyland, headed by John Wells, a leading member of the Church party. A deputation arrives at Croyland, hoping to use its extensive records and chronicles to identify a Yorkist claimant to the throne who might both galvanize and lead the growing opposition to Henry VIII's anti-clerical policies, particularly in the north, where Yorkist sympathies had remained strong in the half-century since Richard's reign. Wells agrees to permit one of his monks, Brother Thomas, to pursue the investigation. *A Trail of Blood* recounts Thomas's investigation as he follows the clues provided first in the abbey's archives and then in a series of interviews, some with persons old enough to have first-hand knowledge of Richard's reign.

In the archives, Thomas discovers an account of Richard's reign written by Bishop John Russell, Richard's chamberlain, during a stay at the abbey in 1486. That account, the second continuation of the Croyland chronicle as it is now usually designated, remains a key source for historians, because its author appears to have been an eye witness to some of the events leading to Richard's usurpation. Its authorship remains controversial, but John Russell is a leading candidate.[16] Potter's account depends on the correctness of that attribution. The chronicle mentions that rumors of the princes' death were circulating during summer 1483, but nowhere states that they *were* dead, a significant silence, according to Potter. Given Russell's access to information, Potter concludes that the rumors must have been false, else Russell would have confirmed them. Brother Thomas also discovers in the Croyland archives a copy of Titulus Regius, which Russell consigned to the abbey for safekeeping. The document convinces Brother Thomas that Richard had no motive to murder the princes, once their bastardy had been revealed. Potter ignores the question of whether their illegitimacy, even if true, would have constituted a permanent barrier to the succession.[17]

Armed with the archival clues that suggest that one or both of the princes may have survived Richard's death, Brother Thomas sets out to reconstruct what had happened fifty years before. He discovers that the boys had been spirited out of the Tower by one of Sir Robert Brackenbury's men, Walter Skelton, when Buckingham came to the Tower intent on killing them. The boat carrying the escaping princes overturned and Edward V was drowned. Skelton managed to save the Duke of York, however, and took him abroad, returning just in time for the prince to be reunited with his uncle on the eve of the Battle of Bosworth. There, York would have died fighting loyally at his uncle's side if Viscount Lovell had not helped him to escape. Two years later, at the Battle of Stoke, Lovell again saved the prince's life but at the cost of his own, whereupon the boy turned to one of the few surviving Yorkists on whom he might call, Bishop Russell, who accepted him as a novitiate and brought him to Croyland. Now a man in his early sixties and Croyland's abbot, Russell's noviate, Potter imagines, is really the surviving prince, Richard, Duke of York.

P. C. Doherty's *The Fate of Princes* offers a different survival story. The novel covers the period summer 1483 through summer 1487, as seen through the eyes of Francis Viscount Lovell, one of Richard's closest confidants and his chamberlain after the execution of Hastings during June 1483. Amidst rumors of the princes' deaths, the king receives a letter from Sir Robert Brackenbury, informing him that the princes were unaccountably missing from the Tower when he became constable during mid-July. Richard commissions Lovell to find out what has happened to them. He eventually discovers the truth, but not until after Richard's death. In the final interview of his investigation, Lovell comes face to face with the surviving prince, Richard, Duke of York, whom he finds living incognito near Leicester, apprenticed to a stonemason.

The boy tells Lovell that Richard himself had taken them from the Tower sometime after his coronation on July 6 and before July 17, when Brackenbury became constable. Edward, seriously ill, had died the night they left the Tower. For the princes, Richard had substituted two boys of similar age and appearance. These were subsequently poisoned by the Duke of Buckingham, and their bodies walled up in an unused Tower room. With Edward V dead, Richard had arranged for the younger boy to be cared for by a London merchant, a former stonemason. On the eve of the battle at Bosworth, Richard had sent for his nephew and assured him that he would be cared for if the battle went well. If it did not, the boy was to tell no one of his identity. As the boy explains to Lovell, " 'they [Henry VII's agents] would not only send me back to the Tower but undoubtedly kill me. . . . I am happy and safe as a stonemason" (176-77).

Like Tey, Doherty believes Richard had no motive for killing the princes. In a postscript, he characterizes Richard III as a man of his age, "a 15th century warlord who fought for survival," but denies that his survival depended on eliminating his nephews: "Suffice to say that Richard had no real motive for killing them. He had already usurped their position." Moreover, "his innocence might account for Elizabeth Woodville's capitulation to Richard in [leaving sanctuary in March] 1484. She must have been given some assurance that the man who had killed her brother, Earl Rivers, declared her marriage [to Edward IV] invalid and her sons bastard issue, had actually not killed her children" (190).

Doherty offers no rationale or explanation for Richard's decision to remove the princes from the Tower. Was it an impulsive act of compassion in response to Edward V's deteriorating condition, undertaken with little consideration of the consequences? Or did Richard have some plan for the boys, a plan that began to unravel with Edward's death and Buckingham's unanticipated poisoning of the two imposters Richard had substituted for the princes? What was Richard thinking? Doherty simply asks his reader to imagine that Richard was concerned enough about the condition of the princes during early July 1483 to weigh various courses of action, the best of which involved not only finding two suitable substitutes to take the place of the princes in the Tower (for how long?) but arranging for the care and safety of the princes, whose identity would have to be kept secret indefinitely. Doherty's fictional reconstruction, like Potter's, is "plausible" in this limited sense: it is not ruled out by the surviving record. On the other hand, there is no evidence to support the claims of either novelist. No professional historian today takes seriously the argument that one or both of the princes survived Richard's death at Bosworth, and few historians today, if any, would disagree with Ross:

In the final analysis, Richard III remains the most likely candidate by far to have murdered his own nephews. It is scarcely possible to doubt that they met their deaths by violence during the summer of 1483. He had by far the strongest motive, as well as the most obvious opportunity. Nothing of what we know about his character in general, and the conditions of his upbringing in particular, makes his having committed such an act at all unlikely. (103-04)

More recently, Pollard has arrived at a similar assessment:

It cannot be proved that Richard III murdered the Princes in the Tower. It is not known when, where, by what means and by whose hands they met their deaths. It is probable, however, that they were killed with the knowledge of the king before the middle of September 1483. (137)

Tey, Potter, and Doherty, as well as historical novelists generally, have argued otherwise. Both historians and novelists are ultimately dependent on the same body of surviving evidence, although novelists—Tey is a good example—probably rely more on historians than on their own independent assessment of the primary sources. Indeed, it is that dependence, unacknowledged by Tey, for example, that partly explains Townsend's animus toward her. And it is the absence of conventions permitting systematic acknowledgment that leads to comments like Wood's, quoted in the epigraph to this essay, namely that "in popular culture, no clear principles exist to enable the interested to distinguish fact from fancy" (305).

The historical record in the case of Richard III is fragmentary and inconsistent, and a document such as *Titulus Regius*, containing the allegation that the princes were illegitimate, provides conflicting "evidence," depending on whether it is taken at face value or not. Tey appears to accept the allegation of the pre-contract between Eleanor Butler and Edward IV as true simply because Richard brought the charge, and "he was a man of great integrity" (174). But it is precisely the nature of Richard's character that is at issue. It is Tey's assumption about his character that makes *Titulus Regius* evidence that Richard had no motive for murdering his nephews. But the quarrel between Tey and historians, and by extension between novelists and historians, is not simply about the character of Richard III. It involves the respective claims of fiction and historical writing to furnish true accounts of past actions. In making a bid for the authority of fiction, Tey makes plain her view that novelists, like alienists and magistrates, are more likely to be interested in "what makes people tick" than historians. The quarrel may also be fueled by a populist sympathy aroused by the spectacle of the machinery of state seeming to be brought to bear in falsely accusing an individual—the spectacle of "Tudor" propagandists blackening with impunity the reputation of a man who could not respond. That reaction, needless to say, also begs the question of Richard's character.

At the deepest level, the quarrel may draw its energy from two very different convictions about human nature. Accepting that Richard ordered his nephews killed shortly after his accession invites at least two inferences, both of which may be unsettling—that Richard had had his eye on the throne for some while and was simply biding his time or that the unexpected prospect of the throne overwhelmed his loyalty to his kin. Was he a masterful dissembler, whose loyalty was expedient? Or was he a tragic hero: "So much promise and potential . . . ruined by a ruthless disregard for the rights of others in the pursuit of power" (Pollard 229) and thus an instance of the corruptibility of integrity when tempted by the prospect of great power—a "truth" about human nature which some may wish to deny in the strongest terms.

In this context, it is worth contemplating for a moment what befell Anthony Earl Rivers and William, Lord Hastings, both of whom were caught off guard by Richard's bold, decisive actions. Both were experienced in the ruthless, faction-ridden politics of the day, and both knew Richard personally. Hastings had been Edward IV's chamberlain. Yet neither anticipated that Richard would destroy them to satisfy his ambition. Why not? One answer surely is that they failed to consider that the sudden prospect of power would tempt Richard to actions that even those who knew him well would not think him capable of.

In all of this, there is a fact of the matter. Richard III either was or was not responsible for the deaths of his nephews. It is unlikely, but not impossible, that evidence may still be found to bolster one side or the other. After all, Mancini's first-hand account of events in the summer of 1483 was not discovered until the 1930s. Previously, its very existence was unsuspected. In the meantime, two very different images of Richard III continue to circulate and to find their adherents. The plausibility and persuasiveness of those images, however, derive less from what is known about the man and more from the theories and assumptions about character and human nature in general that novelists and historians and their readers continue to rely on to flesh out and make sense of the relatively few surviving records in the case of Richard III.

## Acknowledgment

I am grateful to Tom Frank and John Caughey for helpful suggestions on an earlier draft.

## Notes

1. See Ross, *Richard III*, Introduction; Hanham, *Richard III and His Early Historians: 1483-1535*; and the bibliographies in Ross, and Pollard, *Richard III and the Princes in the Tower.*

2. *The History of King Richard III*; the quotation is from John Rous, in Ross (xxii).

3. See, for example, Ross, 96-104, 227-29, and Pollard, especially Chapter 5, "The Fate of the Princes." Alison Weir's popular history, *The Princes in the Tower*, also convicts Richard III, but her documentation is difficult to trace.

4. A summary is available at the Richard III Society web page: http://www.r3. org/triaVtrial2/htm.

5. *History of the Life and Reign of Richard III.*

6. See, especially, Sutton and Hammond, 13-27; Ross, 63-95; and Pollard, 90-114.

7. "It totally passes belief that she would have been willing to support a plan which would automatically disinherit her sons by Edward IV unless she had excellent reasons to believe them already dead (and she was well able to find out)" (Ross 100).

8. The portrait hangs in the National Portrait Gallery, London. Interestingly for Tey's argument, it is a copy (sixteenth century) of a Tudor portrait, i.e., one painted after Richard's death but based, perhaps, on a lost contemporary likeness (Pollard 58, 219).

9. For other instances of this argument, see Myers, 200-01.

10. On the pre-contract, see especially Levine and Helmholz.

11. See Hanham, *Richard III*, 65-73, and Ross, xli-xliii.

12. *Historic Doubts on the Life and Reign of Richard III*; see also Kendall, *Richard III: The Great Debate*, 147-239, and Myers, 192-95.

13. For a response to Levine, see Helmholz, whose essay was not available to Townsend.

14. Richard III's father had violated sanctuary in 1454; his brother in 1471, according to Ross (87).

15. For a recent assessment of the skeletal evidence, see Hammond and White.

16. See Hanham, *Richard III*, 74-100, and Ross, xliii-xlvi.

17. On this point, see Pollard: "even if it had been proved that Edward V and his brother were illegitimate, deposition was not the only course open to the protec-

tor. The stain of illegitimacy could have been removed by the ritual of coronation. Edward V, like Elizabeth I later, could have been declared legitimate and all doubt removed" (101).

## Works Cited

Boucher, Anthony. *Multiplying Villainies: Selected Mystery Criticism, 1942-1968.* Ed. E. Robert Briney and Francis M. Nevins, Jr. [n.p.]: A Bouchercon Book, 1973.

Doherty, P. C. *The Fate of Princes.* 1990. New York: St. Martin's, 1991.

Gairdner, James. *History of the Life and Reign of Richard III.* Cambridge, 1898.

Hammond, P. W., ed. *Richard III: Loyalty, Lordship and Law.* London: Richard III and Yorkist History Trust, 1986.

Hammond, P. W., and W. J. White. "The Sons of Edward IV: A Re-examination of the Evidence on Their Deaths and on the Bones in Westminster Abbey," in *Richard III.* 104-47.

Hanham, Alison. *Richard III and His Early Historians: 1483-1535.* Oxford: Clarendon, 1975.

——. "Richard III, Lord Hastings and the Historians." *English Historical Review* 87 (1972): 233-48.

Helmholz, R. H. "The Sons of Edward IV: A Canonical Assessment of the Claim That They Were Illegitimate," in *Richard III.* 91-103.

Kendall, Paul Murray. *Richard III.* London: George Allen & Unwin, 1955.

Kendall, Paul Murray, ed. *Richard III: The Great Debate. Sir Thomas More's History of King Richard III; Horace Walpole's Historic Doubts on the Life and Reign of King Richard III.* New York: Norton, 1965.

Levine, Mortimer, "Richard III: Usurper or Lawful King?" *Speculum* 34 (1959): 391-401.

Mancini, Dominic. *The Usurpation of Richard III.* Ed. and trans. C. A. J. Armstrong. 2nd ed. Oxford: Oxford UP, 1969.

Markham, Clements. *Richard III: His Life and Character.* 1906. Bath: Cedric Chivers, 1968.

Myers, A. R. "Richard III and Historical Tradition." *History* 53 (1968): 181-202.

Peters, Elizabeth. *The Murders of Richard III.* 1974. New York: Mysterious P, 1986.

Pollard, A. J. *Richard III and the Princes in the Tower.* New York: St. Martin's, 1991.

Potter, Jeremy. *A Trail of Blood.* New York: McCall, 1971.

Ross, Charles. *Richard III.* Berkeley: U of California P, 1981.

Sutton, Anne F.. and P. W. Hammond, eds. *The Coronation of Richard III.* New York: St. Martin's, 1984.

Tey, Josephine. *The Daughter of Time.* 1951. New York: Simon and Schuster, 1995.

Townsend, Guy M. *To Prove a Villain.* Menlo Park, CA: Perseverance, 1985.

Walpole, Horace. *Historic Doubts on the Life and Reign of Richard III.* 1768. Ed. P. W. Hammond. Gloucester: 1986.

Weir, Alison. *The Princes in the Tower.* 1992. New York: Ballantine, 1995.

Wolffe, B. P. "When and Why Did Hastings Lose His Head?" *English Historical Review* 89 (1974): 835-44.

Wood, Charles T. "Richard III and the Beginnings of Historical Fiction." *The Historian* 54 (1992): 305-14.

# C. L. Grace:
# Kathryn Swinbrook,
# Fifteenth-Century Physician and Sleuth

## Jean Coakley

A fifteenth-century English woman practicing medicine seems fanciful to many readers. Yet medical historians Kate Campbell Hurd-Mead and Monica Green provide clear evidence for C. L. Grace's portrayal of Kathryn Swinbrooke, Leech and Physician.[1] Women physicians and surgeons were "openly acknowledged as necessary for the care of the sick and wounded" until universities intellectualized the craft in the thirteenth century, teaching Greek and Arab medical theory and arguing that all practitioners should be male university graduates (Hurd-Mead 265). Despite papal edicts

forbidding [them] to practice medicine or surgery under pain of imprisonment . . . women doctors continued to practice, with or without registration, in the midst of wars and epidemics as they always had, for the simple reason that they were needed and could not be repressed. (Hurd-Mead 306, Grace's frontispiece)

As Grace indicates in the "Author's Note" which prefaces *A Shrine of Murders* (1993), the first title in the series,[2]

Kathryn Swinbrooke may be fiction, but in 1322, the most famous doctor in London was Mathilda of Westminster; Cecily of Oxford was the royal physician to Edward III and his wife Phillipa of Hainault; and Gerard of Cremona's work (mentioned in the novel) clearly describes women doctors during the medieval period. In England, particularly, where the medical faculties at the two universities Oxford and Cambridge were relatively weak, women did serve as doctors and apothecaries, professions only in later centuries denied to them.

While Henry VII's mother—the formidable Margaret, Countess of Richmond—practiced in her own hospitals, where "she personally attended the needs of patients, dressed the sores of the wounded, and prescribed for the sick" (Hurd-Mead 307), less well-connected women doctors like Grace's protagonist minimized friction with their university-trained colleagues by practicing in poorer neighborhoods, where their services were less well rewarded.

C. L. Grace's books include four titles: *A Shrine of Murders* (1993); *The Eye of God* (1994); *The Merchant of Death* (1995); and *The Book of*

*Shadows* (1995). Beginning with the first book in the series, which introduces the continuing characters and their milieu, each is built around a Chaucerian analogue and a historical occurrence, both of which play significant roles in plot development. As in Ellis Peters' "Brother Cadfael" series set during an earlier civil war, Kathryn Swinbrooke's pharmaceutical and medical expertise provide the rationale for her involvement in murder. Her first case calls upon her to solve a series of poisonings centered around Canterbury's most important tourist attraction: the Shrine of St. Thomas á Becket. In others, she is caught up in Court intrigues which place her and those she loves in danger. Each novel interweaves a series of carefully integrated subplots, unobtrusively planting clues while paying close attention to the nuances of psychological motivation.

In all four, Grace, a pseudonym for P. C. Doherty, uses a variant on the successful paradigm he has employed in better than three dozen medieval mysteries he has published under a variety of pseudonyms since 1986. Each novel begins with front matter contextualizing the narrative—an overview of "Historical Personages Mentioned in the Text" and a map of the "Main Streets of Canterbury, c. 1471" preceding *A Shrine of Murders* and a short "Historical Note" ushering in each of the later novels. These are ordinarily followed by Prologues linking the subtleties of milieu and motive to the action which follows. As *Shrine* opens, for example, the connections between Chaucer, magic, murder, and medicine are palpable:

> Wizards and warlocks proclaimed it to be a killing time. . . . Strange sights were seen: legions of hags flew through the dark watches of the night, leading convoys of the dead to black sabbaths and blasphemous Masses. . . . Such whispering spread even to Canterbury itself . . . [where s]trange deaths were reported, mysterious fatalities among those who flocked to Canterbury to seek the help of the Blessed Thomas a' Becket, whose battered corpse and cloven skull lay under sheets of gold before the high altar of Canterbury Cathedral. . . . In the west . . . Margaret of Anjou . . . plotted with her generals to seize the throne for her witless husband. . . . In London, Edward of York . . . drew up subtle plans against the She-Wolf's approach . . . and plotted the total destruction of the entire House of Lancaster. Truly a killing time, and those who could remembered the somber lines of Chaucer's poem about
>
> > *"The smiling rascal, concealing knife in cloak;*
> > *The farm barns burning and the thick black smoke.*
> > *The treachery of murder done in bed,*
> > *The open battle and the wounds which bled."* (1-3)

There is a delicious Chaucerian irony in Alderman Newington's nomination of Kathryn Swinbrooke to investigate the murders threatening Canterbury in this first novel. While the job is essentially Swinbrooke's by default, every other physician licensed by the Corporation being suspect, Newington has taken a calculated risk in recommending her.

The remaining members of the committee have equally compelling reasons but a good deal more practice in vetting candidates. Thomas Bourchier, Cardinal Archbishop of Canterbury and Edward IV's kinsman,[3] is a sharp negotiator who misses little and forgets nothing. Having known and trusted Kathryn's father, "A good doctor" (*Shrine* 26), he trusts her to be an objective medical examiner. With Satan said to be poisoning pilgrims and Cathedral and Corporation revenues at stake, a thorough medical education, an unbiased mind and a reputation for probity are far more meaningful than gender. It is worthy of note that in appointing Swinbrooke Bourchier stipulates she "will be retained by this Corporation and by me" (*Shrine* 31). Since the Archbishop of Canterbury historically could grant doctorates at will, the appointment is not arguable. Bourchier has put his imprimatur on Kathryn's medical training, leaving malcontents like Newington's son-in-law Matthew Darryl high and dry. Thomasina, Kathryn's housekeeper, recognizes his shrewdness when she says, "They call Bourchier a fox and rightly so. He may be an Archbishop, but I wouldn't buy a horse from him" (*Shrine* 32).

Colum Murtagh, Edward IV's special commissioner in Canterbury and its new city coroner, is an equally good judge of competence. As marshall of the royal household, soldier, king's messenger, and master of the royal stable, his very life hangs on his ability to appraise individuals and predict consequences. While he maintains a politic silence throughout most of the meeting and silently concurrs with the Archbishop's judgment (as is meet), he moves swiftly afterward to cement his alliance with Swinbrooke and her household, inviting himself to supper as the first step in this strategy.

Simon Luberon, the Archbishop's waspish principal secretary, is another canny judge of character. Little escapes his attention in sacred or secular Canterbury, where gossip travels quickly. Piqued at first by the Archbishop's decision and Kathryn's deft rejoinder to his crack that "[she] should have been born a man" (*Shrine* 30), Luberon soon grows to respect her, becoming both her partisan and her intelligencer.

As Grace's four novels to date demonstrate, Swinbrooke is no mere quasi-professional stopgap chosen for her gender. The only child of a physician-father trained at Paris' prestigious St. Cosmos School of Medicine, she has been educated to his exacting standards and is modest but truthful about her professional credentials (*Shrine* 30). Following the British practice of pupilage that continued well into the twentieth century despite strong university pressure to end it, she was then rigorously examined and licensed by the Corporation as an apothecary, leech, and physician.[4] Despite a drunken husband who has decamped to the Lancastrians leaving her in uncertain widowhood and the recent death of her beloved father, she has retained her reputation, her self-esteem, and her medical practice. She is thus a propertied woman and professional physician excellently positioned to ferret out crime.

Essentially a ratiocinative detective who resembles fellow herbalist Brother Cadfael in her calm capacity to bring murderers to justice, Swinbrooke solves her first case by linking the murderer Sir Thopas's[5] grievance against the shrine with his grandchildren's fondness for Chaucer's "Knight's Tale." Like Cadfael, Kathryn is refreshingly human, with a ready sense of humor, a keen appreciation of her limitations, a sustaining faith, and an eye for truth. Unlike that "verray parfit praktisour," Chaucer's greedy Doctor of Physik, who found gold such a cordial,[6] Swinbrooke finds homeopathic medicine more effective than horoscopes. Henceforth, she will use her God-given diagnostic skills and knowledge of *materia medica* to heal the body politic by bringing murderers to justice. According to Grace, who modeled Swinbrooke after her real-life contemporary Margaret Paston, Swinbrooke is:

industrious, composed, single-minded and committed to the world of work. . . . [a model] of propriety in an age where emotional outbursts or sexual impropriety by a woman could mean public and private disgrace.[7]

The Archbishop's and the Corporation's £60 per year retainer (*Shrine* 31) is concrete proof of how seriously the authorities regard her abilities. Since Edward IV paid Thomas Saintlegere, his "assayer of . . . gold and silver coinage," and Sir Richard Beauchamp, his "constable of Gloucester," £26, 13 shillings, 4 pence[8] and 40 marks (equivalent to £26.40)[9] respectively in 1471, even when we factor in their maintenance and other perks, Swinbrooke's compensation makes her a woman of substance.

While fifteenth-century England saw worth as primarily a function of wealth and birth, Grace, like Chaucer, measures his characters against seven more important yardsticks: these are the three theological virtues—faith, hope, and charity—and the four "natural" or "classical" virtues—prudence, temperance, courage, and justice. By the end of *A Shrine of Murders*—having risked her life to warn Colum Murtagh of danger, unmasked the poisoner, thwarted his plan to kill her, and taken in the waif who came to save her—Swinbrooke has established both her competence in apprehending murderers and the moral climate of the series.

Aiding her in this medieval comedy of manners is the male protagonist Colum Murtagh, assisted by five subordinate characters—Thomasina, Agnes, Wuf, Luberon, and Father Cuthbert—whose individual permutations on the human condition counterbalance Swinbrooke's intelligent rationality. Grace draws on his familiarity with the era—its historiography, its personalities, and its literature—to define each of these supporting characters by their demeanors, dispositions, and humors with consummate skill.

Colum Murtagh, master of the royal stables at Kingsmead and Edward IV's special commissioner of the peace in Canterbury is an Irish permutation of tested Doherty heroes like Nicholas Chirke and Hugh Corbett. He is a complex fellow: part soldier, part courtier, part would-be lover, part enigma. A black Irishman born outside the pale of Dublin c. 1433-34, he was trained as a page from about age eleven "at the manor of Gowran, a great sprawling place in the countryside near Dublin" (*Shrine* 59), where belief in supernatural evils like the Deargul was bred into him (*Shrine* 60-61). Sometime in his early teens he was recruited by the Hounds of Ulster, a native Irish brotherhood fighting English hegemony. Captured by the English at about age fifteen, he was convicted and condemned to hang others taken in the same raid. Something about the way he carried himself impressed the present king's father, Richard, Duke of York, Henry VI's viceroy in Ireland 1449-1450, who rescued him from the scaffold and made him his page (*Eye* 40). Since Murtagh left Ireland fifteen years earlier his skill with horses has won him promotion from page to royal marshal and king's messenger (*Shrine* 53). Meanwhile, the Hounds have branded him a traitor and mounted an unsuccessful vendetta to kill him. Their assassination of John Tuam, the lad pardoned with him who had become a Dominican lay brother (*Eye* 41-42), demonstrates the unreasoning fury with which the Hounds pursue Murtagh. Although he is confident he can prevail against these assassins, "who want not only [his] head but the Eye of God," the marvelous sapphire pendant modelled after the Middleham Jewel (*Eye* 197), Colum fears for Kathryn's safety when Fitzroy enters her house by a ruse to leave him a ritual warning (*Eye* 131-34).

A quiet man whose carriage, courage, and quickness with weapons mark him as the veteran of more battles than he likes to remember, Murtagh is both a peacemaker cut from the same bolt as Chaucer's knight and a man with his own ghosts. When we first meet him he is tired, saddlesore, disgusted by the bloodshed at Tewksbury, yet still doing his job. He demonstrates his admiration of Kathryn from their initial meeting, becoming her lodger and gradually her friend. As the spartan austerity of his room and refusal of the sacrament demonstrate, he is a private and conscientious man. He cannot partake because he hates the Lancastrians who killed his Welsh wife and child (*Merchant* 140-43). Like Chaucer's Knight, he is a moral exemplar true to his religion and his vows and thus an excellent parallel for Kathryn.

Thomasina, Kathryn's duenna, surrogate mother, housekeeper, confidant, and self-appointed guardian, is the most fully rounded of Grace's auxiliary characters. This tough-minded but soft-hearted romantic is a feisty permutation of Chaucer's wife of Bath with the same sanguine view of marriage. Married and widowed three times after she lost her first love to the church, she recalls each spouse with affection and would marry again if a proper candidate presented himself. Childless since her babes died young, she has mothered Kathryn since infancy, tending to her needs and all too often lecturing her for her own good. When Kathryn's philandering husband fakes suicide and joins the Lancastrians, Thomasina prescribes her own remedy: "What you need is a man," she tells Kathryn when we first meet her,

"I have known you since you were thumb-high to a buttercup, Mistress. Aye, you are married, but your husband's gone, fled to the wars, and the ugly bastard won't be back. . . . You need a man. A woman is not happy unless she has got a man between her thighs. I should know." (*Shrine* 9)

When Kathryn accepts Colum Murtagh as her lodger and colleague, Thomasina is faced with a dilemma. This battle-hardened Irishman is both the exact remedy she's prescribed and a potential threat to Kathryn's reputation. When she learns that a blackmailer has accused Kathryn of murdering her husband Alexander Wyville, Thomasina takes immediate action, catching the culprit and reminding her what will happen if the threats continue (*Shrine* 171-76). Besides enhancing her self-esteem, Thomasina's success as a detective prefaces a more important awareness as time passes: Colum is not the predatory male she took him to be; instead, he's in love with Kathryn and a staunch ally whose moral code sorts with Thomasina's own. As the mysteries unfold, her intrinsic loyalty, unsolicited commentary, and verbal sparring reinforce her role as the series' resident dragon, revealing her reservoir of strengths, and adding markedly to the comedy.

While Thomasina functions as Kathryn's surrogate mother in the domestic comedy that undergirds the mysteries, Agnes and Wuf complete the family unit as Kathryn's, and Thomasina's, surrogate children. Agnes, now a teenager, was brought home by Kathryn's soft-hearted physician father after her parents died and placed in Thomasina's care. When Agnes develops a crush on Wormhair, Father Cuthbert's altar boy, Kathryn makes it clear she regards her not as a servant but as a younger sister. What is Kathryn's is her family's; Agnes will have the best dowry and wedding they can afford. Wuf is a more recent addition to the family. A "very thin, very small, and very hungry . . . [and] very brave" waif "with only vague memories of a mother and then a life of scavenging like a puppy amongst the rubbish of different camps" (*Shrine* 192-93), he comes to her aid when the murderer springs a trap to kill her and quickly wins a place in her heart. Later, in *The Merchant of Death* (143), Kathryn's chance observation of her clever adopted son at play shows her the ruse the murderer used to drown Vavasour.

Simon Luberon, the Cardinal Archbishop's multifaceted principal secretary, and Father Cuthbert, priest of St. Mildred's Church and infirmarian of St. Mary's hospital for aged priests, are stock ecclesiastical characters. Luberon, the diminutive elderly chauvinist who exemplifies the bureaucratic role of the church, is the consummate fussy official grown plump in its service. Persnickety at the outset, he thaws under Kathryn's influence, becoming her point man as well as her official liaison with the city and the archdiocese. Although he is clearly celibate and almost certainly in minor orders for the legal protection and comfort it affords, he begins to appreciate the advantages of marriage as the series progresses, becoming a more sympathetic character as he pictures life with a woman like Kathryn. Like Chaucer's poor parson, who was "riche . . . of holy thought and werk[,] . . . [b]enigne, wonder diligent, and in adversitee ful pacient[,]"[10] Father Cuthbert is a "leech of souls" who exemplifies the pastoral role of the church. Whereas Chaucer's Friar might disclose the secrets of the confessional, wink at adultery, and devise a pleasant penance, Cuthbert like his namesake takes the cure of souls far more seriously. Aware that Kathryn loves Colum and that the Irishman regularly refuses the Eucharist, Cuthbert investigates Colum's background and confronts him with it, probing until he lays bare the hate festering inside him (*Merchant* 140-42). When the questioning ends, Colum can grieve openly for his dead wife and son, while he and Kathryn contemplate the future.

Having set the standards by which Kathryn and her associates measure their actions, Grace immerses readers in the day-to-day sights and smells of medieval living and leaves it to us to judge where others' conduct falls short of their example. This is particularly true in *The Eye of God* and *The Merchant of Death*, which turn on issues of trust and trickery.

In *The Eye of God*, set after the Battle of Barnet, a fifteenth-century sapphire pendant based upon the real "Middleham Jewel" (197) serves as an objective correlative. Like the gold in the "Pardoner's Tale," it is both a magnet for the greedy and a symbol of perfidy. Consigned by the dying Earl of Warwick to his squire Brandon with orders to take it "to the Monks at Canterbury [as m]y last gift" (7), it will doom four loyal men to lingering deaths in an abandoned crypt and drown a royal traitor in a vat of Malmsey. Here, an increasingly confident Kathryn is caught up in Court intrigue when she and Colum go to London to confer with Edward IV and his brother Richard of Gloucester. While Grace studiously avoids ideological overtones in these mysteries, by and large letting the historical record speak for itself, he portrays the future Richard III as a much more attractive character than the deformed monster Tudor propagandists made him out to be. Summoned to Canterbury Castle to solve a suspicious suicide (80-81), Kathryn gets a closer view of Murtagh's world as she encounters a "Righteous Man" masquerading as a pardoner, who himself being pardoned makes an important prophecy (192-94). Here also, as two corpse collectors set up a "plague" scam to kill two old ladies for their property (62-65, 105-10), Kathryn demonstrates that lethal trickery is not confined to the mighty.

*The Merchant of Death*, set in the winter of 1471, when Edward IV's victory was a *fait accompli*, turns on two new permutations of trickery: adultery and embezzlement. The first, a seemingly simple play on Chaucer's "Miller's Tale" with its May and December marriage, involves the murder of Richard Blunt's young wife Alisoun and her two young gallants Nicholas and Absolom. The second, a more complex intrigue reminiscent of Agatha Christie's *Murder on the Orient Express* (1934), calls Kathryn to the Wicker Man, where the King's tax collector Sir Reginald Erpingham, has been murdered and the Crown's revenue stolen. As the two plots unfold and Erpingham's avaricious clerk Eudo Vavasour is lured to his death in a freezing pond, Kathryn needs more than her forensic skills to find the murderers, reveal their motives, and see justice done.

Grace's fourth novel in the series, *The Book of Shadows*, deals with the black arts. In this darkest and most dangerous of her adventures thus far, Kathryn encounters political intrigue at the highest levels, necromancy, blackmail, and a classic locked room mystery, as well as common spell-casting which lands an eccentric old woman on trial for her life. It is based "loosely"[11] on Eleanor Cobham's and Oxford scholar Roger Bolingbroke's 1441 trials for using sorcery to predict Henry VI's death.[12] This tale arrays Elizabeth Woodville, Edward IV's "Ice Queen," against a guild of shrewd London merchants for control of a murdered magus's book of secrets. The Queen has excellent reasons for concern: besides intelligence of her infidelities with underlings, Tenebrae's "grimoire" contains evidence that Woodville's marriage to Edward is bigamous and thus that her sons by him are illegitimate. Medicine, magic, murder, madness, and the macabre converge in this grim tale as Kathryn catches a killer to save a self-proclaimed witch from burning, solves the locked room murder, is commanded to raise the decaying sorcerer from the dead, and races to prevent the devious Queen from revenging herself on Colum.

Grace plays fair with readers throughout the series, avoiding ideologies, anachronisms and red herrings. True to the historiography of the period, he portrays fifteenth-century Canterbury life with all its warts and occasional glory. As a result, we come away appreciating that while sanitation and medicine have improved somewhat since 1471, human nature remains virtually unchanged. As Chaucer intended in his *Canterbury Tales*, all of us are part of this human comedy and meant to recognize our fellows in the company.

## Notes

1. See Kate Campbell Hurd-Mead, "The Medical Women of the Fifteenth Century," *A History of Women in Medicine* (Haddam, CT: Haddam P, 1938), 291-312; and Monica Green, "Women's Medical Practice and Health Care in Medieval Europe," *Signs: Journal of Women in Culture and Society* 14 (1989): 434-72.

2. The editions of the four novels discussed in this essay are listed below in order of publication and all quotations from them cited parenthetically in the text: *A Shrine of Murders*, New York: St. Martin's P, 1993; *The Eye of God*, New York: St. Martin's P, 1994; *The Merchant of Death*, New York: St. Martin's P, 1995; *The Book of Shadows*, New York: St. Martin's P, 1995.

3. For this relationship, see the *Calendar of Close Rolls, Edward IV,* 2: 227, item 852.

4. Despite the best efforts of the universities and medical guilds in the larger cities to end the practice, medical pupilage during which students walked the hospital wards as apprentices to licensed physicians continued in England until the 1920s.

5. "Sir Thopas" is the pilgrim name Chaucer chose for his persona in *The Canterbury Tales.*

6. "The General Prologue," ll. 413-445.

7. See "Author's Note," *The Merchant of Death*, 181.

8. See *Calendar of Close Rolls, Edward IV*, 2: 185, item 693.

9. See *Calendar of Close Rolls, Edward IV*, 2: 185, item 690. According to "The Pardoner's Prologue," in *The Canterbury Tales*, ll, 101-02, nearly a hundred years earlier Chaucer's Pardoner bragged of clearing 100 marks—slightly over £67—a year.

10. Geoffrey Chaucer, "The General Prologue," *The Canterbury Tales*, 11, 480-81.

11. See Grace's "Author's Note" following page 195, which indicates he has modeled Tenebrae "loosely on Bolingbroke, the great necromancer of fifteenth century England."

12. See E. F. Jacob, *The Fifteenth Century: 1399-1485* (Oxford: Clarendon P, 1961), 484-86. Bolingbroke was tortured into admitting he and others had used sorcery to help Eleanor, wife of Humphrey, Duke of Gloucester, divine the future. He was convicted of treason, drawn, and quartered. She was sentenced to penance followed by life imprisonment.

### Works Cited

Chaucer, Geoffrey. "The General Prologue." *The Canterbury Tales*. 2nd ed. Ed. Helen Cooper. Oxford: Oxford UP, 1996.

Grace, C. L. (P. C. Doherty). *The Book of Shadows*. New York: St. Martin's P, 1995.

——. *The Eye of God*. New York: St. Martin's P, 1994.

——. *The Merchant of Death*. New York: St. Martin's P, 1995.

——. *A Shrine of Murders*. New York: St. Martin's P, 1993.

Great Britain. Public Record Office. *Calendar of Close Rolls, Edward IV*: 2: 185, 690.

Green, Monica. "Women's Medical Practicce and Health Care in Medieval Europe." *Signs: Journal of Women in Culture and Society* 14 (1989): 434-72.

Hurd-Mead, Kate Campbell. "The Medical Women of the Fifteenth Century." *A History of Women in Medicine*. Haddam, CT: Haddam P, 1938.

Jacob, E. F. *The Fifteenth Century: 1399-1485*. Oxford: Clarendon P, 1961.

# Michael Clynes:
# The Recollections of Shallot

## David N. Eldridge, Theron M. Westervelt, Edward L. Meek

*The door swings open, the ghosts beckon me back along the gallery of time, back to London when Henry and Wolsey had the kingdom in the grip of their avaricious fingers. Oh yes, back to subtle ploys and clever plans! To treason, murder and death by a thousand stings. I open the door and Murder, evil-faced and bloody-handed, stands waiting to greet me.*
$\qquad$—Michael Clynes (*A Brood of Vipers* 6)

As revealed by the melodramatic note of dark foreboding with which Sir Roger Shallot reaches back into his past, the six volumes of his 'memoirs' published to date are no ordinary detective mysteries. Rather, they are nightmares. Through the recollections of Shallot—a sixteenth-century rogue made good—author Michael Clynes draws the reader into an England teetering on the brink of the Henrican Reformation, where murder is only a precursor to the terrible bloodshed associated with Henry VIII's divorce. Almost every death is intimately tied to the "subtle ploys," intrigues, and rivalries of the Renaissance courts of Europe. You do not normally read a detective story set some four hundred years ago and expect the assassination of John F. Kennedy or the Watergate scandal to come to mind, but this is precisely the response which Michael Clynes provokes. Quite simply, he is to the sixteenth century what Oliver Stone is to Cold War America: a true advocate of the conspiracy school of history.

Shallot is drawn into the conspiratorial machinations of Henry VIII through his friendship with Benjamin Daunbey. As the nephew of Henry's chancellor, Lord Cardinal Thomas Wolsey, it is Daunbey who is the real sleuth in the mysteries. He combines an interest in history, archaeology, logic, and pedagogy, with a quiet, chivalrous demeanour that hides his true intensity of feeling. In comparison, Shallot is "a veritable rogue, born and bred," with coarse desires and crude intellect, but possessing quick wit, street-wise knowledge, and a heightened sense of self-preservation, all of which serve him well in the adventures he faces (*Gallows* 49). From the first novel, *The White Rose Murders* (1991), set in 1521 at the court of Henry VIII's sister, Margaret Tudor, Shallot and Daunbey demonstrate both their ability to reveal the murderers and to uncover corruption at the highest levels. They also reveal their sense of discretion, which is called for when it appears that the king's sister may have murdered her husband, James IV of

Scotland! These skills ensure that the duo are, at least for the next two years, regularly employed as special envoys and investigators by king and cardinal.

Regarded on the level of detective fiction, Clynes's books tend to be rather contrived and formulaic, heavily reliant on variations of locked-room mysteries. Daunbey and Shallot wend their way through numerous red herrings, with supposedly enigmatic riddles to unravel, and people being inconveniently killed just as they are about to reveal key information. As is traditional in such plots, the murderers and conspirators are eventually unmasked from a line-up of suspects—although locations such as the Tower of London and the English embassy in Maubisson are substituted for the Edwardian drawing room. These formulaic elements are particularly noticeable when the Shallot memoirs are read in conjunction with the other books written by the prolific Paul Doherty—for whom Michael Clynes is one of many *noms-de-plume*.[1] However, as the author notes, "murder in medieval times lends itself to the classic style of detective story." "You don't have police procedures, you don't have pathology. The detective has to solve the murder or the mystery by the application of logic and observation alone" (Rennison 46). Clynes points to Conan Doyle's Sherlock Holmes stories as a major influence in his conception of detective fiction, and the "locked-room" mystery certainly lends itself to such deductive reasoning—Clynes considers the form to be the "ultimate puzzle for the detective writer."[2] And, in fairness, when it comes to choosing a method of murder his inventiveness has developed as the series of books has progressed. *The Gallows Murders* (1995), for example, features four royal executioners, each being "killed in a way prescribed by law for certain felons" by the means with which they themselves carried out "judicial murder" (59). Clynes plays upon the assured vague knowledge of readers about the period, and in *A Brood of Vipers* (1994), he sets up the murder of a Florentine envoy to Henry's court, so that it looks as if a new type of handgun must have been used. And in his most recent tale, *The Relic Murders* (1996), he stages the most extravagant of "locked-room" murders, in which fifteen armed soldiers are all brutally killed one night in an impregnable manor house. If somewhat lacking in literary flair, it is Clynes's historical imagination that sets these books apart.

This imagination was highlighted in an article for *Overseas* in 1989, entitled "History: Fact or Fiction," in which the author lamented the fact that "stories are transmitted from one generation to another which gloss over alternative interpretations or possibilities":

School children are often told how King Harold died at the Battle of Hastings—an arrow through his eye—but the possibility that the King may have only been wounded and escaped to live out his life as a hermit is rejected or ignored. Only occasionally do other interpretations surface in the history books.

Clynes goes on to detail over a dozen other "historical possibilities" from the reality of Count Dracula, to Edward II's survival and escape to Italy, from the standard question of whether the two young princes were murdered in the Tower by Richard III, to whether Elizabeth I was truly a "Virgin Queen," or if a man claiming to be her illegitimate son should actually have been believed. The issue of the Princes in the Tower framed the plot of *The Gallows Murders* (as Henry VIII begins to fear that Edward V may still be alive), and Shallot himself claims that it was his seduction of Queen Elizabeth ("no more a virgin than I am") which resulted in a bastard son (*White* 4). This interest in "possibilities" stemmed from Clynes's dissatisfaction with conventional historical practice—which he became aware of when writing his own doctoral thesis on Queen Isabella, the adulterous wife of Edward II. "When you write a thesis you have, of course, to base yourself in sound empirical evidence. But in history you get the 'what if . . .'— and that is what's possible, or logical, but you haven't got the proof" (Interview 1).

This kind of speculation, based on hints and rumours reported in contemporary sources—such as chronicle accounts and histories, the collected letters and papers of Henry VIII's court, coroner's reports, etc.—provides the element of fact from which Clynes's fiction develops. Each investigation by Daunbey and Shallot is commissioned by Wolsey—often acting through his mystical soothsayer, Dr. Agrippa—and begins either with murder, or with a threat to the king. In the cases that initially appear to be standard murder mysteries, the deaths soon mount up and point to conspiracies of much broader conception. *The Poisoned Chalice* (1992) features the mysterious deaths of members of the English embassy in Paris, political assassinations which are the work of a spy in the pay of the French secret service, and the ultimate result of the torrid sexual politics of the French and English courts. In *The Grail Murders* (1993), members of the *Agentes in Rebus* (Wolsey's personal secret service) are killed one by one, murders that form a pattern of revenge for the execution of Edward Stafford, Duke of Buckingham. The death of Lord Abrizzi, the envoy from Florence in *A Brood of Vipers* (1994), is only the beginning of an escalating blood feud which Daunbey discovers has been deliberately provoked by Cardinal Guilo de Medici—on the eve of his becoming Pope Clement VII in 1523—in order to wipe out his rivals for control of the city:

Cardinal Guilo plots to murder the present Holy Father. Secretly, mysteriously, Adrian will die. There will be a conclave of cardinals. England will back Guilo de' Medici's elevation to the papacy but . . . our good cardinal in Florence does not want to leave for Rome knowing the likes of the Albrizzis might make their bid for power. (241)

Complicating the issues further, Shallot and Daunbey are frequently only pawns in the political schemes of Henry and Wolsey. Henry's Machiavellian sensibilities are illustrated in *The Relic Murders*, in which the deaths of almost twenty men result from the theft of a sacred relic—the Orb of Charlemagne—which occurs just as Henry is due to return it to the Emperor Charles V to seal an alliance against France. The murders and the theft were committed by Lord Egremont, a rogue emissary of Charles, but the sleuths discover that the stolen Orb is actually only a fake:

A replica Orb would be handed over to the Lord Egremont made out of genuine gold with precious stones. The work of a cunning goldsmith, it might be years, if ever, before the Emperor realised he had been fooled . . . Like a trader in a market, Henry had raised interest in the Orb, so why not satisfy it? (224)

Other replicas were therefore surreptitiously sold to the French and the Papal envoys. Henry's publicly stated aims of wanting to win back English lands in France and "outdo the feats of Henry V" were merely a cover; the real aim was to create an opportunity to replenish the royal coffers. Wolsey, however, is an even more inveterate schemer, a depiction that chimes with the claim of court historian Polydore Vergil, that "Henry did not share in all Wolsey's projects, but only in those which turned out well" (Hay 263). According to Clynes, the Cardinal's "one great nightmare" was "how to control the king" and keep his own position secure (*Grail* 11). Accordingly, Wolsey is revealed to be party to Guilo de Medici's plot, backing his elevation to the papacy in return for his agreement, when Pope, to support the annulment of Henry's marriage to Catherine of Aragon. Wolsey's desperation to secure the divorce and keep the king's favor is well known—and Henry's need to destroy evidence that could threaten his case against Catherine forms a subplot in *The Poisoned Chalice*. But taking this conspiracy even further, Clynes suggests that Wolsey has a hold over Henry—they were both party to the poisoning of Henry VII. As Wolsey has revealed this to Medici, all three are bound together in a murderous pact.

Apparent challenges to Henry VIII's security on the throne of England form the opening gambits of both *The White Rose Murders* (1991) and *The Gallows Murders*. In the former, Yorkist conspirators deny the validity of the Tudor dynasty's claim to the crown, murdering members of Margaret Tudor's retinue, leaving the white rose of the House of York at the scenes of the crime; Edward V (one of the princes supposedly murdered in the Tower) returned from the grave and demanding tribute from Henry, in the latter. *The Grail Murders* also presents an insecure Henry, suggesting that the king had lashed out against the Duke of Buckingham in 1522, because he feared that Stafford had "a better claim than he to the throne" (*Grail* 22). But as with the cases of murder, these plots against the crown are only surface ripples of even deeper currents. Buckingham's plotting against the king—crucial to the actual charges of treason brought against him—becomes, in Clynes' imagination, entangled with a secret order of the Templar Knights, with the duke being set up in order to preserve the secret. The proclamations issued under the name of King Edward V are only one part of a murderous revenge taken on the royal executioners. And the Yorkist plot against Queen Margaret is simply a cover for the most complex conspiracy. The White Rose murders are the work of Margaret's own clerk, trying to disguise his assassinations of those in the Queen's company whom she can no longer trust to keep her murderous and adulterous secrets. Furthermore, this intrigue turns out to be all part of Henry VIII's own plans to control Scotland—plotting with his sister to ensure that James IV is brought down, thus dividing the nation so that it poses no threat to Henry's dreams of achieving power in Europe. And again, Wolsey, using Daunbey and Shallot to confirm his suspicions, is in a position to use the information to achieve a firmer grip on the King.

By establishing this dark, conspiratorial era, the author challenges the established history of "progress" under the Tudors. It is a Catholic account of a period that used to be most frequently written about from a Protestant perspective, reflecting Clynes's personal religious beliefs—he trained to become a priest, and is now the headmaster of a Catholic school. In *The Brood of Vipers*, he acknowledges that the Papacy had been "dragged through the mire by men like Rodrigo Borgia" and the Church "needed cleansing"—but finds this insufficient justification for Lutheranism (Shallot claims that Martin Luther's state of mind was a side-effect of extreme constipation) and a miserable pretext for Henry VIII's actions (78). Many of those whom Henry executed—notably Thomas More and John Fisher—are, of course, martyred saints of the Catholic Church, and Shallot pointedly shares their faith: "Secretly I miss the Mass, the priest offering the bread and wine, the smell of incense. I have a secret chapel built into the thick walls of my great hall" (*White* 5). The journeys which Daunbey and Shallot undertake also provide Clynes with an opportunity to lament the glories of the Church which were lost during the English Reformation, from the destruction of the monasteries at the hands of Henry, to the damage inflicted on St Paul's Cathedral by Protector Somerset's iconoclastic wrath. It is something that Clynes feels strongly about:

Roy Strong claimed that Henry VIII did more damage to our cultural heritage than the combined might of the Luftwaffe in the Second World War. And you go to these places and see their beautiful architecture—wiped out. True jewels disappeared—Hailes Abbey, Glastonbury, Fountains, Rieveaulx—all destroyed. (Interview 8)

The self-serving way in which Henry VIII denied papal authority in England and opened the way to the destruction of the Catholic Church is in itself enough to explain the bitter hostility toward Henry VIII that Clynes offloads onto Shallot.[3] But the characterization of Henry is augmented by a particularly regional bias. This stems from Clynes' upbringing in Yorkshire, where the great revolt against the "reforms" of Church and state took place in 1536. As Clynes acknowledges, the memory of the Pilgrimage of Grace "still lingers there—it's in the folklore" (Interview 8). And this folklore is exactly what he preserves in Shallot's memoirs. Henry is referred to, from the very beginning, as "The Mouldwarp"—as the seer Agrippa warns Shallot and Daunbey:

They say King Henry is the Dark One, he is the Mouldwarp, the Prince of Darkness foretold by Merlin, the great wizard of King Arthur's court. According to his prophecies, the king of the twelfth generation after John will be the Mouldwarp, a hairy man whose skin will be as thick as a goat's. At first he will be greatly praised by his people, before sinking down into the dark pit of sin and pride. He is condemned by God to end his reign in gore and destruction. We are the twelfth generation after John and Henry is our King. We see him now as a golden sun but what will happen to him as the day dies and the sun begins to set? (White 119)

Although this is a reasonable paraphrase of the prophecy that appears in Geoffrey of Monmouth's twelfth-century *History of the Kings of Britain*, its application is deliberately distorted. Not only was Henry VIII the *tenth* generation after John, but the prophecy's proper title was that of "The Prophecy of the Six Kings to follow John," with the Mouldwarp associated with Henry IV (indeed, the "moldwarp" is referred to in Shakespeare's *Henry IV*).[4] But because it had been used by the Percy family of Northumberland in their rising against Henry IV, the prophecy retained particular currency in the north of England. The rebel leaders of the Pilgrimage of Grace—which included a number of retainers of the Percies—"found it more than tempting to make Henry VIII the Mouldwarp in place of Henry IV, and otherwise to elaborate the story in consonance with the facts of their time" (Dickens 128).

If it was a false allegation then (as Wilfred Holme sought to demonstrate in 1537), it is likewise misapplied by Clynes, who took the propagandist tradition of his region and projected it back to 1521.[5] But in playing with history so that political propaganda takes on the mystical authority of a prophecy reaching fulfilment, Clynes is able to condemn Henry for becoming the monster he was "destined" to be. Shallot, forced to undertake the dangerous missions or suffer the wrath of the king (which, in *The Gallows Murders*, includes being the "fox" on a royal hunt), is ready to reflect on the emerging dark side of Henry:

So far he had not shown, except to me, that cruel streak of venomous temper which would drench his kingdom in rivers of blood: that was still a few years off. Henry was more concerned about his pleasures. He wanted to be a great wrestler, the keenest of archers, the best dancer, the most ferocious jouster. Henry believed he was a fairy-tale prince, and those who danced with him little suspected that the nightmare would soon begin. By 1523, the worms were eating their way into the marrow of his soul.[9]

It is because these novels are purportedly the memoirs of Roger Shallot that Clynes is able to introduce such extreme subjectivity, yet make it seem almost authoritative. They not only carry the imprint of a first-hand account of the "way it was," but, as Shallot is supposed to be dictating his stories some sixty years after the events, he also has some sense of perspective and distance from Henry's reign, which the reader partially shares. Moreover, this form is ideal for Clynes's type of speculative history, allowing a little manipulation of the facts and the dates with the proviso that Shallot's memory may be playing tricks, and that perhaps his accounts may not be entirely truthful. This sense of doubt is built up through the numerous "tall stories" that Shallot relates: playing bowls with Francis Drake; having a son by Elizabeth I; finding an entire murdered harem at the bottom of the Bosphorus while trying to escape from the Sultan. His frequent asides regarding the different lines and plots he has suggested to William Shakespeare also seem far-fetched and egotistical:

Everything I know about Italy, and Florence in particular, I have told to Will. Read his plays and you will see what I mean. I have met Duke Orsini from *Twelfth Night* and been introduced to two gentlemen of Verona. I witnessed the tragedy of the star-crossed lovers, Romeo and Juliet . . . And the Jew Shylock was one of the most generous-hearted men I have ever met. I was angry with Will when I saw how he had described him. (*Brood* 100)

Shallot is the "hungry, lean-faced villain, a mountebank and threadbare juggler" of Shakespeare's *Comedy of Errors*, and Clynes acknowledges that "you're never too sure whether Shallot's telling the truth, or whether he's making it up." Reflecting his opinion of Henry VIII, the author revels in the irony of Shallot being "a liar working for a liar" (Interview 8). Trained historians are used to treating memoirs with a good degree of scepticism and would rarely rely on them without corroboration from other sources. Thus, as a literary form, memoirs provide an eminently suitable vehicle for the "what ifs" of history that Clynes explores—apparently encouraging the reader to think about the possibilities, but not to take them too seriously.

However, the chosen style of detective fiction makes things problematic. The "rules" of writing unconventional heroes—as epitomised in Raymond Chandler's novels—means that, however much a rogue or coward Shallot may be, his integrity is ultimately maintained in contrast to the characters of the killers and the villains. Integrity is what binds Shallot to Daunbey, and it is a characteristic necessary to reassure the reader that order will be restored in the end and justice will be done. Yet it also undermines the readers' ability to think that Shallot may be making things up. He may invent the little asides, but the reliability of his larger narrative is never really opened to question. The "Author's Notes," which Clynes appends to his novels to point to the historical "evidence" which supports his case, closes it off further. Each book assures the reader that while "Sir Roger can be economical with the facts," "there is a great deal of truth in these memoirs" (*Grail* 243). Notably, this is a very similar approach to that taken by George MacDonald Fraser in his "editing" of the fictional Flashman papers—likewise purportedly written by a rakish braggart in his late eighties, with a penchant for reminiscing about past sexual conquests. In the foreword to the first volume, Fraser wrote that: "I have no reason to doubt that it is a completely truthful account; where Flashman touches on historical fact he is almost invariably accurate, and readers can judge whether he is to be believed or not" (9).

This division between personal and public history informs the presentation of Shallot's recollections. Clynes's notes (which are sparse in comparison to those given by Fraser, or by mystery writers such as Candace Robb or Susannah Gregory) inform the reader that elements of the novels, such as the survival of secret Templar societies or the use of poisôns in the French court, are "well-documented facts" or that his plots, notably Margaret Tudor's plans for James IV, "can be corroborated by historical fact." Other issues about which the reader may have doubts are dismissed in the text; the chaplain to whom Shallot dictates his memoirs frequently expresses his disbelief, only to receive a sharp rebuke and a snippet of evidence that is supposed to prove the veracity of what Shallot is saying. In short, while offering one interpretation, Clynes forecloses the consideration of other possible interpretations. In contrast, Fraser provides extensive footnotes that not only contain supporting evidence but also acknowledges that first-person narrative form presents difficulties in producing a personal perspective that may preclude a balanced or fuller perspective on history.[6]

This is not to say that Clynes can often be accused of getting his history wrong. He makes comparatively few noticeable mistakes. Confusing the de la Pole family with the Poles, as he does in *The Gallows Murders* (55), is sloppy but understandable; consistently referring to Margaret Tudor's second husband, the earl of Angus, as Gavin rather than Archibald is rather more surprising (*White* vii, 29, 243); and occasionally his claims about dynastic relationships—which *are* important in the context of his conspiracies—are carelessly in error (*Chalice* 111). Geoffrey Elton may have disagreed with the secret service agents, particularly the *Agentes in Rebus*, which populate the novels (he dismissed Roger Merriman's claim that Thomas Cromwell had established a system of espionage as "a figment of the hostile historian's imagination") but given the development of such a system in Elizabethan England they seem to be a plausible fiction (329). And Clynes's depictions of surroundings, cities and buildings, engender a feel of authenticity that strengthens the books. Descriptions of London, Leeds, the abbey of Glastonbury, or sixteenth-century Florence are brought to life from a combination of personal visits to the actual locations and information contained both in current day guide books and in contemporary accounts and letters.

Clynes's sense of the courtly style of Renaissance Europe is also well defined. The combination of life-threatening danger and erotic sensuality at the court of Francis I is deftly painted and owes a great deal to the tales of the French monarch's sexual profligacy, which are presented by Pierre de Bourdeille, seigneur de Brantôme, in *Lives of Fair and Gallant Ladies*, based on his grandmother's personal recollections. Brantôme's account of the vicious intrigues provoked by sexual jealousy and the danger of venereal disease is reflected in the motives of the killer in *The Poisoned Chalice*. In the English court, the entertainments are less erotic than bawdy and boisterous, and the emphasis is on the pageantry and revels which Shallot witnesses—and is forced to take part in. These are straight out of Edward Hall's *Triumphant Reigne of Henry VIII* or George Cavendish's *Life of Cardinal Wolsey*, and the descriptions of Henry's love of opulent masques and mummery that Clynes provides are certainly well documented. In fact, while at Richmond in *The Grail Murders*, Shallot witnesses the masterpiece created by Henry's devisor of masques, William Cornish: the siege of "Chateau Vert" in which a fortress was constructed to imprison eight noble women, bearing allegorical names such as Beauty, Constance, and Mercy, who were then rescued by the king and his companions, storming the castle against characters such as Disdain, Jealousy, and Scorn, played by the Children of the Royal Chapel (*Grail* 51, Loades 107). Henry's pleasure in disguising himself—particularly as Robin Hood—is also from the history books, and the descriptions of the way in which the court would be decorated with silks and banners matches those found in Hall's chronicle.[7]

Beyond the court, Clynes generally displays a good sense of the period when referring to the tensions in the wider English society: the petty feuds between families in small towns, as in Ispwich where Daunbey and Shallot normally reside; the abuse of the law by the rich; and the social cohesion that the church provided. Clynes also draws upon Thomas More's *Utopia* in a passage in which Daunbey remarks on the growing unrest among the poor, thrown off their land to make way for sheep farming (Brood 17). According to the author: "Shallot represents the beginning of the sixteenth century. People don't really believe in the Church as they would have done, say, in the 1420s. There's a growing cynicism. And they're not too sure about the king either" (Interview).

The gullibility of the English, on which the Imperial Ambassador Eustace Chapuys had occasion to remark, is another recurring feature. Clynes proves to be well versed in the tricks of the trade of quack doctors and fraudulent relic sellers—the former in *The Gallows Murders*, the latter in both *The Grail Murders* and *The Relic Murders*.[8] He has also undertaken considerable research on the nature of petty crime in the period and the punishments which such crimes received—which provides contrast to the more fundamental crimes of grisly murder, generally committed by the high-born classes.

However, Clynes does not draw attention to the sources he uses to find such information—the London letters (forms of coroners' reports), the letters and papers of the court, reports by ambassadors, contemporary chronicles, calendar rolls, and such like (which is something Doherty emphasises when writing the Hugh Corbett mysteries). Unfortunately the sources that Clynes chooses to recommend to his readers do little justice to the research and study he has undertaken. Unlike Candace Robb, who provides a select bibliography of texts for anyone interested in reading about the topics discussed in her novels, Clynes only mentions three texts over the course of Shallot's six memoirs: Carolly Erickson's *Great Harry*, Graham Hancock's *The Sign and the Seal*, and *The Mystery of the Princes* by Audrey Williamson. Of these, Erickson (who, for unknown reasons, is mistakenly credited as Caroline Seymour in the notes for *The White Rose Murders*) is perhaps the most traditional. Evidently, Erickson grabbed Clynes's attention by treating the Mouldwarp legend as a serious indicator of public perception of Henry, rather than as simply political propaganda (264-65). But *Great Harry* has additional value, as a self-proclaimed "popular history," a biography of Henry VIII in the form of a "personal story" that "makes no attempt to arrive at a fresh assessment of the reign, nor to detail the political accomplishments of Henry" (14). As such, it is informal with an eye for good stories, rumours, and gossip—mainly drawn together from the letters and dispatches sent home by the ambassadors from Spain, Venice, and Milan—making it ideal for a fiction author who needs such personal and first-hand observations to put into the mouths of his characters.

The books by Hancock and Williamson are a different matter. Williamson's book is an investigation of Richard III's responsibility for the supposed murder of the princes, part of the move to challenge the public image of the "evil king" which the Richard III Society has long undertaken. It is, however, one of the most ill-judged attempts to exonerate the Yorkist usurper, with a poor understanding of the realities of politics and government during the Wars of the Roses. It is revealing that Clynes should recommend this work to support his case in *The Gallows Murders*, rather than A. J. Pollard's *Richard III and the Princes in the Tower,* which treats Richard generously while still retaining academic credibility. Graham Hancock's work, as the full title *The Sign and the Seal: A Quest for the Lost Ark of the Covenant* suggests, is no history book, but an account of his research and efforts to discover whether, as according to legend, the Ark of the Covenant could really be found in Ethiopia. This touches on Clynes writing in *The Grail Murders*, when Hancock suggests that the Templar knights had discovered the true location of the Ark when they had occupied the site of the Temple of Solomon in Jerusalem during the Crusades in 1119. The Duke of Buckingham's hunt for the Holy Grail at Glastonbury represents a similar "Templar quest" to the one Hancock believes they undertook for the Ark. But Hancock does not provide a great deal of documentary evidence to demonstrate "the well-documented fact" of the survival of a secret Templar Order, which Clynes suggests is in his book. Hancock's claim that "close links existed between the Templars and the Freemasons, with the latter almost certainly descended from the former," is based on statements made by German and English Freemason historians in the eighteenth century (333). Again, a more "academic," less personal, account of how the Templars went underground after persecution in the fourteenth century—as in Malcolm Barber's *The Trial of the Templars*—could have been recommended. But there is a particular affinity between the Shallot novels and the books that Clynes recommends. As with Clynes's own conspiracies, Williamson and Hancock make cases which rely on highly conjectural readings of circumstantial evidence—which other historians have dismissed—making leaps of faith (in the innocence of Richard III or the existence of the Ark) that other historians would avoid.

That none of these sources are held in serious regard in academic circles is something that would please Clynes. In proposing conjectural and conspiracy theories of history, Clynes sees his work as an alternative to academic history. It is his opinion that what we term "historical truth" is in fact only the product of consensus among historians, and that this consensus is preserved because academics fear that, in questioning it, they would incur the mocking of their peers:

I'm just fascinated by the way professional historians steer away from *anything* which could ruin their reputation. As in Egyptology now, you now and again get people suggesting that there are secret libraries beneath the Pyramids, and such like; and some historians say, "I won't touch that—if I do, people will laugh at me." (Interview 5)

This is an outdated view of the academic community. He fails to take into account the debates over the nature of historical truth which Hayden White and Michael Foucault have provoked, or issues of historical consciousness and public memory which suggest that notions of "truth" may be formed outside of the academy. Quite probably this was a view which was prevalent in the 1970s Oxbridge community in which Clynes was schooled, and against which he is reacting.

If the question of "truth" was left up for grabs, then the novels could be regarded in the light of post-modern commentaries on historical knowledge. But because these conjectural readings of history are presented as fact, the books become very problematic from a historian's perspective. The author admits to "teasing" academics at the same time as entertaining his general audience and, in the end, you cannot help but feel that the Shallot memoirs are something of a game to Clynes (Interview 6). They are certainly not treated with the same seriousness that Doherty applies to his Hugh Corbett novels. Rather, they seem to have been conceived as an opportunity for the author to create his own "Flashman"—who can get away with lampooning Henry VIII and making comments for which contemporaries would have been executed. The Tudor imagery that Henry and his family sought to create through patronage of Holbein and Shakespeare and others is shattered when Shallot discusses the king's impotence, his genitalia ("rather small like a little pig"), or his love of cross-dressing, all apparently in the spirit of gossipy fun. His caustic comments on Henry's love of masks and mummery allow him to accuse the monarch of childishness, while also acting as his commentary on Henry's deceptive nature and his betrayal of friends like More. Clynes clearly relishes the opportunity that fiction allows him, to say exactly what he's always wanted to say about "The Great Beast" and the changes he wrought on England. As well as entertaining his readers, it is an opportunity to redress the balance as he sees it, to show them "another reality" (Interview 5). Yet these books are not representations of reality, they are works of fiction—and Clynes tends to erase the distinction. He accuses Henry VIII of being the "great illusionist," but it is a charge that could equally be made against Michael Clynes himself.

*Notes*

1. Paul Doherty has written numerous works as P. C. Doherty, most notably the series of Hugh Corbett murder mysteries, along with books such as *The Haunting* (a Victorian ghost story), *The Rose Demon* (a Tudor epic), and a number of additions to the "Canterbury Tales." He has also written the series of "sorrowful mysteries" featuring Brother Aethelstan, under the name of Paul Harding, and as C. L. Grace he has started a new series featuring the female physician, Kathryn Swanson.

2. Transcript of Interview with Paul Doherty conducted on June 24, 1998, by Edward Meek, Theron Westervelt and David Eldridge (in author's possession), 18.

3. Clynes makes no bones about his hatred of Henry, who is frequently referred to as "The Great Beast." When we inteviewed the author, he was preparing a submission for a television program which argued that Henry VIII was not the father of Elizabeth. Transcript of Interview, 8.

4. Keith Thomas, *Religion and the Decline of Magic: Studies in Popular Beliefs in Sixteenth and Seventeenth Century England* (London: Weidenfeld and Nicolson, 1971), 394. See also Shakespeare, Henry IV part I, act III, 1.149: "Sometimes he angers me/With telling me of the moldwarp and the ant,/Of the dreamer Merlin and his prophecies."

5. Madeleine Hope Dodd's account of political prophecies refers to Wilfred Holmes's narrative poem account of the Pilgrimage—entitled *The Fall and Evil Success of Rebellion*—which has a section devoted to proving that Henry was not the Mouldwarp. See M. H. Dodds, "Political Prophecies in the Reign of Henry VIII" in *Modern Language Review*, 11.3 (1916): 276-84.

6. See, for example, Fraser's discussion of the background to the slave trade in *Flash for Freedom!* (London: Fontana, 1989), 336, n 14.

7. Compare *A Brood of Vipers*, 41, with David Loades, *The Tudor Court*, 107, and Edward Hall, *The Triumphant Reigne of Henry VIII*, ed. Charles Whibley (London: Jack, 1904) vol. 1, 191.

8. *Calendar of State Papers, Spanish 1531-3*, ed. Royall Tyler (London, 1962-1964), 867. Reflecting on the Pilgrimage of Grace, Chapuys remarked that, among all European people, the English were "peculiarly credulous," being "easily moved to insurrection by prophecies."

*Works Cited*

Barber, Malcolm. *Trial of the Templars*. Cambridge: Cambridge UP, 1989.

Bourdeille, Pierre de seigneur de Brantôme. *Lives of Fair and Gallant Ladies*. Trans. A. R. Allinson. London: Fortune P, 1933.

Clynes, Michael. *A Brood of Vipers*. London: Headline, 1994.

——. *The Gallows Murders*. London: Headline, 1995.

——. *The Grail Murders*. London: Headline, 1993.

——. *The Poisoned Chalice*. London: Headline, 1992.

——. *The Relic Murders*. London: Headline, 1996.

——. *The White Rose Murders*. London: Headline, 1991.

Dickens, A. G. *Lollards and Protestants in the Diocese of York, 1509-1558*. London: Hambledon, 1982.

Doherty, Paul. "History: Fact or Fiction." *Overseas* March-May 1989.

Elton, Geoffrey R. *Policy and Police: The Enforcement of the Reformation in the Age of Thomas Cromwell*. Cambridge UP, 1972.

Erickson, Carolly. *Great Harry*. London: Dent, 1980.

Fraser, George MacDonald. *Flashman*. London: Fontana, 1988.

Hancock, Graham. *The Sign and the Seal: A Quest for the Lost Ark of the Covenant* London: Heinemann, 1992.

Hall, Edward. *The Triumphant Reigne of Henry VIII*. vol 1. Ed. Charles Whibley. London: Jack, 1904.

Hay, Denys, ed. *The Anglica Historia of Polydore Vergil*. London: Royal Historical Society, 1950.

Interview, June 24, 1998, with Paul Doherty, conducted by Edward Meek, Theron Westervelt, and David Eldridge.

Loades, David. *The Tudor Court*. London: Headstart, 1992.

Rennison, Nick. "Murder and Mayhem in the Middle Ages." Interview with Paul Doherty in *Waterstone's Guide to Crime Fiction*. London: Waterston, 1998.

Thomas, Keith. *Religion and the Decline of Magic: Studies in Popular Beliefs in Sixteenth and Seventeenth Century England*. London: Weidenfeld and Nicolson, 1971.

Williamson, Audrey. *The Mystery of the Princes*. London: Sutton, 1978.

# Maan Meyers:
# The Saga of the Dutchman

## Frank A. Salamone

Historical detective fiction is an important sub-category of historical fiction in general. As such, it should be judged by the same criteria applied to historical fiction; namely, that a certain verisimilitude is present. All the events depicted may not have actually happened but the reader should believe that they could have happened. Moreover, when real events are mingled with fictional ones, that mixing must appear to be natural. Additionally, real historical characters must act in accordance with their distinguishing characteristics and in conformity with what we know about them. Martin and Annette Meyers, authors of the Dutchman detective series, know and adhere to these standards. Their careful adaptation of their novels to the demands of the historical genre has made them a model of historical detective writing (Klausner 1).

Pieter Tonneman is the *schout,* or sheriff, of New Amsterdam (*The Dutchman,* 1992). His wife has died, and he has become a drunk, although one who can still perform his work. While sleeping off a drunk, he witnesses a murder but is not sure whether he has dreamed all or part of what he remembers of the scene. The murder, moreover, is even more painful to Tonneman because it reminds him of the suicide of his friend Smitt six months earlier, a suicide that is part of New Amsterdam history. The "suicide" in truth is a murder that was initially mislabeled a suicide. Tonneman is unwilling to accept that verdict and becomes more convinced that it is a murder when he becomes involved with a Jewish woman whose husband is missing. A fire in Jews Alley provides the occasion for their meeting. The woman, Racqel, is the daughter of a doctor, and she is proficient in medical arts.

These personal events are tied to the very real threat of invasion by the British fleet. Pieter Stuyvesant stubbornly holds out against compromise or surrender while the population generally desires peace and prosperity. The English promise to deal equitably with the colony, leaving Dutch law in effect for many daily transactions and not disturbing property rights. They even leave Dutch officials in office.

The two stories are joined, emphasizing the manner in which the personal and the public are linked. The imminent British invasion is the trigger for the murders that ensue. Personal ambitions, stemming from the characters of the actors, drive the action in Aristotelian fashion. Personal goodness and decency, similarly, also emerge in the appropriate setting. Thus, Tonneman gives up drinking and becomes a sober and solid citizen. His ability to overcome the prevailing anti-Semitism of the era is another example of the manner in which character and setting interact.

Tonneman begins the novel with a mild dose of anti-Semitism in that he shares many of the Dutch prejudices against the small Jewish settlement in New Amsterdam. These feelings are not deeply held and are more reflexive than conscious. They do not, for example, prevent him from fighting the fire in Jews Alley nor in rescuing those at risk. Neither do they prevent him from aiding in solving other problems faced by Jews nor from marrying Racqel and, later in the series, converting to Judaism (*Dutchman's Dilemma* 1996).

The Meyers planned *The Dutchman* to stand alone. The series, however, emerged from economic considerations. Even before the completion of *The Dutchman*, the Meyers were offered a three-book contract, on the basis of a synopsis and two hundred pages of manuscript. However, they quickly added artistic conditions. They would do the three books but move about in time. They would not confine themselves to the same village with its limited cast of characters. That would lead, they feared, to an earlier version of Jessica Fletcher's *Cabot Cove*. They would imagine descendents of the Dutchman and move them about in different eras in New York's history. In that manner, they could tell the history of New York in a personalized fashion, mixing real and fictional people together. Their model for this technique is the work of Jack Finney, although other authors such as E. L. Doctorow also come to mind (Interview 1998).

The technique allows for a change in style from book to book since one of their major tenets is not to use any words that were not in use during the period under depiction. Their model was Ruth Hill's book on the Lakota, *Hanta Yo* (1979), that was written in Lakota and then retranslated, with the help of a Lakota Sioux and a nineteenth-century dictionary, back into English. Marty Meyer points out that "You cannot have a character empathize until Freud comes along to invent empathy." He uses the Random House Dictionary to ascertain first usage of a word, as well as books on idiom and slang which he has collected over the years.

This meticulous attention to detail is reflected in each book, and atmosphere becomes a major character in a manner reminiscent of Edgar Allen Poe's stories. It is important to the Meyers that readers know that they are in New York at a specific time. Therefore, the setting must be exact. Marty's cinematic mind comes into play in this phase of the collaboration and is carefully edited by Annette. Even those not familiar through personal experience with Manhattan's geography can easily picture the locations through which the characters move.

There are certain constants in the series that appear in each book. There is a strong Jewish element and the Tonnemans interact with Jews, often falling in love with and marrying them. As other ethnic groups enter the city, they become part of the story. The Tonneman men often have alcoholic problems, as did the Dutchman himself. The medical theme works itself out in subsequent periods, as does that of entering the law. Other professions are represented in the Tonneman family line: newspaper work for example, but police work and medicine tend to dominate the series. Additionally, the series sticks to its goal of depicting the history of New York through the eyes of one family. It frequently achieves this goal through bringing the family members into contact with famous people, or those who should be famous. Jacob Hays, for example, is one such person whom the Meyers believe should be better known than he is.

Jacob Hays was the only High Constable in New York's history and he is credited with inventing modern police procedures. Hays was the first person in the New York constabulary to routinely follow criminals to establish their general patterns of operation—something that seems elementary today. Hays walked about the city to make his presence felt and to get a feel for the city. He is also credited with developing the intensive questioning associated with the "third degree." Hays was an imposing figure who carried a cudgel, using it rather freely to prevent further violence (*The Dutchman's Dilemma* 1996).

In 1808, the date of *The High Constable* (1998), Hays is at the height of his formidable powers. John Tonneman, the hero of *The Kingsbridge Plot* (1993), the *Dutchman*'s sequel, is now getting on in years. The problems of middle age are plaguing him. His sweet wife has become a shrew and his son has become a problem, taking to drink and failing to follow him into medicine or do anything significant with his life. In short, Tonneman faces the problems many men face in middle age.

New York in 1808 was a place profoundly capable of producing a feeling in people of all ages and classes that there was little solid ground upon which to walk. This was the period of the Napoleonic Wars during which the United States tried to tread the difficult waters of neutrality. President Thomas Jefferson had declared an embargo on shipping, severely affecting the economy of New York. Poverty and its consequences, homelessness and crime, increased. Opposition to the President's policies was high and a general disrespect for law-and-order common. In sum, these are the personal and social conditions against which the action plays out. Additionally, this book alone among the series refers directly to an unsolved murder in a previous book.

The general opposition of New Yorkers to wars or anything that might disrupt trade is a constant in the series. Moreover, economic motives are generally at the root of murders in the books. "Follow the money" is a key concept for the Meyers. Philosophically, they take the position that behind much of the rhetoric (religious, political, or ideological), there are economic realities that form the bottom line.

Dr. Tonneman is puzzled by his wife's behavior. His son is rebellious and refuses to become a doctor or to hold any job. He is a drunkard suspected of murdering his boss, the Water Commissioner of the City of New York, and stealing his money. Under the jurisdiction of the Water Commissioner, the Collect Company, the source of the New York water supply, went bankrupt. By 1808, the Collect was also the source of a great deal of disease in the city. When a body is found in the Collect, the reader is introduced to Jacob Hays and his methods and led into a plot that connects with and completes *The Kingsbridge Plot.*

In the earlier novel, John Tonneman returns to New York in 1775 after studies in England. His friend Jamie returns with him. Although vowing to stay clear of politics, Tonneman finds his sympathies turning to the rebel cause. He quickly becomes enmeshed in solving a murder and in politics. The two are as connected in colonial New York as they often are in the modern city. The murders are tied to the plot of Thomas Hickey to assassinate George Washington. The decaying bodies, decapitated victims, and the Revolutionary War are connected. Nevertheless, one murder appears out of place, and Hays serves as a catalyst to bring the two novels together.

The Meyers use Hays whenever they wish to write a short story about old New York. For example, they wrote a story about Dickens's visit to New York in 1842. He wished to visit the Tombs and the dangerous Five Points area. Although his guide has been lost in the dust of history, and a New York City policeman guided him, and there is no reason that Jacob Hays could not have been his guide. Thus, the Meyers had a chance to bring the colorful character back along with Peter Tonneman from *The High Constable* (1998). The fan gets to see Peter a bit older, twenty-four years older to be exact. He has settled into his life as a police officer and is Hays's assistant, rather more conservative than he was earlier in the narrative. Dickens is portrayed true to form and although his dialogue is invented, it is true to his character.

Watching Dickens solve a murder is quite interesting and appears to be in character. He takes on a bit of Sherlock Holmes's manner but otherwise reasons in line with his own character as well as his own fictional characters. Interestingly, he, Tonneman and Hays have each arrived at the same conclusion based on the same clues. They share their insights over a meal at Delmonico's.

The decision to jump back and forth in time in the series is because the Meyers did not want to write one sequel after another. They wanted the luxury of going back to fill in the missing parts, the back-story, of one novel in another one. The method is demonstrated in the way in which *The Lucifer Contract* (1998) fills in material from *The House on Mulberry St.* (1996).

*The House on Mulberry St.* leaps forward from 1808, the setting of *The High Constable. The House on Mulberry St.* is set during the Gay Nineties, the so-called Golden Age of New York. The hero is John "Dutch" Tonneman whose mother is an Irishwoman. Dutch is a direct descendant of old Pieter Tonneman, the Dutchman, and the Meyers provide genealogical charts and maps whenever their publisher permits.

Dutch becomes enamored of Esther Breslau, a photographer, whose pictures lead to the solution of the murder of an immigrant journalist. The corruption of the police force and of New York society in general is presented clearly as an element of the mystery, and Teddy Roosevelt is given his proper place in the setting.

The Meyers did not like Meg, Dutch's mother; however, they wanted to develop something likeable in her character. Therefore, in *The Lucifer Contract* Meg's struggle to free herself from the prejudice of her mother is highlighted. Her brief acting career with the Booths is given prominence as is her bravery and independence. The presence of Meg as a young adult struggling against ethnic prejudice and the circumscribed life of her mother and her failure to adhere to the limits of her Roman Catholicism make a nice contrast with her older incarnation as a biased matron.

Interestingly, *The Lucifer Contract* is the only book in the series in which the Tonneman family fade into the background compared with the plot. Nevertheless, the Meyers manage to fill in significant parts of the overall family history while focusing on the plot to burn New York City and the murders related to it. They also present a lucid view of the city during the Civil War and its fear that war might harm business (*Kirkus Reviews* 1997).

The series is continuing with the characters of *The House on Mulberry Street* entering the twentieth century. The next book has been written and ends with the parade in honor of Admiral Dewey, a parade that turns into a triumph for Teddy Roosevelt. Dutch Tonneman and his cousin Bo Clancy from *The House on Mulberry Street* volunteer for the Spanish-American War and return as veterans.

The Meyers agree that characters must drive the action. Marty calls this the concept of the organic character. Truthful characters provide consistent and truthful action. He states that if you want a character to do something, you must create a character and then place that character in a situation where the action is logical. You cannot just have a character behave in a particular way because it is convenient for the author. It is in this sense that characters take over novels. The Dutchman series is filled with such characters. The Indian Foxman, for example, who appears in two novels, *The Dutchman* and *The Dutchman's Dilemma* is a character with ideal integrity. He behaves consistently, according to his own lights. He is filled with contempt for European ways but will use them to achieve his ends. He can appreciate brave behavior by his opponents and even intervene on their behalf, as when he saves the Dutchman's wife, Racqel, but he is no one's Noble Savage. He is a complex person, unique to his time (Interview 1998).

The Dutchman series is a love story to New York City. Although violence occurs, there is a perception that things will work out fine and that the risk of violence is worth the rewards of living in the city. The city, in fact, becomes a character in the series. Its presence is deeply felt through all the phases of the history. The Meyers are adept at depicting the city through its various social, cultural, and economic changes. Beneath the changes that time brings there is an underlying continuity.

They reflect and depict that continuity amid change through using the Tonneman family in each of their books. That family serves as an essential peg to anchor the reader through New York's history. The reader soon becomes aware of the fact that details glossed over in one book will be the focus of another book in the series and that the authors will, in their words, back fill on the plot in due time.

The family forms a link, then, between books and provides an order, an order that reflects the links between one period of New York's history and another, the continuity between its changes. The family is involved in a relatively limited number of professions over time: medicine, newspaper work, and police work. Moreover, any murders that take place are tied somehow to one of these professions and to specific episodes in New York's history.

### *Acknowledgments and Dedication*

I wish to thank Annette and Marty Meyers for their consideration in being so open and forthcoming about their lives and work. They allowed me to interview them at great length. They have also kindly corrected a number of errors in the manuscript. All remaining errors and interpretation are mine. I also wish to thank Virginia Salamone, my wife, for her encouragement and support.

### *Works Cited*

Anonymous. 1998. Review of *The Lucifer Contract: A Civil War Thriller*. *Kirkus Reviews* 5 Nov. 1997.

Finney, Jack. *Time and Again*. New York: Scribner, 1970.

Gilije, Paul. *The Road to Mobocracy: Popular Disorder in New York City, 1763-1834*. Chapel Hill: U of North Carolina P, 1987.

Goffman, Erving. *Presentation of Self in Everyday Life*. Garden City: Doubleday, 1959.

Hill, Ruth. *Hanta Yo: An American Saga*. New York: Doubleday, 1979.

Klausner, Harriet. Review of *The House on Mulberry Street*. *Feminist Mystery Reviews* 1996. Feminist Mystery Corner. www.feminist.org/arts/mys_revmulberry.html.

Interview with Martin and Annette Meyers by Frank A. Salamone. 1998.

Meyers, Annette. 1998. *History in a Historical Novel*. www.meyersmystories.com/maan.html

Meyers, Maan. *The Dutchman*. New York: Doubleday, 1992.

——. *The Dutchman's Dilemma*. New York: Bantam, 1996.

——. *The High Constable*. New York: Doubleday, 1994 .

——. *The House on Mulberry St*. New York: Bantam, 1995.

——. *The Kingsbridge Plot*. New York: Doubleday, 1993.

——. *The Lucifer Contract: A Civil War Thriller*. New York: Bantam, 1997.

# Bruce Alexander:
# Sir Henry Fielding and Blind Justice

## Donna Bradshaw Smith

Mystery novels set in London during the Georgian period often center around the latter half of the nineteenth century during the heyday of the Bow Street Runners, the police force created by Henry and John Fielding. Many writers have employed Sir John Fielding—the blind, brilliant, compassionate magistrate at Bow Street Court from 1754 to 1780—as a secondary character in their novels. Now Sir John is the star detective. Bruce Alexander, an American author, has written four novels featuring Sir John Fielding and his thirteen-year-old orphan sidekick, Jeremy Proctor: *Blind Justice* (1994), *Murder in Grub Street* (1995), *Watery Grave* (1996), and *Person or Persons Unknown* (1997). Critics highly praise this historical mystery series. In a review of *Blind Justice*, *New York Times Book Review* stated that "Alexander works in a vigorous style that captures with gusto the lusty spirit of the era." *Booklist*'s reviewer remarked, "The novel offers much to treasure: wonderful use of language, a rich cast of characters, and an intoxicating evocation of time and place."

Bruce Alexander is the pseudonym for the noted writer Bruce Cook. He began his career by working in various editorial and public relations posts in Chicago. In addition, he has worked as a freelance writer, a book review editor for the *Los Angeles Daily News*, and a movie critic. As Bruce Cook he has written a wide range of nonfiction and fiction books. His nonfiction works include a study of the Beat Generation, biographies, and a country music and travel guide. His fiction books include a "hard-boiled" mystery series about a Chicano detective, Antonio "Chico" Cervantes, set in California. Now, with his Sir John Fielding series, Alexander joins the ranks of authors who write historical mysteries.

Historical accuracy is a key factor in any historical fiction. It is easy for an author to deal with the general public's beliefs and perceptions of an era, rather than doing some investigation to see if the setting is historically correct. Bruce Alexander has researched his subject well. This historical accuracy, along with the social relevance of the plots and the social conscience of the characters, demonstrates that these entries add a mature element to the historical mystery genre.

In the tradition of a Watson retelling the cases of his friend, Jeremy Proctor retells the cases in which he assisted Sir John Fielding. The series begins in 1768, a time when London was considered the most lawless city in

Europe. In *Blind Justice* we learn the story of how Jeremy and Sir John become a team. New to London, Jeremy immediately becomes involved with an independent "thief-taker." These villains would decoy unwary and ignorant wretches to commit a felony, whereupon they promptly captured them and claimed their reward. True to history, a trumped-up charge is made against Jeremy and he is taken to Bow Street Court so that the thief-taker can collect his reward. Sir John ferrets out the truth and rescues Jeremy from a hanging offense. He takes the penniless orphan into his household as a ward of the court. In the midst of trying to find Jeremy a printer's apprenticeship, Sir John must investigate the death of wealthy Lord Richard Goodhope, who was discovered shot through the head, gun at his feet, behind the locked door of his library. Jeremy becomes Sir John's "eyes" to inspect the crime scene and to observe people's nonverbal reactions. Though the initial finding is suicide, Jeremy notices a clue that points to murder. As the investigation continues, we learn of Goodhope's dissolute life, including extramarital affairs and gambling forays.

In the novels, the reader is informed that these are Jeremy's memoirs, written during the 1790s when he is a lawyer in his forties. Thus, it is after Sir John's death that he decides to share his memories of Sir John's investigative abilities and his "prodigious qualities of character" (*Blind Justice* 1). Alexander's style of writing a historical detective story as a memoir provides a double perspective on events. Jeremy is able to not only look back on Sir John's cases as an adult, but it also allows him to reflect upon his experiences as a teenager. He shares his childhood assumptions and admits to his lack of knowledge (even of sex) as a young man.

Jeremy plays the role of the sidekick in the series. The use of a young, inexperienced sidekick is particularly well suited to historical detection; much historical information can be presented to the modern reader as the detective explains his reasoning to the perplexed assistant. Jeremy, a naïve teenager from Leichfield, is somewhat of an outsider to everyday life in London, thus allowing the author to introduce the conventions of the age. For example, Jeremy is introduced to "press gangs" in *Watery Grave.* Jeremy thinks he has been attacked by a gang of villains, but Sir John explains the history of "one of the most execrable practices of the Royal Navy" (116). Due to war casualties and long tours at sea, the Navy had been granted the power to stop ships and take any of the crew it needed. This power was extended to land, so that the press gangs literally whisked young men from the streets and kept them at sea for years. Local magistrates had to grant permission for press gangs to operate in their jurisdictions. Sir John was one of the few who did not allow this practice.

Since Sir John is blind, he uses Jeremy as his "eyes" which allows the reader to observe through him. History shows that Sir John did use a Bow Street Runner to observe for him (Pringle 135). In the novels, the reader becomes privy to much investigative information since Jeremy reads letters and reports to Sir John as well as writes his letters for him. Also, Sir John usually requests that Jeremy be in the room to observe nonverbal responses when witnesses are questioned. However, in order to keep the suspense in the mysteries, Jeremy is not privy to all of Sir John's interviews and conclusions.

Alexander uses Jeremy's youthful awe and excitement to bring alive London circa 1768. During this period, the streets of London were a seemingly perpetual pageant. The river, the streets, the shops, the coffee-houses and taverns, the parks and the places of amusement were the chief sights of London and very much a part of the daily life of the town. The noise of the streets was deafening with the thunder of iron-shod wheels, clatter of hooves, and street cries. Jeremy relates to the reader the beauty and romance as well as the comedies and tragedies of the streets.

Alexander vividly depicts the disease and violence, filth, falling buildings, drunkenness, and insanity that were a part of daily life for many. It was an age of great poverty; the distinction between classes was sharp. Yet the popular pleasures were common to all classes of society: sex, sadism, gambling, and drinking. Public floggings and whippings were popular, especially when the victims included girls. Foreigners marveled at Britons' enthusiasm for hangings. Crowds thronged the three-mile procession route from Newgate to Tyburn to cheer and jeer the condemned prisoners. Executions were not only entertainment for the working class, but for the nobility also. In the series, Alexander accurately refers to Sir John's opposition to public executions.

Criminals (other than the murderers) play prominent roles in this series. During the Georgian era, Britain had not only the most criminals; it had the harshest Criminal Code. Men, women, and children were liable to be hanged for offenses that were seemingly trivial, such as poaching and stealing. Very few offenses were punished by sentences of imprisonment because the penal system was not designed for reformation. A prison was simply a waiting area for debtors waiting to repay their debts, suspects awaiting their trial, and convicted prisoners awaiting their punishment.

Alexander transports the reader to that dismal world. In *Blind Justice*, Jeremy's narrative evokes a vivid sense of the poor conditions, the stench, and the sounds of Newgate. Prisons were not under official control; they were farmed out and run as private profit-making concerns, so corruption was rampant. As Sir John points out, "what goes on in Newgate is closed to us outside" (304). Since warders were paid little or nothing, they lived on what they could make off the prisoners. So, it is conceivable that a warder could be bribed to kill an inmate, as is the scenario in *Blind Justice*.

Money was a necessity for everyone sent to prison. Each prisoner was required to pay an entrance fee, as well as a fine to the inmates. Failure to pay these fees resulted in the forfeit of the prisoner's clothes. Payment to warders for any privileges, such as better clothing, food, and drink, was expected. Alexander touches on these realities and portrays Sir John as a humane magistrate in a scene in *Blind Justice* when Sir John returns the court fine to an offender he recently sent to Newgate, so that the prisoner may fare better during his imprisonment. Sir John remarks that it was "inconsiderate" of him to have not thought of it during court, and "how desperately those inside need all the resources they can assemble" (201).

London's streets, while a pageant during the day, could be quite dangerous at night. Alexander uses Jeremy's narrative to provide realistic and sometimes graphic details of the city's dangers. Sir John often warns Jeremy to be sure to return to Bow Street by nightfall. Many times a constable arms Jeremy with a pistol, despite his youth. Even Sir John is not immune to attacks as we see in *Murder in Grub Street*. Robbers approach Jeremy and Sir John and are chased away only by Jeremy's threat to shoot. Sir John's famous ego relieves the tension in this scene. He remarks that the robbers must have been new to London since they did not recognize him as the Magistrate of Bow Street.

Despite these unsafe conditions, Britons resisted the creation of a professional police force. They were afraid of losing their individual freedoms and did not wish to alter the Constitution. The British police was eventually brought into being by reformers, humanitarians, progressives, and radicals. Henry and John Fielding created the "Bow Street Runners," one of the earliest attempts to begin a professional police in England.

No one is certain when the term "Bow Street Runners" was first used. One of the first mentions of it was in a poem that appeared in the *Morning Herald* on March 5, 1785 (Leslie-Melville 307). During Sir John's tenure, they were more commonly referred to as "beak-runners," "peace officers" or "constables" (Pringle 126). Their initial job was to apprehend thieves and disband gangs. In the eyes of the law they were like any other private thief-takers, thus the references to the Runners as such in Alexander's novels. As time went on and their skill and sagacity became admired, their duties increased. John's five-word formula for reducing crime, "quick notice and sudden pursuit," became the unwritten motto of the Bow Street police (Pringle 106). Being former constables, they not only knew something about the criminal laws and procedures, but also had an acquaintance with the underworld. They were the first constables to make a serious study of the art of detecting and running down criminals. Their names remained secret, enabling them to mix with criminals without being identified. However, while doing official "Beak business," they were easily recognized by their red waistcoats and their batons with a gilt crown on top. Alexander captures their spirit in the fictional characters of Captain Bailey, Constable Perkins, and the other Runners.

Historical accuracy in characterization is another important element in this series. Using a real historical personage as a detective is common in historical mysteries. Alexander is thoroughly versed in the minutiae of Sir John Fielding's life and displays that knowledge for the benefit of the reader. Small facts are thrown into casual conversations, such as Sir John and Henry did not have the same mother, Henry's library had to be sold to benefit Henry's widow and children, and Sir John preferred drinking beer.

Alexander has portrayed him as the humane and honorable figure that he undoubtedly was. Sir John was known as a magistrate of keen intellect, fairness, and uncommon detective ability. Just as in the novels, when a crime was committed, the "Blind Beak" often took it upon himself to solve it. Indeed, history records a case Sir John investigated in 1756, when Lord Harrington was robbed of money and valuables. Sir John and his detectives solved the crime by examining footprints, chisel-marks on a bureau, a candle-stump, and other clues (Leslie-Melville 236).

Interjected into the main plots are historically accurate portrayals of Sir John in action at the Bow Street Court, dispensing practical justice to Londoners high and low. When seated in court he wore a black silk bandage over his eyes, and carried a small switch in his hand which he used to feel his way. He had a singular gift for distinguishing sounds. It was said of him that he never failed to recognize an old offender, though the only indication he had to go by was the sound of the prisoner's voice. Alexander demonstrates this ability on numerous occasions in the series. In *Blind Justice* Sir John recognizes a repeat criminal in his court by his voice, a feat which leads to Jeremy being cleared of stealing charges. Sir John remarks, "To one such as myself the human voice is as sure and distinctive a means of identification as the human face is to the rest" (16).

Bow Street became pre-eminent as the only court where justice was dispensed in a businesslike manner. But Sir John's zeal for justice was tempered with a wise and discriminating humanity. He was compassionate to the needy and lenient to first offenders. Sir John did not criticize the severity of the laws, but he applied them with humanity and he was critical of indiscriminate hanging (Pringle 139). In *Blind Justice*, Sir John takes the time to explain to Jeremy how he came to his decisions in two separate cases, one where a woman is accused of stealing a silk handkerchief and another where a man physically attacked and robbed a Bow Street Runner. He explains that the law looks upon sneak-thievery and armed robbery as the same, that even stealing an item worth only a guinea (a paltry amount) is still sufficient in the eyes of the law to warrant capital punishment. He admits that England has the severest laws in the Western world, but the trial procedures favor the defendant. Those who wish to accuse thieves must produce witnesses to the act, establish ownership of the item stolen, prove its worth and so forth (92). Thus, Sir John differentiates the crimes by his judgements. The sneak-thief is released because the true owner of the handkerchief cannot be established. The armed robber is sent to Newgate to await trial because several witnesses provided accounts of his theft.

Alexander portrays Sir John's humanity and his ingenuity in rendering justice in a unique infraction in *Person or Persons Unknown*. A murder victim's husband is caught selling his wife's body piecemeal. While this was obviously morally wrong, no exact law existed that covered this offense. Sir John believes he must mete out justice for this heinous act. With laborious thoroughness, Sir John applies the most suitable law possible, which is disturbing the dead. However, it is considered a hanging offense. Sir John does not agree that grave-robbing should be a hanging offense, the same as murder. "What is done to a body after death is not near so serious as killing"

(170). He believes that hanging the husband would itself be unjust, so he offers the husband the alternative of transportation to the colonies if he can provide the names of the purchasers.

In *Watery Grave* we glimpse the civil power a magistrate had in the eighteenth century. During a riot, Sir John must use the "Riot Act" which was passed by Parliament in the early part of the eighteenth century to deal with civil disobedience. "Reading someone the riot act" is a popular saying still today and it originated with this law. When warning a crowd to disperse, a magistrate had to read the "Riot Act" to the crowd first. Then one hour was allowed for the crowd to disperse before military troops could act. It demonstrated the reluctance to use the military against civilians. Thus, a civil authority, usually a magistrate, determined the need for military force. Sir John remarks, "It is a clear instance of the preeminence of civil authority over the military, a principle upon which the laws of our Kingdom rest" (214).

However, Sir John's power as a civil authority does not help in the murder investigation in *Watery Grave*. Here, he must struggle with the differences between naval justice and civil law. The case begins with Vice-Admiral Sir Robert Redmond, a former shipmate of Sir John's, consulting the magistrate in the investigation of the death at sea of a frigate's captain and the court-martial of a senior officer accused of his murder. Although Sir John and Jeremy uncover evidence exonerating the unfortunate officer, the evidence is withheld by the naval court and the court-martial proceeds as scheduled in order to provide the scapegoat and protect the Royal Navy from scandal. Sir John and Jeremy soon realize that the Navy's system of justice was not consonant with Sir John's law in Bow Street Court. Essentially, the captain was the "king of his ship," thus his power was absolute. However, when that power is used to a bad end, there are unjust results. Crew members were often at the mercy of this system because the Navy had in its own interests the need to support the tradition of the captain's absolute power, especially considering some of the unsavory characters "pressed" into service. During this investigation Sir John runs afoul of Navy officers who refuse to recognize his civilian authority and dispute that he has any jurisdiction over them. Because of Sir John's love for the Navy, he feels great pain at the injustices dealt to the involved parties. He realizes that he had not understood the system when he was a young man with dreams of a naval career. He bitterly admits, "It seems the Navy is a law unto itself, a country all its own in which the ordinary rules of conduct and procedure need not apply" (249).

Not much is known about Sir John's earlier life before 1749, when he, Henry, and Samuel Welch opened the Universal Register Office. We do know that he was in the Royal Navy. It was during this time that he was blinded in an accident, although the details are unknown. Alexander provides an exciting version in *Watery Grave* of a courageous young midshipman leading his men into battle. In historical accounts, Sir John referred to his blindness as "an accident which everyone but myself deemed a misfortune" (Pringle 147).

In the series, Alexander does deviate slightly from history in regard to John's marriages. In *Blind Justice*, Lady Fielding dies from "a wasting disease." In the second novel, *Murder in Grub Street*, he marries Katherine Durham, a widower. "Tongues wagged at the short space of time that elapsed since his first wife's death" (306). In real life Sir John was indeed married twice and tongues did wag at the short time between the two marriages. However, the timelines of the fictional marriages do not correspond with the real ones. His first wife, Elisabeth Whittingham, died on May 25, 1774, in Brampton. On the following August 6, Sir John married at Kensington Parish Church, Mary Sedgley of Brampton, the daughter of Sedgley, Esq., of Middlesex.

Sir John, a renowned social reformer, played a leading part in the foundation of three charities: the Marine Society, the Magdalen Hospital, and the Royal Female Orphanage. He inaugurated the immensely important work of saving poor girls and boys from criminal careers. This was reportedly the reason he was knighted. Throughout his novels Alexander refers to Sir John sending boys to sea versus the gallows. At their first encounter, Sir John asks Jeremy if he is interested in life at sea. Later in the series we meet Tom Durham, one of the boys he saved from a criminal career.

A fictional version of the Magdalen Hospital is used in the series. In *Murder in Grub Street* Sir John and the second Lady Fielding create the Magdalen Home for Penitent Prostitutes. In reality, the Magdalen Hospital and the Royal Female Orphanage were founded in 1758 by John Fielding and Samuel Welch. The slight variation from fact will be forgiven by the modern reader for it brings into play the social consciences of various characters and allows Sir John and Lady Fielding to work together as a team on a common cause. The missions of the real and fictional Magdalen are the same—take in girls as apprentices, train them in domestic work, and then send them out to reputable families as servants. History does show that Sir John had a servant that was trained at the Magdalen (Leslie-Melville 125), a fact which is integrated into the series with the hiring of Annie Oakum in *Watery Grave*.

Social issues that were prevalent during the latter half of the eighteenth century are an integral part of Alexander's plots. Sir John and Jeremy want to do as much as they can to relieve or reduce these social ills. In *Blind Justice*, while interviewing a sailor, Sir John is interested in the man's viewpoints on the hauling of "black cargo" by his ship. The viewpoint is clearly anti-slavery, with the remark that human beings "deserve to be treated better than livestock . . . cattle and pigs would be treated better" (284).

These and other social problems, such as child prostitution, child education, insanity, and indigence are also encountered in the novels. Alexander does not distort the facts of everyday life during the eighteenth century, nor does he attempt to graft modern day morality onto his chosen period. Unlike many historical mysteries, the fictional characters never strike one as anachronistically modern in their thinking. History shows that Sir John was an advocate for social change, and Alexander does a remarkable job portraying these honorable qualities.

We see the fate of young prostitutes in all the novels, but *Person or Persons Unknown* addresses it forthright. All the murder victims were prostitutes in Covent Garden, a place notorious for its brothels. Each one had a different reason for becoming a prostitute, such as having a husband die or having no job skills. One victim supplemented her earnings as a thief, which was a common occurrence in that period. As Jeremy observes, "these girls lead hard lives" (130).

Jeremy discovers for himself the tragedies associated with prostitution when he tries to help Mariah, a young girl, leave this lifestyle. The man who claims to "own" Mariah tells Jeremy that he can buy her for ten guineas. Jeremy is quite indignant at the idea of a human being for sale. He cannot understand why Mariah does not have the will to leave this wretched way of life. Jeremy's friends try to explain to Jeremy that Mariah has to want to leave that life and better herself—Jeremy cannot do it for her nor choose for her. But, tragedy strikes and the chance for Mariah to change is lost. Not only is the tragedy of prostitution examined, but Jeremy also learns an important lesson in life about helping others.

Throughout the novels, Alexander does not shy away from the topic of religion. A prominent part of daily life in Georgian England, it influenced social, power, and property relations. Denominational boundaries sanctified social divides more than they cut across them. It is true that private faiths were tolerated, but discrimination based upon one's religion did exist. The Act of Toleration (1689) had guaranteed religious freedom with strings attached. The Anglican Church was privileged and had a strong hold on society. In contrast, the position of Roman Catholics was weak. In London they used chapels attached to foreign embassies for worship services (Cowie 67). Catholics were excluded from politics and they could not enter the Services, the legal profession or the Universities. Priests could be punished for conducting services, purchasing land was forbidden, and children had to be educated at home or abroad (Selley 357).

These restrictions were eventually reversed by the Catholic Relief Act of 1778 by the time Jeremy writes his memoirs, but were in place during Sir John's lifetime. Alexander does not ignore the historical accounts of Catholics being virtual outlaws in their own country, doomed to a life of secrecy. He integrates these societal restrictions into his novels. The surgeon in the series is Gabriel Donnelly, a Catholic Irishman who attained his medical training in Vienna. It was noted in Jeremy's memoirs that although he was Catholic the Royal Navy overlooked his religion because of the great need for surgeons after the French war. Lord and Lady Goodhope (*Blind Justice*) were "closet" Catholics, because they were forced to keep their religion secret in order to retain their status and privileges as nobility. In *Person or Persons Unknown* the victim Mariah, since she was Catholic, had to be buried in a secret cemetery.

Fringe sects existed then as they do today. They were congregations of the "perfect" led by born-again prophets who appealed greatly to the urban lost souls. Sectaries provided visions of a New Jerusalem (Porter 198).

Alexander creates such a fringe sect, Brethren of the Spirit, in *Murder in Grub Street*. The murder investigation of publisher/bookseller Ezekiel Crabb and his family revolves around a manuscript that calls for the conversion of the Jews written by the leader of the sect. Jeremy's inexperience gives Sir John the opportunity to explain that preachers wanted to convert the Jews, so that Christ's second coming could occur. A mathematical formula was created that supposedly predicted the year that the conversion would happen. In the story, the date has passed so the Brethren have reworked the formula for a new date.

The Jewish community had their problems also. Historical accounts show that Sir John was brought into close contact with the problem of the Jews as a police official because of their reputation as receivers of stolen goods. Always a wise administrator, he co-operated with the leaders of the Jewish community in attempting to check the depredations of their dishonest brethren. In 1771 this liaison enabled him to arrest a gang of nine Jewish men who had robbed a household and murdered a servant. After this great crime, every Jew in England was in public opinion implicated, and the prejudice, ill-will and brutal conduct this brought upon the Jews, even after the gang had been detected and punished for it, continued for many years (Leslie-Melville 260-266). We see this scenario replayed in *Person or Persons Unknown*. Rabbi Gershon helps Sir John seek the suspected murderer Yossel because "matters such as this often have a way of turning out for the worse for Jews" (100). A broadsheet, the predecessor of the tabloid, is published naming Yossel as the murderer (despite any solid proof), and repeating many of the calumnies commonly laid upon the Israelites. Sir John is furious at this publication because he realizes that some people believe anything in print. He acknowledges that the more lasting damage has been done to the Jews. "Who knows, when such an evil seed is planted, what may grow from it in years to come? I will not have such filth circulated in my precincts. I will not allow Londoners to behave in the manner of denizens of some benighted province of Eastern Europe" (102).

The publishing of hearsay is also examined in this case. Alexander uses another historical personage, the writer Oliver Goldsmith, to defend the right to free speech—"an author should be free to have his say, and that if he is in error, his errors will be corrected by others writing against him. That is the very nature of controversy, and controversy is the very heart of intelligent life" (167). Sir John acknowledges the needs of journalism, even controversy, so that society may reach the truth. But, he also realizes that, as a magistrate, he must deal with the consequences of careless journalism (178). In order to counter the points in the broadsheet, Goldsmith agrees to Sir John's request that he write a broadsheet pointing out the author's surmises, fabrications and ancient calumnies and correcting them. In the final copy Goldsmith also implores the Parliament to repeal these "outdated primitive laws directed against whole people . . . in order to conform with present reality" (179). Not only was he referring to the Jews, but also to the Catholics.

Using the noted poet, historian, romancer, and physician Oliver Goldsmith enriches the story and adds to the feeling that the modern reader is a time traveler visiting Bow Street Court. Throughout Alexander's novels we meet convincing renditions of famous eighteenth-century personages, such as Samuel "Dictionary" Johnson, the obnoxious James Boswell, and noted actor David Garrick. In-depth research of his chosen period is evidenced by the scattering of lesser-known but engaging bit-players (e.g. Alfred Humber, a member of Lloyd's insurance syndicate) who vividly illustrate the bustle of London toward the end of the mercantilist era. The reader can delight in Alexander's attention to small details even for these secondary characters. For example, Jeremy observes the wolfish table manners of Samuel Johnson in *Murder in Grub Street.*

Alexander's writing retains some of the character and cadence of real eighteenth-century writing. He catches the essence of eighteenth-century prose without becoming embroiled with syntax that could keep the modern reader away. He even recreates authentic London slang from that time which was called "flash-talk."

To present a living picture of the life of a past age in all its varied aspects is always a difficult task. Bruce Alexander has frequently been praised for his vivid, historically accurate, well-written mystery novels. His fans appreciate the subtle nuances in his intricate plots. His contributions to the field are noted by the *New York Times*, designating *Murder in Grub Street* a "*New York Times* Notable Book of the Year," and by *Publishers Weekly,* picking *Person or Persons Unknown* as one of the best mysteries of 1997. An important aspect of any mystery novel is believability and Alexander has the knack of making his tales seem real. The novels allow us to travel back to visit the Georgians and see how they coped with many of the same problems that face today's society. Through the medium of the detective novel, Bruce Alexander explores the triumphs and tragedies of an earlier society. It is his frank willingness to deal with controversial issues combined with his credible, sophisticated style which makes him an influential writer of the historical mystery genre.

*Works Cited*

Alexander, Bruce. *Blind Justice.* New York: Berkley Prime Crime, 1995.

——. *Murder in Grub Street.* New York: Berkley Prime Crime, 1996.

——. *Person or Persons Unknown.* New York: Putnam, 1997.

——. *Watery Grave.* New York: Berkley Prime Crime, 1997.

Cowie, Leonard W. *Hanoverian England: 1714-1837.* London: Bell, 1969.

Leslie-Melville, R. *The Life and Work of Sir John Fielding.* London: Lincoln Williams Ltd., 1934.

Needham, George. Rev. of *Blind Justice* by Bruce Alexander. *Booklist* 15 Sept. 1994: 115.

Porter, Roy. *English Society in the Eighteenth Century.* New York: Penguin, 1982.

Pringle, Patrick. *Hue and Cry: The Story of Henry and John Fielding and Their Bow Street Runners*. New York: Morrow, 1955.

Selley, W. T. *England in the Eighteenth Century*. London: Black, 1949.

Stasio, Marilyn. "Crime." Rev. of *Blind Justice* by Bruce Alexander. *New York Times Book Review* 23 Oct. 1994: 24.

# Keith Heller:
# A Genealogy of Detection in the Eighteenth Century

## Scott R. Christianson

Howard Haycraft, in his never-to-be-outdated history of the detective story, *Murder for Pleasure*, rightly observes that "the detective story is purely a development of the modern age." Haycraft cites, with approbation, George Bates's last word on the subject: "The cause of Chaucer's silence on the subject of airplanes was because he had never seen one. You cannot write about policemen before policemen exist to be written of" (6). There were no "police" in the eighteenth century; therefore, there were no police stories. Yet during the mid-1980s, Keith Heller wrote and published a short but distinguished series of historical mystery novels that features an eighteenth-century nightwatch, George Man, as its detective.

Against the widespread common view that "prison reform" throughout the eighteenth century led to the more "humane" modern prison, Michel Foucault, in *Discipline and Punish*, argued and ably documented that, however genuine those humane concerns, the modern prison came to be because of developments in disciplinary and institutional practices: systems of surveillance, information gathering and classification, and disciplines of practices on human bodies. Similarly, surveillance, information gathering, and discipline made possible the development of the police. As the genealogy of the modern prison can be traced to transformations of knowledge and power in the eighteenth century, so Keith Heller's Man novels provide a genealogy of crime, detection, and the police in the emerging power/knowledge relations in "the Age of Reason." As the modern prison was nascent in the classical age, so was the art of detection.

Keith Heller's three Man novels are only recently back in print; of the three, published first in England, only the first two were published in the United States. Although all three novels received extremely positive critical reviews, their availability has been severely limited. Thus, most readers probably are unfamiliar with one of the most innovative of detective fiction series. Based on that assumption, I begin with a brief description of each of the three Man novels; but in keeping with the traditional practice of scholars and critics of detective fiction, I will not reveal Man's solution of the murders. However, my analysis does involve a theory and an interpretation of what Heller's Man novels accomplish, so if any readers don't want to have their own readings of the novels slanted by my interpretations, they are advised to read them before proceeding to read this essay.

Heller's first Man novel, *Man's Illegal Life* (1984), indicates on the cover of the first English edition that it is "A story of London's Parish Watch, 1722." George Man, our protagonist, is forty-three years old and has already served a long career in the night watch. At the outset of the novel, one of Man's colleagues has discovered a dead body in a house in Drury Lane. Taylor Hoole, who has not been on the watch as long as Man although fourteen years older, is an avid reader about the Great Plague of 1665, incidentally the year Hoole was born. The circumstances of the death suggest to Hoole that the victim had been shut up in his home and starved to death in the same manner that plague victims were interred in their own homes during the previous century. The recent concern about the possibility of a return of the plague inspires the London constabulary and legal system—of which the night watch is the lowliest rung on the ladder—not to pursue the case as a possible murder, which George Man thinks it certainly must be. In the course of his own investigation, conducted against the will and for the most part without the knowledge of his superiors, Man is involved with the notorious Jonathan Wild, "Thief-Catcher-General to Great Britain and Ireland" and rumored to be the center of an organized ring of thieves, prostitutes, and blackmailers. He also meets Thomas Coram, sea-captain, businessman, and soon-to-be founder of the first Foundlings Hospital in England. Man's investigation leads him through the dark streets of London, into the coffee-houses frequented by writers, and into the text-dominated world of the eighteenth century. Man's discovery of the murderer is the product of his nocturnal wanderings, his knowledge of "human nature" based on direct contact with people from all walks of life, and his voracious reading of popular literature and journalism, and his genealogical research into the history of the Great Plague of 1665.

Heller's second Man novel, *Man's Storm* (1986), is set in London during 1703, when a twenty-four-year-old George Man is having doubts about continuing his career in the night watch. The storm of the title is the Great Storm of 1703, which raged for over a fortnight and caused extensive damage in London and throughout the rest of England. On a night shortly before the storm is to reach its height, the wife of an ironmonger is murdered in her shop just as she is getting ready to close for the night. Suspects include the woman's husband, a widow of dubious reputation who is the couple's lodger, a drunken cleric who also lodges with them, a notorious man-about-town, and the inevitable "person or persons unknown" who may have been trying to take advantage of the extreme weather to plunder the ironmonger's shop. Once again, Man pursues his investigation against the will and system of the London constabulary. A young and sexually-inexperienced George Man is introduced to eighteenth-century sexuality, from courtship to whoring to adultery to polygamy to lesbianism, and must cope with his own embarrassment, sense of morality, and sexual urges as he untangles the complex web of human romantic and sexual relations. Man also consults with that marginal figure, on the borders of commerce and literature and of the legal and illegal, Daniel Defoe.

The third Man novel, *Man's Loving Family* (1986), finds George Man out of work in 1727, then as now a serious predicament for a forty-eight-year-old man. Man has run afoul of an impressario of Court and society entertainments, John James Heidegger, who has blacklisted Man off the watch because Man attempted to arrest a rowdy reveler who turned out to be a Lord and one on whom Heidegger depends for favor at Court. Through his strange acquaintance, George Psalmanaazaar—a man who had gained notoriety as "the Formosan" for his tales of that Asian island, at this point largely believed to have been fictitious—Man is put in touch with Abraham Sinclair, importer of wines, tobacco, and spices, who hires Man as a bodyguard for his son, James. An "advertisement" appearing in October for what purports to be another installment of the prophecies and prognostications of "John Partridge," long believed dead, promises that this new almanac will contain "a true identification and explanation of the murder of Mr. James Sinclair, first son of trader Abraham Sinclair, which happen'd the 20th of November 1727" (28). After more than a month of boring duty at James Sinclair's side, Man watches helplessly as his friend, the writer Richard Savage, runs his sword through the very man Man has been hired to protect. With this novel, Keith Heller re-creates a historic murder mystery and trial in which Savage, later defended by Samuel Johnson, appears as the accused. We see Man doubt the evidence of his own eyes as he seeks to find an alternative explanation to the murder of James Sinclair. He employs the services of a young Henry Fielding who, like his satiric hero in one of his future novels, Jonathan Wild, has set himself up in London as a "thief-catcher." Man sits at the trial of Savage and his "accomplices" next to the hunchbacked poet, Alexander Pope. His investigation of the murder—entirely unofficial and flying in the face of the court and the Court—is instrumentally assisted by the information of "the London Spy," Ned Ward.

In "A Note on the Watch" which prefaces the first Man novel, *Man's Illegal Life*, Keith Heller writes:

In the first half of the eighteenth century London was probably the most dangerous city on earth. Gangs of thieves and beggars, prostitutes and bullies, lunatics, and murderers made a battleground of the streets for nobleman and commoner alike. . . . Corruption and negligence were the order of the day, and the legal system was more notorious for its brutality than for its effectiveness. In the midst of this chaos, one astounding fact stands clear: there were no police. (7)

Here, Heller evokes a commonplace about the eighteenth century expressed throughout its own popular press and high literature and endorsed or acquiesced in by most subsequent critics and scholars of the century: that England, and in particular London, was a chaotic and crime-filled place. Documents of the period describe a culture in crisis, in the grip of a rising crime rate that its state and institutions were incapable of curbing.

In *Literature and Crime in Augustan England*, Ian Bell summarizes recent historians who doubt the documents of the time that, universally, proclaim the vast extent of crime in the eighteenth century. Bell acknowledges the chaotic nature of the age but seems to agree with recent historians who question how extensive crime was because the documents that "report" it are so obviously influenced by the rising bourgeois ideology of emerging capitalism (15-17, 55).

Although Heller re-creates an eighteenth century that reflects both traditional and contemporary historians, Heller's novels offer a critique of eighteenth-century ideology without doubting, as Bell and more recent historians do, the depiction of the "reality" of crime in such ideological works. Most importantly, very much in the evocative style of New Historical writing, Heller's imaginative fictions offer a believable and coherent image of life and crime in the eighteenth century which are valid as "history." Heller concludes his "Note" with an admission that: "There is no record of the watchmen's ever having had any lasting effect on the lawless conditions of eighteenth-century London. But they were there" (7). The next section of this paper will explore Heller's genealogy of detection in the person of the night watchman; but his firm insistence on the presence of the watch is crucial in establishing the viability of his genealogy of crime in the eighteenth century. The watch was there, and so by extension were the criminals and their crimes. Such is the "new historical" hypothesis through which Heller constructs his recreation of the "mean streets" of eighteenth-century London.[1]

So, down the mean streets of eighteenth-century London George Man must go, a man who is not himself mean (although his job places him among the lowest of classes) and who is neither tarnished nor afraid. This man of the people directly encounters the "rogues, vagabonds, and nightwalkers" specified by Blackstone as the objects of the watch's duties. In *Man's Storm*, a young George Man is set upon by a "devil's dozen of them that style themselves Hawcubites" (21), and in *Man's Illegal Life* an older Man reflects back "to his own early years, of the long succession of bands roving the streets, wild as wolves: the Hectors, the Scourers, the Nickers, the Hawcubites, the Mohawks" (11). The difference between Man's early career and later is that "now it was continuing, only worse" (11).

Ian Bell describes the furor in the periodical press about gangs like the Mohocks (or Mohawks) that occurred in 1712, including the April 19, 1712, issue of the *London Gazette* which published a list of people claiming to be assaulted by such gangs (53). Bell continues:

Further discussion of these scary figures appeared around this time in Defoe's *Review*, in a number of independent poems, satires, pamphlets, like *The Town-Rakes: or, The Frolicks of the Mohocks or Hawkubites* and *The Mohocks: A Poem, in Miltonic Verse: Address'd to the Spectator*, as well as John Gay's little-known first play *The Mohocks*, published a month later. (53)

Bell remarks, "Such an accumulation of evidence looks very persuasive: here is the press at its most active, giving us copious information about the fugitive night life of Augustan London which we could not otherwise come by" (54). Yet Bell concludes by saying that there is no evidence to establish that such gangs spread terror and violence throughout London. Bell writes, rather unconvincingly: "There undoubtedly was violence in the dark and unpatrolled streets of Augustan London, but that is insufficient reason to accept the press's interpretation of events" (54).

However accurate Bell is in concluding that the periodical press "interpreted" events, as he writes, "to address obliquely all the seemingly intractable problems of urbanisation," it seems wrong-headed to doubt the existence of gangs of hooligans in eighteenth-century London when such a variety of documents from the period testify to their existence. Starting from what Bell grudgingly admits—that there "undoubtedly was violence in the dark and unpatrolled streets of Augustan London"—Keith Heller re-creates in his fiction a plausible reality for that violence and those dark and unpatrolled streets. The reality of the Hawcubites is imaged on the body of a battered George Man:

John Manneux looked thoughtfully across the table at the watchman. He had noticed the bruises on the young man's face and his careful way of walking—as if he suffered from a painful hernia—when he had first come in. Now, close, he could see that the watchman had been badly beaten. The nose was swollen, the lips split, and the skin round the eyes was mottled and puffy. (*Man's Storm* 21)

Bell's properly academic concerns notwithstanding, Heller brings to vivid life the violence of eighteenth-century London which, for its victims, was harsh reality. Man briefly, even embarrassedly, tells the tale:

Last night it was, as I took a turn in Sea Alley. A devil's dozen of them that style themselves Hawcubites. They were against me before I knew which way to turn. Thereafter, they spent a few minutes of their time introducing me to their shoes and their buckles. I'd had one or two of them down with my staff, but then they closed up ranks and I went under. I should have kept them at the staff's length. It is hardly to my praise as a watchman. (21-22)

Man's listener, Manneux, softly voices his sincere concern that Man could have been killed, "as old Dick Adams was two or three year past," and Man dismisses the suggestion with "a miss is as good as an ell" (22). He admits, however, "Not that but I let it come too close to me, though, and all for my own imperfect watchfulness" (22). The night world of the London watch evoked by Heller is a world in which criminal violence always lurks close at hand.

Ian Bell also acknowledges the criminal success of the notorious Jonathan Wild who, among other things, exploited the periodical press to blackmail clients into purchasing personal items, like pocket-books with embarrassing or compromising personal notes in them, which had in fact been stolen. Nevertheless, Bell agrees with recent historians who dismiss the existence of organized crime in the eighteenth century (16). In his extensive treatment of Wild in *Man's Illegal Life*, Heller much more plausibly imagines the real Wild and the workings of a criminal organization that produced the stolen goods Wild sold back to his "clients." George Man has had, in his twenty-seven years on the watch, "some contact with Wild's city-wide organization," his "formidable corporation of thieves, conveyers and informers" (92):

Man knew, as well as any, the extent and effectiveness of Wild's operations. By means of cleverness and ruthlessness, Wild had managed to perfect a system by which he set himself up as the indispensable conduit between the most respectable circles of London society and the ubiquitous underworld. . . . There was no one in London who better manipulated both the innocent and the felon. (94-95)

Heller's—and Man's—conclusion: "Few legitimate business enterprises and no public offices could boast of such model organization" (96). The key word in Heller's description is "legitimate." Above all, Heller effectively describes a world in which the distinction between legitimate and illegitimate, legal and illegal, is being hammered out in society, politics, and the law.

Michel Foucault makes explicit the connection between crime and capitalism and the problematic distinction between the legal and the illegal, the legitimate and the illegitimate, in *Discipline and Punish*. Foucault describes how, in the eighteenth century,

the shift from a criminality of blood to a criminality of fraud forms part of a whole complex mechanism, embracing the development of production, the increase of wealth, a higher juridical and moral value placed on property relations, stricter methods of surveillance, a tighter partitioning of the population, more efficient techniques of locating and obtaining information. (77)

Foucault delineates the class struggle over the law itself, how the bourgeois classes seized and defended their right to determine what was legal and illegal in the economic arena: "the bourgeoisie was to reserve itself . . . to an immense sector of economic circulation by a skilful manipulation of gaps in the law—gaps that were foreseen by its silences, or opened up by *de facto* tolerance" (87).

During the time about which Keith Heller writes, London was still in the grip of "the criminality of blood;" the legal system was more preoccupied with punishment of discovered violent crimes than in the detection or prevention of such crimes. As Foucault describes and analyzes in detail throughout *Discipline and Punish*, the use of torture to secure confession was commonplace; discovery of crime depended upon informers and accusations verified under torture. At the same time, in the course of the emergence and rise of capitalism, the distinctions between legitimate and illegitimate economic practices and ventures were not very sharp. There was a period, in other words, of transition between the "criminality of blood" to a "criminality of fraud" in which crime—in the sense of fraud, theft, etc.—was barely distinguishable from capitalism. It is this transition period that Heller's Man novels capture so realistically.

We have seen that Jonathan Wild's criminal organization is better organized than most legitimate enterprises and more like them than different. In *Man's Illegal Life*, Heller draws a marked parallel between Wild's organized "criminal" activities, which encompassed economic ventures that ranged from the illegal to the legal, and an example of an early stock-and-futures speculation which distinguished early eighteenth-century capitalism. The murder victim, Geoffrey Stannard, had made and lost a fortune in the dubiously-legal South Sea Company fiasco, known as the "South Sea Bubble," a rampant stock speculation in the future of the American slave trade. This bubble burst when an annual tax on imported slaves was imposed and the Company was restricted to sending only one ship each year of human cargo. Man looks at a sheet of notes made from a conversation with a clerk familiar with the South Sea matter: "Why had Man even bothered to write them down? Probably because they gave him a bare outline of the events which had occurred in a part of society with which he personally was not very familiar" (56). In the course of the year 1720, South Sea stocks showed miraculous rises from January to August, followed by incredible drops in September and December to far below the original value; Bank of England stock was similarly affected. "Man could read in these numbers the cold facts of the city-wide chaos he remembered so vividly. . . . The scandal had involved the highest levels of society" (56). Noblemen were expelled and imprisoned; gentlemen and not-so-gentle-men committed suicide as their fortunes, families, and futures were ruined; and "the estates of the Company's directors confiscated" (56). Geoffrey Stannard, who "had managed to escape from the squalor of Drury Lane nine years before," had been forced to move back to that site of the origin of the Great Plague of 1665 (56). Two years later, Stannard is dead and the circumstances recall the treatment of people and households suspected of being infected by the plague.

Heller weaves the Great Plague, Jonathan Wild's criminal organization, the South Sea Bubble, and the precarious profession of writing ("a pen in every hand," reflects a writer Man encounters)—capitalism exercised unfettered—into a complex fabric of criminality and contagion. Wild's criminal operation differs only from the South Sea Bubble in being a better investment—not because it is less legal, or less legitimate, or less moral. Eighteenth-century capitalism emerges and grows like a plague; renewed fears of an actual plague contribute, like capitalism itself, to a spreading chaos.

In the other two Man novels, Heller continues to show the close connection between crime and emerging capitalism. In *Man's Storm*, the murder victim and her husband are "ironmongers" who exist by foraging the city for legally-retrievable iron scraps. Heller makes clear the close connection between this legal operation and more dubious forms of "finding" goods and claiming them as one's own, and the various characters' legal, semi-illegal, and illegal economic activities provide one area of possible motives for the murder. Yet these are inextricably interwoven with the involved parties' sexual lives, which span the spectrum of legally sanctioned marriage to adultery, polygamy, and lesbianism and throw into very high relief the age's struggle over the questions of legality and legitimacy. In *Man's Loving Family*, Abraham Sinclair, trader, is shown to have a virtual monopoly on wine, spices, and tobacco. Heller describes how that monopoly is only possible if it is supported by illegal practices like bribery, favor in the court, and an incestuous control over the members of his own family working in his business. *Man's Storm* details the business of prostitution, and how it provides a rare opportunity for the enterprising female madam even as it exemplifies how women in the eighteenth century are increasingly viewed as property. *Man's Loving Family* illustrates vividly how, then as now, the "business of business" is sometimes conducted in the most questionable of locales. The man whom Man is hired to protect is murdered in a brothel that the victim has visited with a man with whom he is doing business.

The theme of legitimate and illegitimate, legal and illegal, permeates Heller's Man novels. Nowhere is this more poignantly illustrated than in the meaning and significance of the first novel's title: *Man's Illegal Life*. The year 1722 saw the re-emergence of the Plague in Europe; fears of its return to England spawned numerous pamphlets, periodical articles, and books both on the new threat and on its last vicious visitation in 1665—most famously in Daniel Defoe's *A Journal of the Plague Year*. As mentioned, the murder victim, Geoffrey Stannard, is found bound, gagged and starved to death in a chair in his house in Drury Lane—site of the origin of the 1665 plague. In a document which is instrumental in Man's solving of Stannard's murder, the narrator describes the soon-to-be-common practice, during the height of the plague in 1665, of neighbors forcibly tying up suspected plague victims in their homes and then boarding up the houses to prevent said victims from escaping and spreading the disease. Presenting himself as a hero and benefactor, the narrator justifies this murderous practice:

In later and more settled times, some observers may fault us for the precipitancy of our acts, saying that such decisions and such executions lay in the hands of the lawful officers of the town; yet our time was much troubled and the chief officers much confused and lax: and, in such extremes, it behooves the private individual, with the vocal or silent acquiescence of the neighbourhood, which last we had, to move against any visible or hidden threat to the conservation of the peace and strength of the society. (137)

Bringing forward this admission and justification, ostensibly, in 1722 and on the eve of perhaps a new visitation, the narrator offers this chilling conclusion:

[Y]et in these days, when the people are more certain of which due preparations they should effect against a new visitation, it is my thought that most must condone and understand that we then had none other choice but to declare, among the leading citizens of the street, the man's life to be illegal. (137)

Based on historical research into the Great Plague and the subsequent life of the eighteenth century, Heller re-creates an important moment in the genealogy of crime and legality. Foucault writes, "For a long time, ordinary individuality—the everday individuality of everybody—remained below the threshold of description" (191). Foucault's history of "disciplinarity" shows how modern institutions evolved ever more precise practices of individualization of the ordinary person: "The disciplinary methods. . . lowered the threshold of describable individuality and made of this description a means of control and a method of domination" (191). These methods eventually evolved into the prisons, the police, educational systems—the modern institutions with their modern disciplines. Heller's fictionalized re-creation of practices during the Great Plague shows the nascence of such institutions in the acts of local communities: how, during a community crisis, citizens of that community identify ordinary individuals who pose a specific threat to that community—as possible bearers of the plague—and act to judge those individuals' lives "illegal." Although it was to take more than one hundred years to perfect modern "disciplines" and institutions, Heller traces their genealogy to discrete practices of the late seventeenth century and early eighteenth which pre-figure the institutions of police and prisons that emerged to exercise control over the individual bodies of the body politic in the nineteenth and twentieth centuries.

In *Man's Loving Family*, Man's surrogate-father relationship to the young writer, Richard Savage, is rendered more poignant by the revelation of the fact that George and Sarah's only son, Nathaniel, was abducted, at age four, by the "professional kidnappers called Spiriters who would trade them like livestock to the plantations" (16). This "legal" practice of kidnapping children into slavery underscores the age's struggle to negotiate the question of legality against the demands of emerging capitalism, which increasingly reduced ordinary human life to a commodity. "The fathers and mothers on the shore aching with helplessness and misery, none of them rich enough to buy their children back" (16). Such are the harsh realities for working-class people and parents in an age in which it was realized that people are products, to be bought and sold like any other.

The crime and criminality evoked in Heller's Man novels are believable and vivid because the author explores class and gender relations within the context of emerging capitalism. Heller's persistent themes of legality and legitimacy reflect urgent concerns of London society in the first decades of the eighteenth century. From the point of view of his main character, watchman George Man, Heller engages in a critique of emerging bourgeois British capitalism from the perspective of the working class. In bringing the world of the early eighteenth century vividly to life, from its lowliest to its highest persons, Heller creates fictions which are as valuable as history as they are as mystery novels. The Man novels provide a believable genealogy of crime and criminals in the early eighteenth century which, while using methods similar to those of New Historicists, make a persuasive case that crime was pervasive and the City a very dangerous place. But the watch *was there*.

In *Discipline and Punish*, Foucault discusses the importance of the emergence of "the rule of common truth":

The old system of legal proofs, the use of torture, the extraction of confessions, the use of the public execution, the body and spectacle for the reproduction of truth had long isolated penal practice from the common forms of demonstration: semi-proofs produced semi-truths and semi-guilty persons, words extracted by pain had greater authenticity, presumption involved a degree of punishment. (97)

For "the rule of common truth" to emerge in the justice system in the first place, complete information about crime and criminals must be available, which requires at once an "optimal specification" of all legalities and illegalities by the justice system and a network of information-gathering which supplied information for specification and classification. Foucault offers an important observation:

Hence the idea that the machinery of justice must be duplicated by an organ of surveillance that would work side by side with it, and which would make it possible either to prevent crimes, or, if committed, to arrest their authors; police and justice must work together as two complementary actions of the same process. (96)

In a nutshell, all of this means no modern prison and justice system without a modern police institution, and neither of those without the rule of common truth and the principle of optimal specification. The disciplines or institutions Foucault describes emerged fully only in the nineteenth century.

Foucault writes, "Hierarchized, continuous and functional surveillance may not be one of the great technical 'inventions' of the eighteenth century, but its insidious extension owed its importance to the mechanisms of power that it brought with it" (176). Police surveillance made it possible for disciplinary power to become an "integrated" system, "linked from the inside to the economy and to the aims of the mechanism in which it was practiced" (176). More importantly, it functioned as "a network of relations from top to bottom, but also to a certain extent from bottom to top and laterally" (176).

During the early eighteenth century, London—like most of Europe—was still in "the old system of legal proofs," with its "use of torture, the extraction of confessions," etc. Crime was confessed and punished, not detected. Without the complementary systems of the police and the modern prison and legal apparatuses, there could be no "detection" of crime, and hence no "detectives." Against this seemingly factual and logical imperative, Keith Heller invents an eighteenth-century detective, George Man. In doing so, Heller provides as believable a genealogy of detection as he did a genealogy of crime, much as Foucault provided a genealogy of the modern prison and police. Man's art of detection derives from his believably-rendered application of "the rule of common truth," pursuit of optimally-specified information acquired through reading, research, investigation, and surveillance, and his knowledge and experience of individuals gained through close observation on the watch.

In keeping with Foucault's analysis of the birth of the prison and the institution of the police, Heller describes a legal system that is definitely not organized as "a network of relations from top to bottom, but also to a certain extent from bottom to top and laterally." The watch, at the bottom of the hierarchy, is not organized to keep individuals under surveillance or to gather information; the system did not recognize that its relations could work from "bottom to top." The very name of the "watch" is subtly ironic: it is hired to "watch," meaning to watch out for crime and criminals, but it is empowered only to apprehend, not to report all that it has seen.

Moreover, Heller makes clear that the "old legal system" operative during the eighteenth century does not function according to "the rule of common truth." In *Man's Illegal Life*, the constabulary and coroner are more concerned to prevent spreading rumors of a plague outbreak than they are in finding the murderer of Geoffrey Stannard. The official view of the matter is at once that Stannard died and didn't die of the plague, that he died at his own hand and at the hand of another, and that, if the latter, it wasn't murder but a service to the community. Contradictions flout logic and the rule of common truth because the concerns of the legal system are not to detect crime but to prevent panic. In *Man's Storm*, the very question of "truth" is doubted by a coroner who believes they shall be able to discover only as much of the truth "as our just Lord deigns to reveal to us" (115). Constable Burton refuses to consider the widow Woodman as a possible suspect because he finds her, not only attractive, but quite available sexually. Burton also subscribes to the notion that "How a man is born is how he dies. There can be no change at bottom" (56)—an indefensible position, outside "the rule of common truth," but a metaphysical belief in keeping with the beliefs about human nature of the time. In *Man's Loving Family*, the fact that writer Richard Savage didn't even know the man he is accused of murdering is not considered by the presiding judge in the face of the overwhelming truth that Savage's sword entered the victim's body and caused his death. Also ignored is the fact that one of the witnesses, impressario John James Heidegger, hires a substitute to appear for him at the trial. The initial verdict, then, is yet another "semi-truth": Savage's sword ran through James Sinclair; therefore Savage murdered Sinclair. Abraham Sinclair, father to one son already murdered and to another threatened with the same fate, sums up the "unreasonable" attitude prevalent early in "the Age of Reason": when Man asks Sinclair if he does not want to know who murdered his first son, Sinclair replies, "Can't be known; and even if it could, it would hardly profit a man much to know it" (65). It is up to unemployed George Man to replace semi-truths with the whole truth.

According to Foucault, in the modern legal system that replaced that of Man's era, "the truth of the crime will be accepted only when it is completely proven;" and Foucault continues, "It follows that, up to the final demonstration of his crime, the defendant must be regarded as innocent; and that, in order to carry out this demonstration, the judge must use not ritual forms, but common instruments, that reason possessed by everyone, which is also that of philosophers and scientists" (97). The system of Man's era clearly relies on "ritual forms"—torture, confession, presumption of guilt during the trial, public execution—and in all three novels Man's "true" solution to each murder must be verified by the ritual forms and means.

Yet Foucualt's discussion of "the rule of common truth" implies that some understanding of "common truth" existed during the eighteenth century; moreover, "that reason possessed by everyone, which is also that of philosophers and scientists" had been understood and practiced by philosophers and scientists since the late seventeenth century—hence the period's title of "the Age of Reason." The point, here, is that however little "the rule of common truth" figured in the eighteenth-century legal system, the common sense and reason "possessed by everyone" were already enjoyed at the time of which Heller writes. George Man possesses that reason—even though he acknowledges that wife Sarah owns a greater share of common sense—to a high degree, and this important quality helps him develop his art of detection.

Although he is "as sincere a Christian as any," Man has "no patience with the popular notion of divine intervention in the daily affairs of the world" (*Man's Illegal Life* 25); and against "metaphysical speculation" Man prefers hard facts, because for him, "the merely human was too regularly obscure enough" (17). In Man's view, even murder is eventually understandable: "He looked upon any such mystery as being the inevitable last act in an individual human drama, the expression of unknown but ultimately recognizable fears and desires" (25). In the manner of Geoffrey Stannard's death, eerily paralleling the summary judgment of people suspected of carrying the plague, Man believes that there "must be some connection, and some hidden reasoning behind that connection, that must be understood" (51-52). And unlike his superiors, more concerned with semi-truths and restricting public panic about a possible return of the plague, "Man would continue to feel the need to understand even if the murderer were never apprehended" (52). Man's commitment to the empirical method is evident in the following description:

This was part of Man's method, because of which he was so often derided and misunderstood. To find the man who had killed Geoffrey Stannard required only the finding of the one man who must have killed him, who could not help but kill him. Some man who—due to the pressures of personality or circumstances—would not be able not to murder. (113)

This is as clear a statement as any of the principle behind "that reason common to everyone, which is also that of philosophers and scientists" of Man's own day. Man believes "that every mortal action resulted from a motivation that was fully consistent with itself, no matter how idiosyncratic or even mad it might appear to others" (20). Yet Man is also sensible of something that "intrigued and frustrated" him "more than anything else: that for any given sequence of human actions, when seen from the otuside, at least two—and very often more—interpretations could be imagined, each one apparently as accurate and meaningful as any other" (154). For Man as much as for any postmodernist, the "indeterminacy of the truth" (154) is as much a part of reality as the necessity of using reason to understand it.

Man's empirical method of detection relies on reliable information. We have seen that the early eighteenth century lacked a system of police surveillance and information gathering. Like children at the bottom level of the patriarchal hierarchy, the watch at the bottom of the legal one was to be seen and not heard or heeded. Nevertheless, Heller convincingly portrays an eighteenth-century world in which certain of the conditions necessary for the emergence of the modern legal institutions, including the police and the art of detection, were already present. Foucault makes much of the fact that, in France at least, the emergence of the police was materially facilitated by the enlistment of organized criminals as agents of the police. Foucault's two exemplary figures from the nineteenth century are Vidocq, whose memoirs influenced both Edgar Allan Poe and Arthur Conan Doyle in their invention and development, respectively, of the detective story, and Lacenaire, who prefigured Arsene Lupin as a real gentleman criminal and who advanced the "aesthetics of crime" (*Discipline and Punish* 282-85). Based on historical documentation of the parish watch, which, as we have seen, "were sometimes criminal themselves" (as Heller describes in his first "Note on the Watch") as they were also usually old and decrepit, Heller invents an eighteenth-century detective who, as a watchman, is neither criminal nor decrepit but who is able to capitalize on his close contact with criminals, beggars, street porters, thief-catchers, the homeless—the people of the streets of eighteenth-century London.

In *Man's Loving Family*, Man's knowledge and the network by which he obtains it is neatly summarized: "The watchman was for holding back and trusting, as he always had, to the living resources of the street. He was waiting for something, looking for the smallest detail, that would help him find the surrounding context for all that had happened" (134). For Man, "the living sources of the street" serve him as they were later to serve the modern police; and the sources are there to serve such a one as George Man, before Vidocq and Lacenaire and Robert Peel and Poe and Doyle supplied the world with models for the criminal detective.

Yet it is in his reading of the literature and periodical press, and his research into documents of the past, that distinguishes Man as the detective as historian. Heller's eighteenth century, like that of the New Historicists, is a most "textual" age. In *Man's Loving Family*, Man researches the contemporary and historical literature about the Great Plague of 1665 and discovers, in a recent publication, the identity of the murderer of Geoffrey Stannard. *Man's Storm* begins each chapter with a quotation from Defoe's *The Storm* and shows Man to be familiar with the other writings of Defoe. *Man's Loving Family* takes Man to the bookshop of Andrew Millar (eventual publisher of Fielding's *Tom Jones*) to discover the source of the advertisement that predicts the death of James Sinclair, the man Man is hired to protect; and Man involves the young Henry Fielding, before he is writer and novelist, in his investigations and is rewarded with his recall to the watch on the basis of what Fielding did not write about John James Heidegger's involvment in the murder of Sinclair. As he is familiar with the streets of eighteenth-century London, so Man is familiar with its discourse—a discourse available to the empirical and reasoning mind of the eighteenth century that is inclined to solve mysteries. Heller's genius is that he imagines a mind and person in keeping with historical evidence who, before detectives seem to have been possible, was a true detective.

In 1733-34 Alexander Pope published a sequence of poetical essays which were to become his *Essay on Man*. Pope's poem reflects the eighteenth century's preoccupation with human nature before the onset of Romantic individualism: "The proper study of Mankind is Man." Heller's choice of names for his main character has obvious meaning and significance. More than any other age (except, perhaps, our own), "the Age of Reason" was preoccupied with the nature of man in both his universal and particular manifestations. There was a belief in a universal human nature, proclaimed by philosophy and poetry, and unique individuality, presented in fiction and personal journalism. What people thought and felt was put into print, partly because of the enormous appetite for the printed word. The line between discourse and reality, then as now, was believed to be fine if not non-existent. Like our own, the eighteenth century was a textual age. The intervening years witnessed the aberration of the writer as isolated individual, writing against the inexorable mass will of the modern materialistic world and writing for an ill-defined future in which the conflict of the universal and the particular would be resolved in favor of the latter—writing as anarchy, the logic of the enlightenment understanding of the autonomous human subject carried to its drastic extreme.

Lawrence Lipking asserts that "the eighteenth century (far more than any earlier age) remains contemporary" (19) because so many of the age's issues and concerns continue to be our issues and concerns. In creating fictions set two centuries ago, Heller captures both the universality of man which has continued—else we couldn't understand, let alone relate to, the rich texts of the period—and the sometimes shocking differences in language, thought, actions, and beliefs that we, at the start of the twenty-first century, no longer share with the eighteenth. That Heller's Man novels are believable as history is testimony to his skill in invoking both the universals and the particulars of the eighteenth century. That those same universals and particulars—especially the nature of man and of individual human beings— are relevant to us now demonstrates that Heller is aware of what Michel Foucault insists upont: that the only reason for "doing" history is to aid us in understanding the present.

However, that Heller's Man novels are also gripping as detective fiction is testimony to another kind of historical awareness: that of the history of detective fiction. In structure, Heller's novels conform to the so-called "classical" or "English" detective novel. Through gathering of evidence and use of reasoning, George Man solves murders. In perspective, however, Heller's Man novels owe more to the so-called "hardboiled" school, in which "down these mean streets a man must go, who is not himself mean, who is neither tarnished nor afraid." While Heller is not the first to achieve a synthesis of these two broad types of detective fiction—Rex Stout's Nero Wolfe novels come to mind—he is the first and, so far, the only to imagine a detective who goes down the mean streets of eighteenth-century London. Moreover, Heller—like Raymond Chandler, just quoted, above—gives murder back to individuals who have real reasons for committing it. Against what Foucault calls "the aesthetics of crime, that is to say . . . an art of the privileged classes" (284), the aesthetics of the "Classical" detective novel, Heller shows that, in the eighteenth century as now, crime cuts across classes. It is neither the inevitable concomitant of being poor, as Foucault describes it was understood in the eighteenth century, nor the artful privilege of the ruling class (see *Discipline and Punish* 68-69, and Bell 46-91). Heller installs George Man as the fictional predecessor of Dupin and Holmes as he shows that Man also prefigures the tough-guy street detectives like Sam Spade and Philip Marlowe. Heller's Man novels thus provide us with not only a genealogy of crime, criminals, and detection, but a new genealogy of detective fiction, as well as a unique contribution to the genre.[2]

### Notes

1. The New Historicism differs from the old in its belief that documents from history embody ideological perspectives more than universal truths. The New Historicism also differs from the old in the former's serious attention to documents other than the canon of Great Literature. Heller's novels conform to these New Historical principles. New Historicism also resorts to vivid, almost fictional recreations of the life of history, which Heller's novels also attempt to do. New Historical methods came relatively late to eighteenth-century studies, so Heller can be perceived as being on the "cutting edge." Other recent volumes taking New Historical and/or other contemporary theoretical approaches are Laura Brown, *Ends of Empire: Women and Ideology in Early Eighteenth-Century English Literature*; Leo Damrosch, ed., *The Profession of Eighteenth-Century Literature: Reflections on an Institution*; Felicity Nussbaum and Laura Brown, eds., *The New 18th Century: Theory, Politics, English Literature*; and Beth Fowkes Tobin, ed., *History, Gender and Eighteenth Century Literature*.

2. Keith Heller is more recently the author of *Snow on the Moon*, a historical "mainstream" novel set in Spain at the end of World War II. Although the novel does have a mystery element, it is not a "detective novel." The work deserves mention, however, because it confirms the paper's argument that Heller's fiction is also an important evocation of history, and of his status as writer as historian. Not surprisingly, like the Man novels, *Snow on the Moon* is first-rate fiction.

## Works Cited

Bell, Ian A. *Literature and Crime in Augustan England*. London: Routledge, 1991.

Brown, Laura. *Ends of Empire: Women and Ideology in Early Eighteenth-Century English Literature*. Ithaca: Cornell UP, 1993.

Damrosch, Leo, ed. *The Profession of Eighteenth-Century Literature: Reflections on an Institution*. Madison: U Wisconsin P, 1992.

Foucault, Michel. *Discipline and Punish: The Birth of the Prison*. Trans. Alan Sheridan. New York: Vintage, 1979.

Haycraft, Howard. *Murder for Pleasure*. 1941. New York: Carroll and Graf, 1984.

Heller, Keith. *Man's Illegal Life*. London: Collins, 1984.

——. *Man's Loving Family*. London: Collins, 1986.

——. *Man's Storm*. 1985. New York: Scribner's, 1986.

——. *Snow on the Moon*. London: Headline Review, 1996.

Kirkpatrick, Kathryn. "Sermons and Strictures: Conduct-Book Propriety and Property Relations in Late Eighteenth-Century England." Nussbaum and Brown 179-226.

Lipking, Lawrence. "Inventing the Eighteenth Centuries: A Long View." Damrosch 7-25.

Nussbaum, Felicity, and Laura Brown, eds. *The New 18th Century: Theory, Politics, English Literature*. New York: Methuen, 1987.

Tobin, Beth Fowkes, ed. *History, Gender and Eighteenth-Century Literature*. Athens: U Georgia P, 1994.

# Margaret Lawrence:
## An Eighteenth-Century Midwife

### Marie Nelson

It is early in the year 1786—three years since the end of the civil war that made traitors of men loyal to their king and patriots of rebellious colonists. Women reckon time in an alternate manner and so it has been twenty years since the beginning of Lucy Hannah Trevor's "long war" that began with her "foolish marriage" to James Trevor. Fourteen years have passed since the deaths of her three children from a summer diphtheria epidemic in Boston and eight years since her husband, a Loyalist, fled to Quebec, leaving her penniless to fend for herself in a "cold, half-ruined cottage down by the docks" of Rufford, Maine on the banks of the Manitac River (*Hearts* 13). Taken in by her uncle, Henry Markham, prosperous owner of a lumber mill and a grist mill, Hannah has learned midwifery from her Aunt Julia. Her medical skills include the knowledge of herbs and other natural remedies and enable her to provide for her daughter and contribute to the family economy.

Although she is skilled in housewifery as well as midwifery, Hannah is an unconventional woman. "Educated above her station" (*Hearts* 9), she can read and write, keeps a journal, and is the owner of three books, *The History of Rasselas, Prince of Abyssinia*, by Dr. Samuel Johnson; *The Tragedie of King Lear by Mr. William Shakspear, with Improvements by the Famous Actor, Mr. Colley Cibber*; and *Poor Richard's Almanack*, by Mr. Benjamin Franklin. She provokes censure from the other women of the village for any number of indiscretions including refusing to wear a demure cap over her curly hair cut short or, except when it is cold, a decent scarf to cover her bosom. When she uses a horse, she rides astride rather than sidesaddle. And "when a thing seems useless nonsense, she takes pains to ignore it" (*Hearts* 10).

What she cannot ignore is the precarious position she and her daughter occupy in society. While married, James Trevor treated her as a possession as the law allowed. He wasted her dowry, set the constable upon her when she attempted to save their children from diphtheria by taking them out of Boston during the epidemic, used her body as he wanted without regard for her feelings, and prostituted her to pay his gambling debts. When he fled from persecution for his Tory politics, his properties, including personal possessions she brought to the marriage, were seized by the Rufford Committee of Public Safety. His creditors looked to her for payment of his debts, but her dower rights which should have entitled her to a third of his goods were denied her by the patriots' committee who declared that as Tories "kept no laws, they could have no legal wives" (*Blood* 165).

After eight years without any word from Trevor, Hannah mourns not the loss of a husband. Indeed she has no desire to be any man's wife, but she does mourn the loss of her children. Soon after Trevor's flight to Canada, Hannah discretely took a lover in order to get pregnant and have a child "of her own." Though tongues wag that deaf-mute Jennet's birth occurred a bit too long after her putative father's departure, Hannah bears no shame over her daughter's suspect parentage. For her it seemed a rational way to circumvent a social and legal system that denied women independence and self-determination even as that rhetoric served to incite men to war.

Abandoned by her husband and without property of her own, Hannah is dependent upon her uncle for protection and support. But it is a dependence that will last only as long as he allows it, or as long as he lives and is in a financial position to shelter her. And it is not enough to protect her from being summoned to Orphan's Court under the aegis of the Poor Laws to show cause why her eight-year old daughter Jennet should not be indentured until adulthood. Even her Aunt Julia uneasily contemplates how drastically her own circumstances will be altered if she should survive her husband. Regardless of the contributions she makes to the family economy during the marriage, her dower rights entitle her to her clothing and her linens. When her husband's property passes to his heirs, her use of the house or other property will be limited. In a society wracked by intergenerational conflicts, she will be dependent upon the good will of her son and his wife to enjoy any comforts in her later years.

Created by novelist Margaret Lawrence, Hannah Trevor's tale as told in the trilogy *Hearts and Bones* (1996), *Blood Red Roses* (1997), and *The Burning Bride* (1998), transports the reader to a historical moment 200 years ago that is both foreign as well as strangely familiar.[1] Violent crimes, suicides, distrust of government and political leaders, war veterans suffering from post-traumatic stress syndrome, intergenerational conflicts, premarital pregnancies, drunkenness, spouse abuse, child neglect, illiteracy, onerous taxes, housing shortages, hunger and poverty are common. This is not a gentler, kinder yesterday that Ms. Lawrence writes about, but one in which racial, class, and gender conflicts frequently threaten and do erupt into violence when people eager for quick solutions to difficult problems take matters into their own hands.

Inhabited by uneasy, indignant, and fearful souls, it is a messy, chaotic world in which Hannah Trevor finds herself. One of her ways of coping with the uncertainties of life is through quilting. She makes quilts "only partially for use and beauty. Mostly, Hannah work[s] from an almost obsessive need to discover a reasonable pattern in apparent waste and chaos—the same need that leads her into the mysteries of childbirth and of violent and sudden death" (*Hearts* 16-17). It is Hannah's careful attention to patterns and their significance that casts her into the role of detective.

*Hearts and Bones*, set in February 1786, opens with the murder of Anthea Emory, wife of an absent surveyor and mother of two children. Viewed from the perspective of the unidentified killer, the death is a mercy killing of a woman dead in spirit long ago as a consequence of the horrors of war she experienced as a child. When Hannah notices no smoke coming from the chimney of the Emory's house, she sets out to carry coals to Mrs. Emory to rekindle a fire. Stopping at the forge for coals, she shares her concerns with Will Quaid, the constable, a smithy, and Hannah's friend. There is a pattern to village life that all are a part of and, as Hannah and Will talk, they discover several breaks in the pattern that suggest some mishap has come to the Emory household. At the Emory home, they find the mangled body and a letter that Mrs. Emory apparently wrote to her husband, claiming that three men had broken the lock of her door, raped, beat and burned her for three consecutive nights. In anticipation of the third man returning as he has threatened to take her life on the fourth night, lest she charge them all with rape, she has sent her children to be cared for at a neighbor's until his return. At the end of the letter she has written three names, one of which has been scribbled over so that the critical letters are indistinguishable.

Upon the woman's body and around the house are several clues that cast suspicion upon one of those named in the letter, Daniel Josselyn, a friend of Quaid's and Hannah's former lover. Josselyn began his life as a privileged third son of Lord Benbridge. His father bought him a commission in the army and he served in India in the Bengal Rifles and then in Burgoyne's Third Horse in America. It was after the Battle of Saratoga (1777) that he resigned his commission with the British Army and joined the Continental Army. But he was always suspect, believed to be a British spy. In England he was declared a traitor and his wife was no longer received in polite society. Disowned by his father, cut off from his former wealth, wounded and broken by the horrors of war and his part in them, he took respite briefly in Rufford, boarding with Will Quaid and working as a smithy in Quaid's forge.

It was then that Hannah had singled him out for her lover, because he already had a wife and thus would not be in position to expect marriage. When she had conceived, she dismissed him, denying any feelings for him and informing him that he could have no claim upon her or the child. Body healed but heartbroken by Hannah's rejection, he returned to the battlefront. At war's end, having nowhere else to go, he returned to Rufford. In the years since returning from the battlefront, through hard work and benefitting from a substantial inheritance from his grandfather, he has risen to wealth and prosperity, and now lives in a finely furnished mansion with servants and his invalid wife. Although he enjoys the respect of the men he had fought beside and led during the War and now as Major Josselyn commands the Rufford Militia, his wealth and his office set him apart from the yeoman farmers and landless craftsmen who find themselves crushed by increased taxes, rising debt, and worthless currency.

Daniel has made no attempt to contact Hannah since his return, knowing that undue attentions from him, a married man, would only do further damage to her reputation. But he watches her as she goes about her duties and counts the day blessed when he catches a glimpse of her or their daughter. Although Hannah and Daniel have not spoken to each other since the night, four years earlier, when she nursed his wife through a difficult childbirth, they are bound together in spirit as well as by the body of the child they created together. Troubled by the evidence that points to Josselyn as the murderer, a chance encounter between Hannah and Josselyn forces her to confront and admit feelings for him that she had long denied. The crisis serves as impetus for reestablishing a limited relationship between the two and Hannah allows Daniel access to his child. Daniel begins teaching Jennet sign-language based on that used by local woodland natives.

The plot thickens, a patchwork made more complex by a second murder. Artemas Siwall, tormented to madness by the massacre at Webb's Ford following the Battle of Saratoga, is found run through with Josselyn's grandfather's battle sword, just after he had spoken cryptically of Webb's Ford to Hannah. Several of the townsmen, including Josselyn and Quaid, were at Webb's Ford and, because of the atrocities that were committed there, made a pact to never speak of it to others. Though Quaid is ready to carry out his duty, arrest Josselyn and hold him for trial, too many others are ready to take the law into their own hands and string him up, not only because of his apparent guilt, but because he represents a focal point for the class tensions that divide the community. Hannah knows that Daniel is not guilty of the murders of Emory and Siwall—in the many clues she sees too many pieces that fail to fit a proper pattern. As she goes about her duties as housewife, midwife, and mother, she encounters other pieces of evidence. But until she has probed and learned the secrets of events in the past, she cannot make sense of the triangles, squares, and circles that she is compelled to turn and to twist and to try to fit together until the motive and the perpetrator emerge from the patchwork.

*Blood Red Roses* takes place a few months later, at Midsummer's Fair. During the dance, Reuben Stark, a broom seller only recently come into the area with a wife and children, is discovered with his throat slit. Knowing that she will be called upon to attend the autopsy, Hannah carefully studies the murder scene for clues. Near the body is a memorial handkerchief embroidered with the initials of Hannah and James, a recent gift from a neighbor. Closely examining the body, she recognizes it to be that of her husband, James Trevor, long thought to be dead of fever in Quebec. Intending to inform the family of the murder, a group of citizens including Hannah and Daniel Josselyn make their way through the woods to the Stark home. There they discover the bloody bodies of Stark's wife and three children hacked by an ax and carefully covered with quilts weighted down by stones. A footprint and the quilts make it clear that the murders were done by a woman, and Hannah becomes the prime suspect. This time in order to save herself, she is compelled to piece together bits of evidence that include the litanies of lost women and tormented men, physically and psychologically abused, casualties of one war or another.

In *The Burning Bride*, the final installment, Hannah and Daniel are once again chief suspects when, during the fall 1786 hunting season and on the eve of the annual Militia Muster, they discover the partially buried and burned body of Samuel Clinch. Clinch, a crude, arrogant barber-surgeon, more concerned about the size of his fees then the well-being of his patients, had just charged Hannah with drunkenness, lewdness, wrongful prescribing and interfering with his treatment of an elderly woman who died. If Hannah is found guilty of his charges, she will be charged with murder by mischance of the shared patient. Hannah's supposed motive of revenge is matched by that of Daniel's, as it was Clinch who botched the birthing of Josselyn's son by dismembering the infant and butchering the mother's body, making her a permanent invalid. At the murder scene Hannah finds a button from a military coat worn by a member of a particular unit and an almanac that she later discovers has been used to record complex weaving drafts.

Hannah continues to attempt to make sense of the clues she gathers much like she collects patches of cloth to make a quilt design. She also weaves together strands of information obtained from female networks with threads drawn from the masculine world to make a coherent pattern. Central to the plot are the escalating conflicts between militant farmers assembled for the annual muster of the militia and the politicians and merchants. In 1786 the Massachusetts legislature passed a Militia Act, which formalized the structure of the local militia, decreed four days of exercises to be carried out annually, and made a military commander liable for the acts of those under his command. When a member of the General Court is murdered by an unidentified member of the Rufford Militia, Daniel is arrested on the eve of his marriage to Hannah. As a result, Hannah is driven to sacrifice herself to save her beloved with the kind of sacrifice desperate women make too often. As one woman puts it when she tells her husband how his debts were paid when he was in Debtors Prison, "I worked as poor women must, on my back, with a great weight upon me" (*Burning* 200). The psychological traumas of wartime continue to cast their long shadows, demonstrating that the hostilities often continue when the pitched battles are over.

Lawrence's Hannah Trevor bears more than a passing resemblance to Martha Ballard, a midwife in Maine, whose journal covering between 1785 and 1812 served as the basis for Laurel Thatcher Ulrich's Pulitzer Prize winning monograph, *A Midwife's Tale*. The fictional town of Rufford which straddles the navigable River Manitac might be mistaken for Hallowell, Maine, a community built upon both sides of the Kennebec River. Timbering and cod fishing are staples of the economy for both villages. Numerous names and events as well as the general social, economic, and political conditions recounted in *A Midwife's Tale* find their parallels in Lawrence's trilogy.[2]

Previous to Ulrich's work with Ballard's diary, a day book comprising brief notations of the weather, terse listings of the mundane pattern of daily tasks and family events punctuated with pious and formulaic religious sentiments typical of Puritan thought, Charles Elventon Nash had made an abridgement that he included in his *History of Augusta*. He passed over many of the "trivial details" of domestic life that Ulrich put to good use, while, in turn, Ulrich, focusing on women's lives, passed over materials more pertinent to men's. The impact of *A Midwife's Tale* upon historians as well as general readers was due in large part to Ulrich's skill in sorting out the snippets left behind by Martha Ballard, piecing them together with historical evidence drawn from other sources and patching into whole cloth a narrative that focused on the complexities and realities of an early American woman's life and illuminated the social networks, "medical practices, household economies, religious rivalries, and sexual mores of the New England frontier."[3]

Nash and Ulrich utilized Martha Ballard's diary in much the same way as two quilters might start with the same fabric and a similar design, yet end up with very different results. Although Lawrence has clearly cut an ample amount of cloth from the same bolt as Nash and Ulrich, Hannah Trevor is not simply a younger, sexier, less pious, more outspoken Martha Ballard, while Lawrence's fictional Rufford is not merely Hopewell in disguise. Lawrence has added in patches recognizable from the research and writings of numerous historians and, unrestrained by the mandates of academic writing, has embellished and enlivened her patchwork with the passions and interior views that historians can usually only surmise or suggest. Like Hannah with her quilts, Lawrence has constructed a complex design of her "sole devising."

Two large historical themes frame the trilogy. The first is the position of women in society. The recently-ended War for Independence, which some had held to be a revolution, has not substantially improved the rights of or opportunities for women, particularly poor or marginalized women such as Hannah. Hannah's efforts to negotiate the strictures of her time and place and the web of relationships in which she is enmeshed illuminate the social and economic dependence and interdependence of women in rural New England during the eighteenth century. Determined to never again marry and subject herself to the will of a man, Hannah's love for Daniel and her need to provide the security for her child that only a man can, is in conflict with her desire for independence and self-determination.

If the revolutionary rhetoric of liberty and equality has failed to significantly alter women's legal status, neither has the War of Revolution improved the circumstances of the growing class of yeoman farmers and landless craftsmen who had marched off to fight bloody battles for the noble causes of Freedom, Justice, and The Rights of Man. Many returned from the battlefront, broken in either spirit and/or body and embittered by the unfulfilled promises of revolution. The unsettled economic conditions and the political and social tensions that characterize the early republic are legacies of the war, as are the lingering effects of wartime deprivations and atrocities experienced by civilians, particularly the women and children left unprotected. Dissension and violence threaten authority and the social order. The great republican experiment seems to be failing. A growing shortage of land in settled communities together with selfish speculation, high taxes, and foreclosures is creating a resentful and often lawless class of men who threaten the premises of republican virtue. There is no stable currency. Payment for burdensome taxes requires hard coin rather than the paper scrip soldiers were paid, and rising debt threatens to rend the fabric of society. The merchant elites have replaced the British aristocracy and their greed and avarice threaten to grind the lesser classes down to nothing.

These conditions provoked the popular uprising known as Shay's Rebellion. Under the leadership of Daniel Shay, formerly a Revolutionary War captain, farmers of western Massachusetts rose up in arms against the propertied elites and politicians in protest against excessive property taxes, restriction of voting by high poll taxes, the actions of debtors courts, the high cost of lawsuits, and the lack of a stable currency. In various actions over several months between summer 1786 and winter 1787, they targeted officials and mobbed court buildings to prevent trials and imprisonment of debtors.[4] As Lawrence's trilogy reminds us, the sentiments and resentments and the very real constitutional and economic conditions that gave rise to Shay's Rebellion were shared by the farmers of Maine. Indeed, as Thomas Jefferson's letter to James Madison dated January 30, 1787, underlines, the scarcity of money, the fears and indignations over the irregularities of administration of public affairs, and the uneasiness of the population, were prevalent throughout New England states. By using these tensions and conflicts to frame her novels and placing Josselyn in the center of the conflicts between the politicians and propertied elites and the farmers and landless of the yeoman and craftsman class, she does a good job of delineating the issues and portraying the class tensions and resentments that continued to simmer in New England and remained unresolved for at least another decade.[5]

With Hannah as a midwife, Lawrence is able to address the changing nature of childbirth and midwifery and the beginnings of a male-dominated medical profession. Hannah and her aunt provide a sharp contrast with the crude, arrogant, self-styled doctor Sam Clinch, a barber-surgeon who relies upon bleeding, blistering, purging, and heavy doses of laudanum, rather than the herbal and folk remedies that Hannah and her aunt use efficaciously. Clinch's use of an ill-designed birthing chair demonstrates either an ignorance of, or a wanton disregard for, female anatomy, both historical characteristics of the medical profession. Hannah and her aunt charge six shillings for their services, one-third the fee charged by Clinch. Clinch receives his pay in hard coin, but seldom are the midwives paid in coin. More often than not they receive goods or services such as wood ashes for making soap, comfrey roots for medicines, a laying hen, sewing scraps to use in their patchwork quilts or traded help with weaving, spinning, or quilting.

Midwives occupied a quasi-legal position in colonial and early America. When attending an out-of-wedlock birth, it was the midwife's responsibility to question the mother as to the identity of the father so as to assign financial responsibility for the care of the child. It was also a midwife's responsibility to witness autopsies, prevent any irreverent behavior or licentious treatment of the deceased by the male attendants, and provide testimony at court. Present at the autopsy of the man who was once her husband, Hannah is able to read in the scars upon his body evidence of the vicious illtreatment he has endured since they parted. The physical abuse James Trevor had suffered at the hands of patriots included clipping, the cutting off of part or all of the ears, branding, slitting the nostrils, and one or more whippings which cut the flesh and left raised scars. Perhaps he had also been tarred and feathered, forced to ride the rail, or pelted as Hannah had been with various objects including sticks, stones, or spoiled fruits and vegetables. All were common forms of punishments meted out for minor infractions of the law, by vigilantes, or overzealous partisans.

Like Hannah, Margaret Lawrence is a quilter, of texts as well as textiles. Her novels combine history, suspense, psychodrama, and romance. Her characters are complex and engaging. Her prose is a pleasure to read. As one reviewer noted, "Lawrence uses the metaphor and skills of quilting to stitch together fictional and real public documents (a quote from Abigail Adams to Thomas Jefferson is particularly telling), recipes, household tips, journal fragments, and easily accessible period dialogue into a book with perhaps a bit more history than mystery but enough delight and dignity to be fully satisfying."[6] So satisfying is Lawrence's writing that in 1997 *Hearts and Bones* was nominated for "Best Mystery Novel" for the Edgar Award, the McCavity Award, the Agatha Award, and the Anthony Award. Critic Carolyn Hart called *Hearts and Bones* "an extraordinary novel . . . Brilliant, passionate, riveting . . . a soul-deep exploration of guilt and retribution, despair and unquenchable spirit," and added, "I am in awe of this elegant, unforgettable, heart-stirring book."[7] Lawrence continued to receive high praise from readers and critics for subsequent volumes.

Lawrence has read widely and deeply and grounded her novels in the pertinent historical literature. Unlike some authors of historical fiction, she provides no list of sources, confident that her writing establishes its credibility on its own. Not until the afterword to *The Burning Bride*, the final volume of the Hannah Trevor series, does the author acknowledge the vast amount of research on which she has based her work. Observing that "historical fiction owes a great debt to the many scholars upon whose careful research we novelists rely," she notes that she consulted "more than four hundred books and documents, many journals on microfilm, cookbooks, song books, books of quilt patterns and weaving drafts, diagrams of the workings of eighteenth-century mills, looms, toast racks—everything that went to build the New England world of 1786."[8] So well has Lawrence blended the material culture, the temper of the times, and the historical issues that it is easy to forget one is reading fiction. Law-rence's attention to the small things of everyday life, the popular literature and music, the tools and tasks, the rhythms and the rituals, provides an almost seamless background for her richly textured work and contributes measurably to loosening the ties that bind the reader to the contemporary world in order to more completely engage with the distant past.

Alex Hailey is reported to have said that "Nobody can write about events that happened 200 years ago that isn't more fiction than fact." Historians operate on the assumption that if they accumulate enough facts, they will have captured historical truth, but by the very nature of the enterprise, historians can at best only approximate a rendering of historical realities. Skilled writers of historical fiction seem to have the best of both worlds. Combining "facts" acquired through careful research with a familiarity with material artifacts and then creating characters with plausible thoughts and emotions, they can engage the reader in history with a multisensory approach. When romance and mystery are added to the design, as Margaret Lawrence has done in crafting her Hannah Trevor novels, the result is the illumination of a historical moment whilst also telling a good story.

## Notes

1. Margaret Lawrence is a pseudonym for Margaret Keilstrup who has also written under the pseudonym of M. K. Lorens. Her works includes several mysteries, stage plays, and screen plays. See *Contemporary Authors*, Gale Literary Databases. 11 Nov. 1998 <http://www.galenet.com>.

2. For example, Martha Ballard's hot-headed, troublesome son is named Jonathan; the girl he gets pregnant and then marries is Sally. Hannah's hot-headed and troublesome nephew is also named Jonathan and the girl he impregnates and then marries is named Sally. Sally Ballard is harsh to her mother-in-law and creates discord in the family. Sally Markham neglects her son, steals her in-law's savings, and, while her husband is in prison for nonpayment of taxes, has an illicit relationship and then runs off with a ne'er-do-well son of one of the richest and most powerful townsman, Hamilton Siwell. Ulrich utilized the diary of Henry Sewall for comparison and contrast with Martha Ballard's diary. Sewall, an army veteran and a town official for more then thirty years, may not have been as greedy or well-to-do as the fictional Hamilton Siwell, nevertheless he was an important personage in Hallowell.

A statute enacted in 1786 made local tax collectors personally liable for the levied taxes for their district. Martha Ballard's husband spent nearly a year and a half in Debtors Prison for failing to collect the taxes his district was assessed. In 1787, the law was amended to allow the jailed debtors to work during the day to pay their debts but required them to spend the nights in the jail. When Lawrence's tax collector refuses to take less than the assessed amount from several of the villagers because he cannot personally make up the difference, violence ensues. In revenge for the death of the tax protester, the tax collector is beaten and left hanging to die. The tensions between the squatters who have settled in the forests on lots that are part of huge tracts of land owned by the proprietors, and the surveyors who are contracted to lay out lots in anticipation of the proprietors selling them and making a huge profit, frequently erupt in violence. Martha Ballard's husband gave up survey-ing for a time after being set upon and roughed up by squatters.

The seemingly bizarre allegations of Anthea Emory claiming abuse and rape by several men which result in her death parallel those of Hallowell's Rebecca Foster, as detailed in chapter three of Ulrich's *A Midwive's Tale*. Wife of an unpopu-lar minister, Mrs. Foster "swore a rape" on a number of prominent towns men and claimed to have suffered great abuses and even feared for her life.

Certainly Ballard's diary provided a wonderful treasure trove for Lawrence from which to draw "patches" for her novels and Ulrich's footnotes provide another rich resource.

3. Laurel Thatcher Ulrich's careful rendering of Martha Ballard's diary earned her a Pulitzer Prize, the Bancroft Prize, and the Joan Kelly and John Dunning Prizes of the American Historical Association.

4. These conditions and tensions that historian David Szatmary detailed in *Shay's Rebellion: The Making of an Agrarian Insurrection* (Amherst: U of Massa-chusetts P, 1984) are central to the plots Lawrence develops. In a brief historical note at the end of *Blood Red Roses*, the author admits to "telescoping" events of Shay's rebellion with "others of similar nature that took place in wilderness Maine nearly ten (sic) years later, long after the new constitution was supposed to have put an end to the mass foreclosures and stabilized the inflated currency. It had not done so, and many sheriff's sales were disrupted by vigilante groups and surveyors set upon by angry farmers, culminating in the Malta War of 1809." Tensions between proprietors and settlers erupted into violence several times in 1807-1808 and resulted in 400 of the militia being called out to put down a rumored attack by squatters on Augusta in 1808. Backcountry settlers resisted the attempts of propri-etors to expel them from the lands on which they had trespassed and squatted with attacks on surveyors, writ servers, sheriffs, and land agents which involved rituals of terror based in military rituals and Indian practices. 1807-1808 was also a time of British and French harassment of American shipping that led to a fourteen-month embargo on trade known as "Jefferson's Embargo." Though the restraint of trade worked a hardship on merchants as well as common folk, merchants were verbally and sometimes physically abused by the angry settlers. Taken together, the events of 1807-08 demonstrate that the tensions and issues which Lawrence uses in plotting her novels were long-term problems for the people of frontier Maine.

5. "A Little Rebellion Now and Then is a Good Thing: A Letter from Thomas Jefferson to James Madison." 29 Nov. 1998 <http://earlyamerica.com/review/sum-mer/letter.htm>.

6. Dick Adler, review of *The Burning Bride* for Amazon.com. 11 Nov. 1998 <http://www.amazon.comexec/obidos/ASIN/0>.

7. Jacket text from paperback edition of *Hearts and Bones*.

8. Lawrence expresses gratitude for the work of nineteen historians, listing them only by name. Included in this list and the major works which she most likely utilized are: Mary Beth Norton, *Liberty's Daughters: The Revolutionary Experiences of American Women* (Glenview, IL: Foresman, 1980); "Eighteenth-Century American Women in Peace and War: The Case of the Loyalists," *William and Mary Quarterly*, 3rd Series, 33 (July 1976): 386-409. Linda Kerber, *Women of the Republic: Intellect*

*and Identity in Revolutionary America* (Chapel Hill: U of North Carolina P, 1980; *The British-Americans: The Loyalists in Exile in England, 1774-1789*; and "Separate Spheres, Female Worlds, Woman's Place: The Rhetoric of Women's History," *Journal of American History,* 75 (1988): 9-39. Laurel Thatcher Ulrich, *A Midwives Tale: The Life of Martha Ballard, Based on Her Diary, 1785-1812* (Westminster, MD: Knopf, 1990) and *Good Wives: Image and Reality in the Lives of Women in Northern New England, 1650-1750* (New York: Vintage, 1984); see also *"Martha Ballard and Her Girls: Women's Work in Eighteenth-Century Maine,"* in Stephen Innes, ed., *Work and Labor in Early America* (Chapel Hill: U of North Carolina, 1988); and "Housewife and Gadder: Themes of Self-sufficiency and Community in Eighteenth-Century New England," in Carol Groneman and Mary Beth Norton, eds., *To Toil the Livelong Day": America's Women at Work, 1780-1980* (Ithaca: Cornell UP, 1987), 21-34. Charles Elventon Nash, *The History of Augusta: First Settlements and Early Days as a Town, Including the Diary of Mrs. Martha Moore Ballard (1785-1812),* published in 1961 by Edith Hary. Mary Ann Mason, *From Father's Property to Children's Rights: The History of Child Custody in The United States* (New York: Columbia UP, 1994). Wallace Brown, *The Good Americans; The Loyalists in the American Revolution* (Fairfield, NJ: Morrow, 1969). Barbara Clark Smith, *After the Revolution: The Smithsonian History of Everyday Life in the Eighteenth Century* (Washington, DC: National Museum of American History, 1987); and *Men and Women: A History of Costume, Gender, and Power* (Washington, DC: National Museum of American History, 1990). Jane Nylander, *Our Own Snug Fireside: Images of the New England Home, 1760-1860* (New Haven: Yale UP, 1994). Alice Morse Earle, *Child Life in Colonial Days; Home Life in Colonial Days; Curious Punishments of Bygone Days; Customs and Fashions in Old New England; and Two Centuries of Costume in America, 1620-1820*; all originally published 1891-1902 and reissued and reprinted variously between 1968 to 1995. Judith Walzer Leavitt, *Brought to Bed—Childbearing in America, 1750-1950* (Cary, NC: Oxford UP, 1988); "'Science' Enters the Birthing Room: Obstetrics in American since the Eighteenth Century," *Journal of American History,* 70 (Sept. 1983): 281-304. Walter Blumenthal, *Women Camp Followers of American Revolution* (North Stratford, NH: Ayer, 1974). Lee Agger, *Women of Maine* (Portland, ME: Gannett, 1982) and *Women of New England* (Portland, ME: Gannett, 1986). Linda Grant DePauw, *Founding Mothers: Women of America in the Revolutionary Era* (Boston: Sandpiper, 1994). Samuel E. Morison, *The Growth of the American Republic* (Cary, NC: Oxford UP, 1981); and *Maritime History of Massachusetts* (Ithaca: Northeastern UP, 1979). Marion L. Starkey, *Lace Cuffs and Leather Apron: Popular Struggles in the Federalist Era, 1783-1800* (Westminster, MD: Random House, 1972); David Szatmary, *Shay's Rebellion: The Making of an Agrarian Insurrection* (Amherst: U of Massachusetts P, 1984).

## Works Cited

Margaret Lawrence. *Blood Red Roses.* New York: Avon, 1997.

——. *The Burning Bride.* New York: Avon, 1998.

——. *Hearts and Bones.* New York: Avon, 1996.

# Stephanie Barron:
# (Re)inventing Jane Austen as Detective

## Anita Vickers

A few years before her own death at the age of seventy-two, Cassandra Austen, elder sister of the famous Georgian era novelist Jane Austen (1775–1817), burned a substantial number of her sister's letters and considerably edited the remainder with a pair of scissors. This destruction and expurgation of correspondence that would have been invaluable to literary scholars and biographers alike has provided the catalyst for some of the great mysteries in literary history: Who was the "real" Jane Austen? Why did her devoted sister find it necessary to rewrite/delete autobiographical papers? And, most importantly, what actually occurred in the novelist's life between the years 1800 and 1804?

The last question reflects not only the loss of key correspondence to Austen scholarship, but also to the dearth of literary output. Between May 1801 and September 1804, no Austen letters are extant. There is also no evidence of literary activity from 1799 when Austen was still working on "Susan" (later to be published posthumously in 1811 as *Northanger Abbey*) and her drafting of *The Watsons* (not published until 1980), abandoned within the same year. The omission of a written record during this time has led one recent biographer to ascertain that these years were "a period of upheaval and unsettlement in her [Austen's] life, of correspondingly little creativity" and that these were subsequently "The Treacherous Years" (Halperin 119).

Perhaps the label "treacherous" is hyperbolic. Yet the mystery remains. Ingeniously, Stephanie Barron has used this historical mystery as the premise for her Jane Austen Mystery Series. Barron's series begins with an intriguing premise: Just suppose that an enterprising mystery writer/ersatz literary scholar has uncovered Austen's heretofore "missing" journals from this time period. And just suppose that the missing piece of the biographical puzzle is that she was not writing fiction because she was busy solving mysteries. Hence the overarching historical mystery nests a series of fictional mysteries which Jane Austen solves, largely due to her keen powers of observation (as evidenced in such works as *Pride and Prejudice* [1813] and *Emma* [1815]).

Within these nested mysteries Barron also attempts to address two other historical mysteries: what was Austen really like and what might have been Cassandra's reasons for destroying the letters. In this series, Jane Austen author becomes Jane Austen consummate detective, a rather reason-

*213*

able premise especially if we consider Austen's reputation as a clever commentator on manners and as an accurate portrayer of personality and character. In fact, Austen's works, characterized by her realistic treatment of everyday life and society, align her writing style more with that of the twentieth century than of her own time. Thus her modernity of style and theme might easily be transmuted into a provocative blend of the high literary and the popular. Using plausible fictionalized events, many set in situations circumscribed and mundane, Barron devises scenarios that simultaneously manipulate and transcend generic convention. The drawing rooms of Bath and its environs (the setting for many of Austen's works) lend themselves both to the comedy of manners and to the intrigues and iniquities that typifies much of detective fiction.

The mixture of biography, literary scholarship, and detective fiction leads to a re-invention of biography. Such a creative composite invariably calls into questions the nature of biography—and how one discerns how and why biography might be manipulated or subverted.

Obviously, the biographer's primary purpose is to establish and support why his/her biographical subject is deserving of such a study. Thus a biography can be laudable (that is, the subject's life and works are meritorious), investigative, and even scandalous. The biographer, in search of his/her subject, invariably becomes a detective. Because the "life" becomes a literary text in itself, the task of the biographer is to fill in details to make the "life" appear authentic. The biographer, now detective, must also become a historian, re-creating the political, social, and cultural constructs of the life-subject's historical period.

In the case of Austen, the historical facts are known and substantiated (birth, death, writing, and publication dates, etc.). The Georgian era in which she lived and wrote has been the subject of a myriad of scholarly tomes. Austen herself has been the subject of numerous biographies, although in tone and intent they vary greatly.[1] In the Barron series, the onus has, however, been shifted to reinvent biography, that is, to use a historical subject to create a fictional subject that maintains historical accuracy and integrity while adhering to the conventions of both biography and detective fiction.

Moreover, the reinvention of biography, under the guise of writing detective fiction, allows Barron to allude to the answer of one of the literary mysteries: Why did Cassandra Austen burn her sister's correspondence from this select time period? Conceivably, the disparity of the saintly portrait perpetuated by the grieving family and the image of the author as an amateur detective (who was strongly attracted to men whose behavior was less than circumspect) would have been anathema to the loyal elder sister. Granted, the detective depiction is far more interesting than, in the words of Austen's nephew, a woman whose

life was singularly barren: few changes and no great crisis ever broke the smooth current of its course . . . There was in her nothing eccentric or angular; no ruggedness of temper; no singularity of manner . . . I have no reason to think that she ever felt any attachment by which the happiness of her life was at all affected. (qtd. in Halperin 4)

Thus in reinventing Austen's biography, Barron has brought into question the validity of this stilted, lifeless portrait of a woman whose works abound with vivacity and purpose. A fictional detective, above all, has a life current that is shifting, sometimes choppy, sometimes serene, often taking unexpected turns. And, above all, Jane Austen, detective, might proffer a more complex psychological study than the purified family portrait.

Unlike biography, which has been accorded "high" literary status, detective fiction has been perceived as being limited as literature. Studies of detective fiction have ranged from apologetics to deprecations.[2] But as many have pointed out, detective fiction can be transmuted into literature. Scholars such as Philip Van Doren Stern identified that at

its [detective fiction's] core is almost always premeditated murder . . . and premeditated murder is one of the greatest themes in all literature: witness such works as *Electra*, *Hamlet*, and *Crime and Punishment*. . . . There is no reason why a tale concerning itself with the most soul-racking deed a human being can undertake should be a silly, mechanically contrived affair. The writer of murder mysteries hold high cards in his hand; if he does not know how to play them, that does not lessen their value. (qtd. in Roth 3)

Consequently, the writer of detective fiction is confronted with a dual task: to create a work that engages the reader, that fulfills his/her expectations based on generic conventions, but also to do so in such a way that transcends good storytelling. Much detective fiction is, as Tzevtan Todorov has identified it, a "story of the investigation" (44-45), which places an additional burden on the writer. This is the "second story" of the book (the first is the story of the crime that has been completed at the onset of the work), and as a "second story" the emphasis is on clues, rather than development of character.[3]

Does the series accomplish its creator's intent? Does the second story go beyond the unfolding of clues, the discovery of the killer? Has Barron reinvented a biography (albeit fictional) of one of the great writers of English literature? How true to history is this reinvention of biography?

The first mystery in the series, *Jane and the Unpleasantness of Scargrove Manor* (1996), adheres strictly to the ruse of the uncovering of the literary/biographical mystery. The "Editor's Forward" somewhat tritely uses the old eighteenth- and nineteenth-century convention of finding a manuscript in an old trunk (in this case, a box of family records discovered in a storage shed in Baltimore). Within the newly recovered Austen family records are not only Austen's notebooks that painstakingly record her activities during this lost period, but also letters to Cassandra Austen that somehow escaped the latter's small epistolary bonfire. Such a discovery would be a boon to Austen scholarship—yet what follows is not a scholarly compendium. Because the "editor" is a close friend of the Westmoreland family (supposedly distant relatives of Austen) and has a keen interest in detective fiction, she (not an Austen scholar) has been asked by the family to edit these "lost" notebooks for publication.

The Forward serves as a crucial frame for the series as a whole. For the uninitiated reader, Barron provides a brief biographical overview, beginning a statement of what the *real* mystery is: "For a woman whose work has endured nearly two centuries, *Jane Austen remains in large part a mystery herself*" (*First Mystery* ix; emphasis added). As a responsible "editor," Barron also furnishes a brief (one paragraph), but accurate, overview of the differences in social morés of the Napoleonic era (the subject of this particular mystery) and the later Victorian era (one with which a general reader would probably have more familiarity). This historical overview succinctly captures the temper of the time, a time where women enjoyed personal and social freedom to a greater extent than what popular perception might be (since that may have been colored by knowledge of the restrictiveness of the Victorian era).[4] Thus "the notion of a lady writing novels—or engaging in detection—was permissible according to the morés of Austen's time" (*First Mystery* x).

Couched within the Forward (and the introduction of the first Jane Austen mystery) is what little biographical information is known of Austen in 1802. (Barron freely acknowledges that her source for her biographical information is Park Honan's *Jane Austen: Her Life* [1987], a more accessible study and more balanced than other works that fall within the range of deification and vilification.) This also provides justification for why Jane Austen, detective, might have been present at Scargrave Manor, Hertfordshire, the setting of this first murder mystery. (Austen had accepted and rejected—within twenty-four hours—the marriage proposal of a stolid, but dull, suitor. The editor conjectures that an invitation to a ball in Hertfordshire would have been a welcomed escape.)

This novel is the most successful at sustaining the edited lost manuscript motif. The journal entries and letters are scrupulously and prudently annotated. For example, one of the suspects in the murder of Lord Scargrave, Fitzroy, Viscount Payne, is a man whose "reserve . . . some might mistake for aloofness and pride" (*First Mystery* 27). Jane notes in her journal that "I must set down something of my sense of Fitzroy, Viscount Payne, for I find him the very type to serve as a character in one of my novels" (*First Mystery* 27). Indeed, the characterization would not be lost on the reader familiar with *Pride and Prejudice*. The editor, however, includes the following footnote:

1. It is possible that Austen eventually turned Fitzroy, Viscount Payne, into her most famous male character, Fitzwilliam Darcy, although strong evidence is lacking. *First Impressions*, in which Darcy is the main male character was written in 1796, and rejected for publication in 1797. Later retitled *Pride and Prejudice*, it was

revised substantially in late 1802 or early 1803, following Austen's visit to Scargrave, and again before publication in 1812.—*Editor's note.* (*First Mystery* 27)

The intrusive editor not only anticipates the questions of a reader who might be very familiar with Austen's life and works, and thus who would challenge the veracity of the journal entry, but also furnishes a credible interconnection between the personages Jane Austen, detective, encounters and the characters limned by Austen, the writer. (Many of the characters within the series are reminiscent of her characters. Mrs. Austen, fond and peevish, shares many characteristics and turn of phrase with Mrs. Bennett in *Pride and Prejudice*. The Reverend George Austen, loving yet acerbic, is very much like the long suffering Mr. Bennett. Jane Austen herself, witty and lively, is possibly a rewriting of Austen's favorite heroine, Elizabeth Bennett.)

The mystery progresses at a fairly even pace. The second story in this instance, however, is more than a series of clues leading to the revelation of the murderer. Because Austen's journals and letters back home structure the narrative and because they emulate her writing style, the second story has evolved into a curious interpolation of the historical and the implicitly biographical. As an example, the Coroner's Inquest (held at a local tavern, the Cock and Bull) illustrates the efficacious blend of fiction and historical verisimilitude.

Decidedly, this is not the pastoral setting of Austen's novels. The Cock and Bull is rife with those not of the privileged class—and is in direct contrast with the concerted impressiveness of the King's Bench (in a subsequent chapter). Falsely accused Viscount Payne (the Darcy-like character) and Countess Isobel Scargrave (widow of the murder victim) are brought before the Coroner (and the good townspeople) to determine whether they should be brought to trial for the murders of the Earl of Scargrave and a maid who had purported to having damning information about the Earl's murder. The inquest scene (episodically related in Chapters 11 and 12) deftly encapsulates the class conflict inherent in early nineteenth-century English society (once again shattering a popular misconception of Georgian English courts). The jury is crammed into the main tavern room, "redolent of the smoked hams that hung from its rafters and the yeasty aftermath of spilt beer" (*First Mystery* 154). Worse, the poor (as represented by a disreputably clothed and shrieking woman named Lizzy Scratch) are filled with a "virulent animosity" toward the accused (*First Mystery* 154-55). The result of inquest is that after very brief jury deliberations, Isobel and Fitzroy are found guilty with a verdict handed down of death.

Justice does, however, prevail—mainly through the efforts of Miss Jane Austen and Lord Harold Trowbridge (a rakish character who holds particular romantic appeal for Jane, against her better judgment). Trowbridge, it is learned at the end of the novel, is a spy for the Crown. (During the Napoleonic Wars, espionage was sometimes the avocation of the aristocracy.) The status quo is restored. The British judicial system has triumphed in the end. Jane Austen has not only solved a murder mystery, but garnered invaluable material for future writing—and the quixotic—yet dangerously dissolute—Harold Trowbridge has been proven to be a fit romantic interest for Jane Austen because, despite his Byronic pose, he is loyal to King and Country.

The second mystery, *Jane and the Man of the Cloth* (1997), attempts to answer still another Austen biographical mystery. Jane Austen scholarship has often focused on and attempted to uncover evidence of a thwarted romance. In the summer of 1804, Austen visited the coastal village of Lyme Regis where it is has been conjectured that she became romantically involved with a young clergyman.[5] The romance, while promising, ended sadly. Most Austen scholars agree that the young clergyman died soon afterwards. The only evidence that the romance did occur was related by a niece who was told the tale (sans names) by the protective Cassandra many years after Austen's death at forty-one.

Like the first mystery, *Jane and the Man of the Cloth* vacillates between the genteel halcyon setting of Austen's novels (and her own life) and the more sordid side of English society. Through a carriage accident, Jane and her family encounter a sinister group of men led by the enigmatic Geoffrey Sidmouth. (The editor's candidate for the historical "Reverend" of Austen biography. See note 5.) Again, the background for this mystery was carefully researched. Barron, in the "Editor's Forward," cites Geoffrey Morley's *Smuggling in Hampshire and Dorset: 1700—1850* (1983) as well as John Fowles's *A Short History of Lyme Regis* (1982) as essential for "editing this volume" (*Second Mystery* xi-xii).

Not only does the second mystery sustain the edited papers motif, but it depicts a fairly accurate historical profile of smuggling and the British government's active support of French Royalist plotters during the Napoleonic era. (Sidmouth, not the smuggler he appears to be, is a Royalist. Like Harold Trowbridge of the first mystery—and who makes a brief appearance at the end of this one—Sidmouth, whose almost ruthless sexuality seems to captivate Jane Austen, is proven not to be the villain of the piece. He is also not the notorious smuggler "The Reverend.") Keeping true to Austen legend, this budding romance (or misalliance, depending on interpretation) ends unsatisfactory. The misidentified "Reverend" is parted from Austen, not by death, but by necessity. (To escape his enemies, he flees to America.)

The third mystery, *Jane and the Wandering Eye* (1998), shifts to a theatrical setting—and emphasizes the more dramatic emotions and pastimes traditionally associated with murder: fiery sexual passions, irresponsible flirtatious behavior, sinister activities (such as involvement in the opium trade), and a lust for vengeance. Detective becomes actress here—and a fairly adept one since her playacting aids her in coming up with clues crucial to solving the case. Historical personages populate this latest mystery more so than in the previous novels, notably those of the art community: the acclaimed portraitist Sir Thomas Lawrence, artists Richard and Maria Cosway, and members of the Siddons and Kemble acting families. Even the death of Austen's dear friend, Madame Anne Lefroy, is interwoven within the mystery. (Anne Lefroy was killed in a riding accident, which Barron faithfully records in the novel.) However, there is more than a faint insinuation in the mystery that this may have been no accident. The liberty Barron takes with historical facts here is to generate a sense of fear and suspicion of the insidious events that unfold throughout the novel.

For although crime and criminal elements abound in the series, this is the first novel where Jane Austen becomes a victim of a random act of violence. While mulling over prior events (murder, blackmail, and her constant attraction to Lord Harold Trowbridge), Austen is accosted and subsequently robbed by common footpads in her sedan chair. Once more in the series, the brutal reality of nineteenth-century England invades the heretofore bucolic setting of her world. (The third mystery is set in Bath, a resort town that was subject of many of Austen's works.)

The third mystery apparently relies more on the known biographical than the previous mysteries—which in a way diminishes the effect of the investigation of the crime. In addition, the time frame employed in this novel might have proven problematic. Aficionados of Austen's life and works might be cognizant that the events of the third mystery take place within days of her beloved father's death. Although the usually intrusive editor does not make note of this, Cassandra Austen (as a novelistic character) makes reference to the poor state of George Austen's health at this time.

Thus the novel ends on a portentous note. Although the mystery has been solved quite neatly, Jane thinks not of success but of "Anne Lefroy, divided forever from her comfortable hearth, the table surrounded by children, and [I] shivered with a sudden chill" (*Third Mystery* 262). With the conclusion of the third mystery in December 1804, the overarching mystery has been "solved." The "missing years" have now been accounted for: Austen, while solving mysteries, has been accumulating material for her great works to come. The "real" Jane Austen (as fictionalized by Barron) was a woman of great intellectual power and discernment—and sexual vibrancy. And this portrait of the novelist, that of a spirited woman drawn to sexually experienced and less-than-reputable men, was not one that the Austen family would have wanted perpetuated.

Overall, the Jane Austen Mystery series successfully accomplishes what it was intended: reinvention of biography. Barron, under the guise of a textual editor, has, in many respects, become a historian. The series, which suitably imitates Austen's prose style and appropriates much of her subject matter, reconstructs the social and economic issues of the Georgian era, thereby providing a forum for learning from the past. Although the mysteries themselves are fictional—and the answers to the overarching mysteries are works of fiction themselves—the biography of the novelist and the depiction of the time in which she lived and worked are in many ways truer than the apocrypha proliferated by overprotective family members and fanatical devotees and by popular misconceptions of history. What remains is a fully developed portrait of a woman artist, a fairly accurate representation of the good and the bad social conditions of Georgian England—and three engrossing murder mysteries.

### Notes

Since this essay was written, the fourth and fifth Jane Austen novels were published.

1. Briefly, Jane Austen biographical scholarship includes, but is not limited to, such works as Elizabeth Jenkins, *Jane Austen* (1949), still considered to be the authoritative work, John Halperin, *The Life of Jane Austen* (1984) which purports to counteract the benevolent portrait of the novelist as perpetuated by her family and subsequent scholarship; Park Honan, *Jane Austen: Her Life* (1988); and Jan Fergus, *Jane Austen: A Literary Life* (1991). An abundance of information can also be found in J. David Grey, ed., *The Jane Austen Companion: With a Dictionary of Jane Austen's Life and Works* (1986).

2. For more complete discussions of the formula of detective fiction see George N. Dove, *Suspense in the Formula Story* (1989) and Gary C. Hoppenstand, *In Search of the Paper Tiger: A Sociological Perspective of Myth, Formula and the Mystery Genre in the Entertainment Print Mass Medium* (1987).

3. See Todorov's *The Poetics of Prose* (1978) for a more in-depth discussion of narrative and narrativity in detective fiction. Todorov's structural analysis concentrates of the geometricity of the whodunit. The terms "story of the investigation" and "second story" that I use here are from Todorov.

4. Even though Honan's book is the primary source for Austen scholarship in this fictional series, Jenkins's work imparts a more detailed look at the eighteenth century from the standpoint of living conditions that is worth mentioning here. The renewed interest in Austen's books (recent cinematic productions of *Sense and Sensibility*, the A & E airings of *Pride and Prejudice* and *Emma*, and the movie and television *Clueless*—a contemporary adaptation of *Emma*—attest to this popular interest in the works of a Georgian era writer) has perhaps perpetuated a false notion of idyllic tranquillity of this time. (Because Austen's works are comedies of manners that dealt with middle to upper class Georgian rural society, the sordidness and misery of urban society are omitted in her works.) Nonetheless, Jenkins's book places Austen's life and works in their social context. She presents a balanced historical view living conditions during this era. The later eighteenth and early nineteenth centuries might have been depicted in Austen's fiction as simply elegant and tranquil, but these were also periods of tremendous poverty, hygienic squalor, and rampant criminal activity. The bipolarity of such an environment, the pastoral and gentility of Austen's Hampshire contrasted with the wretchedness of the urban poor, often affords Barron's series with a fecundity of social issues amid the mystery/biography subtext. Thus, for those readers interested in the verisimilitude of the mystery series, Jenkins's work offers a credible historical resource.

5. The identity of Austen's suitor is unknown. In the "Editor's Forward" of the Second Mystery, Barron lists a variety of potential candidates, among these the Rev-

erend Samuel Blackall and Captain John Wordsworth (brother of the poet). The editor hypothesizes that Austen's suitor was not a clergyman per se, but rather a notorious smuggler known only as "The Reverend" (*Second Mystery* xi).

## Works Cited

Austen, Jane. *The Complete Novels of Jane Austen*. New York: Grammercy, 1994. Includes *Pride and Prejudice, Sense and Sensibility, Mansfield Park, Emma, Northanger Abbey, Persuasion,* and *Lady Susan.*

Barron, Stephanie. *Jane and the Man of the Cloth: Being the Second Jane Austen Mystery*. New York: Bantam, 1997.

——. *Jane and the Unpleasantness at Scargrave Manor: Being the First Jane Austen Mystery*. New York: Bantam, 1996.

——. *Jane and the Wandering Eye: Being the Third Jane Austen Mystery*. New York: Bantam, 1998.

Dove, George N. *Suspense in the Formula Story*. Bowling Green, OH: Bowling Green State U Popular P, 1989.

Fergus, Jan. *Jane Austen: A Literary Life*. New York: St. Martin's, 1991.

Grey, David J., ed. *The Jane Austen Companion: With a Dictionary of Jane Austen's Life and Works*. New York: Macmillan, 1986.

Halperin, John. *The Life of Jane Austen*. 1984. Baltimore: Johns Hopkins UP, 1996.

Honan, Park. *Jane Austen: Her Life*. New York: St. Martin's, 1987.

Hoppenstand, Gary C. *In Search of the Paper Tiger: A Sociological Perspective of Myth, Formula and the Mystery Genre in the Entertainment Print Mass Medium*. Bowling Green, OH: Bowling Green State U Popular P, 1987.

Jenkins, Elizabeth. *Jane Austen*. New York: Grosset, 1949.

Roth, Marty. *Foul & Fair Play: Reading Genre in Classic Detective Fiction*. Athens: U of Georgia P, 1995.

Todorov, Tzvetan. *The Poetics of Prose*. Trans. Richard Howard. Ithaca: Cornell UP, 1978.

# Kate Ross:
# Where Have All the Dandies Gone?

## Jerry L. Parker

From 1811 to 1820, the future King George IV of England served as Prince Regent during the final years of his father, mad George III. It has been claimed that Romance writers have created more dukes, counts and no-accounts in this nine-year period than have ever existed in the entire history of the British Empire.

The fascination for the period is understandable. Not since the Norman Conquest of 1066 had there been more societal change occurring in England than during and immediately after the Regency period. England was on the brink of greatness. By the middle of the Regency period, Napoleon had been defeated, while the Union Jack flew from the Atlantic shore to America's Pacific Northwest. English nobility and aristocracy, standing as examples for the rest of the world, grew and expanded in march-step to the growth of the Empire.

When an aristocracy expands, there are those who take advantage of the supposed increased freedoms and liberties high rank offers. This had been apparent in the middle eighteenth century when Francis Dashwood's Hell-fire club flourished so young nobles and rakes could experience debauchery firsthand. The practice continued on into the nineteenth century and was even more pronounced, although it was given the color of royal approval.

The future George IV was one who enjoyed the pleasures found in "dens of iniquity." He gambled, drank, and wenched with little thought for the future of his soon-to-be role as King. In his endeavors, the Prince Regent was assisted and guided by a young hanger-on, one George Bryan Brummell, better known as Beau Brummell.

It is Beau Brummell, and his copycats, that set the tone of the Regency period. Soon known as the Dandy of all Dandies, Beau Brummell's every move, every action, every thought was quickly copied by those young and unoccupied scions of the nobility and aristocracy who wished to be considered the leading figures of nineteenth-century society. If Beau cut his hair differently, there was a run on barbers. If Beau tied his cravat in a different manner, valets were put to practicing until they mastered the new style. If Beau donned a new style of clothing, tailors experienced a brief period of prosperity duplicating his clothes. Newspapers even maintained a watch on Beau and the Dandies in order to report the latest changes, the beginnings of the fashion and society pages.

Beau Brummell destroyed himself with a thoughtless, hurtful comment about his friend and benefactor, the Prince Regent. But there remained a large number of Dandies to take his place. The life and activities of one of them has been carefully detailed by Massachusetts lawyer Kate Ross in a series of four books. His name is Julian Kestrel.

To be fair, it must be stated that Julian Kestrel's main period of activity is in the post-Regency; 1820-1830. In fact, in her latest epic, *The Devil in Music* (1997), set in politically fragmented Italy, Ross is careful to point out that, during the Regency, Kestrel was in France being trained by a mysterious benefactor in all the social graces. Under the amused tutelage of the Comte Armand d'Aubret, Kestrel was turned from a potential street urchin living on handouts in Paris into a socially aware young man with a natural gift for song and music. A gift that Kestrel will eventually abandon, as told in *The Devil in Music*, in favor of returning to London and pursuing the art of being a Dandy.

Beau Brummell went from an Eton education and inheriting a fortune to dying, broke, in a charitable asylum in France. Julian Kestrel began life as the child of an actress and Richard Kestrel, the son of a Yorkshire county squire, who was disowned by his family for the "improper" marriage. Just what happened to his parents is not made clear by Ross. In one place, she states that Julian's mother died when he was born. In another, Julian and his mother lived for a time with Julian's unimaginative money-loving uncle. This individual discourages, even forbids, Julian from playing the piano. It is clear that Richard Kestrel played a role in the young Julian's education and early upbringing. Just what happens to the father is not mentioned but becomes a guiding force in Julian's decision to become a Dandy. Whatever happened to his parents, Julian finds himself spending his early teenage years with an uncle who does not understand him. The result is that Julian runs away at the age of sixteen.

It is the summer of 1815. The Battle of Waterloo has awakened among the French upper classes an interest in all things English. Julian flees to Paris assuming that someone would be willing to take him in as a tutor in English manners and customs. Instead, Julian finds himself unable to understand Parisians; the French his father had taught him was inadequate, and he is reduced to starving on the streets. With no money and nothing left to pawn, Julian found his manners and breeding made any effort to beg implausible; while his clothing, torn and wretched from his experiences on the streets of Paris, was still of sufficient quality as to forbid anyone from trusting him to do honest work or labor. Consequently, Julian eventually faints from hunger, providentially within the sight of the good Comte Armand d'Aubret. Rescued and fed, Julian begins his new life in France.

It is here, detailed in the last few pages of *The Devil in Music*, that Kate Ross commits her most detectable error. Integral to the plot of *The Devil* is the political intrigue and espionage of Austria and Italy. Most of the action takes place in Lombardy-Venetia, Austrian Italy, in the early 1820s. It is a time when Nationalists such as the *Carbonaros* worked to unite Italy.

And a time of oppression, when Italians could be imprisoned, even executed, for the crime of eating a watermelon. The Austrian occupiers believed the red, white, and green of a watermelon slice represented the red, white and green of the banned Italian flag. Eating a watermelon was a statement of nationalism and anti-Austrian feelings.

Julian Kestrel had been recruited by the *Cabonaros* on December 26, 1821, on a mission to protect the reputation of Comte d'Aubret. Kestrel would have been twenty-two. Yet the narrative of this mission has it beginning during March 1821. A minor point that should have been caught by Ross's editor, this discrepancy clouds the chronology of her earlier books.

While not an irreversible error, Ross needed only to change one date on page 431 to make everything balance. While most historical detectives are not harmed by such indefinite settings, Julian Kestrel is set in a period of great social change. Indeed, in 1829 Sir Robert Peel gains passage of the Metropolitan Police Act, the fore-runner of modern police forces and practices. There is little room between 1825 (the end of *The Devil in Music*) and establishment of London's finest for Kestrel to conduct many inquiries into murder and mystery. The three cases Kestrel had already solved are neatly sandwiched between the first and the second parts of *The Devil in Music*.

*Cut to the Quick* (1993), the first Julian Kestrel novel, proves most difficult to place chronologically. But internal clues in the three books enable us to put a tentative date to the work. One character in *Cut to the Quick*, Colonel Fontclair, is described as having been wounded "some dozen years ago" while serving with the Duke of Wellington in Spain. The Peninsular War lasted from 1808 to 1814 and ended with Napoleon's abdication. This places *Cut to the Quick* at somewhere between 1820 and 1826. Since we know that Kestrel had returned to London somewhere around the latter half of 1821 or early 1822, the action must take place around 1823 or 1824.

*A Broken Vessel* (1994), the second Kestrel work, is clearly placed as taking place in late October or early November 1824, by a dated letter accidently stolen by one Sally Stokes, a street prostitute. In *Whom the Gods Love* (1995), Julian Kestrel is asked to investigate the murder of Alexander James Falkland, who died before early May 1825, which is where the story opens. Mention is made in *Whom the Gods Love* of Philippa Fontclair, a precocious twelve-year-old whose acquaintance Kestrel made during the events of *Cut to the Quick*. Since she was described as being eleven in that book, it is safe to place its time period as pre-May 1824.

How many more crimes can Julian Kestrel solve before the creation of London's Metropolitan Police in 1829? At the current rate of two a year, Kestrel faces eight to ten more challenges before societal changes render his persona as a Dandy null and void. Why is this an issue? Because in 1830 the sixty-five year old Duke of Clarence assumed the throne as King William IV. The age of the Dandies was over, killed by outside events.

Between 1825 and 1830 there were a number of economic and financial disturbances. Economic booms were rapidly followed by collapses. The

1830 revolution in France for a time threatened political stability in Europe. An inconclusive general election in 1830 drove Prime Minister, the Duke of Wellington, out of office and brought into power a Whig reformist government under Earl Grey. Great Britain was entering a thirty-five-year period of social, political, economic, and scientific reforms and growth that was to eclipse the Dandies.

Kate Ross alludes to these coming changes in each of her stories. The issues are occasionally subtle, occasionally hard hitting. Each story reveals another aspect of the changes to and in English society.

*Cut to the Quick* opens with the Fontclair family being blackmailed into accepting a marriage between Maud Craddock and Hugh Fontclair. Maud's father, Mark Craddock, is a man who manipulates the flow of money, a middle-class tradesman along the likes of Dickens's Ebenezer Scrooge. So disreputable is Craddock that the marriage between the aristocratic Fontclair and his daughter is totally out of the question. Here Ross paints an enthralling picture of class differences and class revenge.

Julian Kestrel is drawn into this affair by Hugh Fontclair. Thankful for Julian Kestrel's timely intervention at a gambling house where Hugh has embarrassed himself by over-indulging in alcohol, Hugh asks Julian to be his best man at the wedding. Intrigued, Julian accepts and proceeds to the Bellegarde estates of the Fontclairs. There Julian discovers the body of a young woman, not of the Fontclair's social class or status. She has been murdered in Julian's room at Bellegarde and he must solve the mystery or be accused of having committed the foul deed himself. In the course of his investigation, Julian also resolves the conflict that lead to the blackmailing of the Fontclairs and steadies the course of true love.

*A Broken Vessel* offers the reader a peek into the life of a street prostitute who accidently steals a letter that leads to uncovering a murder and a child prostitution ring. Julian Kestrel becomes involved in this highly unlikely world because the prostitute who lifted the letter is the sister of Kestrel's valet, Thomas "Dipper" Stokes. "Dipper" was a nickname earned from his prior occupation of pick-pocket. The author states she is being held in a place of correction against her will. Julian, alarmed by the tone of the letter, begins an investigation. His inquiries lead him, and the reader, into the world of prostitution, reform and recovery houses, and the horrors of misplaced love and trust. The conclusion comes with as nice a bit of heroics as anyone could wish.

Julian Kestrel's success with these two mysteries leads Sir Malcolm Falkland to request Kestrel to attempt to solve the apparently motiveless random murder of his son, Alexander. In *Whom the Gods Love,* once again, Kestrel looks into the life of an aristocratic family and uncovers its darker side. This time, he has been invited in when the proper authorities have failed to resolve a case of business jealousy or spousual feuding. The deceased, Alexander Falkland, appears to be a devoted husband and social reformer, yet as Julian investigates, mask after mask is stripped off the participants until a different picture is finally revealed.

In *The Devil in Music*, Julian Kestrel is forced to reconsider his past as he makes his way to Italy and the on-going investigation into the murder of the Marquis Lodovico Malvezzi of Milan and the corresponding disappearance of Malvezzi's young progeny, Orefeo. As mentioned above, the book is divided into two parts; the first details the events of March 1821, leading up to the murder and disappearance. The second part deals with Julian's efforts to solve the murder without the singing Orefeo being convicted or even discovered. While so doing, the reader is given a fascinating tour into the worlds of Italian music, Italian nationalism, international espionage and Italian family relationships. *The Devil in Music* is, perhaps, the best of Kate Ross's four mysteries, despite its unusual setting and relatively slow progression. Her careful build-up of the murder, the investigation, and the solution is as meticulous as her occupation of trial lawyer would imply.

Solving crimes is the primary function of the historical detective. He or she must be able to do so when existing authority has failed or is unable to act. Given the almost mystic status of the London Bobby, it might be appropriate to place Kestrel in proper perspective to the history of England's police organization.

Prior to the Norman Conquest, individuals were expected to be observant of what was going on; to raise a warning in case of trouble, and to pursue criminals when needed. Naturally, if every man was busy watching out for trouble, no one would be tending to the crops and livestock. So families would band together in self protection. A group of ten families was called a tithing and selected one individual to serve as a guard. Ten tithings constituted a hundred and was supervised by a constable, the first real police officer. The constable and his assistant-guards were not excused from the daily routine of farming, grazing livestock, or tending to a craft. Law enforcement duties were above and beyond the struggle for livelihood.

Unlike that of the shire's reeve who was appointed either by the king or the local land-owning aristocrat to supervise the shire, it fell to the office of *Sheriff* to maintain order and enforce the noble's laws. The constable protected the village and the sheriff protected the land owner. In simpler times, it was a system that worked.

But the constable, having to work for his living, was rarely able to watch over the village during the night. The sheriff often lived and worked in locations remote from his appointed shire. As villages grew into towns and towns into cities, a better system had to be found. Especially as the threat of fire began to exceed the threat of criminal activity.

Sometime during the thirteenth century, the Watch System was created. Permanent watchmen were hired to stand watch at select locations and sound the alarm at the first sign of fire or robbery. This freed the local constables to investigate crimes, gather evidence, and give testimony. The watch system proved so workable that it survived for some 500 years.

Social conditions in England took a serious down-turn in the eighteenth century with the introduction of gin, a cheap hard liquor. The increase in consumption of alcohol lead to an increase in crime; robbery, burglary, assault, rape, and murder. The demands for street patrols were rebuffed by constables and watchmen who refused to abandon their watch boxes. In 1748, Henry Fielding found a solution when he created the Bow Street Runners.

Created as a patrolling police force, the Bow Street Runners were expected to intercept and prevent crime on the streets and in public places. To them was also given the power to investigate and solve crimes. Their favorite method was to place advertisements of rewards for information regarding specific crimes. While this method proved effective in many cases, in those incidents where there was no witness to give information, crimes went unsolved.

It is against this background, the Bow Street Runners, that Julian Kestrel is pitted. Of course, Julian had no intention of going into the private detective business in competition with the Bow Street Runners. He is, after all, one of the leading Dandies in London. But Julian is forced to solve his first case through the need of self-preservation and a desire to protect his man-servant, Dipper. His second case comes about as a result of the involvement of Dipper's sister. The third, where he first actively pursues an investigation for its own rewards, was brought to him by invitation. In his latest escapade, Julian Kestrel must solve a three-year old murder in northern Italy or again face being prosecuted for committing the murder himself.

Rhona Martin states in *Writing Historical Fiction* that the best reason for writing a historical book is that the situation portrayed springs from the period depicted and could not possibly happen at any other time (9). While any of Kestrel's four mysteries could be placed in the twentieth century, the methodology of solving them would be far different. Solving the crimes is secondary to Kate Ross. Of far more importance is her depiction of human nature in post-Regency England and the impending changes.

If there exists a secret to the popularity of historical fiction in general and historical mysteries specifically, it lies in describing human nature. But the manner or method of description itself needs defining.

The practice of describing the past was long considered an art, a branch of literature (Grossman 227). At the beginning of the nineteenth century, the two split apart. Literature began to become less concerned with telling the facts and more inclined to tell the story. History became less concerned with the story and more scientific in compiling facts. So much so that historian R. G. Collingwood was able to propose three rules for history: 1) the historian must, unlike the novelist, localize his story in time and place; 2) that all history must be consistent with itself since there is only one historical world; and 3) the historical imagination is not completely free but rather bound to work from the evidence alone (Grossman 248, Collingwood 246).

It is clear from these rules that the novelist has far more freedom of expression than the historian. She may wander in time and place with little fear of disturbing the historian, so long as she allows the reader to become anchored in the work. The writer may take liberties with historical fact for literary considerations, as Ross admits in *The Devil in Music* by having the renowned tenor, Giovanni Battista Rubini, sing in Milan in 1825 rather than in Paris as actually happened. In the third rule, the historical novelist becomes bound by the same demands that the historian faces; the rule of evidence.

The debate in scholarly circles over the role of narrative in writing history has lasted for decades. While the art of narrating a story has been present in every age, place, and society, some scholars hold that there is no place in modern writing for more than the bare bones necessary to tell the facts. Using a narrative style only obscures the telling "as it was."

Doris Ricker Marston, in *A Guide to Writing History*, identifies several methods of using history in fiction (152-58). The most important for this essay is the fourth form, the factual novel or novelized history. A concept reportedly developed by Truman Capote to describe his *In Cold Blood*, this is the dramatic presentation of true events which have little or no evidential proof. Allan Eckert is arguably the greatest modern proponent of this style. His Narratives of America series, six books detailing the opening of the Trans-Appalachian West, use a great amount of dialogue. Dialogue based on the written reports of the participants recorded at a later date. "In order to help provide continuity and maintain a high degree of reader interest, certain techniques normally associated with the novel form have been utilized, but in no case has this been at the expense of historical accuracy," he assures us in the author's note to *The Frontiersmen* (*vi*).

It is interesting that Eckert's paperback publisher, Bantam Books, released the series labeled as historical novels. This says more about the debate over the form of the factual novel than the question of whether Eckert wrote fiction or not. Richard Current worries that novelists exert greater influence on the public's conception of the past than do historians. But even Current recognizes that there is a difference between Historical Fiction and Fictional History (147).

While historical fiction presents the writer's imaginary characters and events against presumably historical facts, the writer of fictional history "pretends to deal with real persons and events but actually reshapes them— and thus rewrites the past." Examples abound, reaching from the obvious to the insidious. Gore Vidal's openly proclaimed *Lincoln: A Novel* is clearly fictional history. But what of William Safire's *Freedom*? While it is written in acceptable interpretative narrative, fictional and factual elements of the events leading up to the issuing of the Emancipation Proclamation are so intertwined that *Freedom* required nearly 150 pages of explanatory notes separating fact from fiction.

Kate Ross needs no such separation. Her works are found on the mystery shelves of the local library. At no time does she attempt to do more than present to her readers a plausible description of a long-past world that is relevant to our modern lifestyle. Julian Kestrel's Dandyism is no more than the individualism of today's Hollywood and Society Jet-Setters although, in solving murder mysteries, it is given far more meaning than the Jet-Setting class receives today.

The societal ills Ross uncovers, and the potential cures implied, are mere reflections of our own ills and solutions. The class distinctions mirror today's race, sex, and religious blindness and bigotry. The deep and hidden family problems Ross is so skilled at describing may be found any day on the front pages of modern newspapers.

There is nothing new in what Kate Ross does, projecting an image of our lives through the medium of the printed word. Yet she does it so skillfully and so entertainingly that the reader absorbs the message without noticing the method. Rare is the individual who realizes as he witnesses this Dandy solve the inscrutable puzzle that he is being challenged to rise above his station or lot in life and make a difference. Perhaps what this world needs is more Dandies.

*Works Cited*

Braudy, Leo. *Narrative Form in History and Literature*. Princeton, NJ: Princeton UP, 1970.

Current, Richard Nelson. *Arguing With Historians*. Middletown, CT: Wesleyan UP, 1988.

Day, A. Grove. *James Michener*. Boston: Twayne, 1997.

Gossman, Lionel. *Between History and Literature*. Cambridge, MA: Harvard UP, 1990.

Klein, Gregory, ed. *Women Times Three: Writers, Detectives, Readers*. Bowling Green, OH: Bowling Green State U Popular P, 1995.

Lu, Sheldon Hsiao-Peng. *From Historicity to Fictionality: The Chinese Poetic Narrative*. Stanford, CA: Stanford UP, 1994.

Lukacs, Gyorgy. *The Historical Novel*. London: Merlin P, 1962.

Marston, Doris Ricker. *A Guide to Writing History*. Cincinnati: Writer's Digest, 1976.

Martin, Rhona. *Writing Historical Fiction*. London: A & C Black, 1995.

McCullagh, C. Behan. *Justifying Historical Descriptions*. New York: Cambridge, Cambridge UP, 1984.

Mink, Louis O. *Historical Understanding*. Ithaca, NY: Cornell UP, 1987.

Windschuttle, Keith. *The Killing of History*. New York: Free P, 1997.

# James Brewer:
# Sleuths and Carpetbaggers
# along the Mississippi River

## Lawrence A. Kreiser, Jr.

When the Civil War ended in 1865, the federal government undertook the difficult job of bringing the former Confederate states back into the Union. The dramatic and controversial process of Reconstruction lasted twelve years and comprised two distinct phases. During Presidential Reconstruction, which ran from the end of the war through 1866, President Andrew Johnson advocated mild readmission policies and attempted to minimize any social, political, and economic upheavals in the defeated South. His plans fizzled when most southern states rejected the Fourteenth Amendment and civil rights for blacks and, instead, passed restrictive Black Codes. Their brazen defiance helped Radical Republicans, who advocated universal manhood suffrage and strict readmission criteria, to gain control of Congress during the 1866 state elections. By early 1867, the Republicans had swept aside Johnson's lenient policies and initiated the period of Radical or Congressional Reconstruction. The Radicals divided the South into five military districts and enfranchised black males while disfranchising many ex-Confederate soldiers and politicians. Each southern state could gain readmission to the Union only after it had elected new governments and received the approval of Congress. The Radicals' policies met with violence and bitterness throughout much of the former Confederacy, primarily directed against carpetbaggers, or people who had moved from North to South after the war, and former slaves.

James Brewer uses the turbulent times of Radical Reconstruction as the historical backdrop for his engaging and well-written mystery series, which he first began in 1992. Throughout, the action swirls along the lower-half of the Mississippi River and through the geographic heart of the Reconstruction South, from St. Louis and Memphis in the north, to Natchez and New Orleans, hundreds of miles below. Brewer's works make a welcome addition to historical fiction on America during the mid-nineteenth century, because so few writers focus on the people and events of Reconstruction. In fiction as well as non-fiction the war years dominate, and the transition of the men who wore the blue and the gray to civilian society has received little attention. In an interview with the author, Brewer describes how he eagerly accepted the challenge to write about the too-long neglected times of Reconstruction and to "tackle this complicated period in our history." He also remarks that "I didn't set out to write social or historical commentary, but if you're doing your research, and paying attention to human nature, it cannot but ooze from the pages when you deal with such a fascinating and volatile time."

Brewer brings an interesting perspective to his stories because his family and personal history reflect the divided loyalties that the nation struggled with during the Civil War and Reconstruction. Two of Brewer's ancestors labored as small farmers during the 1850s, one in Illinois and the other in Tennessee. With the start of the Civil War in 1861 both men joined the cavalry, but one fought to preserve the Union and the other to win the Confederacy's independence. In his own life, Brewer has witnessed the different regional attitudes that the country still takes toward the Civil War era. Born and raised in eastern Tennessee, Brewer grew up among people where "one's present-day cultural, familial, political, and socioeconomic circumstances is a direct result of the war." But Brewer also has taught at West Point, the alma mater of such renowned Union generals as Ulysses S. Grant and William T. Sherman. Perhaps appropriately, the author now lives in Kentucky, a former border state!

In *No Bottom* (1994), Brewer introduces an eclectic and redoubtable cast of characters. The book begins in St. Louis during fall 1872, where Luke Williamson, a former Union sailor and currently the captain of the riverboat *Paragon*, receives word that the ship piloted by his business partner and wartime friend, Edward Smythe, mysteriously has sunk. Williamson and his first mate, Jacob Lusk, the only black to hold such a prestigious position on the Mississippi, search for answers as they run passengers and goods to and from New Orleans. But a Yankee and a black often are snubbed in the Reconstruction South and the two men quickly realize that they need help. The unlikely duo of Masey Baldridge and Salina Tyner comes to the rescue. Baldridge, a Confederate veteran hobbled by a wartime leg wound and a weakness for strong liquor, investigates the sinking for an insurance company and discovers valuable clues and leads along the river banks of Natchez. Tyner, a former riverboat prostitute who is scorned by polite society but who possesses considerable grace and inner-strength, provides Williamson with valuable insights about his passengers. The group of four, all of whom encounter insurmountable difficulties when they investigate individually, form a formidable team when they work together. They slowly discover the truth about the sinking and, in the process, uncover a plot that involves advances in military technology that the Confederacy had employed during the last days of the Civil War.

The heart of *No Bottom* lies in Brewer's portrayal of the struggle that many southerners experienced to move forward from their recent defeat. The early 1870s represented a crossroads in the South's history, particularly along the Mississippi River. The region was beginning to recover from the devastation of the war and to make strong economic strides, as suggested by the abundant farm goods and wealthy passengers that Williamson routinely transports down the river. But many southerners remained trapped in their nostalgia for the past and blamed the war and the death and destruction that followed on unscrupulous and greedy northerners. Victor Burl, the main protagonist of the story, is such a man. A wealthy but moody riverboat gambler, Burl refuses to let go of the bitterness of the war. He despises carpetbaggers and Reconstruction and, to avenge a wartime tragedy that befell his river-based family, he continues to wage a private struggle against veterans of the Mississippi Marine Brigade, a Union naval squadron. "[T]he war's still on whether you know it or not," Burl declares in an attempt to win a fellow southerner to his cause. "Oh, maybe they're not shooting at us, but they're killing us just the same . . . You can call it Reconstruction if you want to, but what it amounts to is the *de*struction of the South" (199-200). An intriguing element of the story is the interplay between Burl and Baldridge. Both men were wounded during the war, one emotionally and one physically. But while Baldridge attempts to move on with his life, Burl defiantly remains locked in the past, a self-proclaimed soldier in a deadly and personal war against the North.

In *No Virtue* (1995), the action takes place in Memphis and New Orleans during early spring 1873. After a dead prostitute is found aboard the *Paragon*, a Memphis sheriff arrests Lusk on circumstantial evidence. For their own reasons Williamson and Tyner believe that the first mate is innocent, and they quickly convince Baldridge of the same. When the three find a rare $20 Confederate gold piece in the victim's cabin, they decide to investigate its origins. The search leads them to the whereabouts of a fortune in similar gold coins, previously thought scattered and lost during the chaotic last days of the war. But they also inadvertently uncover a plot of corruption and murder that involves the fictional William Jenkins Dodd, a Union veteran and powerful Republican politician in Memphis, who plans to use his seemingly endless supply of money to run for governor. The sleuths realize that Dodd and several of his cronies have long ago discovered the Confederate gold and now are using the money to illegally finance their operations, but they have to determine how and where the men are minting the loot into United States coins. In addition, Williamson and his partners also have to link Dodd and his gang to the murder of the prostitute, whom they killed after accidentally passing her a Confederate coin.

Williamson and his companions have to hurry to solve both cases, because Lusk stands little chance of receiving a fair trial in a Memphis courtroom and Dodd is becoming suspicious of their activities. The three detectives split ranks to cover more ground and their chase takes them from the bars and waterfront of New Orleans to the Federal marshall's office in St. Louis; and from the grandeur of Jefferson Davis's home on the outskirts of Memphis to the run-down boarding houses and saloons inside the city. They finally collect the evidence that they need, but Dodd and his men have come too far to abandon their schemes without a fight. The book builds to a dramatic climax in an abandoned Union fort outside Memphis, where Dodd has retreated with the remainder of the gold and where Williamson and Baldridge have to follow to complete their case.

Brewer's portrayal of Reconstruction in *No Virtue* fits well with his description in *No Bottom*. He again plays on the theme of southern society in flux, but where the chaos and destruction of the war had destroyed Burl, they are the making of Dodd. A Union officer of little influence in Memphis at the end of the war, Dodd eagerly seizes the opportunities presented when he stumbles across the lost Confederate gold. The new-found wealth allows Dodd to turn politician, and, astutely reading the coming political trends of Reconstruction, he throws his lot with the Radical Republicans. After the war he exploits the black vote as often as his ill-gotten gold and, before he runs into Williamson, Baldridge, and Tyner, he is poised to make the stunning climb from nondescript soldier to governor of Tennessee. "A penniless man has little influence in matters of state," he explains of the combination of pragmatism and greed that drives his actions. "Few men heed the counsel of a pauper. So, after the war, I determined to make myself heard" (182-83). But exploiting the confusion of Reconstruction for personal gain is a trait that extends beyond carpetbaggers, and Dodd is assisted in his political schemes by several well-paid southerners, some of whom are Confederate veterans. A lust for power and wealth motivates these former combatants and, except for a careless mistake in passing the Confederate gold piece, they come close to success.

In contrast to Dodd and his partners who put aside past wartime differences to pursue personal gain, Williamson and Baldridge frequently erupt into squabbles over their former loyalties. Distinct ideas about the war threaten to divide the two veterans, especially when Tyner is not present to reign in their emotions. The trouble starts when Williamson brings Rolf Pittman, a federal marshall from St. Louis, to help investigate Dodd and the Confederate coins. To Williamson's surprise, Baldridge takes considerable umbrage at his guest's connections to the federal government. In an argument over whether Pittman should be involved in the case, Baldridge heatedly tells Williamson, "I'm just amazed that you Yankees could fight us for four years and still not know what the war was about." Williamson objects that he knows perfectly well what the fighting was about, only to have Baldridge shout in response, "It was about Southerners settling their own affairs, without Yankees sticking their nose in our business!" (143). Williamson ultimately wins and Pittman helps to investigate, but tensions again spill over when the three men track Dodd and one of his gang to the old Union fort. Pittman wants to deputize the two detectives for the remainder of the case in order, as he explains, "to do this right." Baldridge objects, even when the group comes under gunfire from Dodd and his companion. "The hell you say!" he responds to another request from Pittman. "I ain't swearin' to no *federal* nothin'!" (217). Baldridge eventually relents, but the different attitudes that he and Williamson express toward the Civil War and Reconstruction is a theme that Brewer picks up several times in his later works.

Although Brewer realistically portrays the motives and personalities of men such as Dodd, Williamson, and Baldridge, he is much less convincing in his description of Elijah Rawls, a black citizen of Memphis. The one black character of the series beside Lusk, Brewer describes Rawls as a "free Negro since long before the war" who, when the Federals occupied the city during 1862, "made it very plain . . . that he hated Yankees more than any white Southerner ever did" (48). Rawls's dislike of northerners carries into the post-war, and he chastises Baldridge for working with Williamson. He also criticizes white Republicans, but saves most of his venom for blacks who have joined the party of Lincoln. "They listen to the promises of all those scalawags and carpetbaggers," he sneers, "I tell you, it makes me sick to see folks of my color being led around like mules" (53-54). Because Brewer is so careful about the accuracy of his other details and descriptions, his portrayal of Rawls may leave readers with an incorrect perception of the wartime sympathies of free blacks. Very few, if any, blacks actively cheered the Confederacy's war effort, as Brewer implies of Rawls. Additionally, Brewer's depiction of black Republicans is considerably outdated by current scholarship. Several recent historians have convincingly argued that freedmen played an active role in the politics of Reconstruction, rather than being "led around" by whites. All and all, Rawls as an anti-northerner adds little to the plot and he is an anomaly among Brewer's otherwise well-researched characters.

Word of the three detectives' success in foiling Dodd spreads quickly, and in *No Justice* (1996) they become involved in a new case. Set in April 1873, the action takes place primarily along the stretch of river between St. Louis and Memphis. The story begins with Tyner and Baldridge in Chicago, where they have a meeting with the famous Pinkerton Detective agency. The Pinkertons want investigated the robbery of a riverboat, during which the bandits killed the captain and a crew member, but made off only with two unidentified crates, rather than any money from the passengers. To Baldridge's disappointment the Pinkertons only want him to serve as a guide for the investigation, but to Tyner's even greater disgust they refuse to hire a woman in any capacity. While the two finish their business, Williamson begins the maiden voyage of his new boat, the *Edward Smythe*. The journey proves to be anything but routine when Williamson discovers that one of his passengers is Addison Sweeney, a wartime friend who now works as a special assistant to President Ulysses Grant. Sweeney informs Williamson that the President is preparing to make a secret trip to Little Rock, Arkansas, to meet with several of his military commanders who are fighting against the Modoc Indians in California. He shocks Williamson when he tells him that Grant will sail on the *Edward Smythe* from St. Louis to Memphis, a voyage that will bring the captain and his boat tremendous publicity but that must be kept quiet until the conclusion of the Little Rock meeting.

With Sweeney's news, the action quickly heats up. Only Baldridge survives an ambush that the riverboat bandits set for the Pinkertons, but the

Confederate veteran still manages to discover the contents of the missing crates. At the same time, Tyner, working independently and determined to prove that she is as good a detective as any man, cunningly pieces together enough information to link Sweeney with the bandits and their activities. When the two rejoin forces they come to the stunning realization that Sweeney plans to use the items in the crates to assassinate Grant while he sails aboard the *Edward Smythe*. Little goes right for the detectives after their discoveries and, in a piece of particularly bad luck, Sweeney and his gang capture Tyner. They hold her at their camp along a sharp bend in the river, where they have prepared a deadly trap for Williamson's boat. With *Edward Smythe* rapidly approaching the same bend and its crew and passengers unaware of the lurking danger, Baldridge has to figure out how to free Tyner and how to stop Sweeney's apparently fool-proof plan.

The who's and why's of the mystery in *No Justice* are the weakest of Brewer's series, but the author still manages to build a tremendous amount of suspense as he moves the action toward a climax. Brewer drops enough hints that readers quickly will determine who are the bad guys and what they intend to do. Early on, the finger points to Sweeney. "But though Sweeney had kept much of his old ironic wit, Williamson couldn't help noticing a certain cynicism that came out when he talked of his work," Brewer writes of the reunion between the two friends. "The tailored suit, the manicured nails, the expensive cigars—all seemed to have come at the price of some humor that he recalled in his old friend. Sweeney had a harder edge now than the captain remembered" (30). The real mystery lies in how Baldridge and Tyner will disrupt Sweeney's assassination attempt. Brewer does an excellent job of crafting Sweeney's motives and plans for killing Grant and the result is an intriguing and fast-paced story. The would-be assassin's only mistake is to underestimate Tyner and Baldridge and, in an ironic twist, the southern prostitute and Confederate veteran are the only people who can save Grant, the hero of the Union.

In *No Remorse* (1997), the three detectives become involved in a case that confronts them with dangers that are more subtle than those posed by Sweeney and his men but that are equally threatening. Set in St. Louis during summer 1873, Helen Van Geer, the wife of Williamson's chief riverboat rival, asks the sleuths to investigate the recent murder of her husband. Her son, Stuart, has confessed to the crime and meekly awaits trial. Van Geer believes that Stuart is innocent and she offers Williamson and his friends considerable money to investigate the case. The three accept, more because they want the work than because they believe that Stuart has been wrongly-accused. In a riveting adventure that ranges between a run-down plantation in Louisiana and the rail yards of St. Louis, the detectives battle a formidable array of opponents, including the terror tactics of the Ku Klux Klan and the supernatural powers of voodoo. The three eventually become convinced that Stuart is innocent and that somebody or something is forcing him to confess to the crime, but they face an uphill struggle to convince the police of their suspicions. The detectives' task becomes more difficult when

Baldridge falls mysteriously ill and more puzzling when Williamson finds a voodoo mojo, or curse, in his cabin. In a mystery that continues to take unexpected twists and turns until the very end, the detectives finally discover Van Geer's real killers, but bringing them to justice proves to be a difficult and dangerous task.

Brewer adds two significant wrinkles to his series during *No Remorse*. The first is Tyner's struggle to overcome her past. At the end of *No Justice*, Tyner forms the Big River Detective Agency with Baldridge and Williamson, and the three plan to investigate mysteries that occur along the river. But where Brewer's male characters often use the confusion and opportunities created by Reconstruction to forge new beginnings, Tyner almost daily is confronted by professional and social obstacles because she is a woman and a former prostitute. The agency threatens to flounder when Williamson becomes too busy with his riverboats and Baldridge takes to the bottle, but Tyner holds the business together through her energy and determination. She makes the most of the Van Geer case and pressures Baldridge to stay sober and Williamson to pick up information on his journeys up and down the river. She also displays considerable grit as she investigates the murder and discovers several valuable clues that her partners and the St. Louis police have overlooked. How Tyner performs as a businesswoman and a detective and whether she can surmount her checkered past are interesting subplots that add considerable depth to Brewer's mysteries.

Brewer also introduces the growing importance of railroads in the nation's economy through the character of Robert Van Geer, Helen's oldest son. At the start of the story, Robert has forsaken his father's steamboat business to work for a railroad company. His decision elicits bemusement among many riverboat captains, who complacently believe that steamboats always will haul more tonnage than the railroad. But Robert has correctly foreseen the economic future of the country, and the 1880s ushered in the golden age of the railroads as well as the beginnings of a steady and ultimately fatal decline in the steamboat industry. Among the riverboat captains described in the story, only Williamson fully recognizes the emerging threat posed by the trains, which moved goods and passengers more quickly and to more places than riverboats. "Everywhere you look someone's building a new rail line," he warns his fellow captains. "But they sure as hell aren't building any new rivers" (12). The looming economic danger of the railroads makes a fascinating backdrop to *No Remorse*, because the struggle is one at which Williamson and his fellow sailors ultimately will fail. With such historical hindsight, readers may find themselves in agreement with Baldridge's reaction when he meets Robert in a rail yard. Brewer writes that when Baldridge first sees the depot he "would probably have thought of it all as progress, as everyone else seemed to, if he hadn't come to know Luke Williamson. Spending time on the packets and living in the elegance of the riverboats made him share some of Williamson's dislike for the railroads' iron monstrosities . . . He had been there less than fifteen minutes, and already he felt dirty" (83).

When Brewer's series is examined in its entirety, several common themes emerge. The first is the author's attention to historical detail, a task that makes his stories come alive. Brewer conducts extensive research before he writes each mystery, from reading contemporary newspapers for details about what people ate and how they spoke, to consulting 1870s river and city maps to ensure the accuracy of his physical descriptions. "I almost always try to visit the places I write about," Brewer declares, "and since I enjoy research and travel, I get an added bonus from my writing. If I tell you what a Winchester sounds like when it's fired in a backwater slough in western Kentucky, you can bet I've been there and fired one." The result of Brewer's research is a historical richness that adds greatly to his already intriguing plots.

In addition to getting the details right, Brewer also focuses on characters who are common people rather than well-known military or political leaders, such as Robert E. Lee or Andrew Johnson. When asked why he writes about ordinary folks, Brewer passionately responds, "Isn't it time somebody told the story of the average people who carried the weight of the war, and its aftermath, on their backs? Most of them didn't get a cushy job as president of an insurance company after the war [Davis], or president of a university [Lee], or the chief executive [Grant]. Most of them went back to the weed patches that were once their farms, or the boarded up businesses that once were their livelihood and tried to make the best of it." Brewer does an admirable job, and fans of works such as those written by historian Bell Wiley on the common soldiers of the war will very much enjoy the series.

Despite Brewer's emphasis on the common people, he occasionally dabbles with the famous. Jefferson Davis makes a brief appearance in *No Virtue* and, as portrayed by most historians, he comes across as an aloof and proud man. What is more interesting than Brewer's description of Davis is Baldridge's attitude toward his former commander-in-chief. While waiting to meet with the former president, Baldridge eyes a present given to Davis on a trip to an English cotton factory after the war. Baldridge becomes momentarily angry when he thinks that many ex-Confederate leaders had left the country after the war, to the abandonment of their defeated followers. "Reconstruction was proving to be almost as bad as the war," Brewer writes of Baldridge's thoughts. "And for him and thousands of other rank-and-file troopers, there had been no European aristocracy to fawn over them and help them lick their wounds. Baldridge figured the Liverpool Cotton Exchange wouldn't have had the time of day for a *real* soldier" (103). Although Davis provides Baldridge with some extremely helpful information during their meeting, the veteran still clings to much of his resentment and he never fully forgives the ex-president for his postwar activities.

Brewer proves non-partisan, and in *No Justice* Grant has several talks and visits with Williamson. Brewer portrays Grant as discouraged by a series of political scandals that have rocked his administration and exposed him to bitter personal attacks. In ways Grant's outlook is reminiscent of that of Victor Burl, the riverboat gambler and ex-Confederate in *No Bottom*, because he longs for the clarity of purpose that came during the war. "I wish there was something in this world that I loved that much—something I could put my heart and soul into," Grant wistfully declares after Williamson describes the importance of the river in his life. "The war was like that for me. Not that I loved it, because I didn't. God knows it caused far too much suffering. But at least the war was something I could give myself to completely. Something that was me" (175). In an interesting twist to Grant's personality, Brewer gives the President something of a suicidal streak. After Grant momentarily is confronted by a gunman, he ruefully declares, "Hell, in some ways, I wish he *had* pulled the trigger" (235). Whether the reader agrees with Brewer's interpretation, Grant's trip aboard the *Edward Smythe* makes for a colorful voyage.

The most powerful and unpredictable character in the series is the Mississippi. At times, the people who live along the river temporarily harness its energy. The river is full of boats loaded with cargo, primarily cotton and other agricultural goods, headed for New Orleans and for eventual shipment to the rest of the country and the world. Farmers and riverboat captains seem masters of the situation and the Mississippi subject to their will. "The main thing is, you can't let her know you're afraid," Williamson describes of the river to a new pilot in *No Bottom*. "Like any woman, if she senses you're scared, or if she thinks you'll hesitate, then she's got you" (16). But steamboats and their captains are only guests and the river ultimately calls the shots. Snags and sandbars can snare complacent pilots and wrecks litter the bottom in mute testament to the river's wrath. "Old Man River . . . could swallow a boat whole and just keep rushing toward the sea," Williamson reflects in *No Bottom*, "unmindful of the lives that he'd snapped up or changed forever. Nobody could see past his muddy surface, or know his soul, or tell him what to do. And just when you though you had him tamed, he'd up and surprise you" (184). The captains who fare best on the Mississippi are those such as Williamson who recognize the tremendous energy of the river but who also respect its potentially destructive powers.

For the many who will enjoy Brewer's work, the series continues to thrive. Brewer recently has written *No Escape* (1998), set in Memphis during the 1873 yellow fever epidemic. Baldridge and Tyner solve a series of murders and robberies in the stricken city, while Williamson waits out both the quarantine of his boat and an outbreak of fever among his crew. Brewer also currently is at work on another book that "will be strongly influenced by the Panic of 1873, and the unemployment, greed, and hunger that was common to the times." He also hints that "Baldridge gets an incapacitating toothache treated by a 22-year-old, thin, pale, Doctor of Dentistry who is riding a steamboat from north Louisiana to St. Louis to buy medical equipment. Recently having moved his practice from Atlanta to Dallas, the young dentist gets involved in the exploits of our main characters, and they discover that he's not only a medical man, but a pretty good hand at the card table and gunfight." Brewer's attention to historical detail and accuracy throughout his series and his willingness to tackle the too-long neglected period of Reconstruction greatly add to our understanding of the era. For those interested in a great mix of mystery and history, Brewer's books will make for an enjoyable read.

## Works Cited and Suggested Reading

James Brewer's mystery series is published by Walker and Company, 435 Hudson Street, New York, NY 10014, (212) 727-3800. Brewer also has written the nonfiction, *The Raiders of 1862* (Praeger Military Books, Greenwood, 1997), about Civil War cavalry raids in the western theater.

Foner, Eric. *Reconstruction: America's Unfinished Revolution, 1863-1877*. New York: Harper & Row, 1988.

Gosnell, H. Allen. *Guns on the Western Waters: The Story of the River Gunboats in the Civil War*. Baton Rouge: Louisiana State UP, 1949.

McPherson, James M. *Battle Cry of Freedom: The Civil War Era*. New York: Oxford UP, 1988.

Wiley, Bell I. *The Life of Billy Yank: The Common Soldier of the Union*. Reprint; Baton Rouge: Louisiana State UP, 1993.

——. *The Life of Johnny Reb: The Common Soldier of the Confederacy*. Reprint; Baton Rouge: Louisiana State UP, 1993.

# Peter Heck:
# Mark Twain as Detective

## Ray B. Browne and Lawrence A. Kreiser, Jr.

Following the death and destruction of the Civil War (1861-65), the United States entered into a period of rapid industrialization and urbanization. By the late nineteenth century, railroad and telegraph lines criss-crossed and connected the nation, millions of immigrants poured into cities on both the west and east coasts, and, on the world stage, America flexed its growing economic and military might. Trumpeted as an era of progress and opportunities, numerous problems also accompanied what many historians now refer to as the "modernization" of America. Deplorable working and living conditions marred many factories and inner-city neighborhoods, while the working classes missed out on much of the wealth that their labor had produced. At the top, a series of political scandals and corruption rocked the country and, quipped some political pundits, "the Man on the Moon had to hold his nose when passing over America." The culture of the late nineteenth century received its name, and a satirical denouncement, with the publication of Mark Twain's *The Gilded Age: A Tale of Today*, coauthored with C. D. Warner, in 1873. Twain suggested that the glitter of the Gilded Age was only surface deep and he lambasted the culture of his country as one of blind lust after wealth and material goods, corrupt politics and politicians, and misplaced faith in the promise of America.

In Peter Heck's mystery trilogy, set during the 1890s, Mark Twain is at the height of his fame and the Gilded Age is in full swing. Heck takes advantage of Twain's mounting debts, the result of several bad investments and wasted financial opportunities, and he sends the famed author on a fictional lecture trip to recoup some of his losses. In a nearly continuous series of journeys, Twain travels by train from New York City to St. Paul, Minnesota; sails on a riverboat down the Mississippi River to New Orleans; and, after an extended stay in the Crescent City, takes a transatlantic voyage to England. Although these trips are products of Heck's fertile imagination, they have a firm grounding in reality, as Twain had largely given up a permanent residence by this time and had become a wandering citizen of the world. Twain wrote numerous accounts of his travels and, in an interview with the authors, Heck acknowledges that these stories "greatly influenced" him and that it was inevitable that he "send [Twain] on the road." By sending Twain across large sections of the country, Heck effectively develops many aspects of Gilded Age culture, both good and bad, that swirled around his famous subject; a culture of rapid, almost terrifying bursts of energy and activity that constituted the gild of the period, but that too often was only skin deep and underlain by a much baser metal.

Recreating the quick wit and homespun stories of Mark Twain is a challenge for any author and, to meet the task, Heck relies heavily upon the writings of his subject. Heck asserts that readers familiar with Twain's stories "will recognize many of the anecdotes and quips herein as being adapted from his work" (*Death on the Mississippi* ix). Although a detailed familiarity with Twain's writings is not essential to enjoy Heck's work, such knowledge greatly adds to the texture of each book and sets the stage for many of the mysteries and allusions that occur.

Twain was interested in virtually all aspects of the times in which he lived and he experimented with all kinds of fiction, including detective stories. While Ernest Hemingway may have overstated Twain's accomplishments when he declared that all American literature began with *Huckleberry Finn* (1884), nobody is going to urge that Twain be considered the forerunner of American crime fiction. Twain wrote several detective stories, none of which are considered among his best works. At times, Twain's efforts at detective fiction were logical attempts to further develop material about the Mississippi River, which he knew very well, and New Orleans, which he had visited many times during his early days as a riverboat pilot. At other times, out of rage and envy, Twain tried to ride the back of the literary success of other authors, especially Arthur Conan Doyle and his popular series about Sherlock Holmes. Doyle wrote *A Study in Scarlet* in 1887 and followed three years later with *The Sign of Four*, both published in cheap bindings and immediately well-received by the public.

Twain's first effort in detective fiction was *Tom Sawyer, Detective* (1896). The basis of the book was "Tom Sawyer's Mystery," an article that Twain had written before he heard the wife of a Danish diplomat outline the plot of the novel *The Minister of Veilby* (1829) by Stephen Steeson Blicher (1782-1848). Fascinated by the story, which Blicher had based upon a famous murder case in seventeenth-century Denmark, Twain rewrote his original mystery almost completely. In a footnote used to authenticate the resulting book, Twain wrote that the incidents were not inventions but facts. He took them from an old-time Swedish criminal trial, changed the actors, and transferred the scenes to America. He added some details, but only a couple of them were important ones.

Twain's version of Blicher's story, naturally, involves a trip down the Mississippi River. Tom and Huck, bored and aching for an adventure, are told by Aunt Polly that Aunt Sally and Uncle Silas have invited them down to Arkansas, where they are having trouble with a neighbor. The two boys eagerly catch a steamboat for the trip, where they notice that one passenger never comes out of his stateroom, even to eat. Sensing excitement, Tom and Huck force their way into the stranger's room, where they discover Jake Dunlap, a ne'er-do-well related to Uncle Silas's neighbors. Jake tells the boys that he is in hiding from three thieves, who want to murder him because he has stolen two of their ill-gotten diamonds that are worth thousands of dollars. Jake manages to remain hidden throughout the voyage and the crooks are seen escaping when the boat docks during a raging storm. Tom and Huck also disembark and, while walking through a woods on their way to Uncle Silas's farm, they see an unidentified man murdered and buried.

The boys arrive at the farm the next day, where they are startled to see Uncle Silas being arrested for the murder of Jubider Dunlap, his neighbor. Silas had been seen arguing with Jubider and, in a fit of rage, hitting him over the head with a shovel. Tom and Huck believe that their uncle is innocent, but Silas, who has been acting peculiarly anyway, confesses to the murder. At the trial, Tom is at his most brilliant. Seemingly half asleep in the courtroom and only casually interested in the events that are transpiring, Tom breaks into a rigmarole that confuses everyone when the time comes to question the witnesses and he adeptly proves his uncle's innocence.

The defensive intuitions of Tom are a burlesque of Sherlock Holmes and a satire of Doyle's work. Tom observes that people always do things with their hands which are so individualized that they create gestures almost as personal as finger prints. With this insight into human behavior, Tom reveals that the dead man is Jake, not Jubider as everyone had mistakenly believed, and that the murderer is Jubider. For this incisive detective work, Tom becomes the star of the courtroom and the town. All this he has accomplished with, in a reference already a cliché, "just an ordinary little bit of detective work."

*Tom Sawyer, Detective* is considered one of Twain's weaker works. Coming over a decade after *Huckleberry Finn*, the mystery too closely echoes the earlier book, where Huck tells the story and Tom stars. Twain uses too many of his favorite devices: twins, switched identities, sleepwalking, a counterfeit deaf-and-dumb character, and a murder trial. Repetition of these old tricks weakens the story, while the plot rests on generalizations, rather than on strongly presented evidence. Twain's development of his characters also is thin, especially that of Tom. Adult readers, for whom Twain was writing, are not going to believe Tom's humorous speech to free Uncle Silas, while his pretended assumption of adult intuition is shaky at best. However, although Twain's writing is uninspired, at times he flashes his vintage style. For example, when Tom and Huck are walking through the woods to Silas's house, they see a stealthy figure slinking away. They keep their wits and conclude that the figure was ethereal rather than a ghost because "*You can't see the bushes through it.*" In general, however, the prose walks on much heavier feet.

Twain's other major venture into crime fiction was *A Double-Barreled Detective Story* (1901). In the story, Archy, a young man with an extraordinary sense of smell that enables him to track anybody anywhere, seeks revenge against his mean-spirited father, who has humiliated and abandoned his family. Archy finds his dad in Denver, where he is a prosperous quartz-miner and goes under the name of Jacob Fuller. In a series of mismanaged identifications, Archy loses his father and ends up in Hope Canyon, a silver mining camp in Colorado. At the edge of the settlement, Flint Buckner, the black sheep of the camp, holds an English lad, Fetlock Jones, in virtual slavery. After a series of improbable twists and turns in the plot, Sherlock Holmes, of all people, arrives and immediately is hailed as a great man. Fetlock, however, who as it turns out is Sherlock's nephew, realizes that the vaunted sleuth can only solve puzzles when the stage is set up beforehand, a not-so-subtle jab by Twain. Soon after, Buckner is killed by an explosion and Fetlock confesses to the crime and is put in jail. At Buckner's funeral, Archy discovers a man who has gone insane from fear that Holmes is chasing him. The angry miners, who believe that Holmes is responsible for the man's insanity, seize him and prepare to burn him at the stake. The sheriff arrives in time to rescue the beleaguered Holmes, but Jones is discovered to have escaped, although nobody really cares. To round out the story, a tale that few people would want to read twice, Twain reveals that Buckner's real name was Jacob Fuller and that Archy, after all, has accomplished his revenge.

*A Double-Barreled Detective Story* was published in *Harper's Magazine* in 1902 and subsequently reissued as a book with illustrations by Lucius Hitchcock. But no kind of praise could make a purse out of this sow's ear and Twain displays himself at very nearly his worst. In trying to make Sherlock Holmes a caricature, Twain turns common sense on its head and the plot becomes difficult to follow and, often, burlesque. The book is filled with much of the culture that was familiar to Twain, but little of his art.

With Twain's two detective works in the bookstores and the much more successful *Tom Sawyer* (1876) and *Huckleberry Finn* very much a part of everyday literature, Heck has a promising subject for his mystery series. Heck's first novel is *Death on the Mississippi* (1995), a play on Twain's *Life on the Mississippi* (1883). In keeping with Twain's works, Heck introduces a number of well-drawn characters, whom he skillfully animates as he moves them in and against Twain's world of the early 1890s. Wisely, Heck decides against an attempt to recreate Tom Sawyer or Huck Finn. Instead, he chooses Wentworth Cabot, a slightly obtuse Yale graduate (Heck graduated from Harvard), to serve as Twain's personal secretary. Cabot has never read any of his employer's stories, and he provides an eager audience for the retelling of many tales. When Twain chastises his secretary for being unfamiliar with his works, Cabot prepares the way for many stories and anecdotes when he protests, "But sir, I have you here to tell it all to me" (69). Equally important, Cabot acts as prompter and sounding board for the loquacious Twain and, throughout the series, Yale and Hannibal mix in a free-flowing chemistry.

In *Death on the Mississippi* (1995), Twain and Cabot are in New York City, completing the final preparations for a lecture trip that will take them the length of the Mississippi River, from St. Paul, Minnesota, to New

Orleans. Before they leave, they receive word that one of Twain's friends from his riverboat days has been murdered while waiting to meet with them. This unexpected event forces Twain to reveal to Cabot that the lecture trip is something of a cover, and that he also is looking to recover a long-buried treasure near Napoleon, Arkansas, and to return the money to its rightful owner. Others of fewer scruples also know about the treasure and they want to follow Twain to its location, an occurrence that might place anyone suspected of being in cahoots with the famed writer in danger, as evidenced by the murdered man. Cabot still agrees to go and, on their journey to St. Paul, they discover that they are being trailed by a New York detective, who has been assigned the task of protecting the two and capturing the murderer. The trio form an uneasy alliance and they soon suspect that a group of roughs who have followed Twain aboard the steamboat are responsible for the earlier killing and that they also have designs upon the treasure. When another man is found murdered only hours before the steamboat reaches Memphis, Tennessee, Twain and Cabot realize that they quickly have to find the killer so that, as Twain declares, "I can go find that treasure without having to worry who's behind my back" (228). In a mad scramble, Twain and Cabot complete some astute detective work and trick the killer into revealing himself, just in time to be turned over to the Memphis police.

Heck's closest use of Twain material comes, as he says, with his recounting of the story about the treasure in Napoleon. Unlike Twain, however, Heck treats the story as true, rather than a folktale. In Twain's account, the writer tells two of his fellow travelers on a journey down the Mississippi that he is going to disembark at Napoleon. Twain thinks that his companions are going to continue downriver, so he recounts for them a story of murder and death that ends in information about a $10,000 cache of gold hidden in Napoleon. Twain declares that if he recovers the gold, he is going to return it to the son of the man whom the original storyteller had mistakenly murdered. His companions argue, however, that Twain should send the son only half the fortune, because he has not done any of the recovery work. They keep reducing and justifying smaller amounts that should be sent until they finally are down to nothing. Then having saved the money for the group, they squabble over the spoils. When the three prepare individually to get off the steamboat at Napoleon, the captain tells them that years before the river flooded the town and washed everything away. "Nothing left but a fragment of a shanty and a crumbling brick chimney," he says. Twain and his companions continue their voyage, since there is no need to try to find the fortune. Twain's moral is that God disposes over human beings' greed and dishonesty, and he ends his account in irony. As he and his fellow travelers bemoan their loss of the gold, Twain turns to praising the countryside and river. The lost money is only the loss of a moment compared with the eternal beauty of nature.

Heck has a different moral for the story and he has Twain leave the boat and find the money. Since Napoleon is no longer in existence, Heck moves the site of treasure to Hellena, "an easy day's run down the river" from the destroyed town, the captain informs Twain and Cabot. Behind the stone foundations of an old building, the two discover and take possession of the gold. Twain's wavering between greed and responsibility is handled quickly by Heck. "I want nothing more than to get it [the gold] out of my hands," Twain magnanimously declares, "and to its rightful owner as quickly as possible." But temptation in the person of Cabot is not far behind. "That doesn't seem much reward for all the trouble and danger you've gone through to find it," he prompts. "What do *you* get out of it?" Twain responds that he gets the satisfaction of giving the money to one who needs it. "And, best of all," he adds, "of having a story that'll have the audiences on the edges of their seats all the way from here to New Orleans" (289-90). Indeed Twain did, and he told the story often. And what Heck gets out of the story is a delightful mystery and a yarn that may well circulate more widely now than it did when Twain first told and published his version.

Heck's second novel *A Connecticut Yankee in Criminal Court* (1996), is a take-off on Twain's *A Connecticut Yankee in King Arthur's Court* (1889). After having arrived in New Orleans, Twain and Cabot spend several weeks conducting research and giving lectures. Their journey to and around the Crescent City is historically-based, as Twain took a trip down in Mississippi in 1882 while struggling over the composition of *Huckleberry Finn* and *Life on the Mississippi*. While doing so, Twain refreshed his memory of river culture and found material to strengthen and lengthen both books. These stories provide fodder for Heck's mill, and he capably weaves them into *A Connecticut Yankee*.

A significant figure in the book is George Washington Cable, a close friend of Twain's and one of the first significant literary figures of New Orleans. Twain and Cable visited each other's homes for years and from fall 1884 to early 1885 they toured the United States and Canada in a very successful lecture circuit. Twain despised these tours because of their physical inconveniences, but he liked the money and public adulation that he received and he often referred to such speaking engagements as "The Highway Robbery Business." Twain's relationship with Cable was always respectful and friendly but somewhat strained because of the different directions of their personalities. During the last months of their tour, Twain wrote to his friend William Dean Howells that Cable "has taught me to abhor and detest the Sabbath-day and hunt up new and troublesome ways to dishonor it" (Feb. 27, 1885). Other notables also make appearances. Heck draws vivid and realistic portraits of Buddy Bolden, a respected jazz musician; Eulalie Echo, a famous "hoodoo" woman and grandmother of Jelly Roll Morton; Charley Galloway, a band leader who gave Bolden some early gigs; and Tom Anderson, the "Mayor of Storyville," the vice-district of New Orleans.

The book begins with Cable telling Twain about the mysterious poisoning of John David Robinson, a leading figure in the social circles of New Orleans and a possible mayoral candidate. When the police arrest on flimsy charges Leonard Galloway, Robinson's black cook and a former employee of the Cable family, George Cable attempts to convince his friend to investigate the case. Twain protests that he wants nothing to do with the murder, but Cable persuades him that the two should right the injustice. To do so, Twain and Cabot interact with the upper-crust families who had employed Galloway and with Eulalie Echo and the voodoo culture of New Orleans. Disaster strikes when Cabot is challenged to a duel by a jealous husband after he is caught in what is perceived as a compromising position with the man's wife. The duel is carried out and serious injury is avoided, but Cabot is arrested by the police for firing a pistol in a public place. After spending the night in jail and threatened with all kinds of long-term sentences, he is released into Twain's custody because the judge has read and appreciated the works of the great author. With the help of Cable and Eulalie Echo, Twain and Cabot stage an elaborate ceremony, during which the killer reveals himself, a resolution somewhat similar to the one in Heck's first mystery. In the end, justice prevails and Galloway is freed from suspicion and released from jail.

A delightful side-aspect of the book is Twain's frequent references to the Civil War. Twain had an interesting relationship to the war. He served for two weeks in a volunteer company raised in Missouri to fight for the Confederacy, during which he claimed to have been "hunted like a rat the whole time," and which gave him his fill of military service (Aaron 133). After the war, he played a major role in helping to publish and market the memoirs of Ulysses S. Grant, the highest-ranking Federal officer of the war and President of the United States from 1868-76. Twain was immensely proud of his work with the books (published as two volumes), although he suffered scurrilous attacks from critics that he served as a ghost-writer. In *A Connecticut Yankee*, Twain wastes little time defending his actions when questioned by an old-line family of New Orleans about working both sides of the fence during and after the war. "I took it as my patriotic duty to erect a monument to the man who brought the War to a conclusion and ended four years of bloodshed," he declares. "I am as proud of having helped that book come into the world as anything I have written myself" (111). His remarks stir some controversy among his audience, which includes several Confederate veterans. Twain soothes the moment with humor, all of which comes as no surprise to Cabot. "Mr. Clemens had half-jokingly told me, earlier that day," Heck writes of Twain's secretary, "that when a Southerner talked about the war (there was only one of any consequence, to them), you could practically hear the capital letter on the word" (104).

Twain goes on another trip in *The Prince and the Prosecutor* (1997), which, in the by now familiar play on titles, Heck bases on *The Prince and the Pauper* (1881). This time, Twain is going to visit his wife and daughters in England, where they temporarily had moved to benefit from what Heck describes as a "cheaper cost of living" (vii). In reality, Twain made the first of his many trips to Europe and the Mediterranean in 1867, the result of which was *Innocents Abroad* (1869), a book that established him as one of

America's great humorists. On Heck's voyage, Twain has more simple plans, and he wants to enjoy the trip while putting the final touches on the manuscript on which he has been working since his recent trip down in the Mississippi River. Heck takes some literary licenses during the book, and he revives Mittel Reuss, a German principality that had ceased to exist during the early seventeenth century, as the home of one of his characters. He remodels the *City of Baltimore*, "the historical version of which was a much smaller and older ship than the one portrayed here" (viii).

Heck also includes Rudyard Kipling, the English author, and his wife, Carrie, as passengers, a fictional event but one that makes for an intriguing crossing. Kipling was just beginning to write at this time, and he looked upon Twain, whom he called "the great and godlike Clemens" as his literary hero. In 1889, a few years before Heck's voyage, Kipling had stopped by unannounced to see Twain in Elmira, New York. Although Twain failed to recall the name of Kipling during their first meeting, he was a good host and he later came to know and admire the English writer and his works on India. Both men received honorary doctorate degrees from Oxford in 1907, the same year that Kipling also received the Nobel Prize for literature, a recognition never accorded Twain.

On the *City of Baltimore*, Twain and Cabot, who again leaps at the opportunity to work for his former employer and to see the world outside of New England, mingle with a mixed group of passengers. There is the pleasant but quick-tempered Prince Heinrich Karl von Ruckgarten of Germany; Giorgio Rubia, a pretentious Italian artist and critic who Cabot suspects Twain views as a professional rival; and the obnoxious and unruly Robert Babson, who is traveling with his wealthy father, a Philadelphia lawyer, and his fiancée, Theresa Mercer, a prominent socialite, and her family. Robert quickly alienates most of his fellow passengers with his boorish behavior and, several days later, he ends up in the ocean, the victim of accident or murder. Prince Karl is arrested because he had argued with Robert the night of the supposed murder and because Twain and his fellow passengers believe that he is an impostor and that his royal lineage is doubtful. Twain, however, has second thoughts and he decides to launch an investigation of the case, to Kipling's surprise. "If that lawyer has his way," Twain counters Kipling's objections, "the whole ship will believe the prince killed that boy. Well, that ain't my idea of fair, Kipling. Prince Karl deserves a better show than that, and I mean to see that he gets it" (165). The mystery builds to a surprising conclusion and, although Twain is not in his own world as much as he was in the first two books, his sleuthing skills are as strong as ever.

Much of the plot rests on Twain's scorn for the social elite. Twain enjoyed a restless spirit as a youth and, in addition to working as a pilot on the Mississippi, he also lived and worked in California and Nevada. He later married Olivia Langdon, the daughter of a wealthy, genteel family. Twain apparently felt somewhat inferior around the Langdons and he entertained a healthy disrespect for the socially pretentious. One of his more despised classes was the upper-crust of Philadelphia society. In an oft-quoted characterization, Twain sarcastically quipped, "In Boston, they ask, how much does he know? In New York, how much is he worth? In Philadelphia, who were his parents?" Thus, when the Babsons and the Mercers disparage the passengers in steerage and the crew of the boat, "nothing more than scum from the gutters," as Mr. Mercer likes to remind those who will listen, Twain promptly turns the tables and reminds them that "scum usually rises to the top" (303).

Overall, there is much to admire in Heck's series. The author has learned a great deal about his subject and Gilded Age culture, and he skillfully recreates both. Most importantly, Heck attempts to recreate Twain as he lived, rather than how Americans in the late twentieth century might have wanted him to live. Heck quotes and paraphrases Twain frequently, as he should, and allows the famed writer to tell familiar anecdotes and adventures. If the recreated Twain is not the Twain that readers know from his own books, Heck presents a character who is a reasonable and enjoyable facsimile; if not an identical twin then a twin nevertheless. When Livy, Twain's wife, burst into a string of oaths, in a desperate attempt to shock her husband into giving up the use of profanity, which she deplored, Twain listened through graciously. He then smiled and replied, "Livy, you've got the words but you're missing the tune." Just how Twainian are Heck's books and does he have "the tune"? An example from each will illustrate his rendition.

In *Death on the Mississippi*, Cabot, while looking out the window from an upper-story hotel room in Chicago, remarks that people on the street below look like "a colony of ants." Twain laughs and replies:

Not a bad comparison, Wentworth. I've heard far worse. I once watched an ant climb to the top of a blade of grass, carrying a big dead beetle. I figure it amounted to a man my size taking hold of a railroad car and climbing up the steeple of the church next door, and thinking he'd done something to be proud of. Some silly fellow back in Aesop's time decided that ants were a model of industry—and the bulk of the damned human race has been fool enough to believe that ever since. (53)

Cabot, aghast at such a broad generalization and his sense of New England democracy aroused, vigorously protests. Twain backtracks slightly, but then comments the man who they suspect committed the murder in New York City is "one hundred percent pure, guaranteed original, unmitigated humbug" (53). Heck adeptly has worked in a well-known Twainian tale and then, just as skillfully, quickly brings the conversation back to the plot at hand.

After Cabot fights his duel in *A Connecticut Yankee in Criminal Court*, rumors circulate around New Orleans that he has killed his opponent. Twain erupts, "Your reputation is made, Wentworth! *Shot a man down cold!* And on the field of so-called honor. Half the women in the city will be swooning at your feet. With a six-foot tall cold-blooded killer to protect me, there's not a man in New Orleans who'll look at me cross-eyed" (207). Compare this to Twain's description of honor and dueling in *Pudd'head Wilson* (1894). Twain was vitriolic toward both, although he attempts to soften his descriptions with humor. "En treckly dey squared off en give de word," a former slave describes a duel between two twins, "en *bang-bang* went de pistols, en de twin say, 'Ouch!' ag'in, en I done it too, 'ca'se de bullet glance on his cheek-bone en skip uphere en glance on de side o' de winder en whiz right acrost my face en tuck de hide off'n my nose—why, if I'd 'a' be'n jist a inch or a inch en a half furder 'twold 'a' tuck de whole nose en disfiggered me. Here's de bullet; I hunted her up" (Ch. 14). Heck has managed to convey clearly and briefly Twain's attitude toward such "affairs of honor" and, similar to his first book, he again does so without detouring far from the advancement of the plot.

*The Prince and the Prosecutor* elaborates on Twain's attitudes toward politics and politicians. Twain never had much respect for Washington and its political inhabitants. After several visits to the city and a brief stay during 1867-68, Twain wrote several satirical pieces about life in the capital, including "My Late Senatorial Secretaryship" and "Cannibalism in the Cars." Twain returned to Washington several times during his later years, once in 1905 to dine at the White House with Theodore Roosevelt and, the following year, to testify before Congress on copyright, a matter very important to him. The latter trip is significant to Twainian culture because the famed author made his debut in a white suit, an attire for which he became famous thereafter. Heck clearly states Twain's attitude in his third book. When, on the *City of Baltimore*, Kipling jokingly tells Twain that he has seen a ship of the Royal Navy coming to "reclaim the colonies" he gets an unexpected response from his friend. "Hell, they already tried that once," Twain declares. "Burned Washington to the ground and chased away Congress. Now, that could have been a real service—Congress is the only indigenous American criminal class. But the invasion didn't do us a bit of good, in the end. After the war was over, the damned congressmen came back and built the whole mess up again, worse than ever. I suppose it couldn't hurt to burn it down again, especially if you could be sure the congressmen didn't get away this time. In fact, I'd contribute to the cause" (77).

Throughout Heck's series, Twain and the Gilded Age culture in which he lived and wrote are richly detailed and re-created. The quips and the anecdotes, as Heck proudly admits, strengthen the texts. Like Livy in trying to out-Twain Twain in her rendition of his profanity, we should say of Heck, "He's got the words." If he is missing some of the high trills and bass notes of the tune, it is only because he is playing in a different orchestra. But the melody is still the best that we are likely to get, and Heck's series will likely please fans of mystery and of Twain.

Authors' note: *The Guilty Abroad: A Mark Twain Mystery* (New York: Berkley, 1999) was published after this essay was written.

## Works Cited

Aaron, Daniel. *The Unwritten War: American Writers and the Civil War.* Madison: U of Wisconsin P, 1987.

Heck, Peter J. *A Connecticut Yankee in Criminal Court.* New York: Berkley, 1996.

——. *Death on the Mississippi.* New York: Berkley, 1995.

——. *The Prince and the Prosecutor.* New York: Berkley, 1997.

Kaplan, Justin. *Mr. Clemens and Mark Twain.* New York: Simon and Schuster, 1966.

Rasmussen, R. Kent. *Mark Twain A-Z: The Essential Reference to His Life and Writings.* New York: Oxford UP, 1995.

Smith, Janet. *Mark Twain on the Damned Human Race.* New York: Hill and Wang, 1962.

Turner, Arlin. *George W. Cable: A Biography.* Durham: Duke UP, 1956.

# Caleb Carr:
# Running Away from the Darkness

## Douglas Tallack

The issue of historical authenticity within a fictional genre—which is one of the concerns of the present collection of essays—has two inter-related dimensions in Caleb Carr's work. In two best-selling novels, *The Alienist* (1994) and *The Angel of Darkness* (1997), Carr re-creates New York City in the 1890s, a historically recognisable world but one which is popu-lated by a mixture of fictional and historical figures. As a history graduate but, equally, as a writer of stories of detection, Carr evinces a sustained commitment to detail and fact (as is apparent in his Acknowledgments), which he skillfully integrates into overarching historical themes, notably the emergence of urban modernity. The other dimension to Carr's work, though, is the highly imaginative use of the detective story genre to confront a more complex historiographical challenge than achieving period authenticity: how to write a history of unconscious fears and their irruption into daily life. In a 1919 essay, Freud terms this phenomenon the uncanny and we might, therefore, summarise Caleb Carr's contribution as an effort to represent the hidden *historical structure* of the uncanny.

The uncanny tends to strike us on the slant: we know it when we encounter it: in a painting of a strangely familiar urban scene by Edward Hopper; in the aural and visual close-ups in, respectively, *The Conversation* and *Blow-Up*; or in the hints of the extraordinary (rather than in the ghosts and the double or second self) in, respectively, Henry James' *The Turn of the Screw* and Poe's "William Wilson." Accordingly, Freud tells us that while the uncanny "is undoubtedly related to what is frightening—to what arouses dread and horror . . . [o]ne is curious to know what . . . allows us to distin-guish as 'uncanny' certain things which lie within the field of what is fright-ening" (Freud 339). The uncanny has much less in common with the fantastic, monstrous, or mysterious than one would expect (see Todorov 41 and 41-48). As Freud further notes, the uncanny is the troubling intercon-nection of the familiar and unfamiliar: "the uncanny is that class of the frightening which leads back to what is known of old and long familiar" (Freud 340). The original German word, *unheimlich*, literally translates as unhomely. Using the less technical words of John Schuyler Moore, the introspective narrator of *The Alienist*, the uncanny is "the darkness [Ameri-cans] know to lie behind so many apparently tranquil household doors" (8). And in *The Angel of Darkness*, when tidying up a counterpoint to the central investigation into the serial prolicide, Carr has his new narrator, the ex-street "arab" Stevie Taggart, return to the same theme:

The "savage" Thorn and the "deluded but redeemed" Mrs. Nack (as the D.A. labeled them) turned out to be, in fact, very ordinary people, while the "monsters" what everyone in town had originally thought were responsible for the crime—the grave robbers, mad anatomists, bloodthirsty ghouls, and the like—were just shadows, dreamed up to glorify policemen, sell newspapers, and scare unruly kids. . . . the real monsters continued, then as now, to wander the streets unnoticed, going about their strange and desperate work with a fever what looks to the average citizen like nothing more than the ordinary effort required to get through an ordinary day. (*Angel* 802-03)

It is precisely because the uncanny is not the outlandish and monstrous that Caleb Carr—even while apparently trading in appalling events—is most effective when he anchors his stories of serial killings within a historically documented public record.

*   *   *

*The Alienist* and its sequel, *The Angel of Darkness*, are carefully anchored in American social and political history. In the first novel John Schuyler Moore is living in a house which still has one gas lamp but in which the telephone is part of daily life and a constant irritant to his grandmother: "John! . . . Who in the world was on the telephone?" (*Alienist* 30). The New York elevated railroad clatters along Sixth Avenue; the "dozen-storied" National Shoe and Leather Bank looks down on "squat, ornate Victorian monuments" (*Alienist* 152 and 153); and "the electrical chair is increasingly usurping the gallows" (*Alienist* 37). Americans are being educated into European culinary tastes; *The Prisoner of Zenda* is playing at the Lyceum; Koster and Bial are showing the first projected films in the city; and the electric signs of prominent places of leisure illuminate otherwise dark city nights. Politically, Manhattan is about to become part of Greater New York, although still

precariously positioned at that moment between the powerful wave of municipal reform that had swept into New York with the findings of the Lexow Commission on police corruption a year earlier (of which Roosevelt was a strong exponent) and the perhaps greater power of that same corruption, which had existed for as long as the force and was now quietly biding its time, waiting until the public wearied of the passing fashion of reform and sank back into business as usual. (*Alienist* 22)

The chronology of the two novels loosely corresponds with that of Theodore Roosevelt's early career. Thus, with his departure for Washington, DC to take up the office of Secretary of the Navy, the city portrayed in *The Angel of Darkness* is already slipping away from reform, while public interest has shifted to the international sphere and the coming war with Spain. Carr re-creates the historical texture in ways that have been used effectively by popular biographers of Roosevelt. The scenes in and around Police Headquarters on Mulberry Street have the liveliness and sense of "being there" that the relevant chapter of Edmund Morris' *The Rise of Theodore Roosevelt* conveys (Morris 221-76). And, having re-created the texture of daily life, Carr can allow Roosevelt, Jacob Riis, Cornelius Vanderbilt II, Elizabeth Cady Stanton, Clarence Darrow, and other historical figures to come and go. Rarely are their appearances used as background authenticity, however; instead, these figures become part of the relationship between the familiar and unfamiliar which is central to the phenomenon of the uncanny. Before considering how Roosevelt and other figures function in this unusual way, it is worth looking at how Carr portrays the more material aspects of urban modernity because these, too, contribute to the representation of the uncanny.

Early in *The Alienist* there is a description of New York street life that warrants comparison with Georg Simmel's theorisation of modern urban life. In "The Metropolis and Mental Life" Simmel comments on "the rapid crowding of changing images, the sharp discontinuity in the grasp of a single glance, and the unexpectedness of onrushing impressions" (410). Here is Carr's version, mediated through his narrator:

When I reached [Sixth Avenue] the force of air suddenly changed directions as it swept under the tracks of the New York Elevated Railroad line, which ran above either side of the street just inside the sidewalks. The shift blasted my umbrella inside out, along with those of several other members of the throng that was hustling under the tracks; and the combined effect of the heightening wind, the rain, and the cold was to make the usually bustling rush hour seem absolute pandemonium. Making for a cab as I struggled with my cumbersome, useless umbrella, I was cut off by a merry young couple who maneuvered me out of their way with no great finesse and clambered into my hansom. I swore loudly against their progeny and shook the dead umbrella at them, prompting the woman to scream in fright and the man to fix an anxious eye on me. (*Alienist* 31)

The over-stimulation of urban life—the sidewalk collisions, the concatenation of signs, the roar of the El, and so on—produces a metropolitan anxiety that Ben Singer, summarising Simmel but also Siegfried Kracauer and Walter Benjamin, aptly calls a "neurological conception of modernity" (72); while Anthony Vidler, also influenced by Benjamin, observes that the uncanny was "born out of the rise of the great cities, their disturbingly heterogeneous crowds" (4). By filtering the narrative of the first novel through John Schuyler Moore, a character caught up in and assailed by the sensationalism (in the literal sense) of the city, and thereby rendered as anxious as the man he threatens on Sixth Avenue, Carr is able to create an undercurrent of instability even as he conveys the local color of this or that New York scene. Of course, metropolitan anxiety has other outlets and manifestations but Carr's fiction confirms Jacques Lacan's insight that "the uncanny . . . situates for us the field of anxiety" (qtd. in Vidler 224).

To appreciate more fully the relevance of Carr's novels to the idea of the historical structure of the uncanny, we can turn to the elaborate narratives of *The Alienist* and *The Angel of Darkness* and particularly to their opening pages. According to Giambattista Vico in *The New Science*, human history began with burial. What Vico means by this is that burial signifies continued residence in a place and the beginnings of an order, sometimes in the form of a story, which connects the living with the dead. *The Alienist* gives Vico's insight into burial and continuity an interesting twist. Its opening chapter begins with a burial, that of Theodore Roosevelt on January 8, 1919, and ends with a story beginning to be told from its beginning, "nearly a quarter-century ago" (6). This story turns out to be one of serial murders and of their detection by Roosevelt, Laszlo Kreizler (the alienist), Moore, and a team of amateur or moonlighting detectives. The team includes Stevie Taggart, who then becomes the narrator in *The Angel of Darkness* and, in this capacity, perpetuates the structure of re-tellings. Detective stories regularly begin with a death and even a scene around a graveside and the ensuing story is the investigation of the murder and usually the apprehension of the murderer. The past—leading up to the death and burial—and the future—discovering how, why and by whom the murder was committed—are thereby connected. Yet, in *The Alienist,* the burial is of one of the detectives and it signals not the initiation of the process of detection but, more intriguingly, the point at which the story of detection can at last be told. The burial of the historical figure, Theodore Roosevelt, is the stimulus for Kreizler and the narrator to meet again and, more importantly, for the telling of a story that had lain hidden for many years.

The narrator has hitherto regarded this as an un-tellable story. For his part, Kreizler wonders whether the public will accept it, even many years later. However, Roosevelt, as a public figure, symbolises an already distinctive historical period, one characterised by a struggle between reformers and chaotic urban growth and political corruption. Consequently, his burial, following on from the end of the First World War (during which his son had been killed), and the onset of the Jazz Age (which we, as readers, know comes next) together signal discontinuity more than continuity and serve to put the 1890s and the murders firmly in the past. The period, the people of that period, and places such as Delmonico's, where the three detectives used to meet, are "on [the] way out" (*Alienist* 7). It is as though only this conjunction of a public and private ending of an era and only the security of facts—"January 8th, 1919. Theodore is in the ground" (5)—can supply the distance necessary for this story of horror to be told. The sad but familiar and well-documented death and burial of the twenty-sixth president becomes the narrator's way into the uncanny.

In the later novel an urban Huckleberry Finn—Stevie Taggart—and his more upbeat, optimistic narrative serve to edge John Schuyler Moore towards the stranger members of Carr's cast of characters. The events at the centre of *The Alienist* and the difficulty in getting an account published have left Moore gloomy about the future of American society and he has become a heavy drinker. For all these differences, Carr still employs the same technique of anchoring the narrative in the very different post-World War I world. The present of the storytelling is June 1919, a few months after the death of Roosevelt, when Americans are ready for a "good time" after the "grimness" of the Great War. In contrast, for Stevie, Moore and their friends the past "was a strange and dangerous time, when [they] learned things about human behavior that most sensible people would never want to know" (*Angel* 2). *The Angel of Darkness* returns to the subject of serial killings but adds to it a focus upon a woman who killed her own and others' children. As in *The Alienist*, the driving force of the detection is less the race against time to catch the murderer than a search for explanations for these awful crimes. These two novels of detection, then, do not slip comfortably into the thriller end of the generic spectrum but reveal an ambition to be histories of competing ideas. Moore confirms as much near the beginning of his narrative when he introduces "the subject of psychological determinism . . . the philosophical conundrum that wove irrepressibly in and out of the nightmarish proceedings, like the only hummable tune in a difficult opera" (*Alienist* 7). Finally, it is the question of what can be known which associates the detective story with the uncanny.

Carr employs a trio of principle detectives in *The Alienist*. They represent a range of philosophies which seek to explain the appalling in terms of the ordinary and Carr only slightly varies the formula and the lineup in *The Angel of Darkness*. Dr. Kreizler, the principle detective in both novels, is interested in the pathologies which drive the actions of those "suffering from mental illness [who] were thought to be 'alienated,' not only from the rest of society but from their own true natures" (*Alienist*, Note n.p.). The second detective in *The Alienist* is Theodore Roosevelt and he serves firmly to locate this story of detection in the tangible historical world of New York in the 1890s. More specifically, however, he represents the dual Progressive drive to rid society of terrible crimes and of a New York police force riddled with corruption. When Roosevelt briefly returns in *The Angel of Darkness* it is to lead a bizarre U.S. Naval attack upon Lower East Side gangs whom the police force leave largely alone. The third detective in *The Alienist* is John Schuyler Moore who, in telling the story, tries to make sense of the different explanations of Kreizler and Roosevelt. These explanations have different philosophical bases, and Carr includes as an epigraph this statement from William James's *Principles of Psychology*: "Whilst part of what we perceive comes through our senses from the object before us, another part (and it may be the larger part) always comes out of our own mind" (*Alienist* 3).

Other members of the little band of detectives include Miss Sara Howard, the brothers Lucius and Marcus Isaacson (two principled, if eccentric, members of the police force), Stevie Taggart and Cyrus Montrose (two of Kreizler's employees and former criminals). They are joined by a pigmy called El Nino whose portrayal is quite ridiculous, to the point that one is tempted to treat his inclusion as a deliberate unsettling of the historical real-ism. The heterogeneity of this team of detectives can also be attributed to Carr's interest in using these characters to explore positions in intellectual debates of the period. For instance, Sara Howard assumes more prominence in *The Angel of Darkness* because Carr foregrounds the argument about the "nature" of women, and arguments about what is excessive to nature relate closely to definitions of the uncanny. Elizabeth Cady Stanton appears as a defence witness in the trial of the "angel of darkness," Libby Hatch, to argue that no mother could murder her children unless she was insane, really a man, or had been driven to it by men. Howard, in contrast, stands for a dif-ferent kind of feminism, one which looks to social causes, and especially to patriarchy, but uses these factors to argue that "the simple accident of being born a woman doesn't necessarily bring with it a talent for nurturing—or even an inclination towards it" (*Angel* 190). However, it is the two police detectives, Lucius and Marcus Isaacson who are used most subtly in relation to the developing theme of the uncanny.

In the pursuit of John Beecham, the serial killer in *The Alienist*, the Isaacsons defend the recent use of forensic science in detection. As such techniques as finger-printing have been augmented by DNA modeling and networked information systems, detective fiction has responded and the police procedural novel of Maj. Sjowal and Per Wahloo and, more recently, Patricia Cornwell has made some inroads into the generic authority of the hard-boiled and classic staples (see Messent passim). Carr's work is part of this generic shift. Of more relevance here, though, is the way in which situ-ating what were then highly suspect forensic procedure developments in a historical moment introduces the uncanny:

> Marcus spoke confidentially. "It's called dactyloscopy."
> "Oh," I said. "You mean fingerprinting."
> "Yes," Marcus replied, "that's the colloquial term."
> "But–" Sara broke in. "I mean no offence, Detective Sergeant, but dacty-loscopy has been rejected by every police department in the world." (*Alienist* 115)

Marcus Isaacson demonstrates the new technique with a photograph of a fingerprint of the murderer on a nail of a victim, even though the victim has become a skeleton, recently exhumed from its coffin. In this instance, the uncanny appears as a qualitative excess: "a permanent image of one physi-cal attribute" (*Alienist* 119) of the murderer produced by a new investigative technique. The uncanny does not appear as an quantitative excess of gore, occultism or (in words quoted earlier) a preponderance of "grave robbers, mad anatomists, [and] bloodthirsty ghouls." Insofar as the uncanny repre-sents qualitative excess, it has arisen, in the operations of the Isaacsons, at least, as a consequence of concentrated and highly rational methodologies of detection which find the traces of what is invisibly present at the scene of the crime. In the sequel, Stevie Taggart articulates the impression which such methodologies can produce, thereby confirming that it is an increase in knowledge and not the abandonment of scientific detection for fantastic projection, which results in the uncanny:

When an unknown, unnamed person you've been pursuing—without even knowing for one hundred percent sure if they exist—stops being a bundle of descriptions and theories and becomes a living individual, it produces an eerie, frightening feeling. (*Angel* 173)

Freud, himself, is dismissive of a rival theory which attributes the uncanny to "intellectual uncertainty" (341) because eventually, he assumes, this state will be resolved by further intellectual activity. The episode of the fingerprint in Carr's novel suggests that the uncanny and intellectual investigation need not be at odds. The space of the crime and the time of detection are linked through the fingerprint but it is the historically specific moment, one in which fingerprinting is not common and accepted knowledge, which makes the appearance of the past in the present uncanny. Freud prefers to argue that manifestations of uncanny feelings have deep-seated causes (for example, fear of being buried alive or fear of blindness) but we should not rule out the supposition that the uncanny can also be historically specific because it is related to the state of knowledge, a pervasive concern in Carr's detective fiction.

Traces such as the fingerprint or the threads of the rope used by John Beecham to scale buildings to commit his appalling murders are signs of a former presence. In a story of ideas it is not surprising that other marks are literally textual ones: indications that someone has thought this before and that someone else is now thinking the same thoughts. In *The Alienist* there is a suggestion that even the security of the detective's self can be breached in this form of intellectual doubling. The murderer knows Kreizler's own writings. A page torn from one of his own monographs and befouled by blood and excrement is left in Kriezler's carriage at the start of the search for the murderer. "As I glanced at Kreizler," Moore writes, "I saw a trace of real apprehension in his features; but then he seemed to force the trace away, and when he spoke it was in a determinedly casual tone" (*Alienist* 70). Kreizler, in common with Dupin, Sherlock Holmes, and Father Brown, recognises how close to home the "other" has come. We hardly need Freud to remind us that the theme of the double is prominent in the literature of the uncanny but his summarising observation is particularly germane: "finally there is the constant recurrence of the same thing—the repetition of the same features or character-traits or vicissitudes, of the same crimes" (356).

The serial murders at the centre of *The Alienist* are located as part of the crime-waves that Roosevelt faced during his tenure as president of the Board of Commissioners of New York City's Police Department. In that post Roosevelt sought to illuminate the darkest recesses of the city; quite literally, to the extent that he encouraged the police reporter, Jacob Riis, in his efforts to light up the tenements by means of flash photography. Carr neatly positions the historical Roosevelt and the fictional Roosevelt (that is to say, the Roosevelt who knew the fictional narrator and the alienist) on the watershed between what Robert Wiebe calls "the search for order" in Progressive reform (Wiebe passim) and the welling up of the nightmare of serial murders. Carr seems to be asking what kind of detection is needed to explain the historical and psychological causes of serial murders of a particularly horrifying kind, involving as they do torture and butchery of young, male prostitutes. And insofar as there is a preferred answer in what is, after all, not a treatise but a novel, Carr suggests that enlightened detection should be scientific but that, in the historical moment in which such detection brings enlightenment, it is implicated in its opposite. Hence, the narrative frames to both novels which dramatise the difficulty in getting these stories told. It is this insight into the ways in which rationality and a "search for order" can engender the uncanny in specific historical circumstances that finds expression in the central character of the alienist.

Kreizler's version of alienism attracts plenty of criticism, notably in the second novel in which his Institute is closed during an investigation into the suicide of one of the boys in his charge. For all their excitement and suspense, then, the plots of both novels can also be understood as Kreizler's efforts to prove his theory of context: that "every man's actions are to a very decisive extent influenced by his early experiences, and that no man's behavior can be analysed or affected without knowledge of those experiences" (*Alienist* 52). This definition differs somewhat from the Progressive reformers' understanding of context as primarily social and economic, a context that they investigated in surveys, maps, photographs, and muckraking journalism. Kreizler also differs from William James, who argued for the power of free will, and from Roosevelt who is presented as an enthusiastic champion of James, but who comes, eventually, to recognise that it is Kreizler, even more than those who know the depths of the city, who can discover the identity of the serial killer. "No one needs to tell me," Roosevelt protests, "that depravity and inhumanity have taken on dimensions in New York unheard of anywhere in the world. But what unnameable nightmare, even here, could drive a man to this?" (*Alienist* 62). In *The Alienist* Kreizler, having hypothesised that the motives behind the murders lie in the childhood of the murderer, reverses the usual procedure and works back to the evidence from the psychological causes. Accordingly, he and his detectives follow the urban traces of the murderer's unconscious:

The killer could have gone on hiding his victims forever—God only knows how many he's killed in the last three years. Yet now he's given us an open statement of his activities. . . . Some buried, atrophied, but not yet dead part of our murderer is growing weary of the bloodshed. (*Alienist* 67)

Similarly, in *The Angel of Darkness*, the breakthrough comes when Sara Howard tracks down Libby Hatch's family and the grave of the first child she murders. Up until that point, Hatch's trial is being controlled by the out-of-town defence lawyer, Clarence Darrow, whose role in the now well-documented historical public domain is used by Carr to define an alternative explanation to that offered by Kreizler; that is to say, that Libby Hatch could not murder her own children unless she is insane (this would be against nature) and since neither the defense nor the prosecution are claiming that she is insane, she must be innocent. Kreizler's theory is that Hatch and also John Beecham are sane but are driven by a logic which society at that time, at least, refuses to recognise. To John Moore this insight is sufficiently shocking for him to italicise it: "there was evidence in the [mutilation of] the bodies *not of the murderer's derangement but of his sanity*" (Carr, *Alienist* 138). And in *The Angel of Darkness,* Stevie reports Kreizler's explanation of Hatch's contradictory behaviour as ministering angel and killer of children:

Something connects the two sides of the character, the two faces of the coin. We don't know what that connecting element is yet, but the connection exists. So that what we are faced with is not an inconsistency so much as a troubled unity. (*Angel* 184)

Miss Howard is the first of Kreizler's group to understand the implications:

if you allow that inside she's not just one or the other [nurse and murderer], but both, what does that say about all the other women in town? How will you ever be able to tell what's actually going on in their hearts—and heads? (*Angel* 471)

It is not surprising that Kreizler, when comparing the earlier case of John Beecham with their investigation of Libby Hatch, surmises that they are "in an even stranger land. . . . And with fewer maps" (*Angel* 221).

The uncanny is a difficult issue to write about historically because structural oppositions, whether political, social, economic, or gendered, tend to get treated developmentally by historians. Oppositions get resolved in historical time, allowing the historian to employ the past tense with a reasonable degree of security or at least more security than literary and cultural critics (see King passim). By contrast, in the uncanny, as Freud explains it, the two positions are implicated in each other: the familiar in the unfamiliar and vice-versa. Given this difficulty, Carr's recourse to the techniques of fiction-writing gives him an advantage in writing about a historical instance of the uncanny. His past tense is devolved to his two narrators; and although Moore and Taggart succeed in getting their stories written those stories leave their marks on the story-tellers. *The Alienist* ends with Moore describing an event three years after the denouement of the investigation. He revisits the Croton Reservoir, the site of the final confrontation with the serial murderer, just as it is being demolished to make way for the New York Public Library. The physical signs of the Reservoir are about to disappear but the implication is that the psychological effects on Moore will remain and this is confirmed when Stevie Taggart sets out to tell his story some years later. Stevie is a more resilient character and narrator but his optimistic closing paragraph has been preceded by the acknowledgement (quoted earlier) that the ordinary surfaces of life are never to be taken at face value. For both narrators, the act of remembering—"to dredge it all up and put it finally before the public" is Moore's way of putting it (*Alienist* 7)—at once fixes the past securely and opens up a space for uncertainty. As Stevie contemplates telling the story of Libby Hatch he experiences "bumps on [his] skin" and "shivers in [his] soul" (*Angel* 9).

In addition to a more explicit use of a narrative persona, Caleb Carr has a further advantage over historians in writing about the uncanny. And this is perhaps the most significant achievement of this new historical detective novelist. When the historicising of ideas needs buttressing by other techniques, Carr draws upon a characteristic of much fiction and probably all detective stories: a preoccupation with space. Classic country-house detective stories, building upon Edgar Allan Poe, emphasize space. *Where* the murder took place can be as important as when it occurred. The urban detective story from Poe through Hammett and Chandler to Walter Mosley continues to accord space significance, extending it to include the wider city. In *The Alienist* the first iruption of "the darkness" in the form of the butchered body of Georgio Santorelli is, of course, recounted as an event in the past (1896) by the narrator writing in the novel's present (1919). Nevertheless, the discovery of the body strikes the reader as more of a spatial "event" than a historical one as we accompany the narrator in the calash driven by Stevie as they cross part of the city, from the gentility of Washington Square North, down Broadway:

We were heading downtown, downtown and east, into that quarter of Manhattan where Laszlo Kreizler plied his trade and where life became, the further one progressed into the area, ever cheaper and more sordid: the Lower East Side. (12)

And then

to Delancey Street—which was in the midst of being widened to accommodate the expected traffic of the new Williamsburg Bridge, whose construction had only recently begun—and then we flew on past several darkened theaters. Echoing down from each passing street I could hear the desperate, demented sounds of the dives: filthy holes that sold rotgut liquor laced with everything from benzine to camphor for a nickel a glass atop a dirty plank that passed for a bar. Stevie did not slacken the pace—we were headed, it seemed, for the very edge of the island. (*Angel* 13)

Jacob Riis's account of leaving the elevated railroad at Franklin Square to "stand upon the domain of the tenement" (27) is echoed in the narrator's phrase, "the very edge of the island." For John Schuyler Moore, as for Riis, this is "a neighborhood that knew little of laws, man-made or otherwise" (*Alienist* 14).

The combination of three elements in this account is noteworthy. First, the particularity of the descriptions of licit and illicit ways of life in the

Lower East Side is not mere antiquarianism but points towards the focus of the political reformism associated with three historical figures identified in chapter one of the novel: Roosevelt but also Jacob Riis and Lincoln Steffens. Second, the historical vision of a modernising city symbolised by the construction of Williamsburg Bridge (where the body has been found) is important because the relationship between the past and the present is crucial both to a historical sense and to the emergence of the uncanny. It is the intrusion of modernity that defines parts of the Lower East Side as liminal. And, third, there is the mapping of what Anthony Vidler calls "spatial fear" (Vidler passim), of which the early morning carriage-ride downtown is only the first example in these two novels. It is immediately evident in the description of that ride from affluence to the "very edge of the city" that the idea of a spatial uncanny abuts upon objective social, economic and political alienation. It is by fastening upon the profession of the late nineteenth-century alienist and then making an alienist the central character in a detective story (rather than following the precedent of much urban fiction of the period itself and making a Progressive reformer or slum-dweller the central figure) that Carr is able to explore the psychological dimension of alienation. Through the investigations of the alienist/detective—as mediated by John Moore, who knows the theory as narrator even as he experiences the night-time ride as an actor in the drama—a compelling psycho-geography of the city can be mapped (see, also, Vidler, Donald, and Pile). In this psycho-geography alienation from the self is as significant as the socio-economic alienation which Progressives addressed.

Throughout *The Alienist*, the little group of detectives unearths traces of past events, usually crimes, so that a different, hidden city is glimpsed beneath the everyday city. In their base room, the detectives pinpoint the dates and locations of Beecham's killings on a map of Manhattan but it is only as a pattern emerges that links the everyday trajectories signified by roads, railroads, and waterways with the trajectory of these monstrous crimes that the uncanny makes its "appearance" on the map and leads Roosevelt to conclude that they are hunting "a man familiar with the city" (*Alienist* 160). A little later in the investigation, Moore and Marcus Isaacson have been tracing the steps of the murderer on his labyrinthine cross-city routes on the roofs of buildings but it is only as they descend to ground level that the unhomely impacts upon the routine, making Moore "feel very detached from the normal rhythms of city life and very uneasy about the immediate future" (200).

The everyday is an indispensable element of the uncanny precisely because the uncanny has a dominant spatial dimension to it. Routine events and a dreadful murder *take place* in the same place. They do not take place at the same time, of course, but the detective's investigations and re-visiting of the scene of a crime create a framework in which they appear to do so. The detective's inhabiting of the same space as the criminal points to a more intimate but, admittedly, more speculative venture into the past than that of many historians in their texts, while the detective's interest in familiar objects and daily detritus is, until the advent of material history, rivalled only by that of the amateur local historian and antiquarian. It is the specialised interest in the spaces of crime, above all, which connects the detective's micro-analysis of evidence with the larger theme of the uncanny. The particularities at the scene of the murder of Georgio Santorelli are gruesome, even fantastic, in their extremity but it is Kreizler's cryptic note to Roosevelt which introduces the uncanny as a pattern in time: "TERRIBLE ERRORS HAVE BEEN MADE. . . . THERE IS A TIMETABLE" *(Alienist* 23). Ernst Bloch catches this connection in *A Philosophical View of the Detective Novel*: "Something is uncanny—that is how it begins. But at the same time one must search for that remoter 'something,' which is already close at hand" (qtd. in Vidler 3). It is "the type and the genius of deep crime" which Poe's narrator eventually encounters in the face of "the man of the crowd" (188) but it is also Freud's uncanny in a very particular sense. Kreizler gradually convinces his team that they are tracking a murderer who—of course—is seeking to evade them but who unconsciously wants to be caught. The detectives are, it is reasonable to suggest, deciphering traces of an unconscious mind left on buildings and on bodies. Freud refers to dreams as the "royal road" to the unconscious. Carr's detectives follow the "dark road" *(Alienist* 200) of the uncanny across New York City.

The spatial dimension of the uncanny appears throughout *The Alienist* and the use of the Croton Reservoir for the dramatic culmination of the investigation also confirms the importance of a relationship between one place and a larger space. The Reservoir collects and distributes water across the city and, as Kreizler concludes from the locations of the murders, water is a crucial link. In *The Angel of Darkness* the spatial uncanny is given a persistent domestic orientation. The ostensible explanation is that the later novel focuses on Victorian maternal and domestic assumptions as these are challenged by the murders committed by Libby Hatch. Freud's persistent theme of a family romance and a tendency to imagine the mind as a home suggest a less obvious but related explanation for the succession of houses that the narrative temporarily inhabits. These are not haunted houses but they are all disquieting, none more so than Libby Hatch's nondescript house in New York City: number 39 Bethune Street. Reading the descriptions of its rooms without, as yet, quite knowing what exactly is amiss, we can understand why Freud was drawn to quote this contradictory statement from Friedrich Klinger's *Theater*: "every corner is *heimlich* [homely] and full of terrors" (347). Freud comments:

Thus *unheimlich* is a word the meaning of which develops in the direction of ambivalence, until it finally coincides with its opposite, *unheimlich*. *Unheimlich* is in some way or other a sub-species of *heimlich*. (347)

Appropriately, entry to the house begins with Libby Hatch inviting the group of detectives in for tea.

The uncanny does tend to strike us obliquely and, therefore, concluding with a definition is somewhat paradoxical. Insofar as it can be pinned down, then, the source of the uncanny in *The Angel of Darkness* is the growing suspicion that there is an invisible space. And, sure enough, 39 Bethune Street turns out to have a secret room, a "deep recess" (*Angel* 275) in the basement where the kidnapped baby at the centre of the initial investigation is being kept and will be mercifully killed (according to Hatch's logic) if the detectives cannot find her. Nothing grows in the house's back yard, a motif picked up when Stevie visits "the old Hatch house" in upstate New York. Other strange houses are subsequently visited by Stevie, who remarks after one visit that "the memory of those spaces is burned so deep in my brain that I could probably re-create them right down to the thousand tiny cracks that were spread out through the walls like so many dying blood vessels" (*Angel* 456). Importantly, though, the house that proves most crucial to the investigation of Libby Hatch's past and therefore her character initially seems entirely different from the other dark houses Stevie and his companions have visited. It is "a small but pleasant-looking little house, its clapboards bearing a fresh coat of white paint and its neatly clipped lawn bordered by pretty little flower patches" (*Angel* 653). However, the farm is, on the one hand, the homely environment in which Hatch grew up and, on the other hand, the start of the story of child-murders and of an inter-relationship between bodies and built spaces. In the barnyard, they find the grave of Hatch's first victim, her just-born baby, buried under a gravestone apparently for her dog (which she had also killed) with this inscription: "Love Always, from Mama." Stevie's reaction (which is also a turning point in the detection because a connection is established) is about as close as Carr gets to describing the effect of the uncanny, a phenomenon which even Freud can illustrate at length but decides not to theorise too firmly.

As I read the last line [Stevie recalls], I felt as though somebody'd run along my back with the hard-end of a goose-quill: they were the very same words what were carved on Thomas and Matthew Hatch's graves in Ballston Spa. (672)

Repetition is the essence of familiarity but it is also the source of the uncanny.

## Works Cited

Carr, Caleb. *The Alienist*. London: Little, Brown, 1994.
——. *The Angel of Darkness*. London: Warner, 1998.
Donald, James. "The City, the Cinema: Modern Spaces." *Visual Culture*. Ed. Chris Jencks. London: Routledge, 1995. 96-122.
Freud, Sigmund. "The Uncanny." *The Pelican Freud Library, Volume 14: Art and Literature*. Ed. Albert Dickson. Trans. James Strachey. Harmondsworth, Middlesex: Penguin, 1985. 339-76.

King, Richard. "The Discipline of Fact/The Freedom of Fiction?" *Journal of American Studies* 25 (1991): 171-88.

Messent, Peter. "Patricia Cornwell's Unnatural Exposure and the Representation of Space: Changing Patterns in Crime Fiction." *Clues: A Journal of Detective Fiction* 21.1 (2000): 37-45.

Morris, Edmund. *The Rise of Theodore Roosevelt.* London: Collins, 1979.

Pile, Steve. *The Body and the City: Psychoanalysis, Space and Subjectivity.* London: Routledge, 1996.

Poe, Edgar Allan. "The Man of the Crowd." *Selected Writings of Edgar Allan Poe.* Ed. David Galloway. Harmondsworth, Middlesex: Penguin, 1967. 179-88.

Riis, Jacob A. *How the Other Half Lives: Studies Among the Tenements of New York.* New York: Dover, 1971.

Simmel, Georg. "The Metropolis and Mental Life." *The Sociology of Georg Simmel.* Trans. and ed. Kurt H. Wolff. Glecoe, IL: Free P, 1950. 409-24.

Singer, Ben. "Modernity, Hyperstimulus, and Rise of Popular Sensationalism." *Cinema and the Invention of Modern Life.* Ed. Leo Charney and Venessa R. Schwartz. Berkeley: U of California P, 1985.

Todorov, Tzvetan. *The Fantastic: A Structural Approach to a Literary Genre.* Trans. Richard Howard. Ithaca: Cornell UP, 1976.

Vidler, Anthony. *The Architectural Uncanny: Essays in the Modern Unhomely.* Cambridge, MA: MIT, 1992.

Wiebe, Robert. *The Search for Order: 1877-1920.* New York: Hill and Wang, 1967.

# Anne Perry:
# Victorian 'Istorian and Murdermonger

## Linda J. Holland-Toll

In *Daily Life in Victorian England*, Sally Mitchell makes many cogent points, among the most interesting of which is:

Many of us have vivid mental pictures of Victorian England: a Charles Dickens Christmas with a large happy family surrounding a table crammed with food [and] the dark and terrifying slums. . . . "Victorianism" remains a living concept in social and political debates, although its meanings are contradictory; it is used to describe exploitation and class division, sexual repression, hypocrisy, values of hard work and self help, moral certainties about family life, and a wide variety of arrangements intended to solve public problems. There is some truth in all of these ideas. (Mitchell xiii)

If this description sounds very much like the setting of Anne Perry's Thomas and Charlotte Pitt detective series, there is good reason. The series accurately portrays the Victorian era after the War (1856) with the action occurring between April 1881 and March 1891.

Anne Perry's main detective, Inspector Thomas Pitt, is assigned to investigate murders that take place in an artificial world of social privilege, where appearance is all that matters. Appearance is, quite literally, to die for. Charlotte's and her sister Emily's access to and understanding of this tightly circumscribed social world frequently provide Inspector Thomas Pitt with the necessary domestic and social knowledge he would otherwise lack to solve the crime, which is quite often an attempt to preserve appearances at the expense of any morality or common decency whatsoever. For this series to engage the reader, several plot constructions must be believable. The reader must accept the absolute importance of appearance, family, blood and position, the inability of the police to penetrate the facade erected by High Society, and most importantly of all, the actions of Charlotte Pitt and Emily, Lady Ashworth, her sister-in-sleuthing.

To accomplish these rules of engagement, Perry has carefully grounded this detective series in late Victorian times, in the middle and upper classes, and speaks, in skillfully woven detective narratives, not only of issues extant in Victorian times but also to contemporary issues. She is extremely conscientious in following the historical chronology; each novel is carefully placed in an identifiable time frame, and each sequential novel reflects not only changes in the Pitts' lives but also in the culture they inhabit. As Pitt gains promotion, their domestic life improves, and Perry's fiction makes the changes perfectly clear; the novels also faithfully record such changes in transportation, communication, politics, and daily living as occurred. Even a historically unaware reader can follow the narrative and understand the basic tenets of Perry's Victorian setting.

One of the problems for a historically unknowledgeable reader, one steeped in the mores of twentieth-century American life, lies in accepting that a world so artificial and superficial could be important enough to commit murder to preserve. Is syphilis really the end of the world or someone's sexual orientation an issue of enough importance over which to kill several people? Is owning slums really social ruin? To many contemporary Americans, no. In order, therefore, to engage the reader in the text, Perry must re-create the times vibrantly enough so that a reader who lacks a historical base and who simply enjoys mysteries can engage Perry's world. Thus, Perry not only details everyday life with a very sharp eye, but also privileges the private sphere enjoyed over the public sphere. We may, for example, be indifferent to the plight of the long-dead slum dwellers of Victorian England in *Highgate Rise* (1991), the eleventh novel of the series, but Charlotte's admiration for Clemency Shaw, ostensibly a victim of the monied and landed interests who wish neither to disgorge nor acknowledge their ill-gotten gains, and her determination to capture Clemency's murderer does engage us.

In order to invite the reader into her characters' world, Perry employs several strategies. Most importantly, she carefully sets up the class distinctions by which the Victorians ordered their lives; she accurately depicts the gradations within each rank, the very well understood but unarticulated cultural models by which Victorians understood class ranking to occur. Perry also articulates a keen awareness that class stratification is not as rigid as the standardly accepted three-tiered structure would indicate. "The middle class," as Mitchell notes, "included successful industrialists and extremely wealthy bankers . . . it also included such poor clerks as Bob Cratchit [of Dickens' *The Christmas Carol* ]" (20). She understands the slippages and the increasingly mobile class boundaries where extremely complicated alliances might bring upper-middle-class people into social contact with the more minor aristocracy.

The Ellison family is a prime example. Charlotte's family has neither extensive land in the country nor a title, which excludes them from "Society," that very limited number who meet the requirements of birth and property. Charlotte's family has four servants and a very comfortable house, large enough for the extended family who live there. Edward, her father, makes a very good living as a merchant banker, belongs to a gentlemen's club, and is a household tyrant. Caroline, his wife, manages the house rather than actively participating in domestic duties and subjugates her will to her husband's; her life revolves around social calls, helping the Vicar and entertainments. They are obviously situated in the upper-middle class, however; Caroline Ellison's life mirrors the lives the landed gentry lived on a slightly lower scale. The life Sally Mitchell describes "society women" as indulging in, "shopping, paying calls, going to concerts and sporting events and giving entertainments," as well as "making marriages" is certainly a fair description of the Ellisons' lives (152). While the Ellison daughters will not be presented at Court adorned with white ostrich feathers, Caroline is preoccupied with making good marriages for her daughters and presents them in her society with a view to so doing. Although neither Sally Mitchell nor Joan Perkin mentions a specifically upper-middle/lower upper class, Perry recognizes that the rigid Victorian ideal had to have gaps and interstices and here she positions the Ellisons. Thus, it is not entirely out of the question that the eldest daughter Sarah marries within her class, the youngest sister, Emily, marries above it, and Charlotte marries below it.

Second, Perry takes great care to not only provide the details of dress and society more commonly found in a novel of manners but also grounds each novel in everyday life. Her novels faithfully reflect the social minutiae of calling, of leaving a card, of the length of afternoon visits, the strategies involved in the precise timing of those visits, the allowable topics, length of stay, and gradation of refreshments offered. Perry effectively captures the maneuvering behind the seemingly dull facade of afternoon calls. Perry's knowledge of fashion is as precise as her commentary on the methods to "re-do" or "turn" last year's dress into this season's dress. A quick scan of any history of Victorian fashion reveals that as the century progresses, crinolines disappear, bustles appear, dominate, and then decrease in size, evening wear becomes more daring, and bloomers make an occasional appearance. Perry uses the fashions to flesh out the characters and reflect their status; in *The Cater Street Hangman* (1979), the first novel of the series, a second or third dress purchased within a month for Emily is worthy of comment; Lady Emily Ashworth gives away as many dresses to her lady's maid; Charlotte, two years after her marriage to Thomas Pitt, the police inspector she marries for love, is still wearing her trousseau and does not expect to replace it, out of fashion though it may be.

Nor does Perry limit her research to the middle and upper classes; she also delves into the life of the working classes, both the "respectables" and the "roughs" (Perkin 123). Her understanding of the lower orders, the working poor, the basically unskilled labor who comprised the vast majority of the English population, is well articulated. She integrates a great deal of knowledge into her narratives on what life for a poor unskilled laborer was like as well as a good understanding of the Victorian underworld of whores, pimps, and thieves, and the social forces that created them. Her comprehension of the forces that drove the Victorian economy is quite specific; she is both precise and accurate in her knowledge of wages paid versus the cost of everyday living. In *The Cater Street Hangman*, Pitt tells Charlotte that a woman gets two and one-half pence for sewing an entire shirt and asks, "Do you sew, Charlotte? Do you know how long it takes to make a shirt? Do you do household accounts? Do you know what two and a half pence will buy?" (215). Belle, the "ruined" maid turned prostitute, would have had to sew eighty-six shirts weekly to gain a subsistence living. Pitt then explains that faced with starvation, many women are forced to turn to prostitution. Mitchell notes that "a standard quartern of bread cost 6d. in 1895" and further comments that "Social scientist Charles Booth determined that the poverty line was 18 s. weekly" (32). Maude Pember Reeves, writing in 1913, notes that "round about a pound a week" was the minimum needed to keep a family (qtd. in Perkins 173). Perry does not go into this much detail, but makes it very obvious that two and one-half pence does not buy very much. She is also well able to bring the misery of the London poor to the readers' senses. No reader of *Highgate Rise* or *Resurrection Row* (1981), the fourth novel in the series, can readily forget the descriptions Perry dishes up on the squalor and despair in which the poor lived.

In addition, Perry has thoroughly researched both lower-class speech, in London generally referred to as Cockney, and "thieves' cant," which is almost a separate language altogether. Such details add verisimilitude to her evocations of the world of the "rookeries," the world of the unprivileged and poverty-stricken as well as to the typical speech of a Londoner. She is obviously well aware that the gap between the so-called Queen's English and the rural and London dialect was a result of the Education Act of 1870, the act that established the proper English for the upper and middle classes. The lower classes were not particularly affected by it as very few attended the preparatory schools and universities at which "the Queen's English" ruled. One of the ways Perry employs dialect is as a class marker; both Gracie, Charlotte's maid, and the typical police constable drop their "h's," render isn't it as in't, and substitute "f/v" for "th," as in bruvver, reflect an intrusive "r" as in "gorn" for gone and barf for bath, all of which are dialectically correct. The constable who finds Denbigh, a policeman killed while trying to infiltrate a Fenian group, says, for example, " 'E's one of ours, sir . . . 'E went orff ter summink special. Dunno wot" (*Ashworth* 1). Characters in Perry also use "yeah," a word until recently "confined to small areas of . . . south London" (Bryson 112).[1]

One of many effective and humorous scenes takes place in *The Cater Street Hangman* when Charlotte Ellison visits Pitt's office and encounters a thief. She and the thief might well be speaking different languages instead of variations on the English language.

"Me father was crapped in forty-two, year I was born and me grandfather got the boat, so they said." . . .

"What is crapped?" she asked.

He drew a hand across his throat, then held it up to imitate a rope. . . .

"And your grandfather went to sea? Didn't he return?"

"Bless you, miss. You really is from another world, ain't you? Not went to se° miss, but got sent to Australia." (Perry, *Cater Street* 140)

As the series progresses, Perry renders the underworld speech dialectally, although again, she does not belabour the dialectical differences, a device that can all too easily become tedious.

Pitt, because he had an upbringing unprecedented for an inspector of police, has the language patterns of a cultured man. Certainly Perry captures the euphemisms used by the gentry for rape, murder, and other mayhem, which are generally reduced to being "interfered with" or "unpleasantnesses." Perry's diction generally represents the more formal Victorian style, complete with Victorian sentiments and reflecting Victorian systems of value. Ainsley Greville, a minister from the Home office, when directing Pitt to direct his energies from pursuing Denbigh's killer, reflects both when he says, concerning a conference on the pernicious "Irish Question," "I personally would appreciate yur assistance, Superintendent, for reasons which I shall explain. . . . And which I regret profoundly. But if we can move even a single step forward in this matter, the whole of Her Majesty's government will be in your debt" (*Ashworth* 4). The diction is very formal, as is the veneer of courtesy; a minister of her Majesty's Home Office has no need to request a mere Superintendent's assistance. The centrality of Her Majesty's appreciation is also very Victorian; a reader familiar with contemporary Victorian novels will feel at home in the dialogue. While Perry's direct dialogue reflects her knowledge of the period, her narrative is slightly less complex than the typical Victorian narration, and therefore more accessible to people who are reading mysteries and not Victorian novels.

Perry certainly understands the small details of servants' lives and vividly depicts their "downstairs" lives, which are as rigidly stratified as the classes they serve. She also shows the reader the amount of hard work it took to keep the middle and upper classes in comfort. Her descriptions of servants' duties, including the separation of duties, which are also strictly codified as by rank are very accurate. In *Ashworth Hall* (1997), the seventeenth of the series, for example, Pitt's sergeant, Tellman, who is unwillingly acting as his valet, must leave last as Pitt is the lowest-ranking gentleman (Huggett 35-36). Perry also accurately describes the separation of duties by rank, by which a "tweeny," often a pre-adolescent girl, will toil up the servants' stairs loaded with a heavy coal scuttle or cans of hot water while a gentleman's valet carries a tray loaded with a single cup of tea (Huggett 24-26). In *Silence in Hanover Close* (1988), the ninth of the series, Emily masquerades as a maid and experiences more daily drudgery and physical discomfort in a few short weeks than she had ever encountered in her life. Emily discovers how very arduous is her own lady's maid's work and also how utterly dependent such a maid is on her employers. She works until she is too tired to see straight at a variety of arduous tasks and then shivers at night in an unheated attic room, even covering herself with the floor mat. "She was used to a fire, and a feather quilt, and thick velvet curtains over the windows. These curtains were plain cloth and she could hear the sleet lashing against the glass" (*Silence* 136). Having a character we know and like in the maid's role works well to bring home the social chasm between classes and brings a lady's maid to life.

Again, it is obvious Perry has read her social history and matched the number and types of servant to the social status of her characters. The Ellisons come from the upper-middle class and have at least the requisite four servants; Lady Emily Ashworth has at least ten per residence as befits an aristocratic life style; Charlotte, after her mesalliance, is lucky to have one maid-of-all-work and occasional help with the very heavy work. The descriptions of the women's activities also works well to place them in their class. Caroline Ellison gives orders to her staff and consults with the butler and cook; Emily must occasionally ask the name of a servant, though she is capable of rallying the servants to the flag, so to speak, when crisis strikes as it does in Ashworth Hall, but it is doubtful she could actually cook a dinner. Charlotte makes her own bread, does her own cooking, including preserving and pickling, and often does the wash, activities which clearly mark Charlotte as working class, at least in the earlier novels. When Pitt finally gains promotion, she has a woman in to clean and do the laundry five days a week, instead of relying entirely on Gracie, a maid-of-all-work. But with only one live-in servant, Charlotte still has not even come close to attaining her family's standard of living, let alone Emily's. Perry's precise deployment of these mundane details, from the specific duties of the maids to the necessity for good looks in the parlourmaids and height, good looks, and good calves in the footmen as well as to the methods for creating body in muslins, her descriptions of how laundry was done, for example, her knowledge of the number of courses, the types of food each class ate, and the cultural amusements in which they indulged all create the requisite engagement necessary for the reader to enjoy the story without being over-whelmed by dry and uninteresting historical detail (Huggett 21-39).

One of the more important elements in Perry's work is the police force; she frequently describes how it worked, what political pressures it experienced, and how the London citizenry regarded it. The example most familiar to modern readers is that of "Jack the Ripper," the psychopath the Metropolitan Police did not capture; this failure was one of the causes for the resignation of Sir Charles Warren on December 1, 1888 (Emsley 14). In *Belgrave Square* (1992) twelfth in the series, Pitt notes that "while the terror and outrage of the Whitechapel murders had died down, the police were still viewed as a failure for not having caught the worst murderer in London's history, whom the newspapers had called, 'Jack the Ripper'" (1). Perry correctly emphasizes the class concerns of the era as well as police-men's social standing, or, to be more accurate, lack of such standing. At this time, the public police force was relatively new and recruited, except for the ranks of Superintendent and above, from the ranks of the unskilled laborers (Emsley 181). Mitchell lists police constables as on a par with such unskilled labor as soldiers, sailors, etc., who made up the largest class and who also made perhaps £45 yearly; police inspectors earned £150–£200 yearly. In the later novels, judging from his increasingly good addresses,

Pitt's salary has risen to an amount close to the middle-class standard of £300 (Mitchell 36-37).

Perry is adept at integrating new technologies into her works, which adds a richness to the series and a sense of a dynamic society as opposed to a static one. As Mitchell points out,

London—the capital of an Empire that covered one-fourth of the globe—had subway trains and electric streetlights; telegraph messages sped around the globe in minutes [. . .] Between 1837 and 1901 social and technological change affected almost every feature of daily existence. (xiv)

Telephones, typewriters, "Hideous thing, Sounds like a hundred urchins in hobnailed boots," the Underground, and an increasing reliance on trains are all present in the narrative (*Bethlehem Road* 39). When Charlotte is sleuthing in *Ashworth Hall*, she boards trains from and to London as a matter of course, not a novelty. One of the details that informs us that Pitt is an important man is that he has a telephone in his house. Not only does the technology flesh out the life of characters in which we are interested, but it also adds a sense of diachronicity to the series. Perry's utilization of detail telescopes the distance between us and the Victorians, a distance which often is more chronological than substantive.

Perry's historical knowledge rarely impinges on the narrative, although the reader who follows the series may get a bit tired of hearing about the social distress invoked by the dread police showing up at the door, or may feel that the comments that women were not allowed to read the newspapers are at times a bit tedious. But, since Perry is writing a series and cannot assume that all readers have read every novel, she cannot avoid a certain amount of the repetitious.

Anne Perry obviously has a feminist slant and a social conscience which manifests in her penchant for revealing social injustices, interests which are very apparent in many of the themes and social issues to which she addresses herself and in which lie much of her relevance and importance; not coincidentally, many of the issues which surface in her Victorian mysteries are also of importance to contemporary twentieth century society. This ability to focus on the present through the filter of the past makes her novels both valuable and relevant instead of merely entertaining.

Although Perry restricts her murders to upper-middle-class/aristocratic situations, she positions the murders within a cultural matrix that reflects the grim social realities of the time. While the murder victim is often an upper-class man or woman, the victims are frequently found in a place inappropriate to their public persona. Setting her murders, as she so often does, within a wider social network indicates Perry's awareness that the superstructure, the elegant ladies and men of leisure, the afternoon calls, the elegant teas, the rich dinners, the preoccupation with culture, scandals, and lives free from economic anxiety are based upon and buttressed by the "tweenies," young adolescent maidservants who struggle up the back stairs loaded down with hot water and coal scuttles, women who sew themselves blind in sweat shops, child prostitutes who cater to unmentionable appetites, and income which derives from the misery of others. Thus her novels are well buttressed by the social history of the time. Various social issues such as housing for the poor, the fate of women prostitutes, the sexual abuse of women servants, the exploitation of the working poor, the limited rights accorded women, and the penalties with which any social transgression was punished are showcased against a background of hierarchy and privilege, which effectively illuminates the dichotomies of the "Victorian Era."

Perry's earlier books are set in the realms of classic detective fiction, in which a character in a limited group of characters commit murder for an economy of gain, and intersect only slightly with the world outside that of privilege. Her earlier novels have the basic detective motif of bringing hidden knowledge to the light of day, exposing the "monster" behind the mask, and revealing the sordid and ugly reasons for murder, which Perry would have us believe, probably accurately, have not changed in one hundred years. *The Cater Street Hangman, Callander Square* and *Paragon Walk*, novels which work within the more classical tradition of finding the murder within an enclosed society, are located in this tradition. *The Cater Street Hangman*'s murderer reacts to a religious monomania concerning the filth engendered by women. The infant murders in *Callander Square*, which start the investigation, occur because the children are diseased and miserably deformed. The murders in *Paragon Walk*, complex though the plot is, are caused by simple jealousy. It is easy to see Charlotte Pitt working to good advantage in these situations, mingling, listening, catching the false notes and eventually figuring out the motive for murder. It is quite understandable how her husband, Thomas Pitt, could not obtain this information. Thomas Pitt, kindly described as disheveled, his collar awry, his coat pockets stuffed with odds and ends, his hair standing on end simply cannot be portrayed balancing a teacup, ears pricked for social innuendoes.

Many of Perry's later novels, more concerned with the intersection of social and political issues with the personal, depart from the realms of classical detective fiction and have wider social issues as the basis for murder. *Resurrection Row* and *Highgate Rise* deal with slum housing and slum lords; in *Resurrection Row*, the motive for murder revolves around maintaining a spotless social reputation; the necessity for protecting what turns out ultimately to be an unwarranted belief in a Church of England bishop and a set of conservative beliefs generates several murders in *Highgate Rise*. "Respectable" gentlemen are found drowned in sewers as occurs in the fifth novel, *Bluegate Fields* (1984), or murdered outside brothels in an unsavoury part of London in the seventh novel, *Death in the Devil's Acre* (1985), or are linked to the torture-murders of prostitutes, as in the sixteenth novel, *Pentecost Alley* (1996). As Charlotte Pitt pithily thinks, "All the adjective [respectable] really meant was that they were clever or fortunate enough to have maintained an excellent facade" (*Death in the Devil's Acre* 25).

In the tenth novel, *Bethlehem Road* (1984), Vvyan Etheridge, an MP, declines to aid a woman in regaining custody of her child; Perry sharply reminds the knowledgeable reader that until relatively recently women had neither child custody rights nor individual rights under law. As Mary Lyndon Shanley notes, "Under the common law a father of minor children enjoyed such control of his children that he could effectively bar his wife even from access to them" (131). When Naomi Royce, Garnet Royce's wife, starves to death rather than give up her religion, no charges can be considered against him. William Blackstone makes this perfectly clear:

the very being or legal existence of a woman is suspended during marriage, or at least incorporated and consolidated into that of the husband, under whose wing, protection and cover she performs everything. (qtd. in Perkin 20)

As Micah Drummond, Pitt's superior, bitterly acknowledges,

Garnet Royce only exercised the same rights and responsibilities any man does over his wife. A man and his wife are one in law: he votes for her, is financially and legally responsible for her, and he has always determined what her religion should be and her social status as well. (*Bethlehem Road* 299)

The social issue in *The Hyde Park Headsman* (1998), fourteenth in line, is wife-beating as both a dark secret and socially acceptable, with its emphasis on the wife's fault, "It was . . . accidental . . . he . . . it was my own fault. If I were less clumsy, less stupid . . . ," resonates uncomfortably in the reader's ears (315). Perhaps an earlier Victorian woman would have accepted her husband's right to apply a little home correction, but Perry sets the Pitt series in a time when such beliefs were coming under fire, when women were gaining more rights, and men were subject to more restrictions. As Perry acknowledges, "It was the Victorians who pioneered the emancipation of women" (Perkin 2). Because she is a twentieth-century woman writer, however, Perry is more aware than a Victorian woman would be that women were unjustly treated by a repressive patriarchy and that remedies would eventually exist, even though domestic abuse is still a contemporary concern. Because she has researched her novels well, Perry also peoples her novels with women who wholeheartedly endorse the "separate spheres." For every woman like Florence Ivory or Zenobia Gunne, there were women like Lady Mary Carfax and her daughter-in-law Helen Carfax, who actively embrace the status quo, women who believe that "It is unnatural for women to desire to dominate public affairs. We do not have the brusqueness of nature; it is not our place." Equally important, Perry's acknowledgment of the division in women's thinking, avoiding a polemical tone and the strident feminism which would be out of sync with the times, also adds to the strength of the series.

A continuing political thread in the novels beginning with *Silence in Hanover Close* is concern with "The Inner Circle," an enclave of privileged and influential men who wield power secretly, far out of proportion to their numbers, and who, like all wielders of power, eventually fall into corruption. Likely, the "Inner Circle" is a conventional device rather than a real political tool. Although it is not at all unlikely that certain men or groups had influence disproportionate to their actual political standing.

These novels closely intertwine political issues such as the rampant and overt anti-Semitism in England, which is examined in *Farrier's Lane* (1993) and the problems which arise when powerful politicians, members of "The Inner Circle," are vulnerable to blackmail and matters of Empire become intermingled with sexual politics, as in *Silence in Hanover Close* and *Belgrave Square*. Ironically, in *Pentecost Alley*, a novel that explores the relationship between justice and class, Pitt is caught between his liberal supporters, who unjustly believe him guilty of hanging an innocent man, a lower-class man, to shield the alleged murderer, Finlay FitzJames, and members of "The Inner Circle," who Pitt despises and whose patronage he has rejected, but who mistakenly support him because they believe that he is shielding FitzJames, whose father is a member of the heinous circle. *Ashworth Hall*, the seventeenth Charlotte and Thomas Pitt novel, is something of an anomaly; the actual murder is politically inspired and not a murder committed to conceal social ruin; set in the 1890s, it also resonates quite strongly with the 1990's "Irish problem." Quite realistically, while Pitt manages to win the battle and expose the murderer, he and Jack Radley, now an MP and a rising star within his Party, lose the war. The conference fails to provide a solution to the "Irish Problem." It is in *Ashworth Hall* that a question arises concerning Perry's historical authenticity, although an entirely possible alternate argument might well be that Perry is reflecting the English views of "Irish Question." Perry is firmly aligned with the English side of the question, though, and her attempts to debunk as politically useful fictions the many tragedies in an Ireland undoubtedly oppressed by England rings rather false to any marginally knowledgable reader of Irish history. The idea expressed by Eudora Greville that "The hunger was to do with the potato blight [. . . ] And that was neither Catholic nor Protestant. It was an act of God," may accurately express the pious platitudes the upper-class English and Anglo-Irish used to soothe their consciences and deny responsibility, but it completely ignores England's oppressive economic policies which reduced Ireland to dependence on a single crop and then refused economic relief in order to protect British revenues (*Ashworth Hall* 47). The political skein running through this book, ironically enough, blames writers of legend and fiction for writing false tales of oppression to inflame anti-British feeling in Ireland to further their own political agenda. Undoubtedly some of this occurred, but the British also willfully misrepresented events to gain ascendancy in Ireland. Perry's deliberate resistance to widely known instances of British oppression, while somewhat of an anomaly restricted to this novel, does call into question her politcal agendas for the remaining novels.

Since Perry is not writing history, but historical detective fiction, however, it is unreasonable to expect her to be absolutely historically accurate.

She inhabits twentieth-century culture and cannot avoid the weight of historical knowledge and social consciousness that shape her work on a doubled level. She does not, as the cover of her books claim, write a "Victorian mystery" in the sense that it is contemporaneous with that time and place; she writes a mystery which is informed by the Victorian era, from a century's distance, and also informed by the connections that she believes exist. Thus, when she writes about the Fenians and the "Irish Question" she is informed by her own beliefs and prejudices, and her knowledge of twentieth-century history, as well as by her historical knowledge. It is considerably less obvious to a British citizen, living in the 1890s, that the only solution for Ireland is "Home Rule," or that it is the responsibility of the government to regulate wages, working conditions, worker's and women's rights than is the case today. Since Perry is a resident of a culture that accepts these concepts, it is difficult for her to avoid foregrounding this knowledge in her narratives.

Most importantly, however, she is bound by the conventions of detective fiction, which is usually engaged in the restoration of social order and which employs many stock plot devices and coincidences to achieve that order. Her setting must occasionally give way to the requirements of her genre and depart from the strictly historical, as indeed even the best of the historical novelists do. The coincidences that occur in her detective narrative are typical of those in most detective fiction.

One of the ways in which Perry brings the Victorian era out of dry factual history and into the living breathing present is through the characters. These characters must come from different classes, must have different points of view, and must provide a feeling for what the Victorian era was like, which would be absent if Perry described Victorian society too realistically; she is, after all, writing detective fiction, and if Charlotte is a pattern card of respectability, she cannot possibly function as a social detective. In Dorothy Sayers's *Gaudy Night*, Peter Wimsey advises Harriet Vane to make her characters more human. Harriet says, candidly, "I admit that Willard is the world's worst goop, but if he doesn't conceal the handkerchief, where's my plot?" (255). Perry is also circumscribed by the demands of the genre. If Charlotte does not have more than a tincture of elixir of today's woman, what happens to the plot? Charlotte would not marry Pitt, for one thing, and abiding by the "separate spheres/ angel in the house" domestic ideology, would not meddle in her husband's business. And then where's our plot?

It is highly unlikely, on the face of it, for example, that the "good" sections of London average the number of society murders a year which Pitt investigates. An amazing number of people known to Emily are murdered; one wonders why the ranks of society are not depleted by the bloodletting and subsequent disgrace. Why are not British aristocrats headed, lemming-like, to the sea, since their primary source of amusement seems to be murder? This problem is common to any detective fiction that deals with murder, which is to say the vast majority of it, and must simply be accepted as one of the necessities of the genre. It is also unlikely that no one ever realizes that Charlotte Pitt, neé Ellison, always shows up when a murder is committed, often with a slightly different identity. But then, it is unlikely that Jessica Fletcher ever gets invitations to dinner, either! By the time that Charlotte has masqueraded as Emily's unmarried sister, or a distant relation from the country, as she does in *Silence in Hanover Close*, it seems to strain even the bounds of generic credulity that someone in this tightly knit circle would not comment that she is an impostor. Her appearance is distinctive enough for her face and figure to be memorable, after all, but no one ever says, "But I am sure when I met you last year you were Miss Elizabeth Barnaby!" But Perry's plots demand that Charlotte be able to infiltrate the society without giving away her identity as a policeman's wife. Because, of course, if anyone realizes that she is a policeman's wife, she would be having tea with the servants, and that would never do!

But if Perry has a weakness, it lies in the main women characters, who sometimes seem a trifle too contemporary. The Ellison women are all rule breakers: why would Perry, who well knows the boundaries of the times, create what to Victorian eyes would have been an unholy trio? The Victorian preoccupation with blood and insanity would seem likelier to dismiss the whole family as mad, rather than accept them in society. They have neither Lady Vespasia Cumming-Gould's social status nor enough wealth to cloak their eccentricities, and lacking these two qualities, would probably not be tolerated in society. Emily, having married so far above herself, must constantly watch her behavior. Naturally, Charlotte's working-class marriage is even worse and would undoubtedly remove her completely from Victorian society, if this were a realistically rendered novel.

Even though Charlotte, we are informed, has a disastrous tongue, it strains belief, to grant that she, a young and unmarried woman, would confront her brother-in-law, Dominic Corde, over a sexual peccadillo with the maid:

A new angry thought occurred to her and as soon as it was in her head, it, too, was on her tongue.

"How would you feel if Sarah went and made love to Maddox?" [the Ellison's butler]

"Don't be ridiculous!"

"What's ridiculous about it?' she asked coolly. "You lay with the maid, didn't you?" (*Perry Cater Street* 218)

While this conversation would be unremarkable in the late twentieth century, the idea that a young and virginal woman would so confront her brother-in-law, and lay bare such an impropriety shades into the ludicrous. Not even Perry's careful delineation of Charlotte's character can carry this off believably, especially for the reader reasonably familiar with Victorian proprieties. As Perry well knows, and comments on often, women were expected to ignore such peccadilloes, dismiss, without a character, any maid impregnated by the gentlemen of the household, and in general maintain a well-bred reticence. But for Perry's plots to work, Charlotte must overturn a great many Victorian conventions.

To create a society in which we can believe, Perry employs more class slippage than actually existed, especially in one family. In the course of the series, consider the number of mesalliances contracted, since actually very few people married out of their own social class. Certainly the occasional "poor connection" made a brilliant match; occasionally, the son of the house may even have married the governess as occurs in the second novel, *Callander Square* (1980). But consider the family that Perry creates and then skillfully subverts. Grandmother Ellison, Edward Ellison, Caroline Ellison, his wife, and Sarah, the eldest daughter, are pattern cards of the expected respectable. The grandmother is a widowed old harridan who makes life utterly miserable for everyone; Edward is almost a caricature of the Victorian *tyrannus domesticus*; Caroline is the dutiful wife, submissive to Edward in everything, and Sarah, the eldest daughter, makes the expected good marriage to Dominic Corde. Charlotte and Emily, and the later Caroline (Edward's widow), however, are not pattern cards of the respectable. During the course of the series, each of them marries out of class.

When Charlotte Ellison, a well-connected upper-middle-class young woman, decides to marry Inspector Thomas Pitt, a man who is on the margins of the lower-level professional class, her life changes dramatically. Charlotte, on a level defined by the social conditions of the time, is obviously a loser; she not only loses her upper-middle-class social status and becomes a part of the lower-middle class; she also loses any property rights she would possess as an unmarried woman. When she marries, she ceases to be an individual and becomes, in law, "one body." Perry, very cleverly, mentions the situation only indirectly. Pitt, noting that several Married Women's Property Acts have become law, remembers that at least one person, on learning of his betrothal, congratulated him on improving, not his social status, which he does not, but his ownership of property (Shanley 103).

Even granting that an inspector has a higher income than a constable, the gap between Charlotte Ellison and Thomas Pitt is almost insurmountable. Nor does Perry attempt to deny the harsh consequences of Charlotte Ellison's awful decision to marry "beneath" her. As Aunt Vespasia points out, her social ostracism in a natural consequence of such a decision as she is unable to acknowledge her marriage or keep up a social appearance (*Ashworth Hall* 259). Although Charlotte is not disowned by her family, as might well have occurred, her marriage does place her in a different world. Perry makes Charlotte's new social and financial status quite clear. In the first years of her marriage, Pitt makes between £150–£200 yearly, which means that Charlotte is clearly keeping house on half the £300 yearly, which marks the border of middle-class income (Mitchell 36). Emily, tactful in her Christmas gifts, knows quite well that "as a constable, Pitt had earned about as much as a chimney sweep, and even now as an inspector, his entire month's salary was less than her monthly dress allowance" (*Silence in Hanover Close* 57). Charlotte Pitt must learn to run a household, not on a supervisory level, where she must know how to do things to instruct the maidservants, but must actually be able to do things. When she is helping Thomas solve crimes, she must borrow a dress and accessories from either Emily or Vespasia in order to appear in her former social circles.

Perry, however, skillfully avoids making Thomas Pitt a Romantic hero or a man more than slightly tinged with the twentieth century. Although Charlotte and Thomas have a very loving relationship, it is not, in contemporary terms, an equal relationship. Since Thomas is a man of his times, her "meddling" bothers him a great deal and he has no hesitation at invoking his status as lord and master. In this scene from *Bluegate Fields*, for example, the Victorian belief in the subordination of women comes to the fore. Charlotte has been arguing, as it turns out correctly, in favor of the innocence of a man Pitt has arrested for homosexual rape and murder, and Pitt brings the conversation to a swift and complete halt:

> "That is the end of the matter! I do not wish to discuss the matter any further. Where is my dinner, please? I am tired and cold, and I have had a long and extremely unpleasant day. I wish to be served my dinner and eat it in peace!"

Charlotte, although correct in her reading of the situation, takes a deep breath: "Yes, Thomas," she answered. "It is in the kitchen." (*Bluegate Fields* 111).

On the other hand, once Charlotte decides to pursue a course of action, Pitt often must surrender to domestic force majeure. Says Charlotte, sitting demurely with her sewing,

> "Let's imagine Jerome is innocent and he is telling the truth! What do we know for a fact?"
>
> He smiled sourly at the "we." But there was no purpose in trying to evade talking about it. He could see she was going to talk about it to the bitter end. (*Bluegate Fields* 145)

Pitt may occasionally (and half-heartedly) attempt to contain Charlotte within the "angel in the house" role to which she is so ill-suited, but he hardly expects success, which is fortunate for Perry's readers.

There are times, however, when Perry's Victorian understanding slips slightly.When Charlotte publicly questions Uttley, Jack's opponent in the MP race, she questions him in an apparently guileless fashion, making the point that like many politicians today, he can utter pious platitudes and glittering generalities about the crime problem without possessing a single solution. But when Uttley dismisses Charlotte's concern, saying,

> "If you will forgive me, ma'am, this is an excellent subject to illustrate why women are so naturally suited to making home the beautiful place of art and spirit, which raises fine children and gives the man the resources from which to fight the world's battles [. . . ] You have a different sort of brain, and that is as God and nature intended." (*Hyde Park* 78)

He is saying no more than is generally believed. Such writers as Coventry Patmore, with his mawkish verse novel, *The Angel in the House*, and Sarah Stickney Ellis' *The Women of England: Their Social Duties and Domestic Habits* (1838) have made exactly the same points Uttley has, and these views still inform Victorian society, despite the growing movements for women's emancipation and suffrage.

Emily, Charlotte's younger sister, who has looks and brains and social cunning, carries out a successful campaign to marry Lord George Ashworth at the same time Charlotte is contracting her "unfortunate" mesalliance. In a slight strain of likelihood, Emily marries as far above her station as Charlotte marries below. However, when Emily successfully snags Lord Ashworth, she discovers that she also must make accommodations; she must turn a blind eye to George's infidelities, and must always be conscious that she has married "above" herself. The strain of not making a mistake is very evident when Perry describes Emily's life. In the eighth novel, *Cardington Cresent* (1987), when Lord Ashworth is poisoned, his family immediately suspects her and attempts to have her put quietly away. The family's reaction is that George married badly, and the only possible way of avoiding a scandal is to have Emily committed to an insane asylum. "Bad blood" [says Mrs. March], "It always tells in the end. No matter how fine the face, how pretty the manners, blood counts. George was a fool!" (*Cardington Crescent* 195). Very fortunately for Emily, Pitt is called in to investigate, since it is a "quality" murder, and Charlotte manages to clear her sister. Emily then marries the charming and well-born but penniless Jack Radley. Perhaps unrealistically, Lord Ashworth's family does not interfere with Emily's choice of second husband although they could have had her placed in wardship to prevent an unwise second marriage, especially since her son, the new Lord Ashworth, lives with her and Jack. Nor does Emily's less spectacular second marriage prevent her from becoming an influential political hostess in order to aid Jack's attempts to win a seat in Parliament. But it is very coincidental indeed that Emily marries above herself and then marries a penniless but well-bred man who immediately becomes interested in social issues, precisely the same social interests in which Charlotte and Emily are interested, not to mention a sudden taste for sleuthing.

It is also highly convenient that Emily becomes nearly as avid and sharp a sleuth as Charlotte. For Perry's detective series to work, Charlotte cannot be isolated from her family; the premise, after all, is that Pitt, despite being a gamekeeper's son, has had a good education with the son of the house and acquired upper-class diction. He is thus assigned to social murders and Emily has the entreé into the circles in which the murders Pitt solves occur.

Caroline Ellison Fielding is by far the weakest character in the series. After Caroline is widowed, she chooses as her second husband a Jewish actor seventeen years younger than herself. In Victorian society, especially as Perry describes it, such an alliance would result in social suicide. The worst thing that happens to Caroline is that a few of her friends decide to cut her acquaintance, about which Caroline could care less. She simply makes new and more interesting friends. She also manages to foist her miserable mother-in-law off on Emily. Such behaviours echo and resonate with the twentieth-century way of looking at marriage instead of the late Victorian model. Although Charlotte and Emily are upset at the marriage, which is, indeed, in Victorian terms unsuitable for reasons of class disparity, social standing and "race" difference, they end by wishing their mother well. It is highly unlikely, however, considering the anti-Semitism which was rampant in Victorian times and which Perry brings so vividly to life in *Farrier's Lane*, the class status of an actor, and the age disparity, that Caroline could even continue to live in Cater Street, or other fashionable addresses, let alone be essentially unaffected by her marriage. She is, after all, no strong proponent of Charlotte's marriage; indeed, when Pitt is accused of murdering a prostitute in *Silence in Hanover Close*, Caroline's first reaction is to close ranks:

"You must face reality, Charlotte. You have made a mistake which has turned out tragically for you. If you come home now, take your maiden name again, I can—." (*Silence* 259)

To Charlotte's bitter rejoiners that Caroline is behaving as though she thought Pitt guilty, and her fiercely expressed determination that she will find the murderer and prove her husband innocent as she did for Emily, Caroline can only say, "My dear, that was quite different." And Charlotte cuts to the heart of the "difference" and Caroline's weakness: "Why? Because she is 'one of us' and Thomas isn't?" Caroline reluctantly says, "If you insist on putting it that way—yes." Charlotte replies cuttingly that "Well, you were glad enough to have him as one of us when you needed him!" (*Silence* 259). Scenes like this make it very difficult to believe that, social consequences apart, Caroline Ellison would marry "one of them" for any reason whatsoever. Her attitude over Charlotte's mesalliance, in other words, rings true, but her second marriage does not. Thomas Pitt, at least, is not a Jew, a man of another race, and if Perry portrays a character who wishes her daughter to abandon her marriage vows, deny her husband, and resume her maiden name to avoid the censure of society, it is all too convenient for Perry to suddenly have Caroline marry as would a woman of the twentieth century. Her advice to Emily, who is gloomily contemplating her widowhood is typically Victorian: sit on committees, bring soup to the deserving poor, snare another titled husband, and avoid notice, behaving like Charlotte, falling prey to a fortune hunter or behaving in any way that might irritate "Society." This very conventional Caroline is the character Perry has developed; when Caroline marries a common actor seventeen years younger than herself, and Jew to boot, and the narrator airily dismisses the consequences, too much of the present impinges on the past.

The danger in Perry's circumscribed world is that the reader who imbibes her history via Perry might think that this was the majority attitude. The sharp and intense focus on Charlotte and Emily, on their apparent success in abandoning the domestic sphere in favour of activism and detecting works superbly well, and Perry succeeds in writing historically informed detective fictions, but one must take her history for what it is, the setting for her characters instead of historical fact.

The main characters are therefore, a bit more accessible and comprehensible to Perry's present-day readers without showing an unacceptable degree of anachronistic behavior, especially when one weighs in the requirements of detective fiction, which is an extremely convention bound genre. It is rare that Perry significantly sacrifices the historical reality of her characters, even for the plot, and on the occasions it does occur, as with Caroline, it may be a violation of the Victorian way of life, but it does not violate the integrity of the plot. Caroline is little more than a peripheral annoyance. Neither Charlotte or Emily ever solves a murder in a manner inconsistent with her environment. In *Traitor's Gate* (1995), the fifteenth in line, Charlotte, for example, does not break into the Morton Club, a gentlemen's club, in order to arrest the murdererer: she has Eustace March do that. Furthermore, she figures out the solution to the murder, and then credits him with the solution, saying, "Uncle Eustace, you are brilliant! You have solved it!" (*Traitor's Gate* 409). Had she marched in to arrest a member, it would have been completely incredible; as it is, when she enters and looks in on the scene, a steward, who has just witnessed accusations of treason, murder, and a common brawl, and is sending for the police, sees her, and thinks her presence "the worst offence of all" (*Traitor's Gate* 416).

How well does Perry's succeed? On one hand, she shares the flaw common to writers of historical fiction, in that she has a somewhat idealized view of the past, and her history is run by her feminist agenda and the demands of her chosen genre. While one would not get an absolutely corrupted and inaccurate view of the Victorian Era as occurs in some medieval romances in which the stable boy ends up being knighted and becoming the king's right-hand-man, so that he may marry the heiress who is his one true love, the reader of Perry's novels who mistakes them for history instead of historically informed detective fiction could well come away thinking all the women were brave rule-breakers, commonly married policeman, lords, or actors and spent their time sleuthing. It is a great deal more likely that Caroline would have endured a widowhood shut in the house on Cater Street with her irascible mother-in-law, Emily would not have married George Ashworth, but someone in her milieu and spent a life like her mother's, or alternately frittered her life away as society women did, and Charlotte, if her tongue did not keep her "on the shelf," a miserable spinster living with her parents, and she had finally won their consent to a "bad marriage," one which Caroline laments non-stop, would have been too busy running a household on very limited means to meddle much in her husband's cases. Nor, one must remember, would he have been likely to have allowed it.

On the other hand, she does perform a much needed literary service in writing well-researched novels about a much maligned and misunderstood period. Perry provides another point-of-view on the Victorians who are often considered puritanical, humourless, goody-two-shoes. In the end Perry demolishes the monolithic view of the people who inhabited the time and place we call Victorian.

## Note

1. Bill Bryson, *The Mother Tongue: English and How It Got That Way* (New York: Morrow, 1990) 99-116; *The Story of English*, eds. Robert McCrum, William Cran, and Robert MacNeil (New York: Viking, 1986) 271-83; Thomas Pyles and John Algeo, *The Origins and Developments of the English Language* (Fort Worth, 1993) 212-36, are the texts which I used to check Perry's use of dialect; in addition, such authors as Georgette Heyer, whose use of Regency cant remains unparalled, provided me with a way to check the use of dialectical constructions in fiction.

## Works Cited

Emsley, Clive. *The English Police: A Political and Social History.* Hemel Hempstead: Harvester Wheatsheaf, 1991.

Huggett, Frank Edward. *Life Below Stairs: Domestic Servants in England from Victorian Times.* New York: Scribner's, 1977.

Mitchell, Sally. *Daily Life in Victorian England. Daily Life through History.* Westport: Greenwood P, 1996.

Perkin, Joan. *Women and Marriage in Nineteenth Century England.* London: Routledge, 1989.

Perry, Anne. *Ashworth Hall.* New York: Faxcett Crest, 1997.

——. *Belgrave Square.* New York: Fawcett Crest, 1992.

——. *Bethlehem Road.* New York: Fawcett Crest, 1990.

——. *Bluegate Fields.* New York: Fawcett Crest, 1984.

——. *Callander Square.* New York: Fawcett Crest, 1980.

——. *Cardington Crescent.* New York: Fawcett Crest, 1987.

——. *Cater Street Hangman, The.* New York: Fawcett Crest, 1979.

——. *Death in the Devil's Acre.* New York: Fawcett Crest, 1985.

——. *Farrier's Lane.* New York: Fawcett Crest, 1993.

——. *Highgate Rise.* New York: Fawcett Crest, 1991.

——. *The Hyde Park Headsman.* New York: Fawcett Crest, 1994.

——. *Paragon Walk.* New York: Fawcett Crest, 1981.

——. *Pentecost Alley.* New York: Fawcett Crest, 1996.

——. *Resurrection Row.* New York: Fawcett Crest, 1981.

——. *Rutland Place.* New York: Fawcett Crest, 1983.

——. *Silence in Hanover Close.* New York: Fawcett Crest, 1988.

——. *Traitor's Gate.* New York: Fawcett Crest, 1995.

Sayers, Dorothy L. *Gaudy Night.* New York: Avon, 1968.

Shanley, Mary Lyndon. *Feminism, Marriage and the Law in Victorian England, 1850-1895.* Princeton UP, 1989.

# Peter Lovesey:
# No Cribbing on History

## Margaret L. Foxwell

Confessing to cold-blooded murder, a woman waits in Newgate Prison for the Hangman. Policemen at a London police station conduct a séance, and a detective polices the spirit world. A Keystone Cop plunges to his death. The Prince of Wales investigates the mysterious death of a jockey.

Can you learn any history from a good mystery?

Yes, you can, with the right author.

Peter Lovesey, who has delighted mystery audiences for almost thirty years, is the right author. His historical mysteries have been unanimously praised not only for their witty style, agile plotting and jack-in-the-box surprises, but for their authentic period flavor and solid historical research. He has won a First Crime Novel Award in 1970 for *Wobble to Death*, in 1978 he won a Silver Dagger from the Crime Writers' Association for *Waxwork*, and the Gold Dagger in 1982 for *The False Inspector Dew*. He won the French Grand Prix de Litterature Policière in 1985 and the Prix de Roman d'Aventures in 1987. More recently, he has been nominated three times for Malice Domestic's Agatha Award for his short stories. No author demonstrates more ably that you can settle in to read a great mystery, and also gain thought-provoking insight into another time and place.

Historically, the mystery genre has struggled for acceptance as "real" literature. Perhaps literary critics suspect its wide appeal and global audience, and historical mysteries by association may be regarded as equally dubious. Critics of this emerging subgenre question the validity of using historical backdrops for mystery novels. But avid mystery readers have no such qualms—they know what they like. They criticize not the validity of the genre, but some writers for merely "tacking on" historical details to modern characters and settings. For them the only question worth asking is how well the author does his or her job.

In Lovesey's case, the answer is very well indeed. Although he is first and last a storyteller practiced in beguilement, weaving tales of murderous plots and abundant skullduggery, he is one of the premier writers of the Victorian period, bringing a thorough knowledge of his subject to a body of work worthy of serious analysis. His historical perspective, characters, and plots are not added onto his story, but grow naturally and convincingly out of the time and place, lending his works the double benefit of a satisfyingly authentic tang and a tight organic structure.

Lovesey has enjoyed notable success and has carried the same level of craftsmanship to his writing in other time periods. But his two most recognized series, Sergeant Cribb and Bertie, Prince of Wales, are set in the Victorian era. They offer not only a good read, but also characters, settings and plots that sparely and yet eloquently provide insight into the time period. Although the author's tone is lively and the procedings often amusing, substantial themes are also woven through the narrative. Through the eyes of these very different characters, the discriminating reader can garner historical perspective on such serious subjects as class, criminal justice, the position of women in society, family life, pornography, and extreme politics. However, Lovesey does not lecture the reader upon his research, but allows the story to inform while it entertains. Serious undertones are always balanced with sharp psychology and a wicked sense of humor.

The Cribb novels present a resonant view of Victorian society from the middle- to lower-middle classes. Sergeant Cribb, a working-class, under-appreciated Scotland Yard detective, investigates crimes with his partner Constable Thackeray. They embody the shrewdness and drive particular to their class and times. We see much of the action through their eyes and judge with their Victorian sensibilities. Cribb's investigations also reveal the routine and often thankless life of a policeman that further grounds the narrative in Victorian reality (Critchley 150-75, Wilkes 27-35). As acute and sharp-tongued as he is, Cribb is often at odds with his more politically minded superiors at Scotland Yard.

Cribb and Thackeray lead the reader into fascinatingly low places: they encounter criminals in the sweaty world of bare-knuckled prize fights (*The Detective Wore Silk Drawers*, 1971), in pedestrian marathon matches (*Wobble to Death*, 1970), and in popular entertainment (*Abracadaver*, 1972). But Cribb also pursues criminals into middle-class parlors as well as to the estates of the rich, proving that the human heart can be equally as black behind lace curtains as in the grimy alleys of Whitechapel (Chesney 267-306, 267-78, 280-88).

Turn Cribb's acuity, staunch middle-class morality, sense, and investigative skill inside out and you have Bertie, the Prince of Wales. Building upon the well-documented peccadilloes of the son of Queen Victoria, Lovesey created another series character by posing the question: what if Bertie fancied himself a great detective called upon to solve crimes? The amusing premise offers a lighter view of Victorian society, allowing the reader to rub shoulders with the famous and infamous of that era. Bertie's investigations are unusual. Apparently he is not as great a detective as he thinks. "A stabbed man in a dumbwaiter may not be all that he seems" (*Bertie and the Seven Bodies* 71), he observes when confronted by a corpse. Although Bertie, in pursuit of criminals as well as a good time, often prowls the same low environs as Cribb, he can go where Cribb cannot. Bertie's world of boredom and social priviledge offers a marked contrast to the grittier world of Sergeant Cribb, marking out some distinct class boundaries.

To the Victorians, class was everything, defining thought, position, conduct, expectation, and ambition. Class permeates every interaction between one person and another, and every milieu from the heights of the peerage, to the depths of Newgate Prison, to the worlds of sport and leisure. Therefore, an understanding of the class system is essential to understanding the undercurrents, tensions and motivations of that society (Emsley 56-58, Harris 6-11, 157-59, Himmelfarb 52, Pike 134). Lovesey ably and unobtrusively educates the reader that certain classes merit privileged treatment. A guard assesses a prisoner: "Bell had been prepared to dislike the prisoner as one of the genteel class who thought of themselves as ladies and would no doubt expect to be treated as such, in spite of having savagely murdered a fellow creature" (*Waxwork* 19). And all is not equal in the world of athletic competition. A sports promoter replies to reporters' questions regarding the need for two race tracks segregating the classes of pedestrian racers competing against each other. "Why do we have different classes of railway travel? Why are our public houses divided into different rooms? Why are some of my tickets a guinea and the rest a shilling? You know the answer, gentlemen. The first class is reserved for the best" (*Wobble to Death* 17). Class affects even the most intimate of relationships. A doctor coldly assesses his third wife: "'Went for looks this time. Married a bit beneath my station. Shop-keeper's daughter. Easy on the eye, but a bit of a liability on social occasions'" (*Mad Hatter's Holiday* 65).

Cribb's encounters with crime and criminals, politics, and his "betters," delineate the British class system from the bottom looking up. Cribb's sharpness of mind and tongue run him squarely into the class ceiling. Despite all his talent and drive, he is from the working class, which will ultimately determine how high he can rise in his profession. He understands that the upper echelons of Scotland Yard are reserved for men of birth and education (Emsley 58, Joyce 2-41, Lynd 94-95). Class dictates his professional manner as well as the action he takes toward the people he meets in the course of his investigations. Interviewing a suspected thief, Thackeray unceremoniously seizes him and shoves him up against a pole for Cribb to question (*A Case of Spirits* 50). In sharp contrast, and only a few pages before this incident, Cribb is all respectful politeness when interviewing a well-to-do doctor. Cribb may resent the stifling of his own career and the inequalities of the class system, but he is too much of a realist, as well as too much of a Victorian Englishman, to question the status quo.

As a Scotland Yard detective, Cribb's investigations routinely bring him into contact not only with criminals, but also with the Victorian criminal justice system. From the day-to-day operations and politics within the depths of Scotland Yard to the edge of the gallows, Victorian concepts of crime, punishment, and law enforcement are central to understanding the times. Unlike other novelists, Lovesey provides a look at those outcast from Victorian society. *Swing, Swing Together* (1976) sets a scene in Coldbath Fields Prison, furnishing a glimpse of the penal system in operation. "In twelve narrow stalls convicts were at the treadmill, forcing their feet to keep pace with steps that sank endlessly away as an unseen wheel turned, its revolutions fixed at a rate that took no account of aching calves and skinned ankles" (159). The treadmill was one of the more unpleasant examples of the Victorian treatment of criminals. Prisoners were engaged in such exhausting, repetitive, and pointless labor in order to break down the criminal's will, which directly contrasts modern views of correction and rehabilitation. Lovesey uses this interview scene as an effective reminder of the consequences of crime behind the ordered and serene face of Victorian society (Emsley 58-65, 274-75).

The treatment of women in the penal system and society's views regarding capital punishment are issues that emerge from the background of *Waxwork* (1978), a mesmerizing puzzle set in Newgate Prison. A woman confesses to cold-blooded murder, is condemned to hang, and to all outward appearances waits calmly for the date of her execution. Why did she confess, and why does she appear so unmoved in the face of approaching death are the questions that Cribb must race the clock to answer. The prison atmosphere and the day-to-day routine for the condemned as the hours march toward the inevitable while society looks on compose the structure of this powerful plot (Babington 151-60, 210-14, Emsley 78).

Lovesey's view of Victorian women, criminal and otherwise, is spirited. He draws his female characters from all classes and conditions; they are not stereotyped pale images incarcerated in the home, but sharply drawn characters that are active, intelligent, and determined. Murderesses, twin music-hall acrobats (*Abracadaver*), the leader of an extreme political organization (*Invitation to a Dynamite Party*, 1974), a student teacher turned detective (*Swing, Swing Together*), a widow who personally manages her stable of prize-fighters (*The Detective Wore Silk Drawers*), and an emancipated spiritualist (*A Case of Spirits*, 1974) number among a startling range of imagined characters. Although these are fictional women, the author draws from historical counterparts as, for example, Victoria Woodhull, the American spiritualist and women's activist, and Madeleine Smith and Florence Maybrick, notorious accused murderesses (Hartman 345-47, 350-53). Women also were renowned performers in opera, theater, and the music hall. In the Bertie novels, the Prince's adventures bring him into contact with such celebrated women as the brilliant actress Sarah Bernhardt, who aids the Prince of Wales in one of his cases; Queen Victoria, that most formidable lady who set standards of behavior and gave her name to an age. She is interpreted by the author as an even more formidable mother, who strikes terror into the heart of her son. As Lovesey demonstrates, the roles and expectations society placed upon Victorian women were more restrictive than those of today, but he makes the point through his female characters that women could circumvent these restrictions. They were not passive victims of society, but active members and arbiters of that society (Emsley 78-79, Himmelfarb 53-54, 66-68).

Victorian family life was also subject to similar limitations. Families, Lovesey suggests, could appear the model of decorum in public and be quite different in private. His mysteries examine the often violent results of relationships gone wrong and families seething with private resentments. The particular dictates of Victorian society offers a sharp tension between such realities and the need to maintain the appearance of respectability (Harris 61-95, Himmelfarb 76). In *Mad Hatter's Holiday*, an outsider is the only one who divines the strange relationships in a family. Something is terribly wrong; a wife is drugged into insensibility every night while her doctor husband goes "visiting" an attractive patient, and a teen-aged son is having an affair with his younger brother's nursemaid. In *A Case of Spirits*, a husband pays more attention to his paintings of nudes in "classical" poses than to his wife. During a pedestrian marathon, one of the competitor's wives spends as much time with the coach as her husband does (*Wobble to Death*). Married couples unsuited to each other held in difficult or abusive relationships could not divorce without incurring social ostracism. Rigid standards of conduct, sexual mores, and constricting social rituals created double standards of what was socially acceptable in public and private life. The conflict between the private world of family relationships and the need for individuals to retain their public positions and reputations had often lethal results, as Lovesey illustrates (Himmelfarb 64-65, Marsh 45-47).

Because the consequences of violating society's rules were so severe, the image an individual projected was of critical importance to the Victorians. Lovesey reflects this concern in his novels by his clever use of Victorian imaging. Image and reflection form powerful subordinate themes in *Waxwork*. Here one theme the author plays upon is the public fascination with crime. Madame Tussaud's Wax Museum assures a hangman concerned with how his wax image will be displayed: "If you should consent to sit for your portrait, an appointment could be made at any time convenient to yourself. Be assured that in the presentation of its exhibits Madame Tussaud's has ever observed the highest standards of good taste" (*Waxwork* 81). This same hangman keeps, as a record of his professional career, photographic portraits of every person he has put to death (Rose 58-59). Physiognomy and photography were also popular Victorian preoccupations which the author cleverly employs regarding the subjectivity of images (Briggs 220). A photographer is more devoted to the beautiful images he has made of his wife than to the real woman. Cribb, in search of truth, studies the photograph of the self-confessed murderess in an attempt to gain some unbiased impression of her character that he cannot derive from witnesses. "The camera was objective. If there was much it could not convey, at least it made an honest statement. *Here is a woman*, was what it said, not *Here is a murderess*" (*Waxwork* 63). The public stares at this woman in the dock, fascinated and repelled by her calm impassivity and her admission of guilt, and unsatisfied that she will not provide the spectacle they expect. Nevertheless, newspapers carrying her picture are snapped up by a London hungry for scandal and avid for a vicarious thrill. Every person projects onto her image the product of his or her own prejudices, and these prejudices not only reflect back to the reader images of Victorian attitudes and assumptions, but also suggest that the modern world shares the same fascination.

Images not only reflect subjective and conflicting images; they reflect the darker side of human nature, which transcends time period. The public's fascination with the waxen representations of famous murderers at Madame Tussaud's reveals the human attraction toward evil. In *Waxwork,* Cribb confronts a pornographer selling pictures of young women that threaten to destroy lives and reputations. Captured images and their danger also create a disturbing theme in *Mad Hatter's Holiday.* A voyeur collects images of people with his binoculars like butterflies pinned under glass. Pursuing the object of his interest, he is drawn into the circle of unhappy relations within one family vacationing at Brighton and the circumstances that lead to violence and murder. From the use of these images, Lovesey suggests that Victorian society as well as modern society is always watching and judging and exerting a pressure upon individuals to conform to standards of acceptible behavior, and yet drawn to its opposite (Himmelfarb 29-31).

Class, criminal justice, and standards of behavior were not the only indicators of societal values. How the Victorians played also reveals as much of the time and the culture. Lovesey bases some of his plots upon a number of these sports and popular diversions. Background range from in popular entertainment, theater, the music halls, summer trips to the Brighton seashore, and punting on the Thames. The author also makes use of popular fads like walking races, spiritualism, and photography. All of these create interesting and revealing backgrounds, allowing the reader a grasp not only of the sights, sounds and smells, but subtler indications of the mindset of the time.

*Wobble to Death* takes place at a pedestrian race, a popular sport fad of the 1870s similar to dance marathons of the early twentieth century. The grit and grime of the agricultural hall setting powerfully evokes gaslit Victorian London. Dubbed a "Cruelty Show," this six-day test of endurance will break the bodies, hearts, and spirits of the competitors. They are an odd lot; a gentleman and former Guardsman, a former ostler, a patent medicine peddler, rough laborers, and working-class competitors who find this punishing competition far easier than heavy labor. This mismatched group of characters provides a range of personal, class, and professional conflicts that build the tension toward murder.

*Swing, Swing Together* is about the pastime of punting on the Thames and reflects the Victorian appreciation of nature (Petrie 163-64). During the summer, droves of people escaped the cities to boat along the quiet river. A young skinny-dipping student teacher becomes the chief witness to a murder and aids Cribb and Thackeray in tracking down the killer. Along the way, they meet a host of characters ranging from humble boatmen and city clerks on holiday to Oxford professors, who create a perspective not only of ordinary people at leisure but the flavorsome life of the river (Briggs 206-07).

*Abracadaver* deals with the popular entertainers of the music halls. Artistes are being victimized by cruel pranks which at first seem harmless, but have a far more sinister purpose. The tangy and robust life of popular entertainers such as singers, weight lifters, comedians, female acrobats, and dancers is nimbly crafted into a lively tale. In the course of their investigation, Cribb and Thackeray attend a music hall performance that vividly portrays the rough jollity of working-class crowds, cruising prostitutes, and gaudy acts. With the characters, the reader is permitted past the curtain to probe the backstage lives of the performers (Kift 36-74, 135-54, Macqueen-Pope 102-83, Mander 13-27).

*A Case of Spirits* opens with a séance held in a police station and closes with Cribb himself conducting a séance to unmask a killer. Spiritualism in the nineteenth and early twentieth centuries was a popular preoccupation searching for evidence of life after death. Thrill seekers gathered in darkened parlors to join hands and wait for table-rapping and ectoplasmic manifestations. "It didn't matter to the well-to-do whether there was anything in spiritualism or not; mediums were drawing-room entertainers, as ready to be hired for an evening as the latest velvet-voiced Italian over for the season at Covent Garden" (*A Case of Spirits* 42).

A particular device that Lovesey often employs to reveal historical perspective is how a modern theme might be echoed in the past. This creates a kind of double exposure or parallel effect. The reader not only identifies with the theme but is able to draw a comparison of the present with the past. Matters of pornography, radical politics, terrorism, and assassination might seem to belong more to the modern world than that of the Victorians, but the author points out that this was not the case.

Questions of what constitutes morality and vice are dictated by the times. Both Cribb's and Bertie's investigations touch upon these questions. Working under cover, the solid Constaple Thackeray is pressed into service as stagehand in a private and scandalous perfomance given to select upper-class gentlemen (*Abracadaver*). Thackeray's reaction to very scantily clad female performers and the bawdy procedings is horrified; he shuts his eyes. This amusing, but historically illuminating scene, offers a sharp contrast between the Victorian world and our own. A modern person might smile at the Victorian notion of pornography and the character's reaction to it, but he or she can contrast these views against modern conceptions. In addition, another contrast is offered between Thackeray's simple morality and innate decency and that of the more sophisticated audience.

Politics—domestic, sexual, or national—have always been dynamite. Literally. The modern reader might believe bombers and radical terrorists are creations of the twentieth century, but *Invitation to a Dynamite Party* is centered about radical and subversive action in the nineteenth century and provides another example of an effective historical comparison between the past and the present. Public buildings are being blown up by "infernal machines" set by a cell of resolute agitators who will use any and all means up to the assassination of an eminent person to gain Irish self-determination. Lovesey's plot is based upon the Fenian bombings of London of 1883-1885. The "Irish Question," home rule for Ireland, was as dangerous a political issue in the nineteenth century as it is today. Cribb infiltrates the terrorist group posing as soldier for hire after undergoing a police crash course in making and defusing bombs. The novel offers insight, not only into the arcana of high explosive and bomb construction in the nineteenth century, but also the interior workings of extremist organizations (Thomson 182-815, Wilkes 38-39).

While Victorian London, high and low, are the favorite haunts of both his Sergeant Cribb and Bertie novels and form the largest body of his work, Lovesey employs the same level of craftsmanship and attention to historical detail even when he leaves that setting. Some examples of his other works offer a range of time periods from World War I to post World War II.

Historical comparisons of past to present are also employed to good effect in *Keystone*, a mystery set in Hollywood in 1915. Mack Sennett and his Keystone Cops, who were popular silent-film slap-stick comedians, figure prominently in the case. The plot centers about a Keystone Cop who, while the cameras roll, plunges to his death. The detailed workings of a movie studio in Hollywood's infancy related in the course of the narrative are not only fascinating but also provide a sharp contrast between the largely improvised operation of 1915 to the multi-billion-dollar industry that is Hollywood today.

Like his Victorian novels, Lovesey uses threads of historical fact to base his novel. A transatlantic liner in the 1920s provides the backdrop for the critically acclaimed *False Inspector Dew* (1982). Using incidents from the famous Crippen murder case of 1910 as a point of departure, he weaves a wickedly clever plot that will keep the reader guessing up to the last page. His character reads in the newspapers of Dr. Crippen, a man who was, like him, seeking escape from his rich and unpleasant wife, and he hits upon the idea of impersonating Inspector Dew, the detective who in real life apprehended Dr. Crippen. When a body unrelated to the guilty man turns up, the imposter is asked to solve the case (Harrison 100-106, Shew 50-55, Thomson 198-201).

Even Lovesey's more recent works set in the 1940s reflect the same care as his Victorian novels to establish authentic settings and characters that form the basis for the plot. World War II Britain is the backdrop for *Rough Cider* (1986). A skull is found in a cider barrel and an American GI is accused of murder. The story is told from the point of view of a lonely young boy evacuated from London. Befriended by the GI, the boy is forced to testify against him at his trial. The experiences of children uprooted from their families and sent away from the London Blitz to the safety of the country, as well as those of American GI's in Britain are juxtaposed to build the dramatic situation. The author uses the same technique in *On the Edge* (1989), which is set against a post-World War II Britain. Two ex-servicewomen, who miss the excitement and purpose of their wartime responsibilities, become embroiled in a plot to be rid of their abusive and tiresome husbands.

From the 1880s to the 1940s, Lovesey uses authentic settings and solid historical research work to generate authentic stories and characters who live, work, and play in three dimensions. Against this backdrop play themes that transcend history: the struggle between good and evil, the pursuit of justice for the victim, and the human frailties of passion and greed that lead to crime.

"History is little else than a picture of human crimes and misfortunes" (*L'Ingenu*, ch. 10). Voltaire's observation suggests a link between history and the mystery genre. History attempts to connect the modern world to the past and revolves about the questions of what it means to be human, of where we have been, and where we are going. Mysteries, in their own way, deal with the same issues. Historical mysteries assert that these questions were as valid in the past as they are in the present.

Historical mysteries are not history. They do not claim to be. A mystery goes where history cannot—into the minds and hearts of living characters, breaking down the separation between times and places far from the present, and in the process touching minds, hearts, and imaginations. Good historical mysteries, like those Lovesey writes, for the curious can open the door into serious research. Young readers or those unfamiliar with a study of history can be introduced to other times and places through characters and places in books. And those who are students of history keenly appreciate research well done, as well as the opportunity to put on the characters' skin and take a journey into another time and place.

A good historical mystery is an illusion, but a necessary illusion. Only through fictional characters can we once more walk the streets of fog-bound gaslit London, to attend the raucous music halls, to walk the decks of the Mauritania, to experience war-time England, or stand in Newgate Prison. The hard truth of history is that the past exists now only in documents, in faded photographs, and the few words written down by those long dead. Let us thank the storyteller who allows us to believe, if only for a moment, that those times and places, those people still live, even if it is only in our imaginations.

## Works Cited

Babington, Anthony. *The English Bastille: The History of Newgate Gaol and Prison Conditions in Britain 1188-1902*. New York: St. Martin's P, 1971.

Briggs, Asa. *A Social History of England*. New York: Viking P, 1983.

Chesney, Kellow. *The Anti-Society: An Account of the Victorian Underworld*. Boston: Gambit, 1970.

Critchley, T. A. *A History of Police in England and Wales 1900-1966*. London: Constable, 1967.

Emsley, Clive. *Crime and Society in England 1750-1900*. 2nd ed. England: Longman, 1987, 1996.

Harris, Jose. *Private Lives, Public Spirit: A Social History of Britain 1870-1914*. England: Oxford UP, 1993.

Harrison, Richard. *Scotland Yard*. Chicago: Ziff-Davis, 1949.

Hartman, Mary S. *Victorian Murderesses*. New York: Pocket, Simon and Schuster, 1978.

Himmelfarb, Gertrude. *The De-Moralization of Society: From Victorian Virtues to Modern Values*. New York: Knopf, 1995.

Jones, David. *Crime, Protest, Community and Police in Nineteenth Century Britain*. London: Routledge and Kegan Paul, 1982.

Joyce, Patrick. *Work, Society and Politics: The Culture of the Factor in Later Victorian England*. New Jersey: Rutgers UP, 1980.

Kift, Dagmar. *The Victorian Music Hall: Culture, Class and Conflict*. Trans. Roy Kift. England: Cambridge UP, 1996.

Lovesey, Peter. *Abracadaver.* New York: Dodd, Mead, 1972.

——. *Bertie and the Crime of Passion*. New York: Mysterious P, 1993.

——. *Bertie and the Seven Bodies*. New York: Mysterious P, 1990.

——. *Bertie and the Tinman*. New York: Mysterious P, 1987.

——. *A Case of Spirits*. Hammondsworth: Penguin. 1974.

——. *The Detective Wore Silk Drawers*. New York: Harper & Rowe, 1971.

——. *The False Inspector Dew*. New York: Pantheon, 1982.

——. *Invitation to a Dynamite Party*. Hammondsworth: Penguin, 1974.

——. *Keystone*. New York: Pantheon, 1983.

——. *Mad Hatter's Holiday*. Penguin, Hammondsworth, Middlesex, England. 1973.

——. *On the Edge*. New York: Mysterious P, 1989.

——. *Swing, Swing Together*. Hammondsworth: Penguin, 1976.

——. *Waxwork*. New York: Pantheon, 1978.

——. *Wobble To Death*. New York: Dodd, Mead, 1970.

Lynd, Helen Merrell. *England in the Eighteen-Eighties: Toward a Basis of Social Freedom*. London: Cass, 1968.

Macqueen-Pope, W. *The Melodies Linger On: The Story of the Music Hall*. London: 1950.

Mander, Raymond, and Joe Mitchenson. *The British Music Hall*. London: Studio Vista, 1965.

Marsh, David C. *The Changing Social Structure of England and Wales 1871-1951*. London: Routledge and Kegan Paul, 1958.

Petrie, Sir Charles. *The Victorians*. New York: MacKay, 1961.

Pike, Luke Owen. *A History of Crime in England, Vol. II*. New Jersey: Patterson Smith, 1968.

Rose, Lionel. *Crime and Punishment*. London: Batsford, 1977.

Shew, E. Spencer. *A Companion to Murder: A Dictionary of Death by Suffocation, Death by Shooting, Death by Suffocation and Drowning, Death by the Strangler's Hand 1900-1950*. New York: Knopf, 1960.

Thomson, Sir Basil. *The Story of Scotland Yard*. New York: Literary Guild, 1936.

Wilkes, John. *London Police in the Nineteenth Century*. London: Cambridge UP, 1977.

# Elizabeth Peters:
## *The Last Camel Died at Noon*
## as Lost World Adventure Pastiche

### Gary Hoppenstand

Listed among crime fiction's most famous historical detectives is Elizabeth Peters's intrepid Amelia Peabody. Victorian Egyptologist, noted archeologist, and staunch feminist, Amelia Peabody is, arguably, the genre's most endearing and popular creation. Since the publication of her first adventure, *Crocodile on the Sandbank* in 1975, she has been featured in twelve best-selling novels, her most recent being *He Shall Thunder in the Sky* (2000). A representative assessment of the Amelia Peabody stories can be found in Jean Swanson's and Dean James's *By a Woman's Hand: A Guide to Mystery Fiction by Women* (1994): "These [the Amelia Peabody] novels are particularly noteworthy for the characterizations of the intelligent and adventurous Peabody, her irascible husband, Egyptologist Radcliffe Emerson, and their precocious son Ramses" (169). And yet, though the best of Peters's work is comparable to the finest examples of historical detective fiction—from Robert van Gulik's Judge Dee novels to Ellis Peters' Brother Cadfael series —it is quite obvious to the astute reader that there exists a decided difference between Amelia Peabody's exploits and those of her esteemed literary relations.

Peters gives us an important clue to this difference in the "Acknowledgements" section of the sixth Peabody novel, *The Last Camel Died at Noon* (1991). As did Anne Rice in her popular horror novel, *The Mummy; or Ramses the Damned* (1989),[1] Elizabeth Peters identifies the popular Victorian romancer, Sir H. Rider Haggard (1856-1925), as an important source of inspiration. Peters states:

My greatest debt will of course be obvious to the intelligent Reader. Like Amelia (and, although he refuses to admit it, Emerson) I am an admirer of the romances of Sir Henry Rider Haggard. He was a master of a form of fiction that is, alas, seldom produced in these degenerate days; having run out of books to read, I decided to write one myself. It is meant as an affectionate, admiring, and nostalgic tribute. (ix)

Thus, the fundamental narrative quality that separates Peters's Amelia Peabody stories from those of van Gulik's Judge Dee or Ellis Peters's Cadfael mysteries is adventure. Undoubtedly, the Amelia Peabody adventures are just what they are advertised as being (i.e. adventures), and Elizabeth

Peters's ability to pastiche the romances of H. Rider Haggard, in part, explains why the Peabody mysteries are so well loved by her legion of fans. In a blurb reprinted in the paperback edition of *The Last Camel Died at Noon*, Peters's enthusiastic reviewer, Aaron Elkins, calls the novel "a tricky, beautifully plotted mystery; rollicking, old-fashioned (in the best sense of the word) adventure; romance; and the doughtiest, smartest, most appealing female protagonist in mystery fiction." Hyperbole aside, in her Amelia Peabody novels, Peters has successfully blended liberal doses of screwball comedy, mystery, suspense, and most importantly, slam-bang adventure, creating a heady concoction of escapist fare. Indeed, as her reviewers have noted, Peabody is the Indiana Jones of the crime fiction set.

The Peabody novels, it can be safely argued, are more adventure story than detective story. The problem in discussing adventure, however, is that this category of popular fiction is easy to recognize, yet difficult to define specifically. For example, the hard-boiled Mongo detective novels of George C. Chesbro feature ample levels of slam-bang action, but they are shelved in the "crime and mystery" section at the local bookstore. As with Chesbro, many of Dean Koontz's popular novels embody the narrative intersection between adventure, suspense, and horror but, due largely to the limitations of contemporary marketing practices in the publishing industry, Koontz's books can only be found in the "horror" section.

The most evident characteristic of the adventure story, of course, is adventure. The adventure story emphasizes narrative action, while de-emphasizing lengthy or introspective characterization. In addition, the adventure story often highlights a larger-than-life protagonist (or protagonists) who combats those mortal dangers that threaten life and limb, such as hostile, exotic foreign settings and villainous antagonists. And, since Peters's Amelia Peabody tales feature these significant formulaic adventure motifs, it soon becomes obvious to Peabody's devoted readers that her novels fit more easily into the category of the adventure story than the detective story.

Though all of the Peabody novels (to a greater or lesser degree) lovingly echo the fiction of H. Rider Haggard, it is Peters's *The Last Camel Died at Noon* that serves as her tribute to the master storyteller. In this novel, Peters has written a classic lost world adventure, a story told in the tradition of H. Rider Haggard and Sir Arthur Conan Doyle (1859-1930). Whatever her motivations might be, Peters's efforts at writing imitations of the lost world adventure have been quite successful; *The Last Camel at Noon* is frequently identified by readers and critics alike as the best of the Amelia Peabody stories. A typical assessment can be found in Jean Swanson's and Dean James' *Killer Books; A Reader's Guide to Exploring the Popular World of Mystery and Suspense* (1998): "One of the strongest books in the [Peabody] series is *The Last Camel Died at Noon* . . . Peters's affectionate tribute to H. Rider Haggard's adventure tales" (121).

If Elizabeth Peters has successfully co-opted the literary formula of the lost world adventure, then what defines this type of story and who are its major practitioners? Briefly explained, the lost world adventure is a formula of contemporary narrative fiction in which a hero (or group of heroes) either by accident or intent journeys to an otherwise inaccessible, previously unknown land in a remote region of the world. Typically, this unknown land is fraught with natural dangers, or it is inhabited by a "lost race" of people who threaten the life of the hero. The lost world adventure was at its most popular during the late-Victorian and Edwardian periods in Europe and America. The lost world setting allowed its authors a literary venue with a nineteenth-century imperialist agenda, in which the European or American adventurer establishes political authority over both the lost world environment and the lost race of people.

Africa proved to be one of the most frequently used settings for the lost world adventure, and so it comes as no surprise to learn that it is also employed in *The Last Camel Died at Noon*. Haggard, in particular, was particularly fond of his African settings for his romances. The reason why this region was such a popular choice for authors of adventure fiction was because it historically possessed a remoteness and an exotic appeal that fascinated European and American audiences. The heroic efforts of Sir Richard Burton, for example, to locate the source of the Nile and the exploits of Henry Morton Stanley and David Livingstone exploring Africa's unknown interior helped to fuel the fires of the readers' imagination about the "dark continent" in the newspaper accounts of the period. The writers of imaginative fiction simply took advantage of the public's interest in their own writings.

Historically, elements of the lost world adventure pre-date the nineteenth century. They can be found as far back as Plato's *Republic* (written between 380 and 370 B.C.) and Sir Thomas More's *Utopia* (1516), philosophical works that postulated a fantasy-like "no place" where the moral virtues of a perfect society were debated. As popular fiction, the lost world adventure can be traced directly to the efforts of French author, Jules Verne (1828-1905). In his series of literary "extraordinary voyages," which were scientific romances that mixed adventure with technological extrapolation and which became the foundation for modern science fiction, Verne escorted his readers across the unknown continent of Africa in *Five Weeks in a Balloon* (1863), and he took them to the center of the planet in *A Journey to the Center of the Earth* (1864). Verne even launched his reader to the moon in *From the Earth to the Moon* (1865), but it was his novel, *The Mysterious Island* (1874)—which is a sequel to the earlier published *20,000 Leagues Under the Sea* (1869-1870)—that perhaps best qualifies as the prototypical lost world adventure.

Other scholars of popular fiction argue that H. Rider Haggard invented the lost world adventure in his two best-selling novels, *King Solomon's Mines* (1885) and *She* (first released as a serial from October 2, 1886, to January 8, 1887, in the *Graphic*; and published as a book on January 1, 1887). Haggard's biographer, Peter Berresford Ellis, states in *H. Rider Haggard: A Voice from the Infinite* (1978) that *King Solomon's Mines* was written in a burst of creative energy, only taking Haggard some six weeks to complete. In the advertising hyperbole of its day, it was proclaimed as "The Most Amazing Story Ever Written" and, as Ellis notes, it has never been out of print since its initial publication in September 1885 (1). While evaluating the lasting popularity of Haggard's fiction, Ellis claims that no other writer of the period could match Haggard's long-standing popularity with readers. Ellis adds that by the time of Haggard's death in 1925, only two of his fifty-four novels were out of print (2).

Haggard's most frequently published series character was his "great white hunter," Allan Quatermain, who first appeared in *King Solomon's Mines* and was featured in some fourteen novels and four short stories. During the course of his venturous life, Quatermain usually found himself encountering more than a few lost worlds. Editor Douglas Menville suggests that when Haggard first created Quatermain for *King Solomon's Mines*, he did not foresee that the character would become so popular with readers. "Only his wonderful creation Ayesha, of the '*She*' books," Menville states, "is better known today; yet Haggard wrote only four novels about her" (v). (Elizabeth Peters's own intrepid Amelia Peabody is herself an obvious and direct literary descendant of Haggard's Allan Quatermain.) In any event, both Verne and Haggard influenced generations of popular authors that imitated and elaborated on the formula of the lost world adventure, writers such as Edward Bulwer-Lytton (1803-1873), Edgar Rice Burroughs (1875-1950), Rex Stout (1886-1975), Abraham Merritt (1884-1943), James Hilton (1900-1954), and, of course, Elizabeth Peters.

"Elizabeth Peters" is the pseudonym of the prolific Barbara Mertz, who also writes under the pen name of "Barbara Michaels." She was born in Canton, Illinois on September 29, 1927, and attended the Oriental Institute of the University of Chicago, where she received her Ph.B. in 1947, her M.A. in 1950, and her Ph.D. in Egyptology in 1952. Her academic specialization in Egyptian archaeology has obviously served her well in her literary career, not only in the writing of her Amelia Peabody adventures, but also in the publication of several popular non-fiction scholarly books under her real name, Barbara Mertz (Klein 275). Peters was the recipient of the Grandmaster Award, given at the 1986 Bouchercon, and the Agatha Award for Best Mystery Novel of 1989, given at the Malice Domestic Convention. In addition, she won the 1998 Mystery Writers of America's Grandmaster Edgar Award, a testament to the long-standing critical and popular reception of her work.

Elizabeth Peters has authored two other series in addition to the Amelia Peabody adventures, the Vicky Bliss novels—including *Borrower of the Night* (1973), *Street of the Five Moons* (1978), *Silhouette in Scarlet* (1983), *Trojan Gold* (1987), and *Night Train to Memphis* (1994)—and the Jacqueline Kirby novels—including *The Seventh Sinner* (1972), *The Murders of Richard III* (1974), *Die for Love* (1984), and *Naked Once More* (1989).

Yet, it is the Amelia Peabody stories that attract the most devoted of readers. In a brief interview that appears in the October 1998 issue of the

*Mystery Guild* newsletter, Elizabeth Peters states how she first came to create the character of Peabody:

[I]t was one of those fortuitous things. I'd done a number of Barbara Michaels books set in Victorian England for the simple reason—and I'm giving away a trade secret— it's a lot easier to get your heroine in danger in Victorian England than it is today. I was whining about what I was going to do next, and somebody said, "Why don't you try Victorian Egypt?" And I said, "Yeah . . . well . . . hmmm . . ." That's the way I always react to suggestions until I think about it and decide it was my idea in the first place. (4)

Peters ranks Sharyn McCrumb, Joan Hess, Margaret Maron, Aaron Elkins, and Charlotte MacLeod as among her favorite mystery writers. Her selection appears to be somewhat eclectic, and equally so is her definition of the mystery story itself, which indicates why her work is comfortably at home in both the adventure genre and detective genre: "A mystery does not have to have a murder," Peters argues. "The puzzle has to be solved before you get to the end, and before the protagonist can achieve, if not love, marriage and sex—a respite from other problems. It's not only the problem-solving thing, it's the atmosphere. There has to be some feeling of suspense, danger and menace" (*Mystery Guild* 2).

In an interview published in the Spring 1993 issue of *The Armchair Detective*, Peters (using her "real-life" Barbara Mertz voice) states that, as she was growing up, she read "everything from Conan Doyle to *Weird Tales*." She admits that her focus of late is on writing Amelia Peabody novels: "I've gone back to Rider Haggard and that crowd, whom I adored," and adds, "I like the lost civilization and the wandering around the hinter-land, so I thought, 'The hell with it,' and hauled them out to a lost civiliza-tion for *The Last Camel Died at Noon*" (McDonald 8-9). Peters claims she had a marvelous time "stealing" from Haggard, and "extrapolating" what it would be like for Peabody to discover a lost race dislocated some fifteen hundred years from its ancient origins. "Everything is totally logical and sensibly based," Peters says of *The Last Camel Died at Noon*, "it was won-derful. God, I had human sacrifices and this and that!" (9).

In another interview conducted by Dean James for *Speaking of Murder: Interviews with the Masters of Mystery and Suspense* (1998), Peters mentions that writing the Peabody series is not all fun, that it does possess a number of "challenges." She says that "avoiding anachronisms" is one of these challenges, as is doing the "nit-picking research" that functions as the background for her novels. However, she believes that her "greatest challenge" involves the placement of her Peabody stories during a specific historic period. "I didn't do that deliberately," she adds, "because at the beginning, I didn't intend to write a series" (167).

As do the three Steven Spielberg "Indiana Jones" films, *The Last Camel Died at Noon* begins *in medias res*, in the middle of things. Amelia, her husband Radcliffe, their son, Ramses, and a servant named Kemit are stranded in the deadly wastelands of the Sudan when their last camel expires suddenly. Over six days travel from the Nile ("as the camel trots") and a difficult two-day journey to the nearest waterhole, the Emerson expedition has barely enough water for forty-eight hours, since their native bearers abandoned them the night before, taking with them all of the supplies, except for what little water the stranded four adventurers had on their person. An angered Radcliffe also believes that their camels have been poisoned, which thus can explain why they all perished within a short period of time. And, after relating their dire predicament, Amelia (as the story's narrator) then returns the reader to the beginning of things, to the start of their adventure and the reason that she and her family find themselves in such a dangerous plight.

Peters borrows from Haggard's *King Solomon's Mines* several important plot devices. The first involves a quest by a group of individuals to locate a family member who has disappeared in the wilds of Africa. In *King Solomon's Mines*, Sir Henry Curtis (along with his friend Captain Good) seeks out Allan Quatermain to ask his assistance in finding a missing brother. In Peters's *The Last Camel Died at Noon*, the sinister Viscount Blacktower asks Amelia and Radcliffe during their archaeological expedition to the Sudan to find a lost son, Willoughby "Willie" Forth, who mysteriously disappeared somewhere in the region fourteen years earlier with his young bride in a disastrous attempt to become a famous explorer. Peters applies a new twist to this quest story by including in her plot Willie Forth's young nephew named Reginald "Reggie" Forthright, grandson to Viscount Blacktower, who attempts to dissuade the Emersons from undertaking such a foolish expedition. The seemingly innocent and naïve Forthright, who denies that his motive is his grandfather's fortune, proves by the end of the novel to be a villainous murderer who will, in fact, stop at nothing to inherit his family's wealth.

Peters also uses a variant of the adventure story plot device of the treasure map, which in Haggard's novel shows the way to the unknown African kingdom of Kukuanaland and to the lost diamond mines of King Solomon. The motif of the treasure hunt was earlier popularized in Edgar Allan Poe's famous short story, "The Gold-Bug" (first published in 1843 as a serial in the June 21 and June 28 issues of the *Dollar Newspaper*), and the motif of the treasure map (or the lost world map) was adopted by a number of famous nineteenth-century adventure fiction writers, including Robert Louis Stevenson and Jules Verne. In *The Last Camel Died at Noon*, Viscount Blacktower gives to Amelia and Radcliffe an ancient Egyptian papyrus containing an encoded message from the missing Willie Forth, along with a sheet of paper from Radcliffe's own notebook containing a map to a lost world sketched on one side.

A third device of the lost world story incorporated by Peters involves the political intrigue of the lost world kingdom itself. In Haggard's *King Solomon's Mines*, a native who claims he is an apparent member of the Zulu people and who calls himself Umbopa attaches himself to the Quatermain expedition. It turns out that Umbopa is the displaced, yet legitimate, ruler of Kukuanas, a king whose actual name is Ignosi. With the help of Sir Henry Curtis, Captain Good, and Hunter Quatermain, Ignosi is able to defeat his evil half-brother, Twala, in an epic battle, hence becoming the rightful leader of his kingdom. In Peters's pastiche of Haggard, she has a native servant named Kemit accompany the Emerson expedition to the lost world City of the Holy Mountain. Kemit is, in actuality, Prince Tarekenidal Meraset, half-brother to the evil twin, Prince Nastasen Nemareh (who is otherwise called "Nasty" by the Emersons). Amelia and Radcliffe, in true Haggard-like fashion, eventually assist the good Prince Tarekenidal in overthrowing the villainous "Nasty," an act that brings promised stability and prosperity to the Holy Mountain.

Satirizing Haggard's other classic lost world adventure, *She*, Peters undermines Haggard's depiction of the immortal Ayesha to frame her conclusion of *The Last Camel Died at Noon*. Peters parodies the character of Haggard's ravishingly beautiful "She-who-must-be obeyed," depicting her variant of this character as the grotesquely overweight "God's Wife of Amon." (The reader learns by the conclusion of the novel that this horrible woman is the obscenely transformed missing wife of Willie Forth.) Peters, with tongue firmly pressed in check, transforms the beautiful young wife into a monstrous sexual creature who presents Radcliffe with the so-called "fate worse than death." It is a darkly humorous moment in the novel, one that not only satirizes Haggard's *She*, but that also inverts many similar scenes in traditional adventure fiction in which the woman, rather than the man, is threatened with rape and death. As Peabody describes the horrid scenario:

> And over him [Radcliffe] bent the form of a woman.
>
> I had beheld such a scene before, through the eyes of imagination, but this was a grotesque parody of the original. My husband's ruggedly masculine features bore no resemblance to those of the golden-haired hero of the classic novel, and the shape that hovered over him would have made four of the immortal She. It was as squat and square as a huge toad. (*Camel* 408)

Radcliffe is saved any further humiliation when the lustful and insane Mrs. Forth abruptly dies of a sudden heart attack. In the usual Elizabeth Peters fashion, by the conclusion of the novel the mystery of Willoughby Forth's disappearance is explained, as well as that of his wife. The vile "Nasty" is defeated, and Reggie Forthright's schemes are exposed. In addition, Amelia, Radcliffe, and their son, Ramses, return home with an "adopted" girl, Nefret, the Holy Mountain's "Priestess of Isis" who is really the daughter of Willoughby Forth and legitimate heir to her family's fortune.

Amelia Peabody describes herself early in *Crocodile on the Sandbank*, in a typically self-critical fashion:

> I know the catalogue of my faults too accurately. I am too tall, I am too lean in some regions and too amply endowed in others. My nose is too large, my mouth is too

wide, and the shape of my chin is positively masculine. Sallow complexions and jetty black hair are not in fashion this season; and I have been informed that eyes of so deep a gray, set under such forbidding black brows, strike terror into the beholder even when they are beaming with benevolence—which my eyes seldom do. (5-6)

By introducing her heroine in such a way, Peters is shaping the central protagonist of her pastiche of the lost world adventure after Haggard's Allan Quatermain, who also presents himself in less-than-heroic fashion. In the opening chapter of King Solomon's Mines, for example, Quartermain calls himself "a timid man" who does not "like violence" and is "pretty sick of adventure" (7). Few heroes of popular fiction, however, have performed less timidly or engaged in more violence than has Allan Quatermain. No doubt, Peters understands (as did Haggard) that by constructing her central protagonist in a manner that encourages the reader to underestimate the protagonist's abilities, the reader can thus be pleasantly surprised when the protagonist heroically triumphs over danger and death. The uncommonly common adventurer serves a psychological purpose in popular fiction. This type of hero allows the reader to feel simultaneously both empathy and admiration. We are the physical equal to Amelia Peabody or Allan Quatermain; they appear to be as average as we are, yet we esteem their larger-than-life acts of courage when faced with danger or death.

In developing the character of Peabody's bombastically arrogant husband, Radcliffe Emerson, it seems likely that Peters turned to Sir Arthur Conan Doyle's Professor George Edward Challenger as her model. Professor Challenger, who made his first appearance in Doyle's *The Lost World* (1912), a novel that ranks with Haggard's *King Solomon's Mines* and *She* as one of the prototypes of the lost world adventure story. Officially, Challenger's biography, as provided by a newspaper editor named McArdle in *The Lost World*, reads as follows: "'Challenger, George Edward. *Born:* Largs, N.B., 1863. *Educ.:* Largs Academy; Edinburgh University. British Museum Assistant, 1892. Assistant Keeper of Comparative Anthropology Department, 1893. Resigned after acrimonious correspondence same year. Winner of Crayston Medal for Zoological Research. Foreign member of'— well, quite a lot of things, about two inches of small type" (9-10). Doyle's description of Challenger in the short story, "When the World Screamed" (first published in 1928 in the April and May issues of the *Strand Magazine*), offers a representative portrait of the character. In the story, Edward "Ned" Malone, a young reporter and associate of Challenger, tells the story's narrator, a friend called Peerless Jones, about the good and bad qualities of the notorious Professor:

[Challenger] would think nothing of throwing you downstairs if you have a disagreement [states Malone]. He is a primitive caveman in a lounge suit. I can see him with a club in one hand and a jagged bit of flint in the other. Some people are born out of their proper century, but he is born out of his millennium. He belongs to the early Neolithic or thereabouts."

"And he a professor! [replies Jones]."

"There is the wonder of it! It's the greatest brain in Europe, with a driving force behind it that can turn all his dreams into facts. They do all they can to hold him back for his colleagues hate him like poison, but a lot of trawlers might as well try to hold back the *Berengaria*. He simply ignores them and steams on his way." (5)

When Peters introduces Radcliffe in *Crocodile on the Sandbank*, her description echoes that of Doyle's Challenger:

He [Radcliffe Emerson] was a tall man with shoulders like a bull's and a black beard cut square like those of the statues of ancient Assyrian kings. From a face tanned almost to the shade of an Egyptian, vivid blue eyes blazed at me. His voice, as I had good cause to know, was a deep, reverberating bass. The accents were those of a gentleman. The sentiments were not. (34)

Like Challenger, Peters endows Radcliffe with his own set of impressive scholarly credentials. Peabody lists her husband's numerous accomplishments in *The Last Camel Died at Noon*: "Professor Radcliffe Emerson, F.R.S., F.B.A., LL.D. (Edinburgh), D.C.L. (Oxford), Member of the American Philosophical Society, et. cetera, preeminent Egyptologist of this or any era" (4). And, like Challenger, Radcliffe is usually described by Peabody as being obnoxious, brutish, swaggering, loud-mouthed, arrogant, egotistical, and bombastic—all qualities that she detests in a man. Of course, by the conclusion of *Crocodile on the Sandbank* they fall madly in love (literally) and marry. Theirs is one of the great screwball relationships in all of popular fiction.

As a mystery, *The Last Camel Died at Noon* has relatively little to do with the type of detective fiction written by Agatha Christie or Dorothy L. Sayers. Instead, one of more apparent influences on Peters's novel is Dashiell Hammett's idiosyncratic *The Thin Man* (1934). Hammett scholar Peter Wolfe says that *The Thin Man* is the author's "lightest, most glittering" novel, a story that offers "both a murder mystery and a sophisticated comedy," highlighting "witty repartee, and rich characters" (149).

Indeed, both *The Thin Man* and *The Last Camel Died at Noon* feature a type of screwball comedy relationship between the married protagonists in each story. Nick and Nora Charles engage in humorous and cosmopolitan by-play with each other during the course of Hammett's plot. Though not as cosmopolitan as Nick and Nora, in *Last Camel* Amelia and her husband Radcliffe also enjoy indulging in a zany contest of wills. This droll by-play in both stories frequently reveals the sexual tension underlying the characters' marital relationship. Compare the following excerpts from each novel. The first example is taken from a scene early in *The Thin Man*, illustrating Hammett's preference for a clipped, hard-boiled dialect:

We found a table. Nora said: "She's pretty."

"If you like them like that."

> She grinned at me. "You got types?"
> "Only you darling—lanky brunettes with wicked jaws."
> "And how about the red-head you wandered off with at the Quinns' last night?"
> "That's silly," I said. "She just wanted to show me some French etchings." (5)

The second example is taken from a scene in *The Last Camel Died at Noon*, after Amelia and Radcliffe have been revived from their ordeal in the desert by the descendants of "ancient Meroë," the lost world inhabitants of the City of the Holy Mountain. At this particular time, Radcliffe is desirous of some privacy with his wife, and Amelia describes the sexually charged moment:

> "Go, Handmaiden," he [Radcliffe] said in stumbling Meroitic. "Tonight I am with my woman. It is the time—er—I wish—er . . ." Here his native modesty overcame him, and his speech failed, for his study of the language had not gone so far as to include euphemisms for the activity he had in mind. Resorting instead to sign language, he blew out the lamp and advanced on Mentarit [one of the Handmaidens of the Goddess], pointing toward the door and flapping his hand at her.
> I think she caught his meaning. (216)

One can only wonder what Radcliffe's "sign language" looked like!

For Elizabeth Peters, screwball humor is an important component of her plot in *The Last Camel Died at Noon*, as it is in all of her Peabody adventures. Peters's writing can be uproariously funny, yet her work as literary humor is rarely discussed. She enjoys "romantic elements in books" (McDonald 11), and she structures the Peabody novels as a blending of romance, adventure, and mystery. It's a heady concoction that has found success with her readers. She says in her interview with Dean James that, earlier in her career, she had a difficult time convincing her "then-editor" that she could "get away with humor in a mystery context." Peters adds in her interview that male writers had been successfully publishing so-called "comic mysteries for some time" (James 164-65). Her audience, no doubt, appreciates her persistence. The Peabody adventures have certainly achieved the status of classic comic mysteries.

The process of Radcliffe's domestication is an important component of the Peabody novels, as the characters grow and develop over the course of the series. In *Crocodile on the Sandback*, Radcliffe, who is called "Father of Curses" by his native workers, is the untamable male who becomes tamed by the resolute Peabody, who is herself called, Sitt Hakim (or "lady doctor"). As Sitt Hakim, Peabody is appropriately named, since her work administers to the moral, as well as physical, needs of her "patients." As the series progresses, Radcliffe learns his responsibilities as husband to Amelia, and later as father to their precocious child, Walter Peabody Emerson (nicknamed "Ramses"), without losing the masculine erotic qualities that attracted Amelia to him in the first place. Peters has underscored in Radcliffe's and Amelia's tempestuous romance her idealized view of a relationship anchored in contemporary feminist sensibilities (McDonald 11).

There exists an overt purpose behind Elizabeth Peters's pastiche of Haggard and Doyle, something other than mere entertainment (though Peters might suggest, and rightfully so, that there is nothing wrong with mere entertainment). In her Amelia Peabody novels, Peters has employed traditional narrative formulas, such as the lost world adventure, to insert a feminist worldview in a genre historically controlled by male writers. She has subverted in her work the traditional roles of women in adventure fiction, dramatically reconstructing the female persona in these stories. Whereas in the past, many popular adventure writers—including H. Rider Haggard, Arthur Conan Doyle, and Edgar Rice Burroughs—stereotyped women characters as docile and passive foils when compared to their rugged male counterparts. Elizabeth Peters inverted that stereotype in novels such as *The Last Camel Died at Noon*, creating in Amelia Peabody a personality that is at least the intellectual or physical equal of the men.

Note, for example, Peabody's feminist statement regarding marriage taken from the third novel in the series, *The Mummy Case*:

> I never meant to marry. In my opinion, a woman born in the last half of the nineteenth century of the Christian era suffered from enough disadvantages without willfully embracing another. That is not to say that I did not occasionally indulge in daydreams of romantic encounters; for I was as sensible as any other female of the visible attractions of the opposite sex. But I never expected to meet a man who was my match, and I had no more desire to dominate a spouse than to be ruled by him. Marriage, in my view, should be a balanced stalemate between equal adversaries. (3)

Peters, in fact, was among the first writers of detective fiction (as well as adventure fiction) to feature a strong female protagonist. Addressing the historic role of women protagonists in crime fiction, Glenwood Irons writes: "Though women sleuths emerged as a separate and popular force along with their nineteenth-century male counterparts, the woman detective has seldom been perceived as having an individuality equivalent to that of the male detective" (x). Thus, in the twentieth-century detective story, as well as in the twentieth-century pastiche of the lost world story, Peters created an adventure heroine who applies a modern-day sensibility to a late-Victorian setting, where such socially progressive notions as a strong-willed female heroine were yet to be found in popular fiction. Peters's efforts are thus groundbreaking, and illustrative of how an author can use the expectations found in conventional literary formula to articulate an individualistic "voice" that speaks to significant contemporary issues.

When asked by interviewer Dean James about the "significant changes in mystery publishing," Elizabeth Peters replies that the "great thing that has happened with mystery publishing is the expansion of the definitions and limits of the genre" (165-66). Peters herself, as discussed in this chapter, has contributed directly to this expansion of definitions and limits in her Amelia

Peabody novels. She has successfully incorporated adventure and suspense with romantic comedy in *The Last Camel Died at Noon*, in the process extending her readers' definition of the detective story specifically and mystery fiction in general. Her use of literary pastiche in her reworking of the lost world adventure has been done with explicit purpose: the entertainment of her audience and the exploration of feminist issues. Peters is credited as being one the first authors to develop "successful feminist heroines" in the mystery story (McDonald 11). Yet, she recently expressed a peevishness at "being overlooked by feminist critics" (James 165). Nevertheless, Elizabeth Peters has firmly established herself as not only the premiere author of historical mystery fiction, but also as one of the finest writers of adventure fiction. She has created in her heroine Amelia Peabody something much more than a mere female copy of Indiana Jones. In the pages of her twelve novels, she has produced a wonderful series character that will live forever in the readers' imaginations. Amelia Peabody, ubiquitous parasol and all, must be regarded as one of the greatest adventure heroines of all time. Even the cantankerous Radcliffe Emerson would be proud of his wife's grand accomplishment.

## The Amelia Peabody Novels

*Crocodile on the Sandbank* (1975)
*The Curse of the Pharaohs* (1981)
*The Mummy Case* (1985)
*Lion in the Valley* (1986)
*The Deeds of the Disturber* (1988)
*The Last Camel Died at Noon* (1991)
*The Snake, the Crocodile and the Dog* (1992)
*The Hippopotamus Pool* (1996)
*Seeing a Large Cat* (1997)
*The Ape Who Guards the Balance* (1998)
*The Falcon at the Portal* (1999)
*He Shall Thunder in the Sky* (2000)

## Note

1. A portion of Anne Rice's dedication to The Mummy reads: "to H. Rider Haggard who created the immortal *She*."

*Works Cited*

Doyle, Sir Arthur Conan. *The Lost World & the Poison Belt*. San Francisco: Chronicle, 1989.

——. *When the World Screamed & Other Stories: Professor Challenger Adventures Vol. II*. San Francisco: Chronicle, 1990.

Ellis, Peter Berresford. *H. Rider Haggard: A Voice from the Infinite*. London: Routledge and Kegan Paul, 1978.

Haggard, H. Rider. *King Solomon's Mines*. Oxford: Oxford UP, 1989.

Hammett, Dashiell. *The Thin Man*. New York: Vintage Crime/Black Lizard, 1992.

Irons, Glenwood, ed. "Introduction: Gender and Genre: The Woman Detective and the Diffusion of Generic Voices." *Feminism in Women's Detective Fiction*. Toronto: U of Toronto P, 1995.

James, Dean. "Elizabeth Peters." *Speaking of Murder: Interviews with Masters of Mystery and Suspense*. Eds. Ed Gorman and Martin H. Greenberg. New York: Berkley Prime Crime, 1998.

Klein, Kathleen Gregory, ed. *Great Women Mystery Writers: Classic to Contemporary*. Westport: Greenwood, 1994.

McDonald, T. Liam. "Will the Real Author Please Stand Up?: Digging Up Dirt with Elizabeth Peters, Barbara Michaels, and Barbara Mertz." *The Armchair Detective* 26.2 (Spring 1993).

Menville, Douglas. "Introduction." *Allan's Wife*. H. Rider Hagggard. North Hollywood: Newcastle, 1980. (Reprint of the 1889 ed.)

Peters, Elizabeth. *Crocodile on the Sandbank*. New York: Mysterious P, 1975.

——. *The Last Camel Died at Noon*. New York: Warner, 1991.

——. *The Mummy Case*. New York: Warner, 1985.

Swanson, Jean, and Dean James. *By a Woman's Hand: A Guide to Mystery Fiction by Women*. New York: Berkley, 1994.

——. *Killer Books: A Reader's Guide to Exploring the Popular World of Mystery and Suspense*. New York: Berkley Prime Crime, 1998.

"Talking with Elizabeth Peters." *Mystery Guild* Oct. 1998.

"Talking with Elizabeth Peters—Part 2." *Mystery Guild* Winter 1999.

Wolfe, Peter. *Beams Falling: The Art of Dashiell Hammett*. Bowling Green, OH: Bowling Green State U Popular P, 1980.

# Contributors

**Scott Christianson** is a professor of English at Radford University in Radford, Virginia. His articles on detective fiction have appeared in the *Journal of Popular Culture, The Cunning Craft* (Western Illinois University Press), and *Gender, Language and Myth* and *Feminism in Women's Detective Fiction* (both published by the University of Toronto Press). He has devoted twenty years to reading, researching, and writing about T. S. Eliot.

**Jean A. Coakley** is associate professor of English at Miami University, where she teaches British literature, technical writing, and creative writing, and regularly offers a course in the socio-cultural aspects of detective fiction. Her publications include the Middle School materials for the Charles F. Kettering Foundation's Individually Guided Education (IGE) program, *Aphra Behn's The Luckey Chance: A Critical Edition*, and contributions to *The Oxford Companion to Crime and Mystery Writing*. She is currently writing "Myth, Marketing, and Political Prophecy: Sir Gawain and the Celts of Carlisle," a monograph examining how Arthurian romances set nearby use local legends to strengthen regional unity, legitimize Anglo-Norman rule, and support the Cathedral of St. Mary at Carlisle 1100-1600.

**David N. Eldridge** lectures on American film at the University of Hull, England. He is nearing completion of his PhD at Cambridge University, examining the attitudes toward history held by Hollywood filmmakers and reflected in the films of the 1950s. His studies and research into the cultural value of History have resulted in an article on the Federal Theatre Project, and papers on John F. Kennedy's use of history in the 1960 election campaign, Disney's America, and constructions of memory in Oliver Stone's *Nixon*. His most recent work documents the reports of a CIA agent working in Hollywood in the 1950s, published by the *Historical Journal of Film, Radio and Television* in June 2000.

**Judy Ann Ford** is an associate professor of history at Texas A&M University–Commerce. Her field of interest is late-medieval religion, particularly as it relates to lay participation in English parish communities. She has also published on the Franciscan Spirituals in Italy. The present essay arises from that work.

**Margaret L. Foxwell** is pursuing a master's degree in history. Her junior thesis on Chandler won the 1993 Mennen Award. Her graduate thesis, *Saints and Psychopaths: The Frontier Vigilante and American Identity in the*

*Works of Raymond Chandler and Robert B. Parker*, examines the power and continuity of myth in the shaping of historical identity. Her field of interest is Gilded Age history, and she is currently researching the American theater of that period.

**Linda Holland-Toll** is an assistant professor at Newberry College. Her research interests include genre and cross-genre studies; her book on horror fiction has been accepted by Bowling Green State University Popular Press.

**Gary Hoppenstand** is a professor who teaches in the Department of American Thought and Language at Michigan State University. He has published numerous books and articles on topics ranging from nineteenth-century British and American literature to film studies. He has been nominated twice for the World Fantasy Award, and he has won the Popular Culture Association's National Book Award for his textbook, *Popular Fiction: An Anthology* (Longman, 1998). He has recently completed work on a "Penguin Twentieth-Century Classics" edition of P. C. Wren's *Beau Geste* and a "Penguin Classics" omnibus edition of Anthony Hope's two novels, *The Prisoner of Zenda* and *Rupert of Hentzau*. He is currently writing a book-length study, *The Story of Adventure in Popular Fiction: A Social-Psychological Approach*, for the S.U.N.Y. Press, and the Introduction for a "Signet Classic" edition of Baroness Orczy's *The Scarlet Pimpernel*.

**Peter Hunt** is an assistant professor of classics at the University of Colorado, Boulder. His published work includes *Slaves, Warfare, and Ideology in the Greek Historians* (Cambridge, 1998) and articles on Greek and Roman slavery for the *Macmillan Encyclopedia of World Slavery* (1997).

**Patricia W. Julius** is an associate professor in the Department of American Thought and Language at Michigan State University. Her PhD in Medieval literature followed a long-time interest in mysteries and crime fiction. This study of Margaret Frazer allows her to merge those two interests. She has published in areas ranging from Native American culture and literature to women's studies and Andrew Greeley's non-fiction, with brief time-outs for an article on Dean Koontz and an examination of vampire detective novels. Most recently, she has returned to her early interests to concentrate on crime fiction written by women, with particular attention to hard-boiled women private eyes. She is presently at work on a book-length study of Marcia Muller's Sharon McCone.

**R. Gordon Kelly** is professor of American studies at the University of Maryland, College Park. He is the author of *Mystery Fiction and Modern Life* (1998) as well as an earlier study of fiction for children, *Mother Was a Lady: Self and Society in Selected American Children's Periodicals, 1865-1890* (1974). His essay "Literature and the Historian" is reprinted in *Locat-*

*ing American Studies: The Evolution of a Discipline*, edited by Lucy Maddox (1999).

**Terrance L. Lewis** holds a PhD in European history from SUNY Binghamton and is an associate professor of history at Southern University at New Orleans. His publications include two monographs, *A Climate for Appeasement* and *Dorothy L. Sayers' Wimsey & Interwar British Society*. Professor Lewis is very active in the on-line world, as a co-host of various discussion lists, web author and web-master, and maintainer of "Dr. T's Internet Glossary." His hobbies are primarily writing poetry and reading, especially non-fiction and mysteries.

**Christiane W. Luehrs** is instructor of English at Fort Hays State University, where she teaches English composition and classes in American multiculturalism. Her husband, **Robert B. Luehrs,** is professor of history at the same institution, specializing in European intellectual history. He has published articles on topics ranging from seventeenth-century witchcraft and eighteenth-century utopianism to nineteenth-century religious skepticism and twentieth-century children's literature.

**Edward L. Meek** is currently a PhD student at the University of Cambridge and is presently researching the diplomacy of King Edward IV. He is also the author of "Printing and the Parish Clergy in the Later Middle Ages" in *The Transactions of the Cambridge Bibliographical Society*, 1997.

**Marie Nelson** is empoyed as a historian with the California State Office of Historic Preservation. She has received MAs in history from Brigham Young University and Clark University. She is a PhD candidate at Clark University; she is researching the poetics and the politics of the contemporary quilt movement. Her biography of Earl Douglass, the paleontologist who discovered the quarry in eastern Utah, which became Dinosaur National Monument, was a recent winner of the Charles Redd Center for Western Studies manuscript competition. Ms. Nelson is an avid quilter whose award-winning works have been exhibited in various art galleries and quilt shows.

**Jerry L. Parker** received his master's degree from California State University at Chico. His specialty is the American frontier and western movement experience. Currently lecturing at Truckee Meadows Community College in Reno, Nevada, Mr. Parker is working on a biography of William Brown Ide, the first and only president of the California Republic.

**Edward J. Rielly** is professor of English and chairperson of the English Department at Saint Joseph's College of Maine. He is the author of *Approaches to Teaching Swift's Gulliver's Travels* (1988), seven chapbooks of poetry, and many articles, book reviews, and short stories. Dr. Rielly, who received his PhD from the University of Notre Dame, currently is writing a book on baseball and popular culture and a cultural history of the 1960s.

**Rita Rippetoe** received her MA in English at California State University at Sacramento. She is currently a PhD candidate at the University of Nevada, Reno, where her planned dissertation is on the role of alcohol and drugs in American hard-boiled detective fiction. She has published "Not a Magical Mystery Tour: Locale in Dorothy Sayers' Harriet Vane Novels" in *Para\*doxa* and "Layered Genre Strategies in *Smiley's People*" in *Clues.*

**Jeffrey A. Rydberg-Cox** is an assistant professor of English at the University of Missouri at Kansas City. He holds his PhD from the Committee on the Ancient Mediterranean World at the University of Chicago. His research interests include ancient rhetoric and humanities computing. He is a collaborator with the Perseus Project (www.perseus.tufts.edu), a major digital library of materials for the study of ancient Greece and Rome and the English Renaissance. His academic publications include articles on Greek rhetoric and myth, digital libraries, and computational linguistics. He has just completed a book about several works by the Greek orator Lysias.

**Frank A. Salamone** is professor of sociology and anthropology at Iona College, New Rochelle, NY. He is married, and he and his wife have two children. He has five other children and six grandchildren. Salamone has written or edited over ten books, more than 100 articles, and conducted fieldwork in Nigeria, Kenya, Ghana, Canada, and the United States. He loves jazz and mysteries and occasionally teaches a jazz sociology class.

**Donna Bradshaw Smith** is associate professor of library services at W. Frank Steely Library, Northern Kentucky University, Highland Heights, Kentucky. She is a contributor to *Magazines for Libraries, Recommended Reference Books in Paperback,* and *Electronic Resources Review.*

**Douglas Tallack** is professor of American studies at the University of Nottingham, UK. Among his publications are *The Nineteenth-Century American Short Story* (1993), *Twentieth-Century America* (1991), *Critical Theory: A Reader* (1995), and *Literary Theory at Work* (1987), the last two as editor. Professor Tallack's first publication was an essay on William Faulkner in a Popular Press collection, *Dimensions of Detective Fiction* (1976), edited by Ray Browne and Larry Landrum. The present essay arises from research on urban culture funded by the Arts and Humanities Research Board and Professor Tallack wishes to acknowledge the Board's support.

**Anita M. Vickers** is associate professor of humanities and English at Pennsylvania State University where she teaches courses in American literature, women's studies, and specialized writing courses. She has published articles on Charles Brockden Brown, Zora Neale Hurston, and popular culture. She is presently writing a book-length study on popular culture during the early nationalist period of American history.

**Theron M. Westervelt** is currently a PhD student at the University of Cambridge and is carrying out research on the domestic government of King Edward IV and has previously completed a thesis concerning the Woodville family in the 1470s.